American Television Abroad

AMERICAN TELEVISION ABROAD

Hollywood's Attempt to Dominate World Television

by KERRY SEGRAVE

McFarland & Company, Inc., Publishers
Jefferson, North Carolina, and London

British Library Cataloguing-in-Publication data are available

Library of Congress Cataloguing-in-Publication Data

Segrave, Kerry, 1944–
    American television abroad : Hollywood's attempt to dominate world
television / by Kerry Segrave.
        p.   cm.
    Includes bibliographical references and index.
    ISBN 0-7864-0582-1 (library binding : 50# alkaline paper) ∞
    1. Television broadcasting — Europe.   2. Television programs —
Europe.   3. Television broadcasting.   4. Television programs.
5. Television broadcasting — United States — Influence.   I. Title.
PN1992.3.E78S44   1998
384.55'4'094 — dc21
                                                                98-20086
                                                                     CIP

Manufactured in the United States of America

*McFarland & Company, Inc., Publishers
    Box 611, Jefferson, North Carolina 28640*

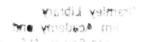

Contents

Preface

Every time one dollar's worth of international television trade takes place, about 75¢ of the dollar goes to U.S. companies. Anywhere from 60¢ to 67¢ of that 75¢ goes to members of the Hollywood cartel, the Motion Picture Association of America members — also known as the "majors." That group of eight film producers formed during the period 1910–1930 and consisted of MGM, Paramount, 20th Century–Fox, RKO, Warner Bros., Universal, United Artists and Columbia.

During the mid–1920s, movies made in the United States constituted about 80 to 90 percent of all film screenings in the world outside of the U.S. Virtually all of those movies were from the majors; the group generated some 25 percent of its total revenue offshore. In 1943-44 the eight majors took 94 percent of the domestic box office receipts. A decade later about 70 percent of the world's film screen time was held by U.S. product, with 42 percent of the cartel's total income coming from abroad. Today, control of the world's film screens is held in the same proportion by roughly the same members of the Hollywood majors club.

The majors dominate television trade to the same degree. However, there have been a few changes in the cartel's membership. RKO died in the 1950s; MGM and United Artists merged into a single unit in 1983. As well, most of them are now parts of larger conglomerates. Thus the eight were reduced to six. Disney was anointed with major status some time ago, while the Ted Turner empire attained that status in the 1990s. No sooner had Turner become a full member of the cartel than it was announced his empire was merging with, or being swallowed by, Time Warner.

To a large extent these seven companies determine what appears on the television screens in American homes and most of what appears on foreign television screens during whatever portion foreign product has carved out for itself in a particular country. It is worth noting, however, that although the U.S. majors at times have generated as much as 50 percent of their total cinema income through offshore distribution, they have fallen short of that mark in television sales, drawing probably no more than 25 percent of their total television income from offshore.

1

This book is the story of how these U.S. producers have tried to dominate the world's television screens to the same extent that they dominate the world's cinemas.

Chapter 1

1940–1962:
International Television,
"An Emissary of Truth"

Back from a six-week trek to Europe in 1954, comedian Bob Hope told reporters he thought global television networks would arrive within ten years, paving the way for promotion of "mutual understanding between the world's peoples." Such links would arrive, he thought, through connections via transoceanic cables.[1]

Such dreams of global networks were widespread at the time. The same year that Hope made his prediction the U.S. Congress established an International Telecommunications Commission, consisting of two senators and five representatives appointed by the president, to look into the possibilities of transoceanic global television. Commission member Senator Alexander Wiley (R, Wisconsin) was enthusiastic about the prospect: "Mankind is offered a golden opportunity of unlimited horizons. It is an opportunity to help improve standards of living, to stimulate education and culture — to improve trade, to increase understanding...."[2]

That dream of global television had actually surfaced earlier, back in the late 1940s, when this new medium was nonexistent outside of the U.S. and U.K. and in existence in these places just barely. Yet at a time when almost no one on the planet owned a television set or received television transmissions, plans for global television were in the works. Although transoceanic cables were often mentioned, the smart money was on the only other alternative considered at the time, the terrestrial-based system of microwave relay transmissions of signals. It went without saying that the coming global television would be run by Americans, controlled by Americans and be programmed by and for American interests, although the rhetoric was often otherwise.

Around 1948 engineer William Halstead was approached by Henry Holthusen (formerly a consultant in establishing the U.S. radio service Voice of America) who sounded Halstead out on the topic of global television.

Holthusen was worried that the Soviet Union would get the jump on the U.S. in television dominance. Halstead suggested the concept could become a reality through a microwave relay system. Enthusiastic about the plan, Holthusen embarked on an around-the-world trip. From that sojourn he concluded that before their plans could be adopted they had to solve the problem of who would look at television in nations where only a few would be able to afford to buy sets. Mass viewing in public places was the answer, decided Halstead, who said, "At strategic places throughout a city like Tokyo large TV sets can be put up. Mobile units on trailers can be parked in front of outdoor audiences."[3]

The pair then outlined their plans at a meeting with Senator Karl Mundt and other governmental officials. The first step to make global television a reality was to induce other countries to install American-style television systems — that is, to use systems operating to the same technical specifications. Once that was done a global network was feasible. Halstead showed how by drawing a path around the world from New York through Canada, across Greenland and Iceland, on to Scotland (via the Faeroes and Shetland Islands), then across Europe, Southern Asia and Philippine Islands to Japan, then across the Pacific by way of various island groups to San Francisco. At no place on that map path was there more than 290 miles between land masses, while the best microwave relay methods of the time, said Halstead, gave television beams a range of 300 miles. Senator Mundt gave a favorable speech about the idea in the Senate with the story picked up by the wire services. After reading about it, a leading Japanese publisher, Matsutaro Shoriki, invited Halstead and Holthusen to Tokyo to present their plans. Following a 1952 debate in the Japanese Diet, Shoriki and his group were granted a license for the Nippon Television Network. One year later the anchor station JOAX went into operation, under the supervision of Halstead's engineering company.[4]

Also enthusiastic about the microwave relay idea was Meade Brunet, president of RCA International. He pointed out in 1952 that the Atlantic Ocean between North America and the northern-most part of Europe was dotted with islands no more than 250 miles apart. Perhaps more realistic than Halstead, Brunet conceded that once a system was found to "increase" microwave transmission to that distance it would be possible to build the necessary towers. Global television would then be a reality. RCA engineers were then at work on that very problem. David Sarnoff, RCA chairman, made a much-reported prediction in 1952 that international television would be a reality in five years, although he didn't specify how.[5]

When global television arrived it would do nothing but good; at least that's how the rhetoric went. Studies from United Nations Educational, Scientific, and Cultural Organization (UNESCO) and others offered glowing possibilities. From one television studio, it was said, classrooms of a whole nation, or many nations, could learn physics or chemistry. Adults could receive instruction in scientific farming, soil conservation and family planning, to name a few. There would be cultural exchanges of programs among nations. Best of all, if television everywhere were structured in the American style, then all of the above would cost nothing — advertisers would pay for it.[6]

During a 1952 Chicago speech RCA vice president E. W. Engstrom told a communications symposium that television programs on an international level could spread friendship and understanding throughout the world and might act as an antidote to the threat of war. Global television could foster world peace by carrying bits of culture from nation to nation, helping people to understand people. Engstrom foresaw a "pattern of adult education that surmounts evening classes and correspondence courses in convenience and effectiveness."[7]

Writing in *School Life*, the official journal of the Office of Education — a part of the U.S. Department of Health, Education and Welfare — radio/television chief Franklin Dunham saw the imminent arrival of global television, explaining that "Some way must be found to finance international television, for there is little doubt that international television will promote world understanding of social, racial and economic problems."[8]

When ABC International president Donald Coyle spoke before a 1961 gathering of the Inter-American Association of Broadcasters he was enthusiastic about the still-imminent arrival of global television's serving the future. "I believe that global television, as an architect of understanding, will help create a climate of unmatched progress and prosperity. I believe that international television, as an emissary of truth, will prove to be freedom's strongest ally," he explained. Briefly commenting on how global television would be of value in the fight against mass illiteracy, Coyle went on to more cultural matters when he said, "Global television, projecting honest experience through programs of information and entertainment, is a window in our separate houses that lets others see in and observe our lives, while we look at theirs."[9]

By that year the reality of the pervasiveness of U.S. television programs on foreign sets, if not global television itself, was in evidence. It became harder to argue along the above lines, but some did so anyway. Norman Katz was the director of foreign operations for United Artists Associated in 1959, then also distributing Warner product overseas. Among the most popular fare in Katz's catalog were cartoon characters Popeye and Bugs Bunny. "I'm not saying that all the peoples of the world can be reached by a feature motion picture or by Popeye. But if that unique individual can be the means whereby the children of the world can start on a common understanding and appreciation then maybe our future generations may live in [a] world free of tensions," pronounced Katz. Those cartoons went out in dubbed form to some nations, subtitled to some, in a "live synchronization" format to Japan, but in English only to some non–English-speaking countries. It was not the easiest task to rationalize the jingoism manifest in such a practice, but Katz was equal to the task. "In many cases the cartoons are not even sub-titled. Maybe in this way we can take pride too in helping people of the world overcome language barriers too, by familiarizing them with English. A universality of language, the ability to communicate in a common tongue may be another step toward international amity."[10]

Another supposed benefit of global television was its use in fighting off the forces of darkness. As Senator Alexander Wiley put it, this new medium "would spread the truth concerning the epic battle of the forces of the free world against Communist dictatorship." Journalist George Wallach saw global television as a challenge for the networks, something more than selling 52 weeks of commercials with discounts. "It's Communism vs the American way of life — and Communism is not commissionable." Wallach concluded that "now is the time for an alert television industry ... to guide and lead government agencies."[11]

NBC president Sylvester (Pat) Weaver announced in 1955 that "it is through television that we can expect to answer the charge of the Communists that ours is an empty society without interest in the better things of life." Speaking before a meeting of the Grocery Manufacturers of America he called upon his government to appropriate "at a cost that would be very small" monies to give all countries television transmitters, relay stations and enough television sets to reach one million people with a single telecast. Weaver estimated the cost of a single-channel transmitter plus relays along with 10,000 sets set up strategically in public places to serve that 1 million (an average of 100 viewers per set) to be "not much more than $1,000,000." Multiply that by the number of nations to be so blessed to arrive at the grand total. Once set up, "this international network" would, said Weaver, offer people "our best television shows in the cultural field" and educational fare such as programs on infant care and crop rotation. All of this could, he concluded, "leave the Russians gasping for breath and out of the running."[12]

Such Utopian visions were rarely criticized. Since most nations did not have established systems the problems of experiencing American-style global television had not yet arisen. However, all had firsthand experience in seeing their theater screens dominated by American product. All had had that experience for 30-some years by the start of the 1950s. One criticism came in 1949 from a Canadian writer in a Canadian magazine — that country was still three years away from establishing its own television system, but the subject was much discussed. Reviewing Utopian claims of education for all, of doctors' being taught new techniques (from the tube and from a great distance) and that international exchange of television shows would mean great things for international relations, Jean Tweed declared those claims "add up to sheer nonsense ... international exchange of film and radio has been going on for years without any appreciable good effect." Canada was the only country whose radio system had been swamped by American product. Tweed noted that in every case American transcription of radio programs were sold in Canada for a fraction of the cost to the U.S. producer, and much lower than the cost of producing indigenous material. That extra money from Canada represented pure profit for U.S. interests and thus "prevented the growth of an important industry in Canada which could be employing thousands of Canadians." Canadian television could be a thriving industry, said Tweed, "provided it does not have to labor under the handicap of cheap importation of American second-hand film." A national public broadcaster, the Canadian Broadcasting Corporation (CBC) was established by Canada's federal government in the 1930s precisely because of that threat. The airwaves were being inundated by American radio shows; those same Americans were also trying to buy up Canadian radio stations. It would be 60 years later before the national CBC television network would announce — and implement — a prime-time schedule containing all–Canadian material.[13]

That nations around the world would want U.S. television shows, would eagerly await them, was another article of faith. Partly that was fueled by general American arrogance and partly by the success enjoyed everywhere overseas by U.S. theatrical releases. When J. Walter Thompson advertising agency executive Harry Hermann returned home after a three-and-a-half month 1952 tour of Brazil, he reported there were two stations operating in São Paulo and one in Rio de Janeiro. Each city had about 12,000 sets in operation, owned only by the affluent. Almost all transmission of U.S. fare was done only in English, "which the people know because of the subtitled films they see," he stated. What must have been of particular appeal to him was that "the commercials, both spoken and superimposed are delivered almost every minute on the minute." Television in Latin American developed along American lines — almost purely commercial with little or no public broadcasting. Of the local fare Hermann did see he dismissed as poor quality and imitative of product produced in other lands partly because "Brazilians have not yet developed their own culture."[14]

Equally bereft were the Australians. Paul Talbot, head of independent television distribution company Fremantle, observed on his return from Down Under that Australia had the potential to be a major market for U.S. television shows, "much better than England." At the time television station licenses had been announced and awarded, but nothing was in operation. Talbot explained that Australia was a "natural" recipient for U.S. television fare since it already took American films and radio programs and "there is no large supply of indigenous talent so the Anzacs might readily turn to the U.S. for shows." Conceded by Talbot was the fact that the U.K. did have some native talent.[15]

When Australian television was just 15 months old the ratio of live to filmed material was about 45 to 55, with most of the filmed material being American imports. That was so, said Keith Cairns, an executive of a commercial station in Melbourne, because "Australians, brought up on American motion pictures, have virtually the same tastes in telefilms as Americans." The fact that his station made big profits by importing cheap American fare undoubtedly had no effect on his opinion.[16]

When U.S. series such as "Highway Patrol" and "I Love Lucy" were riding high on Japanese prime time in 1960, the trade journal *Variety* excitedly stated that the Japanese "love those Yank-styled westerns ... Ward Bond and his 'Wagon Train' cohorts spouting Japanese really sends 'em." Some shows were not dubbed into Japanese but subtitled —"Lucy" for one. Given the complex written language, it meant, noted the report, "superimposed titles frequently can blot out the whole picture." Segun Olusola was a television producer of local shows for his station in Ibadan, Nigeria. Concluding a U.S. visit he said that popular U.S. programs on his station were "Lassie," "Wagon Train," "Life of Riley" and "Highway Patrol." "Highway" star Broderick Crawford was, declared Olusola, "a national hero."[17]

Back from a one-month European tour early in 1962, NBC executive Alvin Ferleger boasted that over 22 percent of Poland's weekly television schedule came from America. Most of the rest of the week's 44 hours were Polish-produced. When asked why Polish television was so heavily Americanized Ferleger replied, "They use American product because they like it," and Poles are "terribly cosmopolitan," seeking to understand the U.S. Just what shows did those cosmopolitans favor? "Disneyland" and "Mickey Mouse Club" "are absolute smashes there." If the Poles' program selection was not everyone's idea of sophistication then certainly their method of viewing was, because "unlike the other countries of the world with television, English-language programming in Poland is played sans dubbing and even without titles." Poles were limited to "summaries" in their native language. At given points in the screening a translator wrapped up live, as briefly as possible, all that was about to happen or had happened.[18]

Sometimes American nationalism covered the entire globe. In 1960 Merle Jones, a CBS executive in charge of the network's global sales, felt the time might come when foreign sales of U.S. television product could approach 50 percent of the industry's total. Asked if he thought that might necessitate a change in program content — to appeal internationally — Jones replied that no adjustment would be needed as "the international appeal now of American programs is just overwhelming." A couple of years later Ralph Baruch, another CBS executive involved in offshore sales, observed, "The likes and dislikes of the television audience are essentially the same here and abroad."[19]

Once in a great while reality intruded into an article. German writer Hans Hoehn noted that in 1958 U.S. product had a hard time getting on

German screens at all. Partly it was because the system was completely state run, with only a minor amount of ads allowed, plus the fact that hours of transmission were also limited. And, said Hoehn, the Germans "want, of course, their own product in the first place."[20]

If the prospects of global television caused excitement, the reason was not because of all the lofty benefits that would soon be bestowed upon humankind. People were to be massed in the millions before the tube not to be educated or informed or enlightened or uplifted — or even to be entertained. They were to be massed together to watch commercials, preferably American ads. They would then rush out to buy stuff, preferably American stuff. For television was the greatest selling machine of all time. People within the industry, in ad agencies and in boardrooms of transnationals in particular, all recognized this from early on. For television with its visual component could do so much more than print and radio, which were limited to words alone or static photos. Television could reach illiterates. It could use and manipulate symbols like no other medium. So the prospect of a soon-arriving global television system caused paroxysms of anticipatory delight in many quarters. It was to become, and did become, the ultimate selling machine.

Work had begun early to try and ensure that everywhere television developed it did so along commercial, and American, lines. When Sarnoff made his 1952 prediction, he also observed that a number of U.S. businessmen and representatives of ad agencies were then at work in Brazil trying to avoid any mistakes made in early American television. Sarnoff declared that "Brazil, through TV, will provide a wider market for American products as soon as the country's dollar indebtedness is overcome."[21]

Two years later Rodney Erickson, a Young and Rubicam advertising agency vice president, told a convention meeting of the American Association of Advertising Agencies that they would be called on more frequently to serve American clients in foreign locals as television expanded. Television, he stated, "will be one of the motivating media" in selling U.S. goods overseas. Even at that early stage Young and Rubicam carefully tracked television's worldwide spread and its style of development. There were then 11 nations with commercial systems, two had systems that were partly commercial, 15 nations had government-operated systems, and 27 lands had television in the active planning stage. Those latter countries were said to be watching how U.S. "commercials and programs" functioned in other foreign lands to guide them in deciding between governmental or commercial systems for themselves. Note the order listed ads before programs. Erickson warned his audience that, for the U.K., "you're going to have to buck some excellent BBC programming for awhile."[22]

Five major U.S. ad agencies billed a total of over $230 million abroad in 1957, led by J. Walter Thompson at $75 million and McCann-Erickson and Grant Advertising each at $50 million. All of them were opening offices abroad in various countries, as were many U.S. agencies below the top five. Grant had recently opened an office in Colombo, Sri Lanka (then Ceylon), as it was one of the few lands in southwest Asia that had commercial radio. Some ads were produced overseas, but many were done in America, by transnationals such as Colgate, Kodak, Singer and GE. A McCann spokesman said his firm's billings had increased 1,000 percent in the previous ten years. Fueling that expansion in part was a general increase of U.S. sales and business activity abroad due to the U.S.'s economic strength and advantages gained from World War II (stemming from both physical destruction abroad and items such as Marshall Plan aid to European lands). But television was also crucial in that explosion. *Variety* observed that "what has prompted the agency colonial policy more than anything else and has turned the ad men's attention to overseas is the advent of television and its foreign possibilities." By then, 1957, 24 foreign lands had commercials with some 375 commercial television stations abroad. That same year marked the spread of commercial television into all major areas of Britain.[23]

London, England, was the site that year of the first World Congress on Commercial Television. Representatives from 14 nations attended the congress sponsored by transnational Johnson & Johnson, which claimed to have staged the event "as a public service to television." Attendees viewed television ads from numerous countries, and the event's whole purpose was to promote commercial television and determine how best to pitch ads worldwide. Decided at the congress was that a one-ad-sells-all approach would not work. It seemed that Mexicans liked a humorous sell, Pakistanis preferred a serious ad, Japanese went for restrained, indirect pitches, and so on.[24]

What the Japanese were getting was a flood of ads. A code supposedly limited ads to 10 percent of air time (about the same as in America) but, reported a journalist, "apparently everybody looks the other way." Ads sometimes ran continuously for seven to eight minutes. "That the Japanese commercial pattern is making the station owner rich is reflected in the NTV story.... Profits are enormous." (NTV was the Japanese commercial network.)[25]

The importance of commercial television's winning out over publicly run television could be seen in the remarks of John McCarthy, head of an industry lobby group, who said, "when a commercial television outlet opens in a place such as Lebanon for example, the foreign affils of American companies are the first to hop on the television bandwagon with commercials."[26]

Late in 1959 a survey was undertaken by *Executive*, a monthly Canadian magazine "for the men of decision." If they had their way those Canadian businessmen would reduce television's role of "enlightening, educating, unifying and informing" in favor of emphasizing its capacity to "entertain, relax and sell." Nearly all of those executives interviewed wanted Canadian television to "meet the U.S. pattern." What they wanted was "more profits for the broadcaster, better selling for the business man." Pointed out by the magazine was the fact that there had been "continued pressure" against Canada's nationally owned public broadcaster, the CBC, with most of that pressure aimed at getting the CBC to screen more mass-interest fare, "fewer ballets, more bullets" and to make it "more commercial, more American." Executives interviewed believed Canadian television would become a better selling tool when programs became "light, bright, antiseptic, wholesome, cheerful, easily understood and escapist — like American television."[27]

No one beat the drum for ads on television as much as Donald Coyle. Few were as enthusiastic, or as self-delusional. Coyle was a vice president of ABC International in 1960, a division of ABC formed a year earlier. Reasons for U.S. industries to expand abroad, he argued, were the competitive squeeze at home — near the saturation point in some cases — and strong growth abroad. Coyle declared, "It is highly desirable from the standpoint of the economies of these countries themselves that television be brought in — so that it can fulfill its natural function as a giant pump fueling the machine of consumer demand, stepping up the flow of goods and services to keep living standards high and the economy expanding." Expounding on his theme a few months later Coyle told a meeting of the Inter-American Association of Broadcasters how the coming global television would serve the future: "I believe that global television, as an architect of understanding, will help create a climate of unmatched progress and prosperity." Continuing, he argued that international television "will serve freedom's future by providing a terrific stimulus to the economies of individual nations, and to productive international trade. We have learned that television, through its sight, sound and motion, creates the emotion to buy. Television performs a marriage between desire and possibility. It brings the consumer to the goods and services available to him. By doing this, television opens new markets. New and better products, designed to meet new needs, create wider prosperity. Television advertising not only lubricates the wheels of the economy, but actually adds new wheels and generates the energy to make them turn." Acknowledging that global television could promote shared experiences through program exchange he concluded that "equally important is the opportunity we have to prove that commercial television's use as an advertising medium can be a vital aid to industrial growth with its accompanying increase in the standard of living."[28]

Coyle felt expansion of television into foreign nations was only in its infancy; it was still a "wide open frontier for the American television industry as a whole." One item that worried him about the coming spread of global television was that U.S. shows had "not been designed for the foreign market" and that the current acceptance of U.S. fare on foreign tubes was "dictated by the need to fill programming time with some kind of acceptable material." Ad dollars would flow into international television, he believed, and be more successful and effective than attempts by magazines such as *Life*,

Time and *Reader's Digest* to hit the global market with local editions. As ad agencies had switched emphasis from regional to national with the advent of radio and television in the U.S., so would they go global with the coming of international television.[29]

The dreams, hopes and greed of the American television industry were one thing; reality was another. As television debuted in country after country its structure tended to echo that which existed in a nation's radio industry. That is, if a nation had a commercial radio system in place it usually adopted a commercial television system. On the other hand, if a country had a publicly owned radio system it generally set up television in the same way. Behind this lay the theory that the airwaves were a scarce resource that belonged to the people and should be owned and operated as such. The number of radio and television stations available in any area was severely limited. Demand for such stations was high. But leaving television to free market rules entirely meant that only a very few rich individuals would end up owning the handful of available stations. To push for global control of television, the American companies used various tactics. One method was to set up distribution offices abroad. By 1954 several independent U.S. distribution firms had opened offices up in Canada, including United Television Programs — a large company in that era. Hollywood's major producers were still more or less boycotting television by not dealing much with the new medium, neither selling much to it nor producing much for it. All that would change drastically by the end of the 1950s. One major even then breaking ranks was Columbia Pictures' television arm, Screen Gems, which in late 1954 or early 1955 established its first foreign office, also in Canada. Before then no company had offices in any other nation, although many were thinking about it and soon would establish many such offices overseas. Canada had eight stations on the air; the U.K. had the BBC; and France, Germany, Italy and some of the Scandinavian lands had operating stations, as did many Latin American countries.[30]

For the fiscal year ending June 30, 1961, Screen Gems (SG) reported foreign gross revenue of $8 million, making it the lead television distribution company abroad, it claimed. Some 60 television series were distributed outside the U.S. to around 50 nations by an SG staff in foreign locales that totaled 100 or so people around the globe. SG's major markets were Canada and Australia. It had sold out its entire catalog in Australia, Argentina, Peru, Venezuela and the Philippines. Setting up a distribution office abroad allowed a company to keep the distribution profits, and just as importantly it prevented the development of an indigenous distribution system. The latter was always a threat because it might grow too big and too powerful and perhaps neglect U.S. product. Also, with no indigenous distribution system in a country it was harder for a native production industry to develop — the foreign distributor could see to it that native product was not distributed (using various excuses) while favoring its own material.[31]

One of the easiest methods, at least in theory, was simply to buy into foreign stations and networks. America could afford it. However, most countries were more than a little sensitive to any foreign control over their communications industries. Nevertheless, the U.S. tried, with little ultimate success. Because Latin American television had mostly followed the U.S. model in going commercial, U.S. companies concentrated their buying efforts in Latin America. One of the earliest deals took place in 1952 when NBC-TV completed negotiations with Goar Mestre's Cuban network, whereby the Havana-based chain became affiliated with NBC. The U.S. network was then trying to strike a similar deal with Emilio Azcarraga's Mexican station XEW. Under such an affiliation agreement one result would be to see "NBC feeding kinescopes of its top shows to both countries and sharing in a program exchange." That network, which formally created its international division in 1956, continued to explore buying into stations but with marginal success. Reportedly NBC was then looking into station buys in Jamaica, Cuba, Spain and elsewhere. A network spokesman hopefully stated that those explorations might only "be the beginning" in the network's global aspirations. As well NBC and its affiliate RCA Great Britain had a 20 percent stake in a mostly British group competing for a commercial station in Britain. It was not the chosen one.[32]

ABC was busy at the end of the 1950s trying to set up a network in Central America. Late in 1959 meetings were held in New York City hosted by ABC with representatives from five Central American nations to set up the Central American Television Network (CATVN). An initial meeting had already been held in Guatemala City. The U.S. network held a minority interest in the only television station in Costa Rica, then under construction. Leonard Goldenson, ABC's president, explained that the meeting attendees saw the proposed network as the first major move toward the establishment of a common market for all Central American nations. After more meetings the birth of CATVN was announced in February 1960. With the perception that rapid growth was happening in that region, ABC foreign division chief Donald Coyle explained that "U.S. industry will be competing with the rest of the world to fill that demand. To compete successfully it must use the most potent selling force known — television, the medium for personal selling and personal communication." CATVN had single stations in each of Tegucigalpa, Honduras; Guatemala City, Guatemala; San Salvador, El Salvador; Managua, Nicaragua; and San José, Costa Rica. All were then on the air except for the still-under-construction outlet in Costa Rica. Coyle added that "CATVN's prime objective is to build the best Central American television cultural, entertainment and sales force possible."[33]

NBC International had "management consultancy" agreements in 1959 with a station in Wales, one in Lima, Peru, and another in Buenos Aires, Argentina. ABC held a 15 percent stake in an Adelaide, Australia, outlet.

CBS was into studio construction overseas for stations as well as being "management consultants." CBS was partnered with Cuba's main broadcasting mogul Goar Mestre in a Buenos Aires television studio. Remarked CBS executive Merle Jones, "The growing stake of American broadcasting interests abroad is not so much in securing minority interests in commercial television outlets overseas, but in securing distribution of American programming." Eighteen months later NBC spread the word to Mexican broadcasters and businesspeople in general that it was ready to give "every aid" in the improvement of existing facilities and the establishment of new stations in Mexico. NBC added that its policy of aid to new stations should not be viewed as a buildup of competition but as a general buildup of the industry there. However, some observers saw the initiative as a prelude to the goal of a Latin American television linkup, a project NBC had been discussing off and on for several years.[34]

South Korea's first station went on the air permanently in June 1956. For the test run in May, nobody in Korea owned a television set. To remedy that 50 sets were dispersed around Seoul for community viewing. Donation of those receivers was done by the operators of station HLKZ, "most of whom are American," per one account. The franchise distributor of RCA sets in Korea was a firm called Korcad, which was headed by American Joseph Miller. He also headed HLKZ. Chuck Levenburg was station vice president. Station manager Peter Ostroff was then in the U.S., buying American shows for his station to telecast.[35]

One American inroad in Europe took place in 1957 when CBS signed an exclusive deal with Spanish government television authorities to furnish tapes of some of its programs. On the way to Spain were "I Love Lucy," "Foreign Legion" and "San Francisco Beat." Until then Spanish television had been broadcasting all live — four hours a day. The coming of taped material hastened the end of live television in Spain and many other places. The pact called for CBS to provide all programs without charge, but CBS had the right to keep all the advertising revenue it could generate.[36]

When Irish television (Telefis Eirann) debuted in January 1962, it did so thanks to an $8.5 million loan from the Irish government. Just prior to startup the approximately 100,000 Irish set owners were picking up broadcasts from France and from the BBC Belfast outlet. Regarding the six-hours-per-day, seven-days-per-week schedule, Telefis Eirann director general Edward Roth stated that half of the broadcast time was tape "mostly of U.S. origin," with the other 50 percent being local and live. Revenue came from a nine-dollar-per-set annual license fee and from commercials, limited by law to a maximum of three minutes per hour. Roth, an American and former NBC executive, had set up television stations in Mexico and Peru before landing the Irish job. Imports included "Father Knows Best," the "Donna Reed Show" and "Have Gun, Will Travel," although "excessively violent" shows such as "The Untouchables" were not programmed in Ireland.[37]

Not every attempt by U.S. companies to buy into foreign outlets was gratefully received. When ABC International made its 1961 bid to buy into Toronto-based station CFTO, Canada's regulatory body, the Board of Broadcast Governors (BBG), quashed the deal, supposedly looking to a new emphasis on Canadian ownership in its communications industry. However, ABC then made a long-term loan of almost $3 million to the outlet. Said *Variety*, "But ABC had managed to maintain its friendly tie-up with the CFTO ownership via the loan to which the BBG had no objection."[38]

If the Americans were trying to buy into foreign television ownership, or gain control in other ways, then back home the strategy was to buy out the competition. In March 1960 United Artists (UA) acquired the independent producing/distributing television company ZIV. It had been one of the largest of the independents. Those independents had sprung up in greater profusion and had attained greater strength and size partly because Hollywood's seven or eight major film companies had been slow to move into television, reacting at first from emotion — fear the new medium would further erode their already declining audience. Of course, that fear was justified. However, the Hollywood majors learned to adapt and survive, although in the short run they avoided television, allowing independents to get more than a toehold. Once Hollywood committed itself fully to controlling the small screen as well as the big screen, it was necessary to remove the competition. ZIV's being swallowed by UA was one example. In the early to middle 1950s those Hollywood majors had very little material on the small screen, either originally made series or movies sold to television. By early in 1961 those majors — led by Warner, Screen Gems (Columbia), MGM and 20th Century–Fox — accounted for almost 25 percent of all material screened by the three U.S. networks during prime-time hours. It was a degree of penetration that would rise.[39]

ABC led the way, signing a contract with Disney in 1954 for the first Hollywood production for television. A larger and more significant deal was announced when ABC contracted with Warner for a package of 40 films for the 1955-56 television season. With that deal, and the many others that followed, the shift in production for television from live entertainment to taped was underway. Around the country countless stations reduced staff and closed expensive studios, turning to film and tape projection. Local programming was abandoned for network fare, Hollywood films and taped series. By 1959 all three networks were heavily into Hollywood movie running; production of series had shifted wholesale to the Hollywood majors. This switch led to an increase in television advertising. From 1954 — the last year before the introduction of movies on television — until 1957, when conversion was complete, the number of television stations operating grew by 32 percent while sales of advertising time were more than twice that, growing 65 percent. National broadcasters and national consumer goods manufacturers were drawn into a closer alliance.

In the fall of 1959 the television quiz show scandals arrived when it was revealed that such programs were regularly rigged. In the wake of that, ABC and the other networks used the incident to justify further network control over program production. Those quiz shows and many others had been produced under contract with sponsors, not networks. Sponsors purchased network time, which they filled with their own shows. Those scandals allowed the networks to reverse the lines of power and reap greater profits. Networks promised more responsibility to the public by taking control of their program fare, by contracting for production themselves and by selling spot time to sponsors. This allowed them to extract new profit-participating deals from shows aired domestically and later exported for foreign syndication.[40]

Another method of gaining control in foreign locales was *block-booking*, whereby potential buyers who expressed the desire to buy a hot series or film for their stations were forced to buy it in a block of other material, much of which they didn't want. Block-booking had been imposed by Hollywood film companies on foreign and domestic movie exhibitors since around 1915. It was a practice declared illegal in the U.S. at the end of the 1940s, when Hollywood's cartel control of film production, distribution and exhibition was ordered broken up by the U.S. Supreme Court on antitrust grounds. Hollywood continued to block-book abroad (and still does) although it remained illegal at home. Domestically the government brought a 1960 antitrust action against several major distributors — including UA, MGM and Screen Gems — for allegedly block-booking feature films to U.S. television stations. It was an unresolved case. Little block-booking took place abroad at that time mainly because most nations didn't have a lot of stations, making it easier for them to resist such pressure and pitting the majors more intensely against each other in an effort to sell their fare to relatively few outlets. Block-booking would become a more important weapon for U.S. majors as time passed.[41]

Then there was the publicity machine driving the American star system. Television stars regularly toured foreign nations to drum up bigger audiences for their shows. CBS sent its "Rawhide" stars Eric Fleming and Clint Eastwood to Japan in 1962 after having sent "Perry Mason" lead Raymond Burr on a tour that included stops in Australia, Italy, France, Germany, Sweden and the U.K. the previous year. Another way to make foreign inroads was to sell cheap. And one way to do that was to not pay the creative talent any residuals when tapes of their shows were played overseas. While the American Federation of Television and Radio Artists (AFTRA) had gotten such residual payments into its contracts for domestic repeats, gaining that concession for foreign airings was much slower in coming. NBC finally capitulated late in 1958 when it included a foreign residual clause in its agreement with AFTRA. However, CBS and ABC were still holding out. The lack of foreign residuals for actors meant a yearly loss to the creative talent of several millions of dollars each year.[42]

Another cost-saving method was employed by Sheldon Reynolds, producer of the series "Foreign Intrigue." With his cost of production at $21,000 per episode, Reynolds proudly observed he took in one third of that cost, $7,500, from foreign sales. French Canada paid only $400 per segment, but the deal had the Canadians pay the cost of the prints and for the dubbing. Thereafter he had the Gallic soundtrack free to use in France, where he tried to get his price increased by pointing out to the French how much it cost to dub a show. He tried to sell his program in the Arab market but decided there just wasn't enough Arab television then in existence to make it worthwhile. So the inventive producer put three episodes together and sold them to cinemas as a feature film.[43]

What was needed by the U.S. television interests was an organization to push American penetration in foreign locales from a united front. Hollywood film majors had their own group in place from the early 1920s that fought in foreign nations and domestically to control the world's film screens, the Motion Picture Association of America (MPAA). In 1945 the majors formed the Motion Picture Export Association (MPEA)—a subsidiary of the MPAA— to work specifically abroad. The MPEA lobbied governments, fixed prices and imposed block-booking—practices that in many cases were illegal at home but perfectly legitimate as long as practiced only overseas. Television producers and distributors began to seriously discuss a plan to form an organization to decide on uniform practices around 1956. Envisioned as a counterpart to the MPAA, this proposed television entity, said *Variety*, "would embrace negotiations with the U.S. Treasury and with foreign governments on reciprocal trade agreements." While it would also function at home, internationally the hope of the men and women behind the plan "is to empower the organization to negotiate with other countries in order to create video arrangements." Although the international television business was then worth only a few million yearly or so, "that investment must be protected from chaotic competition, particularly on an inter-country level." However, by 1957 the initiative was stalled, mainly because the Hollywood film majors had not committed fully to television. They viewed joining an organization containing independent television producer/distributors and the three networks— their perceived enemy until recently—with some suspicion. At the same time, the networks worried that being in an organization with the huge Hollywood majors would overwhelm them, with their interests being sacrificed whenever television interests conflicted with theatrical needs.[44]

Every once in a while plans to organize would surface, only to die out. Some distributors felt problems included that competition among them was too keen for unified cooperation and that the cost of running such an organization would be too great, plus the problems of attracting a man of stature to head such an organization, comparable to MPAA chief Eric Johnston.[45]

What drove the television companies into forming an organization was the rapid growth underway in foreign television plus the beginning of restrictions being imposed in some nations on the import of foreign television shows. In 1958 the MPAA offered to serve the television industry as well as film producers, but the offer was rejected due to the belief television interests would be lost within a film entity. As it looked to some like a power grab attempt, it hurried the coming of an organization specifically for television. Chaired by CBS executive Merle Jones, a committee was formed to bring a television entity into being. On the committee were representatives from MCA, UA, Screen Gems, NBC and ABC.[46]

On September 21, 1959, ABC president Oliver Treyz issued a statement calling for a television industry "state department" to negotiate with foreign governments and broadcasters to allow more U.S. programs in and more dollars out. On the following day ABC-Paramount president Leonard Goldenson called a news conference to emphasize the same point. Merle Jones explained such a lobby group was needed because the U.S. television audience was near its peak. That meant the prices charged by distributors for their product was nearing the maximum, yet producers argued that product prices had to rise still higher if "values" were to be improved beyond current levels. Such a dilemma could be solved in only one way: by expanding abroad, the only direction left. But trade barriers were starting to be erected; Japan had a price maximum for imports, the U.K. had a 14 percent foreign maximum; in the Philippines as well as in Brazil and Argentina currency was frozen; Canada had recently announced a 45 percent maximum of foreign fare on television. Germany had no quotas or other restrictions, but one U.S. network executive complained the Germans were "selective" when buying. The organization would be set up under the Webb-Pomerane Act, an old World War I–vintage law that exempted foreign trade associations from U.S. antitrust laws provided any and all questionable activities engaged in abroad did not take place domestically as well.[47]

Late in December 1959 representatives of 17 firms met and agreed to form the Television Program Export Association (TPEA). Those 17 sold about 90 percent of all U.S. television product sold abroad. Members included all three networks and almost all Hollywood majors. Pointing out the "danger signs" of restrictions on television imports then being imposed in some locales, TPEA organizer William Fineshriber (formerly with SG) said it was "far easier and better" to prevent restrictions coming about than to attempt to repeal them after they had been imposed.[48]

John G. McCarthy was named president of the TPEA early in 1960. From 1950 to 1957 he had been a vice president of both the MPAA and the MPEA. After that, McCarthy worked for the U.S. Department of State as director of the U.S. Office of Economic Affairs. Fineshriber was named a vice president, in charge of television, for both the MPAA and the MPEA. The year following his appointment McCarthy was off on a trip to Latin

America. One stop was in Argentina, where he met with Argentinean senator Benjamin Guzman, who had introduced a bill in his country requiring dubbing in Argentina of all imported television fare. McCarthy maintained he was successful in persuading Guzman to postpone the bill. Later in 1961 McCarthy journeyed to London, England, where he met with British Board of Trade president Frank J. Erroll to complain about the U.K. quota, which, at a 14 percent foreign maximum, limited U.S. shows to no more than one hour per day on each of the BBC and ITV networks. He explained to Erroll that such a measure placed the buyers of television shows in a superior position whereby they "were actually operating a buyers' cartel." Also important was the effect the U.S. quota might have in influencing other markets to adopt similar measures. U.S. distributors were reduced, explained McCarthy, to competing in the U.K. "for a screen time of an hour a day with the rest of the world."[49]

And television was expanding rapidly abroad. By mid–1953 the new medium was a reality in sixteen nations with regular service and in another seven with television in the experimental stage. An estimated 3 million sets were then in use abroad that had an estimated audience of 25 to 30 million viewers, due to community viewing. The following year there were 6 million sets abroad; in 1955 an estimated 10.5 million sets were in use. One year after that 44 nations had regular programming, seen on over 196 stations. By comparison the U.S. then had 37.5 million sets in use and 459 stations.[50]

Scrambling to get a piece of that foreign market were the major U.S. distributors. Screen Gems had offices in Canada, the U.K. and several Latin American markets by early in 1957. Some 200 hours of SG material was playing outside the U.S., one hundred of them in Latin America. Leading the way was "Rin Tin Tin," which netted SG $100,000 yearly in Latin America alone. Altogether the Columbia subsidiary grossed $3 million yearly from television sales to 21 countries. While some local firms signed on as sponsors, mainly sponsors were large U.S. firms such as Proctor & Gamble, Colgate, Del Monte, Goodyear, Max Factor and Bristol-Myers.[51]

ZIV International, one of the largest of the independents, reported in 1957 that it had tripled its foreign take for each of the four years of its existence. Company president Ed Stern remarked that with some exceptions "foreign tastes in telefilms run along U.S. lines." One exception was sitcoms, which "baffled" foreign audiences. Also those audiences did not like "flag-waving," the nationalism found in shows featuring the American military, such as "West Point."[52]

SG vice president Ralph Cohn said enthusiastically at the start of 1958, "We are interested in producing programs for the whole world, and are prepared to go anywhere in the known world to find a market." Cohn noted his company had either branch offices or sales representatives in every nation that had television service. To produce for audiences in 40 countries speaking

12 different languages could be, said Cohn, "challenging and stimulating in a very important way. It demands a freshness, vitality and breadth of vision that will make it better entertainment on any screen." Although he did admit "our primary aim is to please American audiences." SG's then flagship program "Rin Tin Tin" was the subject of newspaper jokes that the dog could bark in 17 languages. Cohn claimed it was then the most widely aired program in the world. Grumbling about overseas problems with quotas, monetary restrictions and censorship abroad Cohn added one overlooked problem: "In Germany, France, Belgium and most of Latin America the sales contracts have to be written in the native language." An effective international sales operation required representatives in most world capitals but also frequent visiting of overseas television centers by home office executives, explained Cohn, an expensive undertaking. He felt the challenge of the global market was "building up one of the main pressures for bigness among television distributors." With the aid of its parent Columbia, SG could count on 40 international sales agents, all but three stationed abroad. Company executive William Fineshriber spent 40 percent of his time overseas. Even then SG was on the lookout to engage in coproduction deals with other nations, as SG was "eminently capable of guiding producers in other countries in the production of programs with the greatest profit potential in every country of the world," said Cohn.[53]

Fineshriber noted that on foreign operations his company was "very nicely in the black," which included the "costs of maintaining representation in every major country that has television as well as dubbing costs." He admitted it was then easy for a distributor to recover his dubbing and sales costs the first time around, particularly in Latin America. A Spanish dub cost around $1,200 per half-hour episode, with that cost recovered in sales to Cuba, Mexico and Puerto Rico — the rest was profit. A dub into French cost the same with sales to France, Luxembourg, Monte Carlo, Belgium and Quebec far exceeding that cost.[54]

Major independent company ZIV dubbed or subtitled in nine languages near the end of the 1950s: Spanish, German, French, Italian, Finnish, Flemish, Japanese, Tagalog and Chinese. Material dubbed into Spanish was distributed by ZIV in 12 Latin American nations and in Spain.[55]

Global television continued to spread abroad at a furious pace. From 1956 to 1958 the number of foreign television stations went from 230 to 566, with 404 of those being commercial outlets. Outside of the U.S. television was then received on 21 million sets, up from 10 million in 1956. Over 100 different American television programs were running every week in 43 nations ranging from a high of 93 half-hour series aired by Australian stations down to just three per week in France. Gross foreign television receipts were around $14 million in 1958, representing some 10 percent of American total world gross. In Latin America sponsors had the opportunity to buy the shows that they thought would do the best job for them and place the shows on the station of their choice. Outside of the Western Hemisphere and Japan, to the extent that commercials were even allowed, the sponsors were not directly involved with the programs, being limited to purchasing spots. The trend to filmed as opposed to live programs continued to grow — it favored American firms, as it was more costly. As well it helped eliminate local competition, which, was generally live. In June 1957, the top 15 shows in Puerto Rico contained nine live, six on film. One year later 12 of the top 15 shows were on tape.[56]

By then some 18 U.S. television companies were doing an estimated $20 million annually in overseas sales. One was the independent Television Programs of America (TPA), which sold 15 properties, from "Charlie Chan" to "Tugboat Annie," in 33 countries. TPA had 19 overseas representatives pitching to 600 foreign stations and 23 million sets. Within America there were 532 outlets and 48.5 million receivers. TPA provided subtitles or "running narration" in a variety of languages, including Thai and Arabic. That rapid growth of television abroad had many U.S. industry executives dreaming of the day sales to foreign television would provide 50 percent of the total gross — as was almost the case in the film industry. One reason U.S. distributors liked to sell directly to a sponsor for airing abroad was that it ensured payment would be received. ZIV, for one, sold series for Latin American airing by going to U.S. transnationals such as Proctor & Gamble, GE and Westinghouse. ZIV sent the bill to company headquarters in America for payment in dollars, avoiding any currency restrictions in Latin America and late payments or no payments at all from a foreign outlet. Having bought a program that way the transnational would then simply buy air time in Latin America. Of the 23 million or so sets outside of America in 1958, 9.3 million were in the U.K., 3 million in Canada, 1.7 million each in Japan and West Germany. No other country had as many as 1 million sets in operation except for the Soviet Union, with an estimated 2.5 million receivers. In any case it was not a market for American television product.[57]

At the beginning of the 1960s U.S. television firms exported material to over 40 nations, grossing about $30 million yearly offshore, 20 percent of the total television revenue. "The Lone Ranger" ("El Llanero Solitario") rode the range in 24 nations. Latin America was a prime target for the U.S. television industry since its commercial television had less government oversight than any other region. At home the growth rate was stagnant relative to foreign television. Also, strict U.S. government regulations limiting the U.S. networks from owning more than five VHF stations each in the U.S. left them feeling constrained. There were then 1,088 foreign television stations beaming to 32 million sets in 56 countries with regular television service. As recently as 1951 there were 10 million sets in the U.S., less than 1 million in the remainder of the so-called free world. In 1960 some 86 percent of U.S. homes had a set, sales of new sets were growing only at a rate of 5 percent a year, and "program time is nearly all taken." Even then the rationale was being developed that foreign sales were necessary for U.S. producers to make any profits or in some cases to "break even." ABC's Coyle remarked that "the industry needs the overseas market to start making some gravy." Optimism reigned, with industry executives still foreseeing 40 to 50 percent of their total revenue coming from foreign sales sometime before the 1960s ended.[58]

Although western Europe had more money and more sets in operation than Latin America did, the latter was a major target for U.S. expansion because of less governmental oversight. NBC was helping to develop two stations in Mexico. Both NBC and CBS were lending financial and technical support to one channel each in Peru while all three networks were trying to get directly involved in Argentinean television. And, of course, ABC continued to develop CATVN in Central America. ABC had assigned itself the task of doing the CATVN program purchasing from a central source "for the benefit of all stations." These expansionary efforts were, wrote a trade journal, "the first stage of what the broadcasting companies hope will be several international networks spanning the western world."[59]

Surveying the world television scene in late 1960 *Business Week* hopefully reported that "foreign television has moved away from government supervision and government subsidization toward commercial operation. On both the sending and receiving end, television abroad is coming to look more like television in America." With rapid foreign growth and less government regulation than at home, in some nations, "U.S. broadcasting interests have been penetrating these inviting situations in whatever way permitted by local regulations: as advisors in France and Germany, as program purveyors in Britain, Canada, Japan; as minority owners of stations in Australia and Latin America; as network organizers in Central America and the Middle East." Proudly the magazine boasted, "The bigger foreign TV gets, the more it resembles the American product. Unquestionably, increased programming, particularly of a less cultural, more commercial nature, has spurred set sales in those countries. Where television operators are allowed to cater to the popular taste, programs run on about the same level as in the U.S. Indeed, U.S. programs, suitably dubbed for the local market, provide the bulk of the most popular fare on foreign stations." Italian television then limited ads to three assigned time periods per day of five minutes each — no other commercials were allowed, nor were programs interrupted. *Business Week* was even enthusiastic about that, claiming that "these commercials tend to be excellent entertainment that hold the audience during the long commercial intervals." Yet all was not as rosy as the magazine pretended. Outside of Latin America and Japan, commercials were nonexistent or severely limited. It caused a schizophrenic reaction among U.S. firms as they moved from area to area looking for El Dorado. Latin America was open but had less sets and money than did western Europe, but the latter permitted little or no advertising. The solution was to have more commercially run television systems, as opposed to state-controlled public broadcasters. That was easier said than done, however.[60]

As early as 1954 *Variety* reported that foreign sources of revenue lay mostly in Latin America with Mexico, Cuba, Puerto Rico and Venezuela leading the way. With the exception of Canada — often considered part of the U.S. domestic market — there were only minor dealings with other nations. Britain was only a tiny source of television buying, but the coming of commercial television to the U.K. was expected to drastically enlarge its share. Even then *Variety* reported that "foreign sales at present cannot even cover the cost of overseas operations" — an illusion.[61]

Three years later SG Latin American director John Manson was bullish on the Latin American television market for U.S. fare. The reason being that in that area, unlike in Europe and elsewhere, television facilities were privately owned and commercially sponsored in the U.S. pattern in all the nations of the region except Argentina and Columbia. With print readership comparatively low and illiteracy high, television was the ideal selling medium for the region. According to Manson, American companies in general that produced consumer products found Latin America a "wonderful" market with strong public acceptance of those products.[62]

That same year, 1957, NBC president Robert Sarnoff, back from a European sojourn, cited European television as at a takeoff point, saying, "The economic facts of life weigh heavily in favor of privately-owned commercially supported TV in the future" in Europe because "many governments simply don't have the money to support a national service of the scope and type their people seem to want." Sarnoff did warn that Europeans would not welcome an indiscriminate flood of U.S. product: "There would be an emotional rebellion against loss of national identity if any foreign product was dominant in any European nation."[63]

At the same time the trade journal *Broadcasting* predicted that foreign television sales would account for 40 percent of gross revenues within the next five years. According to this source no American distributor was then making much, or any, money from foreign sales. Answering its own question as to why then U.S. firms were selling to foreign outlets, *Broadcasting* explained that what extra money did come home meant "U.S. prices may be maintained at current levels" (that is, not raised domestically). Also in answer to that question, *Broadcasting* gave the following reasons: "to upgrade program levels for U.S. advertisers outside the U.S. and give them programs which have proved their worth in competitive U.S. markets"; to build a market for the future when circumstances may be more favorable; "to help build foreign television set sales by use of U.S. stars as box office attractions;" and "to improve the sales picture abroad for both U.S. and foreign advertisers, and thus contribute to the reputation of television film as an advertising medium."[64]

Yet years later Europe remained a hard-to-crack market. In 1961 no continental European nation was close to putting a second channel on the air, except West Germany and Italy. Having only one publicly run network in each nation meant hard times for U.S. fare. For one thing, the price paid could be held to a reasonable level. West Germany's custom was to buy just a few episodes of a U.S. series, to run them, and if the series proved popular, to buy more episodes. American distributors much preferred selling at least in full-series lots and to block-book other material, if possible.[65]

At the end of 1961 the MPEA issued an optimistic report predicting some kind of commercial television in all non–Communist lands by 1965. Yet there were only six nations on the Continent then allowing advertising. It was important because "American exporters' stake in commercial television is that introduction of advertising-supported TV abroad results in more pure entertainment shows being bought, more dollars being paid for shows, and perhaps, the opening of competing, new channels." According to the MPEA one factor stimulating commercial television on the Continent was "the rapidly growing agitation for TV advertising on the part of influential businessmen and the mounting costs of maintaining a sustaining television service which can favorably compare to an advertiser-supported service." West Germany's First Channel (nine state-owned stations) aired only from 8 to 11 P.M. with no sponsorship of shows, only spot ads, 12 minutes per day per station. The Second Channel (due to enter full service in 1962) then carried no ads. Italy's first network, RAI, limited ads to four brief periods per day while that nation's second network, also state run by RAI, allowed no ads at that point during its start-up phase. Only the small European nations of Monte Carlo and Luxembourg had completely commercial television systems. Their significance for the future lay in their coverage beyond their own borders more than in their local service. Between them Tele-Luxembourg and Tele-Monte Carlo reached 180,000 households in France, 70,000 in Belgium, and a lesser number in West Germany. One observer argued "their success in the overlap areas serves to stimulate the demand for TV advertising in these countries." France and Belgium had only one network each, both publicly run with no ads, but the signal spillover from Luxembourg and Monte Carlo added to the pressure for commercial television in both nations, pressure that had been applied for years. Holland's noncommercial sole network received spillover from German broadcasters "and their advertising messages are serving to increase the drive for a commercial service there." Surrounded by commercial television signals, Switzerland allowed no ads on its single public channel, but this policy led to demands from Swiss companies for their own television advertising. Within Scandinavia Denmark, Norway and Sweden had an agreement that no one of them would introduce commercial television without consulting the others. Here the belief was that if one of them went commercial the others would have to follow. U.S. television exporters, of course, all wanted to see commercial television in all nations. There was so much lobbying from domestic sources in each land that the Americans hardly had to lobby at all themselves. Still, commercial television was slow in coming, especially from the American perspective.[66]

One of the problems with public television was its limited hours of operation. Nations moved slowly to add new outlets and to extend the hours of operation of existing stations. On the other hand, commercial outlets tended to expand rapidly both in terms of on-air hours and number of outlets. This, of course, was of great benefit to distributors of programs and advertisers. The more outlets there were, the more demand and competition for programs — which tended to push prices up. In 1954 when Canada had only the public broadcaster CBC on the air — it did accept ads — U.S. distributors found it hard to sell to the CBC, as it was virtually sold out. The only way a distributor could get a series on the air was to sell it to a current sponsor that was willing to drop its present show, subject to CBC approval. As early as 1953 the private broadcasters, through their trade group, the Canadian Association of Broadcasters, was constantly lobbying for television to be taken out of the hands of government and for permission to open private television outlets.[67]

CBC general manager A. D. Dunton remarked in 1955 that Canadians had rich and expensive tastes in video. He admitted that that taste came from watching television shows originating in the U.S. while reiterating that the CBC could import television shows at much lower cost than it could originate them.[68]

Although Latin America was largely open to commercial television, lobbying continued. Mexico's biggest broadcaster was Emilio Azcarraga, who was also a major spokesman for the Inter-American Association of Broadcasters (IAAB), with members from some ten nations, including the U.S. According to Azcarraga the group's mission was for IAAB members to "travel from one country to another throughout Central and South America at their own expense to convince the powers-that-be that radio and television should operate as free commercial enterprises." He was on record as opposed to public broadcasters such as Canada's CBC, the U.K.'s BBC and Italy's RAI. That criticism was cloaked under the rubric that public broadcasters denied freedom of expression. Touring America for the IAAB in 1956 various transnational companies and broadcasters threw galas for Azcarraga and the other members of his group. He explained those U.S. firms "mostly had nothing to sell; they were interested in our principles." Both NBC and ABC promised full support to the IAAB. Discussing his group's mission Azcarraga told reporters, "You know how we can build television in little countries like Salvador is by throwing the kinescopes in their hands. If they only pay $15 or $20 for one of our shows, we will have helped them, and we have nothing to lose…. So we'll help and maybe later on pro-rate our charges to increases in the people watching television."[69]

An example of the importance of commercial broadcasters to U.S. distributors could be found in Cuba's major broadcaster Goar Mestre, who had major links to American firms. Cuba's television was all commercial, and Mestre was a broadcasting magnate. In 1955 he was reported to be the most prolific buyer of both English-language and dubbed television fare in the Latin American market.[70]

Argentinean television was described as being "way behind other South American countries" because it was slow transferring television and radio systems to private enterprise. More channels were considered essential to develop set sales. RCA announced the availability of cheaper receivers in Argentina along with the establishment of a pay-later plan it had set up with a local finance company. Referring to one Argentinean station a report observed that "demand for advertising space on Channel 7 has now sparked extension of schedules."[71]

In the U.K. there was heated debate in the early 1950s about whether or not commercial television should be established there to compete against the sole, publicly run network, the BBC. Harry Towers, head of a large U.K. radio transcription company, said the establishment of a world market for television hinged largely on the approval of commercial television for Britain. Creation of commercial television in the U.K. would influence not only the European continent — then installing television — but the "entire English Commonwealth," he thought. They would all need programming product. At the time, 1953, the BBC aired six hours a day from six stations.[72]

Britain's opposition politicians strenuously opposed the coming of commercial television. In March 1954 a show business delegation that included actors Jack Hawkins and Dame Edith Evans marched on the House of Commons to try to keep U.S. shows from dominating the coming commercial television operation, which had recently been announced as going on the air in late 1955. Marchers wanted a quota of at least 80 percent domestic on the new enterprise. British Actors Equity chairman Gordon Sandison told an all-party meeting of 40 members of Parliament, "The chief menace is the import of films — mainly American — which have already covered their production costs in America and whose cheapness will attract British advertisers." U.S. distributors were said to be offering half-hour films abroad for $150.[73]

With the launch of private television in Britain in the fall of 1955 — and its startup in Australia several months later — U.S. suppliers were elated. These were major English-speaking markets, which involved no dubbing costs. Suddenly the potential of a series through foreign sales could be as high as one-third of the original budget if produced for a U.S. network and close to one-half in the case of a series shot originally for U.S. syndication. If a show could be sold in all or most territories *Variety* noted, "the foreign market now means a fat profit" for the distributor.[74]

As the commercial network debuted in Britain the BBC was reported to be fighting to hold onto the viewing public by bidding against the commercial network "and offering real money" to get the shows they wanted. By the end of 1955 the U.S. suppliers had sold around $3 million worth of product to Britain's commercial system, the take from 25 series ranging from "Gunsmoke" to "I Love Lucy" to "Lassie" to "Amos 'n' Andy." The situation meant American firms could sell blocks of 26 or 39 or up to as many as 78 episodes of a series, compared to the BBC's habit of buying less than a full run when it faced no direct competition. The rivalry between the U.K.'s private and public television systems had "meant lotsa sterling in American pockets and in some cases the difference between profit and loss on a particular series."[75]

However, in Europe generally commercial television was slow in coming. ZIV International president Ed Stern said in 1957 that all Europe was watching the U.K.'s commercial system. Stern felt private television would come soon to all European nations except perhaps to France "where the anti-commercial tradition is strongest."[76]

Early in 1958 Switzerland ended a four-year television trial period with the people then asked if they wished the Swiss government to take over the system and finance it. They said no. The problem was that they also said no to having commercials on television. Solving the problem was the Newspaper Publishers' Association, which reached agreement with the state whereby it would give television $465,000 annually for a period of ten years — on the condition that no commercials would be allowed. The remainder, and minor part, of television funding was to come from a set license fee of $19.50 per year per television home. Thus Swiss television was guaranteed to be ad free for at least ten years. If license fee revenue ever reached the point where it fully funded the system, then the newspaper group could cease its funding. Swiss television was on the air 14 hours a week with 50 to 60 percent of its offerings on film — half of that from the U.S. Still, it amounted to only about four hours a week. Stations were located in Zurich and Geneva, with the latter getting mainly French-dubbed versions of U.S. fare while Zurich received English-language product, "with a short German commentary." Opposition to television in general was the usual reaction from a nation's print media for the obvious reasons: they feared a loss of audience and a loss of ad revenue in countries with commercial systems. Generally a nation's print media were among the most vigorous lobbyists against private television. There were exceptions, though. Australia's print media offered no opposition, only encouragement. But then they owned most of the commercial outlets.[77]

Director of France's state broadcaster Radiodiffusion-Television-Francaise Christian Chavanon stated in 1959 there would definitely be no commercial aspects in the second state-run channel in France, expected to be operational in the near future. He wasn't sure what the situation would be like in five or ten years but was definite on there being no commercial television soon. Chavanon admitted to "pressures being put on the government by private concerns to open television to ads and commercial programming."[78]

Financial considerations often played a major role in determining the type of television a country had. By 1961 five-year-old Spanish television had one government-run network, which allowed commercials, broadcasting six hours a day, seven days a week to 300,000 receivers. Spanish television's annual budget came to less than $400,000 a year, in the neighborhood of what a single 90- or 120-minute spectacular sometimes cost in the U.S. Not surprisingly, many old American series aired over Spanish television, such as "Seahunt" and "Medic." Spanish film exhibitors were said not to be too worried about this as a threat to their business because "Yank serials are popular as time fillers, not as a substitute for entertainment."[79]

West Germany had a single, state-run network consisting of several regional outlets in 1961. By February of that year all the ad time for 1961 had been sold out. While commercials were allowed, they were limited to five minutes beginning at 7:25 P.M. and to the last three minutes before 8 P.M. Thus, for the entire network it was only 56 minutes per day (eight minutes times seven stations), or, as *Variety* lamented, "Throughout all of West Germany, it's right now possible to book only 27 hours of commercials in a month — less than one hour of commercial time daily." Those 27 hours contained 4,000 spots representing around 300 brands or firms.[80]

A somewhat depressed Alvin Ferleger, NBC International director of sales, told a global television forum at the Los Angeles chapter of the Academy of Television Arts and Sciences that U.S. television sales might never get 50 percent of their total gross from foreign sources because television fare was so often sold abroad to government-owned monopolies "who can fix prices." Even when there were commercials allowed, there was much less advertising abroad on television than at home, meaning lower prices for product were the rule.[81]

Although television was barely underway in most countries, the Americans were already into coproductions with other nations, in a minor way. Often these were used as examples of mutual cooperation and as exemplifying cultural exchange; in reality it was a way for American producers to circumvent restrictions against foreign television imports then beginning to arise. One example of a coproduced series was SG's "Ivanhoe," made in the U.K. Wholly owned by SG, it used a British director and crew, which enabled it to qualify as a domestic product, which exempted it from the quota of a 14 percent maximum of foreign fare allowed on television. *Variety* made its own nationalistic slip by referring to the restriction as a "14% quota on American product" — it was 14 percent on all foreign.[82]

Faced with price ceilings on imported American television product in Japan, NBC International director of operations Alfred Stern considered coproduction deals there after a visit by him proved fruitless in raising those price ceilings. Of those potential deals he said, "We would undoubtedly send over an American lead and an American director to make the kind of show that meets the needs of the advertisers. The remainder of the cast would be English-speaking Japanese performers." Stern even thought it may be possible to shoot two versions, the second being in Japanese for the home market.[83]

Returning home from a 1961 trip through Europe, SG vice president William Dozier lamented, "Our family shows are not popular abroad because they don't understand our mores." Citing upcoming coproduction deals with both Canada and the U.K., Dozier was enthusiastic about the concept since the overseas profit potential was so attractive. Explaining the benefits of such deals Dozier said "By making pictures abroad we improve our position as a friendly company with those nations and have better opportunities to have our TV series shown. By maintaining our own offices we know the market better and resultantly get better prices for our series. Producing in these countries takes us out of the quota restrictions. The profit potential abroad gives fiscal soundness to our thinking."[84]

A 1961 account in a trade journal remarked that Australia, one of the biggest foreign markets for American television material, was upset over the almost total lack of coproduction deals in that country. One unnamed high-level Australian television industry executive told the reporter he believed that unless the situation was corrected he saw his country following the quota examples set by others, thus putting an end to the "free market" there. Contrasting the situation with Canada — which had recently imposed a 45 percent minimum domestic quota for television airings — where there were coproduction deals with American producers, this executive said that "Australian television has no quota in effect against American programs. In fact, the Aussie stations' schedules read like most U.S. major market outlets from sign-on to sign-off." There was a connection this executive apparently failed to see. Americans did coproduction deals with other nations only when restrictions of some kind against imported television fare were in effect and the Americans perceived coproductions necessary as a way of increasing their tube penetration. As long as a country was wide open to U.S. offerings — as Australia then was — there was little chance of a coproduction deal. Countries that struck such deals got no real benefit, since American producers always insisted on full control over content, regardless of amount of financial investment. It was the American way, or no way.[85]

The advent of television around the globe brought with it hopes in many lands of true cultural exchange, with the television productions from various nations being seen in many other lands. In particular foreign producers hoped to crack the large, rich American market. Anyone casting even a glance at the structure of the world theatrical film business — then dominated by the U.S. for well over a quarter of a century with exchange being strictly one way, as almost no foreign films made it to U.S. screens — would have realized true exchange would never happen. As with the film business, America imposed no quotas or restrictions on the import and screening of such fare, yet it rarely ever happened.

NBC's Stern also contemplated program exchanges after his nine-week 1958 world tour. This contemplation was due to a worry on Stern's part that foreign restrictions and quotas on U.S. television material could become even worse if the U.S. did not allow some sort of program exchange with other nations, reversing the dollar drain from those regions. During a stop in Australia Stern told Australians that, for example, a recent "Wide, Wide World" episode did a story about doctors. Australia had famed flying doctors who covered the outback country. If Stern's concept had been a reality at the time NBC would have had local Australian broadcasters do a piece on flying doctors and ship it to NBC for use on the program. For the future, NBC might send a list of "Wide, Wide World" projects for the coming season to Australia, along with "recommendations" on what Australians could do. Stern also thought NBC could use taped segments of Australian talent on the "Tonight Show." If the exposure proved popular the Australian talent might come to America for live appearances. When asked why not simply import television fare from abroad as the simplest solution to the problem, Stern quickly replied that that was not possible as no practical way had by then been devised to bring in foreign product, not only because of language differences "but because the foreign networks and producers generally have no idea of the needs of American advertisers." The audience was not mentioned.[86]

Cultural exchange between the U.S. and the Soviet Union became a big news item in the 1950s, with much discussion between government officials and private U.S. firms. Little transpired at the time although there was a much-ballyhooed exchange of theatrical films in the middle of the decade, with ten U.S. features going east while seven Soviet films came west. Television saw no such exchanges, with one reason being that none of the three U.S. networks showed any interest, despite prodding in that direction by the State Department. A major stumbling block to any such exchange was the Soviet demand that U.S. television allow as much time for Soviet product as the Soviet set aside for American product.[87]

At a 1960 forum on global television held in America and attended by industry figures from around the globe there were many complaints that international television was a one-way street, that American telecasters bought no imports. Greeve del Strother of the BBC said there was a lot of "lip service" about international exchanges "but it doesn't mean much if the flow of exports is one-way." NBC International executive Alvin Ferleger retorted, "We represent the greatest market in the world for television programs. We have no quotas, no restrictions," and he added, "we also have virtually no solicitations from foreign television program producers." He urged them to make a "real effort" to sell their product here.[88]

A couple of years later nothing had changed: no foreign fare on U.S. television and plenty of foreign complaints about that situation. Over the years *Variety* felt compelled to do an article from time to time admitting to the fact but suggesting that changes were coming very soon, although qualifiers were usually tacked on. "More of a two-way street is developing in the foreign field, with a greater variety of foreign television product getting American airing, and with U.S. distributors taking on non–American product for distribution in other areas of the world. It's still a long way from being an even-steven operation, if that ever will come or if that is even desirable," said one example.[89]

Pondering why it was that little foreign fare was ever broadcast in America, *Variety*, in another 1962 article, noted that broadcasting executives said efforts to produce abroad were made "time and time again, even under network auspices, but for one reason or another, mainly in the creative area, the projects in most instances don't jell." Other executives pointed to a lack of "sophistication" in a good deal of foreign television shows. As *Variety* pointed out, this lack referred to the failure of foreign product to meet what was held to be "popular American tastes." Hopefully, the article cited some executives from the U.S. industry who labeled the current export/import television program situation as just the beginning "of a developing two-way street." However, other executives pointed to radio, which had always been as domestic as apple pie.[90]

Occasionally during this period Hollywood found time to wallow in self-pity, bemoaning the idea that foreign broadcasters somehow had the upper hand on the Americans, that it was the foreigners who operated in cartel unity against U.S. distributors, driving down the price to the distributors. And there was nothing the Americans could do. Cuba's Goar Mestre formed Television America, S.A. (TISA) in 1958. It was a pact between stations in Cuba, Puerto Rico, Venezuela and El Salvador whereby TISA would buy programs for all its members. U.S. distributors, including NBC and ABC, opposed TISA complaining they were subjected to "tremendous price-cutting" if they sold to TISA. Grumbling that the Latin American market had never been very rewarding financially U.S. firms said the $600 they had been getting for a half-hour program in Caracas had been reduced to $400 by TISA. Although, one distributor did admit it was possible to gross $5,000 in Latin America per half-hour show before it was exhausted. Even when the expense of maintaining a foreign sales force was subtracted, along with the $800 to $900 for dubbing, there was still "good profit." With the exception of CBS, which continued to sell to TISA, all major U.S. distributors were then boycotting TISA. They were in a battle to keep from losing their distributor grip in the region. Mestre had approached Mexico's Azcarraga urging him to join, but the latter declined. TISA was, however, attempting to get stations in Peru, Argentina and Colombia into its group "to make its telefilm buying combine complete and inescapable." TISA soon collapsed when Fidel Castro took power in Cuba, nationalizing the nation's television industry.[91]

When *Variety* dealt with the problems of selling abroad, in 1961, it discussed the usual subjects such as quotas and currency restrictions but alluded to the existence in some foreign nations "of booking combines and cartels to fix prices of American films but there's no way to get around it." CBS executive Robert Levine moaned, "If we don't sell to them someone else will." He also indicated "there has been no unified front by American producers to combat the practice."[92]

One example given was that of the U.K., where, by 1961, the arrival of commercial television had led to the creation of the television millionaires. Unfortunately not everyone was permitted to share in the bonanza, "least of all the foreign vidpic distributor who is taking quite a beating in this buyers' market." With the top price for a one-hour segment sold to commercial television being $7,000, it was all the fault of that 14 percent foreign quota, with the result that "all distribs have to scramble for that restricted playing time." In this case *Variety* chose to ignore all the articles it had run pointing out how much money had been made by U.S. distributors selling to the new commercial operation and how the rivalry between the BBC and the ITV had driven prices up and how even with an unchanged quota, a doubling of airtime in total had meant a doubling of U.S. television imports.[93]

By around 1957 U.S. feature films were in their heyday on domestic television. Always popular, theatrical films quickly became, and remain, a staple on U.S. television. However, in those early years U.S. movies had little presence on foreign screens. *Variety* thought features "will be supplemental programming by and large, and like in the U.S. telecast in many areas during so-called 'off-hours.' At this point, the American cinematics are not seen competitive to any degree to U.S. telefilms, the half-hours making their mark in the foreign market."[94]

One reason for limited penetration of U.S. films on foreign television sets was the limited number of hours those systems were on air compared to U.S. standards. Compounding the problem was the fact that where quotas existed it was easier to book a half-hour show on the air than a one-and-a-half-hour feature film. Also a difficulty was that cinema exhibitors abroad put a great deal of pressure on their governments and on U.S. distributors to keep feature films off the air. They had considerable success. Since those films were distributed to television by the same Hollywood majors who distributed to theaters, they tended to move cautiously. Prices received from foreign broadcasters for feature films were described as "low. For that reason, many companies haven't made much of a plunge in that field. Screen Gems has held back because of that." The big hope of American distributors was that when more stations went on air, especially of the commercial variety, "the market will open up quite a bit. For that reason some distribs are holding back, feeling that the price will climb in future years."[95]

The importance to the telecaster of movies of more channels with longer hours could be seen in the American domestic situation. A survey there showed that 43 percent of all domestic stations devoted from ten to twenty hours a week to feature film telecasting. Independent stations averaged 21 films a week, for an average total time of 36 hours weekly, or 38.3 percent of their total broadcasting hours. Stations affiliated with the networks averaged nine films a week for an average of fifteen hours total, or 13.7 percent of their total weekly broadcasting hours. Of the survey *Variety* commented, "As the number of stations in a market increase, so does the use of feature films."[96]

By 1960-61 the situation remained the same: relatively little exposure of U.S. films on foreign outlets. At the same time the pool of available films for television had grown enormously since the mid–1950s, when the Hollywood majors began to license their films to television in a big way. By 1961 the number of theatrical films available to television had reached 12,209, with 2,651 of those being in the post–1948 category. Little material outside of entertainment fare — series and movies — made it to foreign television sets. For 1961 estimates were that NBC and CBS grossed a total of $1 million from sales of news and public affairs abroad; CBS grossed $600,000 of that; ABC had no such sales to speak of. Total gross for U.S. television distributors offshore was then about $43 million yearly.[97]

In their quest to dominate the global television scene U.S. suppliers received a great deal of government help. As with the film industry, the costs paid out by the government were socialized — shared by all taxpayers — while the profits were privatized, limited to a few very large firms who were very rich to begin with. In 1953 New York television consultant Rudolf Bretz went to Germany to advise on television programming and production. His trip, salary and expenses were paid by the U.S. State Department, which announced he had received a grant under the educational exchange program.[98]

Major independent distributor ZIV Television got to host a traveling delegation of 18 foreign television officials representing 11 nations at their Cincinnati headquarters in 1955. Those officials were touring the U.S. under the auspices of the State Department's Special TV Project.[99]

When television debuted in the fall of 1956 in Australia, it began with three stations in each of the two largest cities, Sydney and Melbourne. Two of the outlets in each location were commercial; one was the government-run ABC (Australian Broadcasting Corporation). Although strict monetary controls were in place in Australia, each of the six stations was allowed to spend up to $100,000 for imported shows. Before television debuted there Winston Frecker, an executive with commercial station ATP in Sydney, was in the U.S. studying the television scene there. His visit was sponsored by the U.S. State Department under its International Education Exchange Service, which was geared to train selected overseas persons, noted a report, "in general television presentation, and also to provide an insight into the American way of life." Thanks to such efforts *Variety* announced, "It can be taken for granted that the majority of the programs televised here will carry the U.S. tag."[100]

The first television outlet to open in Africa south of the Sahara did so in Ibadan, Nigeria. NBC played a major role in its start-up and early operation. A producer of local shows for the outlet, Segun Olusola, spent four months in 1960-61 in the U.S. on a State Department–sponsored tour of American television centers. Not surprisingly the shows broadcast on Ibadan's station included a dominant U.S. presence.[101]

In 1953 the newly created United States Information Agency (USIA), an independent government agency, was set up for overseas information programs. The existing Voice of America was transferred to USIA from the State Department. A dozen years later the separate motion picture and television operations were combined into a single service within the USIA. Tapes and films were produced by the agency for distribution abroad. Over the years it provided invaluable assistance by giving taped material for free to developing television services in poorer nations, thus forestalling excuses from such countries that even if they set up television they would have little or no money left for programming. By doing so the USIA established an American presence while instilling a taste for television in the populace. At the same time the USIA avoided antagonizing U.S. television suppliers by sending abroad only material of an educational or cultural nature — leaving all the entertainment programming for commercial distributors to export. Thus the USIA always took pains to ensure it could not be accused of competing with or taking potential business away from Hollywood.[102]

Painstakingly the USIA counted the number of television sets in operation in all nations around the world, while also tabulating the number of television outlets in existence, hours of operation, whether they were commercial or public outlets, and so forth. Such information was invaluable to U.S. suppliers, as they often based selling prices in foreign lands very roughly on the number of sets in use, as well as the number of viewers per set, with almost all numbers generated from USIA information and data. USIA television chief Romney Wheeler remarked in 1958 that international television growth provided America with a "fine opportunity" to tell the world about the American way of life. But, explained Wheeler, the hard sell would be avoided in that effort: "We only want them to get to know us — to understand us a little better — and to see for themselves that we don't resemble, even remotely, the Communist-inspired image of America."[103]

Courtesy of the USIA one learned that at the end of 1958 the world had 70 million television sets: 44 million in the U.S., 2.6 million in Canada, 23 million in all other nations. Excluding the U.S. and Canada, the rest of the Free World had 19.5 million of those sets with 3.5 million in the Communist bloc. Worldwide the set count had increased 6.5 million in one year. Western Europe had 14.5 million sets in use — 9 million of them in the U.K. Various other breakdowns were provided by the USIA, with all of it of no use to anyone but the U.S. television exporters and their commercial allies.[104]

Government help came in other ways. In 1962 Reykjavík, Iceland, had some 400 television aerials sprouting from rooftops, yet Iceland had no television at all. Those antennae were trying to catch the signals from the U.S. forces base in Keflavík, some 35 miles distant. That 50-watt transmitter, in operation about seven years, broadcast mostly taped U.S. shows for the benefit of the 4,000 U.S. military personnel stationed there. Putting pressure on the Icelandic government to increase the station's power to 250 watts, the U.S. military argued that was necessary because "50-watt equipment is no longer available" and the current equipment was wearing out. That request set off a furious debate in Iceland's Parliament to keep foreign influences out, or to a minimum. In the end permission to increase power was granted. The whole episode had the effect of pushing Iceland to set up its own television service probably sooner than it would have had the country been free of such outside pressures.[105]

Within America in 1950 there were 100 stations transmitting to 5 million receivers; in 1956, 450 stations (many on air 18 hours a day) were broadcasting to 37 million sets. By 1963, 600 television stations telecasted to 56 million receivers. Three out of every four American households had television by 1956.[106]

Contrasting that was the situation in western Europe, which had 3.7 million receivers in use at the start of 1955, 3.5 million of them in the U.K. A survey on the status of television in 28 Free World nations conducted by the U.S. government determined that the BBC had 45 hours of programming per week, moving to 50; Belgium broadcast 30 hours a week to 10,000 sets; Denmark transmitted just eight hours a week; France telecast to 119,000 sets 28 hours a week; West German television was on air two to three hours per day broadcasting to 95,000 sets; Italy had 32 hours of weekly programming and 50,000 sets; Canada had 1 million sets. In South America, Argentina had 35 hours of programming per week and 30,000 sets while the Rio de Janeiro, Brazil, outlet was on air 35 hours a week. The three stations at São Paulo, Brazil, broadcast a total of 98 hours a week.[107]

By 1956 the set count in continental western Europe was 1.25 million with 350,000 each in France and West Germany and 300,000 in Italy. The U.K. then had 6 million receivers. Dubbing costs for a half-hour U.S. program ranged from $1,000 to $1,400 in French and from $1,400 to $2,300 in German. NBC executive Romney Wheeler remarked that dubbing should be done in the nation involved, citing as "worst examples" of ineptness some dubbing of U.S. fare into German at a studio in Mexico City using German refugees, with the result being ludicrous to German ears since members of the same family turned up speaking totally different dialects. Since most countries prohibited telecasting except by their national services, Wheeler stated, "it has been necessary to establish commercial stations in principalities like Luxembourg and Monaco or in the autonomous Saar." Signal spillover from those broadcasters reached into France, Belgium and Germany, putting pressure on those countries to allow domestic commercial television.[108]

As of October 1960, there were 38.6 million sets abroad tuned to 1,353 stations. Six million of those sets were behind the Iron Curtain — 4 million in the Soviet Union. Western Europe had 22.1 million sets; the Far East had 7 million receivers; Latin America had 3.3 million, the Near East and Africa had 170,000 sets. Those statistics were all compiled by the USIA. In the four months ending in October 1960, the USIA reported its television service sent a total of 226 programs to 51 nations with an estimated viewing audience of 135 million. One year later there were reported to be 50 million sets outside the U.S. and 53 million in America. Of the foreign sets, the U.K. had 12 million; Canada, 4 million; Italy, 2.5 million; France, 2 million; Scandinavia, 1.6 million; Brazil, 1.2 million; Australia, 1.2 million; Japan, 8 million; West Germany, 4.8 million; the Soviet bloc had 8 million receivers.[109]

The year 1957 was only the fourth year or so in which the foreign take was important to U.S. distributors, with the total foreign television gross that year estimated at about $14 million — 10 to 20 percent of the total world gross. U.S. fare was on air in 36 nations; thirteen in Latin America, fourteen in continental Europe and four in the Far East. The number-one market was Canada, which accounted for about $8 million of the foreign take. Most of the remaining $6 million came from the U.K., Australia and Latin America. It was possible for a first-run U.S. program to achieve $15,000 per episode if sold in virtually every market abroad, but few shows did that well. By the end of the 1950s the foreign take was estimated at about $20 million yearly.[110]

Then the gross began to take off. For 1960 the foreign television market yielded $30 million. One year later it was about $43 million with $23 million to $29 million from the U.K., Canada and Australia, $5 million to $6 million from Latin America and $4 million each from the Far East and the Near and Middle East. Motion pictures accounted for 20 to 25 percent of that $43 million. Foreign receipts were rising dramatically as television spread rapidly offshore in the number of sets in use, the number of outlets telecasting and the number of hours each station broadcast.[111]

For 1962 the estimated foreign take was $50 million, with $16.5 million from Canada, $9 million from Australia and New Zealand, $7 million from the U.K., $6 million from Latin America, $5 million from continental Europe, $3.2 million from Japan, $2.8 million from Thailand, Hong Kong and the Philippines combined, and $1 million total from the Middle East and Africa.[112]

Chapter 2

1940–1962:
"British TV Is Going American in a Big Way"

As American television programs spread globally, delivering "I Love Lucy," four-legged stars such as Lassie and Rin Tin Tin, and the wit and wisdom of "Father Knows Best," it was discovered that Lucy was not loved universally. Hostility and resentment arose in various lands. When U.S. distribution executive George Caputo returned from a Latin American selling trip in 1956 he commented that he found a lot of hostility to U.S. fare, citing in particular "Latin nationalism and Latin unions." Television had come early to the region, before filmed material was readily available, thus, when U.S. shows arrived on tape they squeezed out the local, live fare. Systems starting later programmed filmed shows from the outset. The overthrow of the Juan Perón regime in Argentina in that era was greeted with enthusiasm in U.S. television circles, as his ouster was hoped to be a step in the direction of opening Argentinean television to U.S. product. Under Perón, wrote an observer, Argentinean television was subject to close supervision "and represented a closed-door not only to American entertainment product but to the American export ad agencies and their clients, the international divisions of dozens of giant American consumer industries."[1]

U.S. television's fledgling lobby group, Television Program Export Association (TPEA), called publicly for the removal in Latin America of any and all restrictive practices against U.S. television product and demanded higher prices for its material. American independent supplier Leo Cagan, headquartered in Mexico City, argued the big restrictive evil in the region was "monopolistic situations"—meaning state control of telecasting. Cagan felt the best way to get more shows on the air, and at higher prices, was to aid the development of competitive stations in as many nations as possible. He argued that such public statements by TPEA only angered station buyers and increased negative reaction. Investment in competitive stations in the Latin region was the way to proceed, he stated. As an example of the power of competitive outlets Cagan pointed to Argentina, where the single Buenos Aires station paid him $80 for a 30-minute show just two years earlier while then he received $300 for the same item while also selling more shows in total. The difference was that Buenos Aires then had three outlets, instead of only one.[2]

Brazil had an unofficial quota of 80 percent domestic product for stations in Rio and São Paulo until 1960, when it was lifted. That quota had been worked out between unions and stations, but as more outlets came on the air the need for product became acute, resulting in the end of the unofficial quota.[3]

Brazilians continued to protest against the amount of foreign television on the air, causing President Janio Quadros to sign new regulations into law in 1961, to take effect at the beginning of 1962. Under the new law, for every two foreign shows on the air one Brazilian show had to be aired. During the evening prime-time hours of 7 to 9 P.M. only 30 minutes of station time could be devoted to taped material — the rest had to be live. During other hours filmed shows could occupy no more than 20 percent of total air time. At the time Brazil had 26 television stations in operation. All those owner-operators opposed the new measures. Pressure for the measures was led by unions, artists and technicians. Immediately U.S. interests tried to eliminate the regulations: "MPEA's Brazilian representative Harry Stone is trying to ease the terms of the decree, joining the station operators, advertising representatives and others." Before 1961 ended, those regulations were put on hold and Quadros was a former president. Early in 1962 the TPEA announced that those regulations had been specifically repealed.[4]

Agitation in Mexico against U.S. shows began in earnest in 1959 around several themes. One was a campaign against the violent content of American shows, called in the Mexican media "a grave danger to our youth." Local television producer Javier Espindola complained in the press about the $40,000 per month spent by Mexico on American television product. Mexico's government had recently passed legislation giving the state the right to control television and to "protect and watch over these vehicles of diffusion to see that they complete their social function." It was all worrisome to *Variety*, which summed it up as "an insidious snowballing campaign." A few months later Mexico's broadcaster Emilio Azcarraga denounced the "criminal themes" in U.S. shows. Reportedly he was able to drive the price he paid for a U.S. half-hour show from $500 to $400. Around the same time Cuba disappeared as a market for U.S. product when Castro nationalized the local television industry.[5]

The Mexican Union of Film Workers urged its government to ban foreign television product if the Spanish dubbing was done outside Mexico — to create more work. While many American shows were dubbed in Mexico, there was also dubbing done in Spain, Puerto Rico, Cuba (before Castro), and other areas, where dubbing fees were lower. American firms tended to pit nations against each other for their dubbing business.[6]

When U.S. Federal Communications Commission (FCC) chairman Newton Minow made his famous remarks in 1961 calling U.S. television a "vast wasteland," he touched off sparks in Mexico. One Mexican government official said it was time to get out from under "inheriting" the worst of American television product. Rodolfo Landa, head of Mexico's National Association of Actors, complained that Mexican television as a whole was merely a "bad copy of the United States." He attacked shows such as "I Love Lucy" and "Father Knows Best" as having family problems and solutions totally outside the normal mode of living in Mexico. Soon coming into force was the Mexican Radio and Television Law, supposedly with teeth, with the power to levy fines and revoke licenses of stations programming material contrary to "national integrity, social morality and human dignity" as well as fostering national injuries to youth. However, that Mexican campaign against excessively violent U.S. shows had been in effect for about a year "without much result it is true," reported *Variety*.[7]

Although Nigeria's sole television station had been established in Ibadan in 1959 with much American financial and technical assistance, there was resentment there. During a U.S. State Department–sponsored 1961 tour of television facilities in the U.S., Nigerian Minister of Education Emanuel Fadayiro explained that his country spent a great deal of scarce capital to establish that outlet, which ran for six hours a day broadcasting to just 10,000 sets, each having 20 to 35 viewers. The greatest weakness he saw was the poor quality of U.S. programs: "Our production funds are limited, and our programming depends largely on antiquated and inferior American filmed shows." Fadayiro added that a "big job in Africa is to instruct people in such basics as health, sanitation and nutrition." Sponsoring such U.S. offerings as Sgt. Preston, Liberace performances, "Topper," "My Hero," "Fibber McGee and Molly" and wrestling on Nigerian television were the likes of Pepsi-Cola, Kent (cigarettes), Bendix (washing machines), Ford, Pontiac and Hoover (vacuum cleaners).[8]

One of the countries most dominated by U.S. programming has been, and remains, Canada. Even Canada's radio system had been dominated by American programming. That situation led to the formation of the national public broadcaster, the CBC, in the 1930s. By the end of 1947 television could no longer be ignored by Canadian politicians. Twenty stations were operating in America; 21 were under construction and a further 100 building permits had been issued. Some 250,000 sets had been sold in America. Canadians in areas near the American border were buying sets and installing exterior aerials. They were directional and "pointed to" the nearest U.S. station. As one Canadian historian noted, "When Canadian stations were finally licensed, it was necessary, often with difficulty, to induce viewers to modify their aerials so as to permit reception from our own stations." The CBC was then both a national broadcaster and a regulatory agency with broadcast industry oversight responsibility. Early on, the CBC decided when granting station licenses it would recommend that the channels necessary be reserved for the national system. When half a dozen license applications came before the CBC Board of Governors in 1948, one came from Famous Players Corporation of Toronto. Objections were raised to granting a television license to an American-controlled motion picture industry firm. In the end all applications were deferred. Discussing the Canadian federal government's attitude toward Canada's coming television system, Transport Minister J. J. McCann told the House of Commons, "The plan by no means provides for exclusion of non–Canadian material from our television channels.... The public will wish Canadian stations, both private and public, to carry some good programming from other countries."[9]

Canada's federal government issued its television policy in March 1949 through the Aird Commission. It said that a truly Canadian entity meant that "television should be established on a national basis. If television was to be developed exclusively by private enterprise, economic pressures might well cause our visual air channels to become mere carriers of foreign programmes." During the late 1940s the CBC was attacked by many newspapers and magazines for "delaying" the introduction of television denying "millions of Canadians" access. That was unlikely since hardly anyone had a set. That pressure was from commercial interests such as broadcasters and television set makers. In 1949 the CBC TV Group was definitely of the opinion it should carry American programs even though tentative program schedules drafted by staff at the future Montreal and Toronto stations showed several options that did not include U.S. fare. By the time those stations went on the air those options had disappeared. Initially the Toronto outlet aired about 50 percent U.S. material. Noted a reporter, "This bulk importation may possibly be CBC TV's financial salvation, but otherwise one must look upon it with great misgiving, for by now it has surely been well-established that, excepting possibly in comedy, American TV has little of value to offer." The CBC could have reduced the number of hours of transmission time, as some draft schedules recommended. Instead the CBC decided to try and go head-to-head against U.S. border stations beaming into southern Ontario.[10]

Canada held a royal commission on the new medium in 1951, the Massey Commission, named for its chair, Vincent Massey. At those hearings the Canadian Congress of Labour, worried about control of the new industry, stated that "our Canadian system of broadcasting will ultimately disappear and we shall have in its place a carbon copy of the American system and a carbon copy made in the United States at that." Yet, wrote historian T. Allard, "at that moment the CBC was substantially the largest importer of U.S. programming into Canada." One recommendation from those hearings was that "all private stations be required to serve as outlets for national programs."

While the lobby group for private broadcasters in Canada, the Canadian Association of Broadcasters (CAB), argued in favor of 100 percent Canadian ownership for television stations, it opposed any domestic content rule for programming. Speaking in the House of Commons about the CAB opposition, member of Parliament M. J. Coldwell said, "It is a powerful propaganda agency, operating, as I believe, against the best interests of this country, and from my point of view likely to destroy the independence of this country and place it more and more under the cultural and economic control of the United States. As I have said already, I regard that as treasonable and subversive activity — just as treasonable and subversive as the activities of those who sell our country to a communist power or to Russia."[11]

The CBC began television transmission in September 1952 from outlets in Montreal and Toronto. In the first month or two of operation the Toronto station placed a newspaper ad soliciting commercial advertisers. In January 1953, the CBC received permission to import programs from all the U.S. networks. Later in 1953 private, commercial television started operations. A 1955 House of Commons hearing on broadcasting revealed that "approximately 50% of all programs in the CBC television system are of United States origin." Canada's federal government passed legislation in 1958 establishing an independent regulatory agency, the Board of Broadcast Governors (BBG), to oversee both the CBC and private stations. Provision was made that station licenses would be issued only if the applicant was a Canadian citizen or to a corporation only if it were at least 75 percent owned by Canadians. The BBG was charged with regulating a "comprehensive broadcasting service of a high standard that is basically Canadian in content and character."[12]

By the end of the 1950s all–Canada rights to broadcast a U.S. half-hour series could be had for $2,000, less than one-tenth what it would cost to produce a domestic series. It was a powerful incentive for broadcasters to load their schedules with U.S. fare. It also meant much less work at home for domestic talent. Writer-director Henry Comor, president of the Association of Canadian Television & Radio Artists told a New York forum of the Academy of Television Arts and Sciences, "You've made it impossible for us to earn a living." That lack of work led to an exodus of talent to the U.S. that included directors Norman Jewison (who directed "Hit Parade") and Arthur Hiller (who directed episodes of "Gunsmoke"), actors William Shatner ("Star Trek"), Lorne Greene (a noted Shakespearean actor who became Pa Cartwright on "Bonanza") and Dorothy Collins and Giselle McKenzie (both starred on "Hit Parade"). Lamenting that talent loss in a Canadian magazine Harry Rasky said, "Had the growth of Canadian television gone a different and more distinguished way, it's possible the early pioneers might still be home saving their talent for a strictly Canadian audience." With more than a little ambivalence Rasky titled his article "Canada's most successful export: TV-talent." Everywhere around the world the image of education and culture said to be the major benefit of the coming of television gave way to violence and banality followed by plugs for cola drinks, cigarettes, headache pills, soaps, laxatives, hair tonics and deodorants.[13]

Pressures for more Canadian shows on Canadian television led the BBG to issue regulations. Originally the BBG proposed a minimum 55 percent Canadian content rule to go into effect in 1960 and to be measured over a one-week period. Also proposed by the BBG was that in prime time (8 to 11 P.M.) stations had to reserve two hours each night for "purposes to be prescribed" by the BBG. At the time the regulations were aimed primarily at the private outlets, as the CBC English network was about 66 percent Canadian, the commercial stations much lower. Both networks had less Canadian content in prime time than in their overall percentage. Those proposals were met with enormous resistance from the CAB, with the result that the BBG backtracked significantly. Until April 1, 1961, the status quo of unrestricted use of imported television fare would continue. On that date all stations would have to air a minimum Canadian content of 45 percent, moving to 55 percent on April 1, 1962. The measuring period was changed to four weeks, instead of the proposed one. As well, the BBG dropped its prime-time proposal entirely. In dropping it the BBG said it would be "concerned" if broadcasting between 8 and 11 P.M. were not basically Canadian in character and content: "That the board would not be satisfied with the performance of networks or stations which meet the regulation of 55 percent Canadian content by broadcasting most of their Canadian programs outside the peak viewing hours."[14]

The sorry state of Canadian television was noted by reporter Dean Walker, who wrote in 1960, "As an instrument of national policy — the cement to hold our national ideas together — Canadian TV has failed." Across Canada 75 percent of all viewing time was spent watching U.S. programs on U.S. stations and/or Canadian ones. In Toronto (where three Buffalo stations, one affiliated with each of the networks, were available) 68 percent of viewing time was spent on U.S. stations, 11 percent on U.S. programs appearing on Canadian stations. Between 55 and 68 percent of all English-speaking Canada was within range of one or more U.S. outlets — some were built solely to attract Canadian viewers. That summer, just south of the Manitoba border a new television station tower was built in Pembina, North Dakota, to capture Winnipeg, which until then had been unable to receive U.S. transmissions. So close was it to the international border that one observer said of the 1,450 foot tower, "If it toppled, it would fall into Canada." In the nation's capital of Ottawa the CBC carried 54.5 percent American content during the 7 to 11 P.M. period. Many Canadian companies ran ads on those U.S. outlets penetrating Canada, drawing more money out of the country. Estimates were that some $5 million to $10 million was spent annually by Canadian firms advertising on U.S. border stations. In 1960 Toronto's CBC outlet telecast the "Ed Sullivan Show" at the same time as the Buffalo station. Despite the obviously better reception from the much closer CBC transmitter more viewers watched the program on the Buffalo station than on the CBC.[15]

Just before the 45 percent rule kicked in, BBG chair Andrew Stewart expressed confidence that stations would have no trouble meeting the quota because when the newer ones applied for their license those applicants "were wholly convinced the target was workable." However, just before the 55 percent rule went into effect, the BBG was once again after a quota for prime time. At that time the BBG wanted to set a minimum of 45 percent Canadian content on all stations between 6 P.M. and 12 midnight (the newly defined prime time). When the BBG dropped its original proposal for a prime-time rule, it worried stations would pack all their Canadian shows into morning and afternoon times, leaving the prestige, heavily viewed prime-time period for American shows. From its own observations the BBG found that in fact stations were "leaving Canadian material out of the 6-to-midnight slot almost entirely." Putting Canadian content programs into prime time gave them access to much higher revenues, which led to bigger bankrolled, better shows.[16]

Toward the end of the 1950s Japan had 6 million television sets in use — 2 million of them in Tokyo — served by six stations, four of them commercial and two channels of the government-run NHK network. The U.S. Nielsen rating service was then setting up shop in Japan. Top-rated shows included the likes of "Highway Patrol," "Lassie," "Father Knows Best" and "I Love Lucy." All were dubbed except for "Lucy," which was subtitled. Other programs were said to be rip-offs of U.S. programs such as "Gesture Quiz" ("Pantomime Quiz") and "Dial 110" (a Japanese version of "Dragnet"). Of the schedule *Variety* trumpeted "Translate it all into English and you could be watching WFIL-TV in Philadelphia or WFAA-TV in Dallas."[17]

Yet the market was less rosy than *Variety*'s words implied. For the fiscal year ending in 1958 the total amount allocated by the Japanese government for the purchase of imported television fare was $325,000, with an unlimited number of programs allowed as long as the dollar total was not exceeded. (Such restrictions were sometimes imposed by countries with balance-of-payment problems, nations trying to control the outflow of hard currency.) For the following fiscal year Japan's government raised the dollar allocation to $458,000, but an additional restriction was imposed in that each of the commercial and government stations was limited to buying a maximum of only nine half-hour foreign series for weekly national showing with a ceiling of $300 per episode. MCA Far East sales executive Irwin Klein grumbled the Japanese market was worse now because while the price per episode may have been higher it was still below standard values and the number of shows was limited.[18]

NBC director of international operations Alfred Stern was dispatched to Japan, where he met with Finance Ministry officials to plead for higher prices for U.S. product. He argued for a grading system with a scale of $300,

$400 and $500, still with a maximum of nine half-hour shows — three in each price rank. Japanese stations would do the grading. Said Stern, "The aggregate payments would be higher than now, but that's only fair. Then if we have a good show, we'd get a better price." Although the restrictions were a sore point with U.S. suppliers, they continued to sell as much as they could. While he was unsuccessful in getting price ceilings lifted, Stern, like others before him, asked for payment in yen if a dollar increase was impractical. Yen would be frozen in Japan, so Stern suggested possible location shoots and/or coproduction deals. He was also unsuccessful in that attempt.[19]

Restrictions were eased somewhat in 1960, when the price ceiling for a 30-minute series went to $450 if used by five or fewer stations, $500 if aired on six or more outlets. Nine key stations in Tokyo and Osaka were allowed to program ten half-hour imported shows each week — up from nine. Under the new regulations there were no fixed limits to the number of feature films or hour-long imports, but the fixed total amount of dollars allocated to each station meant a tight limit on them. Some American distributors welcomed the moves, calling them "limited steps in the right direction." However, most expressed disappointment in the extent of the increase. One major exporter felt Japan should be paying from $3,000 to $3,500 per half hour — similar to the price paid for the New York City market.[20]

One of those disappointed was distributor Warren Lewis, who didn't like the $500 quota: "because of the high quality of our programs I don't know if I can sell them under present Government restrictions. We feel this country is important and we would like to find some way to start some or all of our series here. But the returns are still a handicap to the producer." He added that "we invest more money in our pictures than we expect to receive from the United States. Overseas money is important money, not just found money. If we can just recoup a portion from here, we'd be content to make the profit elsewhere." Lewis also journeyed to Japan, where he joined the queue of exporters who lobbied the Japanese Finance Ministry for more money.[21]

The U.S. suppliers continued to apply intense pressure to Japanese officials. Among those involved were TPEA president John McCarthy and Motion Picture Export Association (MPEA) executive Irving Maas, who both lobbied the Finance Ministry. By then it was reported the MPEA's "various representatives around the world are actively engaged in building the export field for American television interests." It all paid off when the MPEA announced that starting April 1, 1961, the only fiscal limitation in Japan on foreign television imports was in total dollar allocation, $3 million per year, up from $2.1 million the previous year. Most of that money was restricted to series, not to be spent on feature films for television airing. It meant major increases for U.S. exporters. Bidding led to the sale of 54 episodes of "The Untouchables" for $100,000 — 60 percent paid in advance, the balance due within four weeks after broadcast of the first segment. It was a record Japanese deal.[22]

Under the more liberal Japanese regulations, the average price for a U.S. half-hour series was around $750, double that for an hour-long episode. Remarked SG Japanese representative Lloyd Burns, "It's easier to sell here now with quantity ceilings off and better prices permitted. The combination of both factors means we are selling more shows and taking a larger sum of money from Japan than before." Asked if SG was satisfied with the changes in Japan's regulations Burns replied, "No, we never are."[23]

Around the same time, Tokyo's official Communist newspaper *Akahata* (*Red Flag*) launched a heated attack on America's "ever-tightening culture offensive by radio and TV." Writer Yumi Yagama had counted 94 U.S.-made items on Tokyo television taking up as much as twelve and one-half hours a day. "At any time of the day there is at least one channel from which these propaganda beasts are waiting — sharpening their claws — to pounce upon us," he wrote. Yagama slammed "The Untouchables" for promoting anti–Soviet thinking, "Father Knows Best" for propagandizing the American way of life and "Rawhide" for exalting white supremacy — in its relations with Indians. Yagama wrote, "Our land is now completely enveloped" and U.S. shows "slip into our homes — in the guise of amusement or artistic expression — and insidiously, inch by inch, inject America's imperialist policies into our ochanoma [tea-drinking rooms]."[24]

Television came to Australia in the fall of 1956, and by mid–1956 those first six stations had spent an estimated $1.25 million to $1.5 million for two years worth of foreign television product, the purchase of over 40 series, most of them American. Despite that windfall some U.S. exporters complained they had taken a beating on some of the deals, with the reason being "overeagerness for some extra foreign coin on the part of some companies that broke down the price structure before it was even established." All admitted there was little logical base on which to set prices. While the number of television sets in use was often considered it was not applicable in this case, as none were then in Australia. As to pricing structure, some suppliers admitted "that they asked what they felt they could get and that the Aussies countered with what they thought was the least they could get the pix for." Under Australian import regulations only the stations themselves could import film, which meant only they could do the actual program buying. That left Australian advertisers and agencies at the "mercy" of the stations with regard to program selection and price. U.S. suppliers hoped advertisers would fight the regulations and obtain the right to do their own program buying and film importing and simply place it on the stations, American style. Such a setup would be welcomed by U.S. distributors, as it would widen the market and "consequently tend to make prices higher."[25]

Within a year or so of start-up Australia remained one of America's best markets. Already U.S. feature films were making their way into the schedules. Stations were starting up in other major cities while the operations of the commercial outlets were proudly touted as being "strictly along U.S. lines, rather than that of commercial U.K. broadcasters." By law sets had to be manufactured in Australia.[26]

During Australia's 1958 election campaign the Labour Party promised that if elected it would impose a 55 percent local content rule on television. However, when Robert Menzies's Liberal Party was returned to power in November it meant it was very unlikely there would be any restrictions on the import of foreign television fare. A relieved *Variety* wrote "Survey here shows conclusively that the Aussie television fans ... are all for American-brand entertainment, with sponsors backing this opinion to the limit via the major commercial outlets. With no interference from politicians in the Aussie television sphere covering local talent protection, the year ahead should be a boomer for importers of ace teevee programs." U.S. suppliers were even said to be hard pressed to keep up with the demand in the Australian market. One reason was that Australian television did not then air repeats in the summer. It was new material all year long.[27]

In Australia U.S. distributors used a tactic that they used in all nations — selling material at a price drastically under what it would cost to produce a comparable local product. Driven solely by money, commercial stations naturally gravitated toward the cheapest available product; little selling was needed. It was more difficult with public broadcasters since all honored, in widely varying degrees and with mixed success, their mandate of promoting domestic culture, artists, and so on. Money could not be ignored, but with public broadcasters it was never the sole or most important factor. Of the early selling period in Australia, TPEA head John McCarthy told a New York United Nations Educational, Scientific, and Cultural Organization (UNESCO) conference, "We gave them some series for as little as a thousand dollars for a one-hour program, for all of Australia." After a few years, with U.S. fare well entrenched, prices went to $3,000 per one-hour segment, $1,500 per half-hour segment. Local talent pitched its own ideas, but a half-hour Australian-made series cost $20,000 per episode to produce. A potential sponsor would explain he could get a high-rated U.S. series such as "Restless Gun" for $1,400.[28]

Such heavy penetration of the U.S. into Australia's home screens came to elicit resistance, even from the Menzies government. Television was under the control of postmaster general William Davidson, who was then considering a rule whereby each television station would have to broadcast at least 40 percent local material. This would come after the outlets had been on air for three years. Davidson told Parliament, "I am extremely disappointed at the fact that Australian programs are completely taboo in the peak viewing hours." He also told the stations to program at least one hour of local material in the peak period of 7 to 9 P.M. each week, "commencing as soon as possible." These were directives, not laws on the books. However, they came from a source with the power to turn directives into laws. Davidson also announced the government would be taking action under the Australian Broadcasting and Television Act to deal with imported television commercials. He pointed out such ads could easily have been made locally.[29]

More vigorous in attacking the U.S. tube domination were opposition Labour politicians and Australian Actors' Equity, each lobbying for a 40 percent Australian content rule for prime time. Attacking that idea was the Sydney *Sunday Telegraph*, which editorialized that "few people watched the homebrew shows when they had the alternative of watching the world's best." The paper also argued that "no sponsor could afford to spend anything like the money required to give the public the programs they were accustomed to viewing." As it happened, that newspaper was owned by the Packer Group, which also happened to own one of the private television outlets. *Variety* entered the debate when it reported it conducted its own man-in-the-street survey in Australia, finding "that the average Aussie viewer preferred imported fare with No. 1 preference to the American brand." How many were asked just what questions went unstated.[30]

At the end of 1961 the situation in Australia remained rosy for U.S. television distributors. Mounting pressure had not yet translated into definite action. Said *Variety*, "Of all the countries buying telepix product from the rest of the world (which, in the main, means the U.S.), Australia would seem to be the happiest hunting ground and the most satisfactory. That's because the Aussies have no quota system." They also had what was called "strong" commercial television. Melbourne channel GTV9 had upwards of 50 percent U.S. material on its schedule. While in the U.S. on a buying trip that station's manager, Collin Bednall, explained he had been able to find just one half-hour program made in the U.K. that suited his needs. Bednall claimed that by putting a ceiling on television imports, as in the U.K., "it automatically puts the country under such pressures [to fill an entire week's program schedule] as to invite inferior home-made product." Serving up further compliments for his U.S. hosts he added that Australia "recognizes the fact that there just isn't that much quality programming available in Australia and, free from the shackles of a quota system, the world is its oyster." Because the U.K. had to respect quotas and produce so much product domestically, U.K. television shows, claimed Bednall, "must invariably come off second best."[31]

Events moved slowly in continental Europe for U.S. television exporters. Mostly the scene was that of a single, state-run network in each nation with most not allowing ads at all. In countries where commercials aired, they were tightly controlled. Italy's state telecaster RAI had outlets in only Milan and Turin in early 1953. U.S. programs screened were mostly second-tier product such as cowboy shows (Gene Autry, Wild Bill Hickok, Hopalong Cassidy) and "The Trouble with Father." *Newsweek* reported that year that "Italian TV, in fact, looks like the American variety (vintage 1949) at first glance." Actually there weren't that many U.S. programs on the air — a reflection of the limited funding available to RAI. For the year 1953 RAI had a total television budget of $500,000, with just $150,000 of that available for programming. A single episode of the Sid Caesar hit "Your Show of Shows" had a budget of $160,000. RAI's big splurge had been a live version of *MacBeth* that cost the network $3,200, including electricity costs."[32]

France was mulling over the addition of a second network in 1960 but was put off by the estimated cost of $80 million. Also being considered was color television, although again the cost made it prohibitive. With only 2 million sets in use in France, advertising was not considered very attractive. That high cost of adding a second channel fueled U.S. hopes that when it arrived the state would not be able to afford it, thus opening it up to ads. With that hope in mind several Hollywood firms had deals set with local producers in the event a second channel meant a need for commercial programming. Declared *Variety*: "The foot is in the door."[33]

France's sole network, which was state run, was on the air some 45 to 50 hours a week late in the 1950s. Yet only two half-hour American programs were being aired. Some 60 percent of French television was telecast live. One inroad made by U.S. distributors was in the screening of feature films, of which French television aired 160 per year. Seventy of those were dubbed U.S. fare, which usually went for $1,000 per showing. Those U.S. series went for $300 to $400 per episode. Dubbing costs for those half-hour shows exceeded $1,000, but sales to other French markets turned it into a profit. In each French-speaking market U.S. suppliers argued for higher prices, claiming they lost money in each one — citing the dubbing costs but neglecting to mention multiple market sales from the same dub. In contrast the feature films screened incurred no dubbing costs, as most that aired had been dubbed years earlier for their first-run theatrical release.[34]

Continental Europe was not much of a market for U.S. product at the end of the 1950s, either in price or in quantity. It had big potential — if, as hoped, many of the nations adopted the British system of dual public and commercial television. U.S. firms wanted to see the American model imposed but as a first step were willing to accept the British model of commercial television, albeit a tightly controlled and restrained one. Distributor Leo Lax commented that the Germans paid up to $1,000 for a half-hour segment and up to $3,500 for a movie — they paid the dubbing costs. The Italians paid $500 for one run of a series and up to $1,200 for a movie. They also paid for dubbing. France paid a flat fee of $500 to $1,000 for a single run — the seller paid for dubbing. Other French markets included Belgium, Luxembourg, Switzerland and Quebec. Lax explained that there were few U.S. shows on French television because the network was "crowded with native shows."[35]

United Artists Associated executive Manny Reiner bemoaned the fact, in 1961, that most European nations screened U.S. television fare in advance to see if it was acceptable, including cartoons, movies and series. More violent episodes were rejected. In most cases it was government agencies that did the screening. Illustrating the intense selling pressure applied by Americans was Reiner's own schedule. In the first five months of 1961 he was out of the U.S. for 16 weeks on selling trips. On those trips he hit 22 cities in continental Europe and 19 in the Far East. In June of the same year he was packing for a lengthy selling jaunt in Latin America.[36]

One unnamed German television filmmaker accused the U.S. suppliers and the U.S. Information Agency (USIA) of "dumping" television fare in Europe, thus ruining the market for local television producers in many nations. He cited one U.S. distributor who was selling old, already-dubbed material to outlets in Belgium and the Netherlands for $150. With some 700 films in its library, many of them feature length, the USIA was slammed for its practice of giving that material free to stations throughout the world. In some markets, claimed the critic, stations took that free material from the USIA and sold it to sponsors.[37]

Commercial television started in Britain in 1955 with Independent Television (ITV), established to compete with the long-running BBC government network. It was brought in despite enormous opposition to commercial television from many quarters including opposition politicians, trade unions and print media owners. Reportedly the strategy for achieving the commercialization of British television was masterminded by the London branch of the American J. Walter Thompson ad agency, working with a group in Parliament. Their well-financed campaign did not emphasize commercial advantages but shrewdly attacked the BBC at its most publicly objectional point — its monopoly status. That commercialization of British television opened a crucial market for U.S. advertisers and their agents. Equally important was the idea that the British example would be followed by other European nations, increasing the outlets for U.S. television fare, U.S. advertising, and U.S. goods. By 1958 the Thompson agency had 34 branches abroad with eight of them in South America, and eight in Asia.[38]

When its Television Act was going through the British Parliament, demands for a quota for home product was demanded from many quarters, in anticipation of a flood of U.S. product. The government refused to set a quota, saying that as soon as there were signs of a foreign program invasion it would step in and quickly set a quota. With sales to the ITV thus underway, *Variety* described the strategy of the U.S. suppliers thus: "At the moment, it's not so much a matter of profit, as it is a question of getting in on the ground floor." Financial return was not expected to be great for a few years. "But each and every American telepix distributor wants in now, as a means of establishing contacts and doing business in Britain in anticipation of the time when the British playoff of American telepix does have a marked financial effect. While most Yank distribs are trying to place their shows on BBC and the commercial network, it's more for the purpose of setting up contacts than for the coin involved."[39]

Opposition to the import of foreign television programs continued when Labour member of Parliament G. R. Chetwynd rose in the House of Commons to ask Chancellor of the Exchequer Harold Macmillan how many dollars had been expended on the import of U.S. television fare. Chetwynd stated both the BBC and the British Independent Television Authority (ITA)— governing body of ITV — were showing "many rubbishy American films which are a complete waste of money." Three weeks later Exchequer economic secretary Edward Boyle released in the Commons the information that both the BBC and ITV had spent $3,750,000 over the past year for U.S. television product. Labour member of Parliament Stephen Swingler remarked this was a "rather large sum for the sake of getting Hopalong Cassidy."[40]

Late in 1955 a number of trade unions involved with television reached an agreement with ITA to the effect that foreign-filmed television material would be limited to a maximum of seven hours per week out of the total ITA broadcasting time of 50 hours per week. However, initially that agreement was ignored. Some fifteen trade unions and other professional groups monitored a typical month of ITA programming, finding 70 percent of the filmed material came from America and 30 percent was British (note live programs, all British, were excluded here). That finding prompted the unionists to put increasing pressure on government officials in the media to set a formal, official quota. The result was that ITA promised it would abide by the original agreement and maintain a 14 percent quota on foreign fare aired, an informal quota, on its commercial television network. For its part the BBC honored that quota, although it was not a party to it.[41]

When *U.S. News & World Report* surveyed the scene in Britain it reported, "An American visitor watching television in Britain might almost think he was still back home." The piece acknowledged there were no ads on the BBC and those on the ITA stations were on a much smaller scale, because there were fewer of them and they were of shorter duration —"But, other than that, British television is 'going American' in a big way." This was something of an exaggeration, but the U.S. shows all appeared in prime time, which meant their share of the viewing audience was considerably higher than their 14 percent share of transmission time. Everything from "I Love Lucy" to "Dragnet" to "Highway Patrol" appeared. American penetration was increased by the presence of several British versions, counted as home fare, of U.S. programs. There were British copies of "What's My Line?" "This Is Your Life," and "The $64,000 Question." (The British version of the latter placed less emphasis on the prize money; in Britain, the "Question" carried a reward of 64,000 pence, or $4,480.) London's *Daily Express* called the importation of U.S. shows an "indefensible" waste of money. "Why does the Treasury permit this extravagance?" asked an editorial. "It is ridiculous that Britain, struggling to earn dollars, should waste time on such frivolities. Cannot Britain produce her own entertainment?" In answer to that, *U.S. News* noted, "One big reason why so many American programs are offered on British stations is that it is cheaper to buy them than to produce original programs here. Most of the American programs already have been shown profitably in the United States and can be sold to British stations at low cost."[42]

Hostility came from other media outlets. London's weekly *The People* complained, "Is BBC short of British ideas?... A pity the BBC can't devise a British series." Lord Beaverbrook's *Sunday Express* grumbled that the infiltration of American television had become a "persistent, irresistible intrusion,... a tumbling, roaring flood." Chief target of the critics was the ITA. With a reported 50 percent of the time ITA devoted to children's programs taken up by American product the *Express* declared, "Do they imagine that commercial TV was brought into being here in order to turn our children into little Americans?" Responding to the criticism, ITA director Sir Robert Fraser called the attacks "anti–American feeling thinly disguised." Before a Rotary Club meeting in London, Fraser added, "And remember this, Americans have acquired such a mastery of TV film techniques that we can apply no better stimulus to our producers than to let them see how it is done."[43]

Fighting for a 90 percent British quota the Association of Cinematograph, Television and Allied Technicians unanimously passed a resolution deploring the "ever increasing amount of American material" on the BBC and ITA. Also opposed was television violence, most of which was American, claimed the group. Spokesperson Vivian Milroy said, "We say that although we can do nothing about teenage violence, we can do something about the wholesale importation of American films. Nine out of twelve of them are based on crime and violence. The quintessential common philosophy among all their films is that might is right."[44]

Anger continued through 1958 led by the unions, the Labour Party and the media. British Screen and Television Writers Association vice president Dudley Leslie said of ITA's Fraser, "We have reached a point of utter exasperation with Sir Robert and his cheap foreign material." The fight was not so much about the 14 percent quota but about "serious infiltration" of U.S. material into the other 86 percent of television time "which purports to be British." Critics claimed almost all half-hour filmed series were mostly written and produced by Americans (an exaggerated reference to coproductions) that all but one of the quiz shows was a version of an American one, and so on. All the critics were angry that the trade in television material was all a one-way street — that is, the U.S. bought virtually no British shows for telecasting in America.[45]

Little or no letup occurred in the criticism. Beaverbrook's *Sunday Express* slammed U.S. imports on ITA again in 1960. Admitting the 14 percent quota was not exceeded journalist Alan Watkins argued it was more than it seemed because "nearly all the American programs are broadcast at peak viewing times"—which meant they had bigger audiences. Also slammed were "the shows which are produced in Britain by American firms using British actors (who are cheaper to hire)."[46]

Midway through 1960 TPEA head John McCarthy traveled to London, where he met with British television officials and executives, lobbying unsuccessfully for an increased quota. Upon his return he conferred in Washington with State Department officials. From there U.S. embassy officials in London relayed the State Department's support of the TPEA position to British officials. A few months later McCarthy returned to London for more lobbying. But it had no effect. The fierce opposition to the existing amount of U.S. material on the small screen more than overwhelmed U.S. pressure. For the 1959–1960 fiscal period Robert Fraser reported that foreign product occupied 12.15 percent of total transmission time, compared to 12.3 percent the prior year. The BBC had held to its self-imposed 10 percent quota.[47]

Sixteen British labor unions and professional associations formed an umbrella group called the Radio and Television Safeguards Committee to present a report in 1961 to the Pilkington Committee on Broadcasting (formed to investigate what direction U.K. television should follow) that was, among other things, a "plan for safeguards against the domination of British air and British screens by a foreign ethos." It called for a 10 percent quota. Agreeing the BBC provided some of the best broadcasting in the world, it nonetheless slammed it for a "deplorable tendency towards Americanization." As to the commercial outlets the report stated, "They have done much to advertise the American, rather than the British way of life." Among other unwelcome features "probably the most serious are those which have forced British television film companies, and all the artists and writers employed by them, to angle their work for the American market." The Association of Cinematograph, Television and Allied Technicians continued to pass resolutions deploring the continued U.S. influence on British television and demanding tighter quotas.[48]

Formed in 1960, the Pilkington Committee issued its report in the summer of 1962, wherein it criticized ITV as "vapid" and "cheaply sensational," noting that the profit motive and "good broadcasting" were "incompatible." The report praised the BBC, concluding with a recommendation the BBC should receive the immediate award of a second network while the ITV should get a second network only after it was reconstituted and had proved "its capacity to realize the purposes of broadcasting." The ITA was responsible for the commercial network but it produced no programs. It owned the transmitters for the network, leasing those facilities to "program contractors" who provided programs and sold ads (spots only). A total of 15 program contractors existed, but the major metropolitan centers were controlled by the Big Four. The Pilkington report also took a dim view of U.S. programs, with main objections being to the "poor quality of the product and of the values depicted by it."[49]

Evidence of a wider-based hostility toward U.S. product was visible at a global television forum held in Hollywood in 1960 that was attended by representatives from many nations. One persistent theme was that there was too much violence in the U.S. shows with a call for lesser amounts of violence. In response, NBC International executive Alvin Ferleger blamed the foreign telecasters for buying those shows; they had other options. He also blamed quotas for the problem, claiming that NBC had tried to sell opera to the U.K. but the British network would not preempt a Western; the U.K. only allowed "two hours per day of American programming." A second persistent theme was that U.S. television stations broadcast next to nothing in the way of foreign programming.[50]

Hostility to U.S. television abroad arose even from domestic sources on occasion. Speaking in Canada U.S. television producer David Susskind warned Canadian viewers should stop watching U.S. shows or "they will soon get sick and silly ... the whole business is nothing but unmitigated drivel. Canadians should be ashamed to take the stuff."[51]

When John F. Kennedy-appointed FCC chairman Newton Minow described his country's domestic television situation in 1961 as a "vast wasteland," it worried reporter George Rosen because "equally alarming is the fact that these are the basic staples among U.S.-made shows that are shipped to Latin American, Asia, Africa and all other countries."[52]

Minow's statement outraged the TPEA's McCarthy, who denied the implication that America's image abroad was tarnished because of U.S. product telecast in foreign lands. McCarthy warned that all those abroad who wanted to raise restrictions against the import of U.S. programs used such statements of American critics as justification for their restrictive moves. He added, "The export earnings of this industry are an important factor in improving the critical U.S. balance of payments position."[53]

A year later U.S. exporters were still smarting. CBS Films' director of international sales Ralph Baruch, in a speech to the Hollywood Ad Club, complained that the ogre of the undesirable image generated abroad by U.S. television "has been created by those who shout the loudest and whose speeches have been blown up by the public media." Baruch, whose company then served 57 countries, believed "free choice" should be expanded abroad to "open our entire catalog to everyone, leaving the decision entirely up to those who purchase from us." As far as he was concerned, the U.S. broadcaster had "faced his responsibility as a citizen better than those of any other land."[54]

A much-heralded speech to the National Association of Broadcasters was given in April 1962 by famed journalist Edward R. Murrow, director of the USIA at the time. Advance billing had it that Murrow would make a strong attack against television exporters for marring America's image overseas. But it was much milder than anticipated. He did call upon the exporters to show as much concern about a show's impact abroad as they did about the dollars earned. Murrow called television film a "strategic commodity" in the struggle with the Communist bloc. On the eve of Murrow's address, NBC-TV chairman David Sarnoff contended that domestic attacks on television were widely read abroad and an "uninformed opinion created." It meant, said Sarnoff, that "as seen from abroad through the distorted lenses of such reports and comments, American television is falsely depicted as degrading public taste and culture with an unrelieved onslaught of gunslingers and horses and private eyes." Pointing out NBC's commitment to news and informational programming, Sarnoff concluded, "In short, it is an image unjustifiably derogatory not merely to American broadcasting but to our country itself and the level of our culture."[55]

As the 1960s began, restrictions imposed on the import of U.S. television fare in various countries became more of a headache to American exporters. Explained journalist Murray Horowitz "as television grows in area after area, native television industries also grow and there's a demand for native programming as opposed to U.S. fare. Demand may come from government circles, native entrepreneurs, local talent and technicians unions, or a combination of some of all of these groups." Most U.S. exporters subscribed to the "free market" concept in which there should be "open competition of programming from all sources and if American programming is the most popular, it should not be penalized because of its foreign origin." At the time, exporters faced the U.K. quota, a coming Canadian quota, an Australian directive that was considered tantamount to an eventual order, Japanese price ceilings, blocked funds in Italy, and other annoyances. "The dollars are there for most areas. But so are the headaches," concluded the reporter.[56]

When TPEA president John McCarthy returned home from a three-week swing through Greece and the Middle East he called the area an active, growing market. The biggest problem he found in the area was the currency situations, with government and private television interests unable to pay U.S. television exporters in hard currency. With the top price for product in the largest Arabic market — Egypt — being $100 for a half-hour program and dubbing costs estimated at $700, subtitles were used, which McCarthy admitted were "primitive." Twentieth Century–Fox reportedly had a deal to supply Egyptian television with product in return for local currency to be used by the film producer in making *Cleopatra*.[57]

In the middle of 1962, with U.S. exportation of television fare starting to increase rapidly there was much more interest in — and more resistance to and restrictions on — U.S. product in foreign locales. There was much optimism and much pessimism. Optimistic was Edward R. Murrow, who predicted global television via space satellites would be a reality within a matter of weeks. His USIA was deeply involved in forthcoming tests of satellite broadcasting. The National Aeronautics and Space Administration (NASA) had charged the USIA with program responsibility for content of the first satellite broadcast. To that end the USIA had already met with the three networks to take the first step in that project.[58]

Pessimistic was MGM-TV European sales chief John Spires, who was dubious about the presumed bonanza of the international television market, pointing out that something less than 20 percent of the total television gross then came from offshore. A future in which the foreign take was close to 50 percent was a delusional one. He explained, "The decisive difference is that television overseas is generally government-operated and looked upon as a culture-medium, whereas film theaters are private enterprises. Even where there is commercial television, sharp quota restrictions put a severe crimp into sales of U.S. television properties."[59]

Chapter 3

1960s:
"Brazilians Will
Watch Anything"

The 1960s saw a major push by Hollywood to gain a larger share of the expanding international television scene. Often it was frustrated by the slow changes in Europe, where television remained highly regulated, which meant the number of outlets on air and their hours of operation increased slowly. It also meant that private, commercially driven television made only a few inroads in the European market, which, outside of the British Commonwealth nations, was potentially the most lucrative area. At home and abroad the Hollywood major film companies, the Motion Picture Association of America (MPAA) cartel, gained greater control of the small screen.

Dreams of a global television system, so prevalent and fanciful at the end of the 1940s and start of the 1950s, faded away in the face of more routine matters such as U.S. distributors fighting quotas and pushing prices up. Those dreams were revived in the early 1960s as the space race between the U.S. and the Soviet Union heated up with a technological spillover to the benefit of television. Satellite television had its start here but was still some time away. Were it not for heavy government spending on the space race we would not have satellite television today. Several satellite launches, which included communications experiments and tests, led to the 1962 launch of Telstar, which included a brief live television transmission, first from the U.S. to Europe and then from Europe to America. Those early satellites had a relatively low orbit and lacked the ability to be "parked" over a specific location, which meant transmission could occur only in a short interval during each orbit Telstar made around the planet. Continuous transmission to the same spot was impossible. Still, the Telstar launch rekindled global television dreams. *Variety* heralded the event "World TV: a click premiere."[1]

In April 1961, the U.S. Air Force conducted the first transmission of a television picture via satellite. The signals were bounced off an Echo balloon satellite. Telstar was sponsored by the National Aeronautics and Space

Administration (NASA) and built by American Telephone & Telegraph company affiliate Bell Laboratories. Later that summer of 1962 were launched the U.S. Defense Department's Advent satellite and NASA's Relay orbiter. These would "tell engineers many things they must know in the drive toward global satellite transmission." A future was envisioned in which 30 to 50 such satellites would be launched to provide a worldwide relay station system. Writing in *Reader's Digest* Harland Manchester commented, "Since the first TV set was turned on, world-wide television has been the goal of engineers and the hope of viewers." He headlined the event piece describing the article as "Here comes world-wide television!"[2]

Newsweek summed up the event as "Telstar — for all the world to see." Pondering the implications of international television, the magazine stated that one plan being considered by the U.S. government "stresses the urgency of the race between the Free World and the Communists for the minds of men. It is vital, the plan says, to tie all nations into a global TV network while the United States still has the lead." In a more general sense the Telstar launch was seen as a first step toward a sky-based system of picture, voice, data and other types of communication.[3]

International agency UNESCO issued a 1963 booklet titled "Space Communication and the Mass Media," in which it predicted the day was not far off when people around the world could watch the same program: "Single programs may soon be able to reach around the world and allow set owners a choice of shows from almost every corner of the world." That report emphasized the cultural and educational benefits of satellite television.[4]

Speaking in 1964 CBS executive Paul Levitan predicted global satellite television airing in one to two years. As to a likely show to be the first program carried that way he nominated the "Miss Universe" contest because what could be better than an event "to celebrate a dame." Another likely candidate in his mind was "The Ed Sullivan Show." Other suggested events were the opening of the United Nations or a session of the U.S. Congress, all live events. At the time, CBS aired "Miss Universe" live and sped tapes of the show to twelve nations. However, those films reached their destinations after the selection of the winner was known throughout the world. Levitan realized that a distant broadcaster could capture a satellite feed of, say, an "I Love Lucy" episode, hold it, then air it at a later time, yet he thought the use of conventional film and videotape would continue because "There's no reason to utilize a satellite for telecasting 'I Love Lucy' throughout the world when shipping film does the job just as well."[5]

That same year ABC International president Don Coyle predicted a global satellite television network coming within five years. ABC was then the product-buying agency for some 53 television stations abroad that were affiliated with ABC's Worldvision group. With the television set count rising by 1 million a month globally, Coyle explained that advertisers and their agencies should begin to think in terms of world rather than national markets. A global system would, he said, "produce an exchange of the best the nations have to offer in ideas and talents, as well as goods and services."[6]

In the closing months of 1966 ABC sponsored a symposium on global television for its Worldvision affiliates. Coyle enthusiastically declared that "the alertness of global advertisers to the enormous possibilities of centrally controlled worldwide promotion" must be stressed because "commercial television on a global scale will do the same things it has done in the U.S.— the monies generated will help pay for better and more diverse programs, and the stimulus to trade will help uplift economies the world over."[7]

So-called educational advantages of global television continued to be emphasized. RCA board chairman David Sarnoff predicted in 1965 direct-to-home satellite television would be a reality in five to ten years. "The greatest promise of direct satellite television rests on its ability to educate millions simultaneously." Those educational programming prospects "offer perhaps the greatest hope for advancing the world to a higher plateau of understanding and peace," concluded Sarnoff. Some saw those educational aspects in a narrower framework. CBS executive Howard Kany commented on the role television was playing in teaching English in Asia by saying, "If there is an international language developing, it seems to me it is English."[8]

Two years later, in 1967, Sarnoff predicted that within ten years there would be satellites capable of beaming television into homes anywhere on the globe. Through such global broadcasts "illiteracy could be completely wiped out in a relatively short time," he said. It would be a world of instant around-the-globe communications that would also see the emergence of an international language "based largely on English."[9]

U.S. Information Agency (USIA) director Leonard Marks called for a worldwide communications satellite information grid so that all nations could exchange data swiftly and fully. He wanted such a system to be initiated by educational broadcasters and educators and said that "radio and television programs should become an important ingredient of this new reservoir of knowledge and there should be a regular exchange of programming."[10]

When it came to actually establishing something akin to an educational global television system, the networks wanted no part of it. During 1966 the U.S. Senate communications subcommittee met on the Ford Foundation proposal to fund an educational television network from the proceeds of a non-profit communications satellite system within the U.S. Publicly the three networks expressed no harsh criticism, but privately what interest they had in it was only a selfish one. That proposed satellite system would supposedly save the commercial networks some $5 million a year from the $15 million yearly each then paid for distribution over AT&T land lines. As to the second half of the proposal, establishing a permanent financial base for the network, they wanted no part of it, feeling a certain resentment at being asked to play a part in funding a network that would compete with them for the audience, especially the upper strata viewers. Finally, the networks were wary of doing business "with some sort of non-profit, do-gooder operation for program transmission." That idea was the brainchild of McGeorge Bundy and Fred Friendly.[11]

U.S. television spokespersons developed a general philosophy to rationalize their attempts at cartel-type domination of foreign television screens. More and more they cloaked those activities under the guise of protecting free enterprise, free choice and freedom of speech. Responding to domestic criticism of U.S. product abroad which, it was argued, created an image abroad harmful to the U.S., CBS executive Ralph Baruch said that it was all the fault of those foreigners, since it was those foreign buyers who made the decision on what to buy, based on viewing desires. "We do not censor nor do we wish to exert pressure on others abroad when they choose the program fare they feel is best for their own viewers and the programs of their own concepts best suited for their purposes. This is in line with our ideals of the free enterprise of a democratic people setting the example for the rest of the world," he said. Asked for examples of American shows with positive values Baruch cited "I Love Lucy," "Perry Mason," "The Defenders" and "The Phil Silvers Show." Unmentioned was the U.S. practice of imposing block-booking whenever and wherever possible, whereby buyers were forced to take a lot of dross selected by the U.S. cartel to go along with the programs they really wanted.[12]

Another CBS executive, Willard Block, attacked those forces abroad that restricted U.S. television shows as limiting the free market, arguing the foreign broadcaster should have the same right as U.S. broadcasters in choosing what they wanted to telecast. He claimed there was nothing inherently bad in the image of the vast majority of U.S. product being telecast overseas, as they did "represent the American scene, our culture, and the interests of our people." Leading the way among programs sold by CBS Films abroad were "Perry Mason" in 48 nations; "I Love Lucy," 42; "Gunsmoke," 35; and "Twilight Zone," 32. There were then 60 million television homes in the Free World outside the U.S. and 50 million in America. Domestically there were 624 television stations (78 of them educational), compared to 838 stations in the rest of the Free World.[13]

In a report to his board Television Program Export Association (TPEA) president John McCarthy urged an open market throughout the Free World in the television programming field. He believed the best way to approach that goal of elimination of quotas and other limitations was through the General Agreement on Tariffs and Trade (GATT), an international agency that attempted to regulate world trading rules. The creators of GATT's working paper on television, said McCarthy, "will need to be persuaded of the desirability and workability of this overall project and incorporate it as a recommendation in their findings before the parent body of 37 nations can consider the matter in full session." To that end, McCarthy explained that the attention of GATT was being "forcibly directed to the open door policy of our industry in the United States, wherein there are no restrictions on any producer or distributor, from any country, coming here and marketing as much of his product as our broadcasters will absorb. McCarthy's contention was that "only by permitting broadcasters everywhere to select programs from all sources can world-wide television ripen into full maturity." Complaints by foreigners about the impossibility of getting access to U.S. television or that a private, cartel-type system could effectively limit access as successfully as government-imposed rules were unmentioned by the TPEA leader.[14]

By the time a television amendment to GATT came up for a full membership vote in 1963 in Geneva—it did not pass—both TPEA and Motion Picture Association of America (MPEA) were vigorously lobbying for its passage. Had it passed, U.S. television exporters could have, for example, petitioned the U.S. government to ask the U.K. to lower its "unreasonable" quota on U.S. product. Having such a trade agreement in place allowed private companies to formally bring the U.S. government into the picture as a trade ally. Said MPEA head William Fineshriber, "We can use the government more energetically in our dealings and this will give us prestige."[15]

In its 1968 report to its members the MPEA was pleased to announce that in Italy "only a few films are being produced locally for television, since American-made TV films are available for far below what it would cost RAI to produce similar films or series." Also noted was that "very little TV material is filmed in Argentina" and "There is no film production in Chile except news flashes and TV commercials."[16]

Occasionally a report surfaced claiming that Hollywood was at the mercy of the foreign television buyers. One 1962 account said that as more U.S. companies entered the arena with more product, "Some companies in key areas of the world panicked, and in order to move product, sold at rates far below the norm." That situation got so bad in one instance that TPEA called in one of the companies and tried to explain the error of price-cutting over the long term and for the general health of the industry; "Other than persuasion, there's little that the TPEA or any other industry group can do, as each company pursues its individual goals." This combined with the fact that some nations had restrictions on the import of foreign programs meant the overseas market was a "buyers' market with the buyers almost in a cartel arrangement in key areas, swapping information as to prices and other provisions of deals." Cited as examples were Latino markets where "some brokers have become a thorn on the side of exporters. Native brokers, who operate by buying programming and time on stations and selling off that time to sponsors, dictate prices and other contract provisions, according to American exporters." It was a false picture of U.S. exporters as victims, as helpless. Control of the domestic television industry was passing rapidly to the Hollywood majors, the handful of MPAA members. Independent television producers were rapidly disappearing. During the 1963-64 season MPAA firms supplied 26 hours weekly of prime-time material (series, not old movies) on the three networks, up from nothing not many years earlier.[17]

Television in its earliest years in America had a lot of sellers of programs and a lot of buyers. That changed quickly, as the number of buyers was radically reduced. At one time sponsors bought programs directly and then bought air time from stations, which then telecast the program and the commercials the sponsors had inserted. However, the three networks took over the responsibility for programming from the national advertisers in the 1950s. Advertisers insisted the networks made the changes for their own benefit, while the networks countered that the shift in responsibility was made to accommodate advertisers, who could no longer afford the rising costs of sole sponsorship. When the television quiz show scandals broke in the 1950s, U.S. networks used it as an argument that they should do the programming because if they did, such things as quiz show scandals would not happen. When the shift was over the result was a drastic decrease in the number of prime-time buyers, from between 50 and 100 national advertisers to the three networks. Program producers then had to pass through a narrow network bottleneck or face the prospect of not getting their material on the air. Producers of programs and networks signed a "pilot and series" contract stipulating what share of the costs networks would pay for the pilot and also set out renewal option payment amounts for each year up to the fifth, or longer.[18]

That practice effectively eliminated competitive bidding for hit programs. Those networks maintained the practice was thrust upon them by advertisers unwilling to provide development funds. By forcing long-term contracts on producers the networks not only prevented competitive bidding and limited price increases over the life of the contract but were also able to reap the large profits from any hit shows. When a contract expired producers could negotiate with the other two networks, but the right of first refusal rested with the first network. In practice very few programs have transferred from one network to another. On rare occasions a producer could generate a successful series through syndication — selling on a station-by-station basis with no network affiliation and no prime-time telecasting — but such examples were rare. If a producer was denied prime time on all networks the producer's show was essentially dead. This gave ABC, NBC and CBS enormous power over the producers and enabled them to extract valuable subsidiary rights from suppliers, such as foreign distribution rights, profit shares in the domestic syndication market (reruns) and so forth. Allegedly those who refused to go along with network demands were excluded from access to prime time. Things got so bad for suppliers that the government would later step in to enact the Prime-Time Access Rule, which banned the networks from obtaining subsidiary rights such as distribution rights or profit shares in programs other than those that they produced themselves. Since the networks produced little material themselves — news, public affairs and sports were the main fare actually produced by the networks — their powers were somewhat curtailed. Nevertheless, at the start of the 1960s the number of domestic buyers of U.S. television product was effectively just three: ABC, NBC and CBS.[19]

On the other side, the number of program sellers was also reduced. A pattern of a relatively large number of independent producers selling material to the networks and to independent stations held throughout much of the 1950s. For a few years sales to independent stations were just as important as sales to the networks, as the networks had not then established strong control over programming of their affiliates. The U.S. television industry's purpose was to produce material divided into 30-minute segments designed for maximum audience appeal. As one writer noted, "Above all, the trade had to meet the networks' need for a predictable product that could be marketed to advertisers." The obvious choice was the Hollywood film studios. Not interested initially, they all soon came to be heavily involved; by the late 1950s 20th Century–Fox, Universal, MGM, Warner, Paramount, United Artists and Columbia were all involved or soon would be. In less than a decade from that point they dominated. Some 331 companies were listed as television program producers by *Television Factbook* in 1956. Three years later the same publication reported half of them had gone out of business. It became harder and harder for an independent company to survive, harder still to prosper. Twenty years later the number of principal television program suppliers would stand at nineteen. By 1965 those Hollywood majors grossed over $400 million from television sales (mostly domestic) — $100 million more than the gross take for theatrical features in the domestic market. For the 1965-66 television season almost 85 percent of prime-time programs shown on the three networks were produced by Hollywood, majors and independents.[20]

Until 1960 there was almost no competition from foreign distributors in the international market. American distributors had a head start and could draw upon a backlog of material that had already been profitably circulated domestically. They filled a new demand abroad from stations that were desperate for programming. This coupled with the fact those U.S. exporters could afford to sell abroad at low prices gave the U.S. a strong initial position in the world telefilm market. Wrote historian Wilson Dizard, "The international telefilm market is based, for better or for worse, on standards set by American producers which are imitated with little variation, by other Western telefilm companies. The American-oriented 'internationalization' of the product is a formidable barrier for Japanese and other non–Western telefilm producers. They can either have a restricted market for programs of their own style or try to imitate Western telefilm efforts."[21]

There was a lot of money to be made in television, particularly for the distributor. On a television sale, the distribution fee was 35 to 40 percent.

The size of the fee was important, but equally cogent was that it was taken "off the top" in foreign sales. In domestic sales residuals came out before the distribution fee was taken — as would be the case for foreign sales when talent got residual payment clauses in their contracts for such sales. In a typical foreign sale in the early 1960s a one-hour episode might take in a total of $30,000 from all foreign markets it penetrated. That would yield the distributor $12,000 (40 percent). Print costs and other expenses might total $3,000, leaving $15,000 to be divided by the owners. If profit participation was fifty-fifty, each got $7,500 compared to the distributor's $12,000. If one of the profit participants was also the distributor, as was usually the case, the distributor's total share then was $19,500 of the $30,000 sale. Of the total foreign television gross of about $52 million in 1962, distribution fees totaled $20 million. That explained why the Hollywood majors became heavily involved quickly, after they got over their initial fear and loathing of the new medium. It also explained why the networks demanded that if an independent producer's show was to air prime time on their network the independent would have to allow the network to become the foreign distributor of the show and perhaps a profit participant as well. The Prime-Time Access Act would put an end to that practice. As *Broadcasting* magazine wrote, "Producers understandably cling to distribution rights for their properties if they have strong sales organizations of their own. The major motion picture producers, foreign sales arms pre-dating television, to a great extent have dominated the syndication of U.S. television programming abroad.[22]

Attempts to control foreign television stations took many forms. As before, attempts ranged from providing "assistance" to the outright buying into outlet ownership offshore. Television went on the air in Thailand in June 1954. Early in the 1960s the country had two stations; though both were controlled by the government, they were given more or less complete freedom to program as they wished, to operate as many hours as they wished and to sell commercials. Both telecast seven days a week from 7 P.M. to midnight, with an extra seven hours on Saturday and Sunday. Half the nation's 24 million people were within range of the signals, which were received on 100,000 sets to a peak viewing audience of 1 million viewers. Creative arts director for Thai television was Pichai Vassnasong, who spent "much time" in the U.S. acquiring television training before starting his career. One U.S. show aired was "Ben Casey," which Vassnasong personally translated (spending eight hours on each one-hour segment). Then, two men and one woman rehearsed for three hours before doing all the voices live on air while "Ben Casey" was broadcast. Each outlet broadcast 47 to 60 percent live material with 90 percent of the remaining, taped material, being U.S. made. There was no limit on ads with one observer counting ten ads (ranging in length from ten seconds to one minute) in each break. Programs did not always begin at the listed time because of the large number of ads. In the month of December 1962 the

USIA supplied Thai television with 34 hours of programming, free. Thailand also received U.S. loans and grants to help the nation in its "communications fight" with the Communists. Thai television personnel were reported to be all Thai "with the exception of some 'key personnel' from RCA."[23]

When NBC International handed over the Nigerian Television Service Channel 10 to the Nigerian Broadcasting Corporation in 1967 it marked an end to the five-year management and training contract between NBC and the Nigerian government. When Israel launched its television service, personnel were initially trained in New York by CBS, and then CBS experts were stationed in Israel for some time. For many years Israeli television had a contract with the American network for guidance and technical advice. A renewal of that contract near the end of the 1960s cost the Israelis $50,000 for six months.[24]

ABC International continued its quest for a worldwide network that, of course, it would control and program. During 1962 the network spent $3.6 million on buying programs for its affiliates, $8 million the next year. Included were less-than-high-rated fare such as "Glynis" and "The Greatest Show on Earth." The marketing potential of global television had barely been scratched then, but ABC International president Don Coyle was on a U.S. cross-country trip, visiting every major corporation and advertising agency to tell the story of the company's worldwide service.[25]

One such function was held in New York City for 900 agency, advertiser and government guests at a breakfast meeting to introduce those American advertising leaders to ABC's overseas television advertising possibilities. Coyle told his guests "Our overall goal is the creation of a worldwide broadcasting network of active associates, and we are only on the threshold of the future." ABC represented most of those 26 affiliated stations in 17 countries for network and spot ad sales and in the buying of programming. Coyle boasted that costs of commercials for his affiliates were "flexible and down to earth." All of those stations, except for one each in Canada and Australia, used the ABC buying service. With some of them the network had some sort of "consultancy" agreement. In some of them ABC held a financial stake or an option to purchase one.[26]

While ABC was the network most actively involved in station control, it was not alone. One reason for U.S. broadcasters' investing was the Federal Communications Commission limitation on station ownership in the U.S., limiting each network to owning and operating no more than five outlets, and the large profit potential of station ownership. One authority estimated that the payout on carefully screened foreign station investment could be achieved in five or six years as compared to perhaps 20 to 25 years in the case of the multimillion dollar prices involved in the sale of domestic television outlets. The major problem came from political and economic instability, as when Castro nationalized Cuban broadcasting facilities. Cuban broadcaster Goar

Mestre resurfaced and was in partnership with CBS in ownership of a Lima, Peru, television production company. Those two plus Time Inc. owned a Buenos Aires production company, while CBS had a minority ownership position in a Trinidad station along with being in a "mutual assistance" pact with Italian public broadcaster RAI. NBC had financial interests in Mexico, Argentina, Australia, Venezuela and Peru to go along with management contracts in Nigeria and the U.K. The latter contract was with TWW, an independent program contractor for the commercial network. Emphasis for NBC in its overseas pacts was on "management services" ranging from design layout to installation of equipment to training of personnel to "direction." In addition to its Argentinean connection, Time Inc.'s Time-Life Broadcasting had a 2 percent interest in a Beirut, Lebanon, outlet. Warner had a 25 percent stake in ABC Television, a British commercial programming contractor. NBC International had "financial arrangements and associations" with two Argentinean stations, "arrangements" with two outlets in Mexico, its above-mentioned Nigerian contract and a 10 percent stake in another Argentinean outlet. At the time ABC owned minority interests in and represented Guatemala (one station), El Salvador (two), Honduras (two), Nicaragua (one), Costa Rica (one), Ecuador (one), Venezuela (six), Philippines (one), Japan (two), Lebanon (one), Australia (one). Additionally it represented but owned no stock in one Argentinean station, one Panamanian and two Canadian. Columbia's Screen Gems owned a station in Puerto Rico and held a financial interest in a dubbing company in Brazil.[27]

Representatives from 53 stations in 23 lands met in Washington in 1965 to discuss a worldwide television communications network. Those meetings were held under the sponsorship of ABC International and came about after five years of discussion and planning. In addition to the fourteen listed above were Brazil, Dominican Republic, Iran, Mexico, Syria, Nigeria, Japan (Okinawa) and Netherlands Antilles — the U.S. was the 23rd country. A key resolution passed acknowledged the importance of the commercial use of television. Participants resolved that individually and collectively, under the Worldvision banner, the stations would "unite in the promotion of commercial use of TV by an increasing number of internationally minded advertisers and local advertisers around the globe who have never tested the power of the medium."[28]

Often the U.S. producers joined forces openly with domestic lobbyists overseas to try to have their way. Toward the end of the 1960s New Zealand politicians debated the wisdom of adding a second station to the one state-run channel then on air and whether it should be private or public. New Zealand's ruling National party was trying to get a bill through Parliament to set up an agency that would have the power to grant television licenses to private companies and individuals. Opposed was the Labour Party, which agreed that a second network was needed but felt it should be state run. Had that unsuccessful attempt to enact the bill succeeded, one of the front-runners for a television license was a company in which NBC and Time-Life shared an interest of 20 percent, the maximum permitted by law. Pressing hard for passage of that bill, reported *Advertising Age*, were NBC and Time-Life Broadcasting "plus a score of New Zealand ad agencies and hundreds of advertisers."[29]

Brazil became the first Latin American nation to have television, with service inaugurated in 1950. By 1967 some 3 million sets served the nation's 85 million people, who were reported to be avid television fans: "And the blander the fare the better. In fact, Brazilians will watch anything so long as it is not highbrow — that even excludes Alfred Hitchcock." Popularity of the medium was said to be due to the high illiteracy rate, approaching 50 percent and even higher in some areas, making print media of little value. One advertising executive was "particularly pleased with the high tolerance Brazilians have for endless parades of commercials." Staple fare on Brazilian television "are old U.S. films and locally produced serials." Acknowledging that Brazilian television still had a long way to go before it achieved U.S. standard of professionalism, *Business Week* went on to note "But audience acceptance of programming — any programming — is so wholehearted that there appears to be little need to strive for perfection."[30]

Early in the 1960s Time-Life allied itself with Brazilian newspaper *O Globo* and opened a station in Rio, TV Globo, to compete against the company Diarios Associados, which owned 17 of Brazil's 39 outlets. Diarios complained that Brazilian law forbade foreign ownership of communications media. Its political clout forced Time-Life to write a new contract with *Globo* under which it became the station's landlord instead of its part owner.[31]

Even that change did not satisfy critics. Brazilian congressman and broadcaster Joao Calmon called a press conference to declare that Time-Life was "trying to cover all underdeveloped countries with a television web aimed to fight communism." Calmon asserted Time-Life had poured money into TV Globo against 3 percent of earnings for its technical advice and 45 percent for studio rental. He added that TV Globo salaries had been raised to levels unreachable for other television stations and that TV Globo had slashed ad rates by 50 percent. They were willing to lose a lot of money to drive out competitors and for political gain. All the publicity about foreign ownership and control of domestic media brought the problem to the attention of the Asociacion Interamericano de Radiodifusion (AIR), a group of private radio and television stations from all over the continent. In effect it was another front for U.S. lobbyists, as the AIR board was presided over by American broadcaster Herbert Evans. Meeting in Buenos Aires when the Time-Life/Brazilian story was prominent, the group considered the situation behind closed doors, after which it issued a statement: "without giving [an] opinion on foreign participation in those countries where local legislation allows it ... AIR is against foreign interference when it may distort the national character ... or may prevent local competition on radio and television, which neither implies refusing healthy cultural influences from other people nor backing an isolationism harmful to spiritual life's progress." That AIR Declaration of Buenos Aires went on to maintain however, that radio/television "is an activity of public interest not a 'public service' [subject] to government dictates."[32]

Ownership stakes in overseas outlets and companies were almost always a minority position by the U.S. firms, as most nations were very sensitive to the idea of foreign ownership and control within their communications industries. American companies were prone to use euphemisms such as "partners in progress." NBC liked to say that hardware provided by its parent, RCA, was not automatically used by NBC as it made installations abroad. Network executive Joe Klein explained: "We try to dissociate from RCA. As management service advisers we try to get the best equipment for each job at the best prices, from anyone." To the extent that was true it was equally true that RCA benefitted greatly by the general spread of television all over the world. Time-Life vice president Sig Mickelson saw the spread of commercial television as inevitable: "The various underdeveloped countries are having to permit commercials because they can't afford a television system otherwise. And in Europe, where most countries have just come through the development of their second TV system, there eventually will be public demand for a third system, and this will have to be commercial because fees [for the annual licensing of television sets] can only be raised to a certain level and no higher."[33]

In explaining its foreign holdings ABC stated it "follows a policy of cooperation, never of control." ABC International bought programs and provided them to Worldvision stations for a commission that usually was 7.5 percent of the station's highest time rate. However, if the program was one of ABC's own, then no commission was charged. As a sales representative ABC offered to advertisers any time not sold by the Worldvision outlets themselves. The only condition was that the sale had to be international. That is, Worldvision would not sell time to a Mexican advertiser for a Mexican station. But it could sell time on that Mexican station to a Venezuelan advertiser. ABC International's networking service provided that each Worldvision station had to make Class A time (prime time) available within eight weeks from the time any program was presold by ABC. For example, ABC could sell "Batman" to an advertiser and then place "Batman"—along with designated ads—in any country "where the advertiser wants it to appear," said reporter Ralph Tyler.[34]

Taking a different perspective was Chilean Marxist journalist Maximo Humbert. Commenting on U.S. investments in Latin America he wrote in 1969 "North American imperialism has made it clear that it intends to continue its control over this important media, thus completely dominating developing nations such as Chile." He felt U.S. television expanded into Latin America at the end of the 1950s both because of domestic saturation and because growing nationalist movements in Latin America were perceived as dangerous to U.S. interests. "TV would create a desire for consumption throughout Latin America, which in turn would assure continued American ideological domination," he wrote. ABC then controlled 64 television stations in 27 countries, with an audience of 80 million. Humbert noted that any Latin station affiliated with Worldvision "must accept the programs and commercials chosen by ABC for its primetime viewing hours." To Humbert what the U.S. producers were creating in the Third World was "an artificial desire for consumer products — artificial in the sense that it take precedence over more fundamental desires such as education, health and basic economic development." Also noted was the practice of imposing block-booking: "In order to buy the top-rated shows, Latin stations must accept packages that include flops.... TV stations must purchase programming in packages or not at all." Humbert added, "The content of almost all these programs is meant to stupefy our people, to keep them within the imperialistic framework, to make them consumers." Among the free programs provided by the USIA, to any who wanted them, in Latin America was "Horizon Newsreel," in which the Alliance for Progress appeared regularly as the region's "good fairy." In Humbert's own country of Chile an organization called Protab provided programs used by both the commercial and the government channel. It provided the largest number of television programs seen in Chile. It had recently affiliated with ABC's Worldvision. Paparazzi Products made most of the programs not produced by Protab. After several trips to America, paid for by the State Department, its directors were reported to be "working hand-in-hand" with the USIA. "In effect, a major portion of Chile's communications media have been handed over to the North Americans," he concluded.[35]

As the foreign television market potential increased dramatically so did the salesmanship efforts of the American exporters. A meeting of the European Broadcasting Union (EBU) took place in New York City for four days in October 1962; the U.S., Canada, Japan and Australia were among the associate members of that group. In all, 25 nations held full membership; seventeen were associates. Nineteen European countries were represented by official EBU delegates at that convention, as were the four associate countries named above. It was a perfect opportunity for U.S. producers to sell their television fare. Yet, a few months before the meeting took place ABC, NBC and CBS came to a "gentlemen's agreement" whereby they agreed to make no specific sales pitches to any EBU delegates during the period of the convention. Supposedly this was to allow EBU delegates to concentrate on the real business of the convention. That four-day peace treaty was endorsed by the EBU itself, with its headquarters being encouraged to warn all members not to accept private invitations from any of the three networks. However, many EBUers were staying over in the U.S. for a second week. Said one U.S. network executive, "In the second week, it's open warfare." Those three networks drew straws to determine the order of hosting EBU luncheons over the four days; the fourth luncheon was hosted by USIA director Edward Murrow.[36]

Since the agreement not to pitch any wares either publicly or privately to EBU delegates was limited to the three networks, they sought to limit such selling opportunities for all other U.S. suppliers by refusing to release the EBU agenda or details on where the delegates were housed. Despite that agreement, when Don Coyle made his public luncheon speech on ABC's day as host, he made specific mention of ABC programs and then told the audience; "We at ABC propose to seek out each member delegation of this conference for the purpose of discussing what product can be made available to world markets." Naturally, that infuriated personnel at the other two networks. "It's shocking to me, considering the understanding we have," remarked a CBS executive. An NBC official complained, "Yes, it is a sales pitch and we had an absolute understanding — very specific — that there would be no pitches, especially at these luncheons. They're distasteful, and for that reason we agreed to behave and stick to — call them high-level ideas."[37]

Less than one week after that convention closed, ABC hosted 850 foreign broadcasters — including EBU stayovers — advertising agency representatives and transnational company executives at a meeting where it pitched itself, its programs and its idea of an international commercial hookup. *Variety* wrote that ABC was "frankly demonstrating the hardsell approach."[38]

NBC International used the tactic of giveaway. It offered, in the early 1960s, some 125 hours of public affairs shows free to nations "where television is now in the planning stages and where the initiating of programming poses economic problems to these nations." At the time, NBC sold public affairs shows in most nations where television existed "and this provides a fair buck to the American web." The new plan provided free product to countries such as Kenya, Sierra Leone, Uganda and Jamaica which would receive tapes of shows just for the cost of mailing under a plan NBC called Operation Documentaries. After two years of free product, recipient lands would be expected to pay for the material, although NBC allowed it would consider renewing the free status for two years, in individual cases.[39]

Everywhere there was a flood of salespeople. CBS executive Ralph Baruch estimated in 1964 there were 50 sales representatives permanently based in London, England, who pitched U.S. shows to the U.K. market. A large force of salespeople abroad was considered a necessity, to hold frequent screenings of programs and to constantly hype their wares. Some sales were made only with the screening of a pilot, and in some cases, "without the screening of any footage at all." Disappointment often followed sales resulting from limited or no screenings. Still, a powerful buying incentive was the cheapness of American product. Akira Shimizu, a sales agent in Japan for NBC, and others commented that U.S. shows would continue to sell in Japan because they sold for less than the cost of a domestic production. For a Japanese one-hour episode, the domestic product cost $7,000 to $8,000, more expensive than the average U.S. import "even considering the extra expenses of dubbing, shipping, duties and taxes." It was conventional wisdom that regardless of the age of an American television series there was a market. NBC International president Gerald Adler sold the 10-year-old "Hiram Holiday" for a third run on the BBC and in Switzerland and Germany. Still, few nations bought more than six or thirteen episodes at a time. German television bought "Laramie" one episode at a time until the entire run of 42 was purchased. Adler managed a sale of a block of 52 segments of "Bonanza" in Germany, a record for the number of episodes involved. In Adler's mind the best customer was Australia because "They buy everything."[40]

In the summer of 1966 United Artists TV reported sales in 100 foreign lands, reportedly the highest for any American distributor. The country that brought UA to the century mark was Paraguay.[41]

When color television arrived in America it put pressure on other countries to follow suit, even if they could ill afford it. For foreign nations it meant spending a great deal of money on color equipment, leaving less money to devote to their own programming. It also meant U.S. suppliers tried to extract more money for their material. With the advent of color television in the U.K. still a year or more away, *Variety* observed "the needs and demands of the American video business has hyped the era of color production in Britain." Color production costs were at least 20 percent higher than for black and white. One "British" series done in color was the variety show "Hippodrome," slated as a U.S. summer replacement on CBS. A U.S. producer was flown to London to oversee the show, which featured mostly U.S. talent. U.K. producer Lew Grade did some color variety shows from London's Palladium with U.S. artists in the top-billed spots. Both those shows were telecast locally in the U.K. in black and white. That rarely realized hope that foreign producers nurtured of seeing their product break into U.S. prime time motivated them to turn to color. Italy debated the color issue in 1966 when its advent was still several years away. Critics argued that RAI should concentrate on bettering its black-and-white programming rather than experimenting with color. Cost of the changeover for Italy was estimated at $640 million. Those favoring the change to color felt RAI should rapidly adopt color television for reasons of "international prestige."[42]

Star tours remained a popular way for Hollywood to sell its product, particularly if some of the costs were picked up elsewhere. Screen Gems sent a covey of its television stars and executives to Canada in 1967 for a round of interviews in various cities. One aim was supposedly to publicize the World's Fair in Montreal that year, Expo 67; another was to plug "Screen Gems personalities and programs." Some of the expenses of that tour were borne by Screen Gems but some costs were absorbed by Canadian cities, provinces and by the federal government for Expo 67.[43]

Some U.S. suppliers thought foreign buyers would "always" want American shows, even when they were on firmer financial footing, because they could never match U.S.-type per-show production costs ranging from $40,000 to $140,000, and they could obtain those shows at relatively low rents. It was felt that even if the percentage of American shows dropped on one station or network, that drop would be more than compensated for by the opening of more stations and networks. While a half-hour episode sold in the U.K. for $2,000, it went into Ireland for as little as $27.50 "just to get started in the market." Ralph Baruch complained that the dollar grosses were not as good as they looked, saying "If we do a million dollar business in Great Britain this is not a million dollars cleared. Sales costs, producer's share, maintaining overseas offices and staffs, etc., are very expensive. In the end we may retain only $100,000." On the other hand Charles Michelson, an American who bought for an Australian network, complaining of U.S. suppliers, said "It's been all take and no give up to date."[44]

Driving it all was advertising. Prior to the television era the U.S. stood alone among advanced industrialized nations in having its radio system totally commercial. Nowhere else did advertisers pay the bills and direct the medium so completely. In Europe state broadcasters were the rule, with the U.S.-style system a rare exception. However, when television arrived many national broadcasting organizations adopted some variant of the American method. Television developed principally as a commercial medium. Money was a factor, as was signal spillover. Even strong, financially solvent Western nations found themselves forced to modify their longtime stable broadcasting services and accept ads. Media critic Herbert Schiller stated "Nothing less than the viability of the American industrial economy itself is involved in the movement toward international commercialization of broadcasting."[45]

As transnational companies roamed the world for new markets, ad agencies went along. Together they looked for new places and ways to advertise; television was a major one. By early in the 1960s England had 21 U.S.-associated ad agencies, West Germany had 20; Brazil had 15. The McCann–Erickson agency then had 70 offices overseas in 37 nations with 4,619 employees. "The insistence of powerful American sellers, temporarily allied with their local counterparts, on obtaining advertising outlets abroad is overwhelming state broadcasting authorities, one after another," wrote Schiller. "The successful campaign to introduce commercial television in England was largely a matter of industry admen manipulating complex political wires." In 1964 private enterprise spent $21 billion for advertising in fourteen industrial nations, $14 billion of that in the U.S. Wherever that commercial force penetrated, wrote Schiller, "broadcasting is subverted to salesmanship. It is not only a matter of the ubiquitous, jarring commercial. The entire content that illuminates the home screen is fitted to the marketeer's order." Journalist Daniel Karp emphasized that television was neither an art form nor a culture outlet; it was solely an advertising medium: "it seems a bit churlish and un–American of people who watch television to complain that their shows are so lousy. They are not 'supposed' to be any good. They are supposed to make money ... and in fact, 'quality' may be not merely irrelevant but a distraction." Programs themselves often had to follow advertiser dictates, directly or indirectly. In the case of widely shown and popular U.S. shows advertising agency people often sat in it at each stage of a script's development.[46]

ABC's Worldvision network held a 1966 symposium titled "Television in the Space Age — A New Opportunity for the Global Advertiser" that traveled the U.S. and many foreign lands. One of the speakers was Robert W. Young, a Colgate–Palmolive executive who predicted that in the coming five to ten years as much as 40 to 50 percent of a major advertiser's volume would have to come from new products. Young added that those new products would not have to be named or packaged differently from nation to nation. He explained that Colgate had some apprehension about using Ajax cleanser's white tornado television ad abroad because Europeans were not familiar with tornados, but the ad was successful. Compton Advertising chairman Barton Cummings did envision some problems for global television because of both language and commercial content. For example, with regard to the selection of actors for commercials he wondered, "Should they all be Americans, or should some be Europeans, Africans or Latin Americans?" As television technology increased the cost of providing a service, ABC International president Coyle told the gathering, "Television systems are going to have to find a way to pay for this; so they will be forced to go commercial.... The people of the world are ready and willing to accept global advertising."[47]

Expenditure for domestic television advertising moved from $57.8 million a year in 1949 to $2,765 million in 1966; total U.S. ad expenditure was then some $16.5 billion annually. Commented reporter Neil Hurley. "The steady growth of television as an advertising medium has been paralleled by the increase of network affiliates abroad, the cultivation of overseas markets, and the rise in exports of telefilms, videotapes and old Hollywood movies." Exported along with the commercials were television shows that directly and indirectly exported such dubious values as nationalism, materialism (a blind faith in an escalating standard of living), doctrinaire conservatism (social conformity and resistance to change), liberal progressivism (things are getting better all the time) and social Darwinism (survival of the fittest and might makes right) and America's popular illusions such as people's capitalism, consumer sovereignty, unions as labor monopolies, socially responsible management and advertising as a community service and an essential work of public intelligence. One unnamed president of a Latin American country said U.S.-inspired television functioned as a "social narcotic, thus playing into the hands of reactionary conservative forces in favor of maintaining the status quo."[48]

Speaking in 1966, ad agency executive Herbert Zeltner predicted a single advertiser sponsoring a worldwide network program would be a reality within five years, via a satellite system. There would be no language problem because a voice computer — which to date has not been invented — on the satellite would automatically translate the text into as many languages as required.[49]

Profits and sales levels were kept at high levels by practices such as block-booking and lack of residual payments for overseas screenings. Residuals were payments to creative talent for reruns of programs and were extracted from domestic reruns and had been for some time. Such was not the case for foreign screenings, and the unions fought to win such payments. The sales of U.S. television abroad brought a high rate of return to distributors because of, said *Broadcasting* magazine, "the comparatively low cost of selling operations (as compared with domestic sales) and to a more advantageous position vis-a-vis residual fees to talent, particularly actors." In accordance with the contract in effect in 1962 between producers and the Screen Actors Guild (SAG), residuals applied to filmed programs carried in the U.S., Canada and Mexico but not the rest of the world. That was said to "add a substantial financial burden to domestic syndication." Residual fees for television entertainment films applied up to the sixth screening (fifth rerun) of an episode, with a performer who had received minimum scale for the original, getting up to 140 percent of that amount for reruns (35 percent for the first rerun, 30 percent for the second and 25 percent for each of the third, fourth and fifth reruns). Star performers could demand their own residual pay scales. SAG admitted it had tried to impose a foreign residual clause during the 1960 negotiations but eventually withdrew that demand. The other major union, American Federation of Television and Radio Artists (AFTRA), had an overseas payment formula for live shows and tapes of those shows sold abroad, but few of those programs were sold abroad principally because of that clause. Distributors openly admitted residual payments were one factor in choking off sales of those programs overseas. While actors were the biggest beneficiaries, writers, directors and musicians also shared. It was estimated that $7,000 to $8,000 was required to obtain residual clearances domestically on an average half-hour filmed series for six runs, a lower figure for fewer runs.[50]

Distributors admitted foreign critics sometimes asked where the U.S. variety shows, the specials, the live/tape shows were. Those suppliers "knew" those shows were "locked up at home" due to the "high payment scale" demanded by AFTRA. "U.S.-filmed programs flow overseas in abundance for the simple reason that present contracts with film unions do not carry the high talent pay costs live-tape programming does." NBC International did distribute "The Perry Como Show" overseas in 16 nations in 1960 because most performers on the live "Como" agreed to work for an "equitable fee." But other talent did not, with the result that some of the "Como" hours played offshore in formats ranging down to eighteen minutes. On the live "Ed Sullivan Show" some individual acts were "segmented" out for foreign showings of the program, which ranged down to fifteen minutes. As the number of U.S.-produced live/tape programs was rapidly declining, the issue gradually disappeared; virtually all fare would be done on film.[51]

One of the major issues that resolved the Hollywood writers' strike in 1960 was the winning by the Writers Guild of America of a clause whereby television writers would receive overseas residuals. The guild received its first payment in the summer of 1963; $30,000 from $750,000 of foreign sales, 4 percent. In July 1964 agreement was reached between producers and SAG on a new contract in which, for the first time, actors were cut in on the take of U.S. television product shown abroad.[52]

Block-booking could not always be imposed, particularly in nations where the service was government run and not commercial. BBC buyer Gordon Smith never bought programs without screening two or three episodes of a series, and he never block-booked, which meant the buyer also had no opportunity to prescreen the material. Smith said, "We don't entertain package deals, we don't want to buy anything we can't screen."[53]

However, it was a different story where there were many competing networks and/or they were commercially driven. When Nigerian television was eighteen months old in 1962, one in five shows was live and locally produced, but the rest of the fare was mainly filmed U.S. product, much of it second rate. While the Nigerian service allowed commercials, the system was still too poor to pay its way, relying on government subsidies. Worried about image in Nigeria a USIA (actually then USIS, United States Information Service) official said, "We go our own way trying to project one image of America and behind our backs American films on television here create an entirely different impression." Nigerian program director American Roger Bowers (NBC was still running the outlet on its five-year management contract) explained, "Until we can build up more live programs of our own we're at the mercy of the American film industry. Our difficulty is that if we want to get a good show like 'The Defenders,' we have to buy a package that includes second-rate westerns, crime shows, and whatever else is outdated and can't be peddled at home."[54]

Hollywood's two export associations continued to operate into the 1960s. Back from a six-week foreign trip in 1963, TPEA head McCarthy announced his group planned to undertake a campaign to increase the prices paid for American product in foreign locales. He thought prices then paid in many world markets were "inadequate," largely attributable to quotas and "price-fixing arrangements among buyers of U.S. programs." TPEA planned to do a market-by-market analysis of pricing throughout the world. Asked what steps could be taken to raise prices if overseas buyers continued to resist increases, McCarthy replied the TPEA was prepared to take "defensive counter measures" but only in extreme circumstances would suppliers withhold product from a particular market.[55]

On another occasion McCarthy complained that "Western Europe today adheres to a monopolistic or governmental television approach. We are at their mercy on price in a buyer's market. And we won't have a satisfactory picture until competitive commercial TV is introduced." Another time in 1963 McCarthy boasted, "The stranglehold on trading conditions, with which world buyers of U.S. television programs have harassed producers and distributors since the inception of export sales, will be breached by 1964."[56]

Yet there was tension between the two lobby groups, the TPEA and the MPEA television committee, headed by William Fineshriber. In 1963 TPEA members included ABC, NBC, CBS, MCA and a few smaller independent producers such as Four Star and Desilu. MPEA members included the eight majors. Screen Gems, MGM and UA at one time had been members of both groups, but all quit TPEA early in 1963 to stay exclusively with the MPEA film group. On the surface one reason given for dropping out of TPEA was to eliminate any duplication and save on dues. However, the split went deeper. Motion picture interests had invested heavily in television but the two media were not compatible in many situations. By 1963 the composition of TPEA was almost a pure television-oriented membership. On the other hand the MPEA represented companies that historically were the major Hollywood film producers. One observer commented, "MPEA has to look out for overseas motion picture exhibitors who deal with Hollywood. And I don't think MPEA will be behind many bills in foreign lands that benefit TV to the detriment of motion pictures."[57]

At the time it was unclear how much of the television export market each group was responsible for; it was perhaps 50–50 or 70–30 one way or the other. American industry executives in charge of foreign operations were troubled by the duality of the public relations image. While there was no open break in 1963 each organization was quick to get into print to claim credit whenever a foreign restriction fell. One worry was that sooner or later each group would try to weaken the other, with U.S. exports the loser. Those opposed to having two lobby groups argued one needlessly duplicated the efforts of the other. Even those prepared to live with two organizations saw a problem in that television and feature films were sometimes in conflict in certain markets. If film interests outweighed television interests, the former would prevail. With a limited membership each group could lobby only partially. Only companies engaged in motion picture production/distribution could become members of MPEA's television committee. Some argued that McCarthy was too aggressive in his public statements. Fineshriber had helped organize TPEA while McCarthy, years before, had been second in command at MPEA when he split with MPEA/MPAA chief Eric Johnson. One U.S. television executive said, "we do have two organizations. They best learn to live well with one another. There's too much at stake for anything less."[58]

Membership in TPEA continued to decline. Its 10 members dropped to eight when MCA pulled out after acquiring MPEA major Universal. Even the independent producer Desilu had turned in its letter of resignation. The TPEA folded completely around 1970.[59]

One reason for its demise was a leadership change in MPAA/MPEA when Eric Johnson died suddenly in office in 1964. Johnson had never shown much interest in the mutuality of television and movie interests. Things began to change during the interim appointment of Ralph Hetzel as acting MPAA head. It was a change that gained momentum when Jack Valenti was appointed head of the MPAA/MPEA in May 1966. Within a few months of his appointment Valenti and a number of other MPEA executives made their first European trip on behalf of U.S. television exports. That delegation met with government officials and television network heads in London and Paris. For 1965 member companies of MPAA (who represented 95 percent of U.S. film production receipts) grossed $350 million from world television (about $75 million offshore) and $600 million from world theatrical grosses.[60]

Those lobby groups were fighting for a world market that continued to grow dramatically. At the end of 1963 USIA reported 80 million sets abroad, up 15 million from 1962. Western Europe had 39 million of those sets, Japan had 15 million and Eastern Europe had 15 million receivers, 9 million of those in the Soviet Union. In total 83 nations had a television service. There were 3,444 stations abroad (up 800 from 1962); Western Europe had 1,803. By 1968 there were 140 million sets abroad, almost twice as many as in the U.S. Over 100 countries had become markets for American television fare. A successful one-hour U.S. series could expect to sell for up to $7,000 in the U.K., $6,500 in Canada, $6,000 in West Germany, $6,000 in Japan, $4,400 in France, $4,250 in Australia, $180 in Kuwait, $150 in Hong Kong, $120 in Saudi Arabia, $110 in Guatemala, $90 in Taiwan and $60 in Nicaragua.[61]

As to the potential of that world market MCA-TV executive Berle Adams warned that the foreign bonanza would be less than many in the industry hoped. Canada, Australia and the U.K. represented 50 percent of the U.S. foreign gross, with Latin America accounting for another 25 percent. Problems in Latin America were currency devaluations and political instability as regimes came and went. Nonetheless Adams felt Latin America was potentially the best market since private, commercial stations dominated the Latin American scene. Europe was not a good market due to "an intensive nationalism plus control of television there by various governments.... Programs are selected by committees which are extremely sensitive to public and press reaction." That, plus the lack of "competition" didn't make for a good market for U.S. shows, thought Adams. As well, Europeans rarely bought a series, usually taking only a few segments, maybe more later. "Government-appointed committees will screen every print of an American vidfilm before buying," moaned Adams, who also lamented a nationalistic sentiment wherein each nation emphasized its own product in preference to foreign fare."[62]

One foreign buyer pointed out that as most U.S. shows made up their costs at home, overseas earnings were gravy. Yet the Americans asked prices out of line with what the economy of most foreign nations could bear. In reply a U.S. supplier said those foreign buyers "don't love us, but they damn well need us."[63]

As the U.K., France and Holland added second channels (all government run), in 1964 *Variety* pointed out that an expected bonanza from second channel addition was not forthcoming, as stations in these countries were buying a relatively small amount of U.S. product. Adams explained this was so because those new outlets were state owned, were public service outlets and had limited broadcast time. All were making an intense effort to produce as many of their own shows as possible. Since those outlets were basically noncommercial, the "competitive" element was missing.[64]

More optimistic was Screen Gems International president Lloyd Burns. On his return in 1966 from seven weeks overseas he said he didn't equate growing nationalism in global markets with diminution of U.S. television abroad. While that market might level off, it was still good. If American programs had 30 to 40 percent of the market in some lands and if that market had declined, on each station the overall total held up because there were more stations in total. Burns declared, "Australia is a good example where there is wide acceptance for anything American in television." For a long time there, he said, "the licensees were capable of controlling the prices" but a break came when a third commercial channel opened in both Sydney and Melbourne, causing the import market to boom anew. When a second channel opened in Taipei "this ups the price." Burns went on to agree there was unabashed anti–Americanism throughout Southeast Asia but he claimed paradoxically, that nationalism had no effect on sales of U.S. television product.[65]

Also optimistic was Desilu executive Bernard Weitzman, who felt in 1967 that foreign television gross would eventually reach 50 percent of the world total gross. Admitting that a number of nations, such as Germany, were exhibiting more nationalism with a desire to produce more of their own fare he believed they would not be successful because "they don't have the Hollywood style and knowhow, the personalities, creative talent, nor the expertise which makes Hollywood-made telefilms so popular abroad." Foreigners loved action fare because, said Weitzman, programs were dubbed and it was hard to follow the shows if they had too much dialog. Germans continued in their habit of buying only a few episodes of a series rather than the entire run, something Weitzman felt to be an example of their "strange ways."[66]

Twentieth Century–Fox executive Alan Silverbach commented, at a time when Fox had seven and one-half hours of prime-time weekly television fare on the three networks — the most of any Hollywood major — "I think Fox is making a particular type of product with international appeal." Examples cited included "Batman," "Felony Squad," "Lost in Space" and "Voyage to the Bottom of the Sea." Silverbach explained that "Even though these programs are initially tailored for the American networks, which has to be the major consideration because of the economics of the business, we also produce with an eye for the international market." He reinforced the myth of the financially strapped American producers by claiming, "The cost of a show today is so high that in almost all cases you don't get your investment back from American network sales. You also need the income from syndication in the U.S. after the network runs and from overseas sales."[67]

The battle to impose commercial television in Europe continued, although successes were limited in the 1960s. In regions such as Latin America the battle was over, but it was a somewhat hollow victory, as money was limited there. Swiss television capitulated to commercials on the home screen when the 11-year-old, state-run service first allowed ads in February 1965. Each night of the week except Sundays, three four-minute periods of commercials were presented at fixed times; the first was at 7 P.M. Ads were finally permitted as more revenue was needed to expand programs. When commercials were allowed, the service was expanded to seven nights a week of television instead of six — Tuesdays had been dark for reasons of economy. Better and more programs were promised with no increase in the annual license fee of $20 per set. Commercials were expected to add $4 million in yearly revenue to the $10 million obtained annually from set license fees.[68]

Holland's 2 million sets were served by two noncommercial channels that were shared by five nonprofit broadcast groups. However, Dutch viewers could receive close-to-the-border German stations that did carry ads. Dutch businesses agitated for domestic commercial television explaining they were losing business to those German advertisers. Further pressure was applied in 1964 when a pirate station, TV Noordzee, was established just off Holland's coast; it broadcast much American fare, and ads. The Dutch navy was dispatched to shut it down. Politicians were so divided on the issue of whether or not to allow commercial television that Dutch Prime Minister Victor Marijnen (who favored commercial television) resigned when he couldn't get his cabinet to fully endorse the idea.[69]

One problem in the middle 1960s in Germany, where television households paid a monthly license fee of $1.25 to the government, was "black watchers," those who had sets but didn't register and pay the license fee. In the month of July 1966, in Frankfurt alone the government tracked down and fined 1,098 black watchers. Adding to German television's financial woes was the coming of color transmission, then just a year away. It would up the cost of providing a television service considerably. To cover increasing television costs the annual television license fee (the norm in Europe) could be increased, but such a move was always fraught with political peril. When France increased its annual fee from $17 to $20 yearly in 1966 it marked the first raise since 1960. Belgium's fee was $16.50 per year, West Germany and Italy were at $14 to $15 while Japan imposed a $9 annual levy. Commenting on the French license increase *Variety* commented that it "is also expected to set back the long contemplated plans for commercial programs and ads, at least for a few years. Ads are discussed every year but somehow always either get avoided, pushed back or superseded by some other move."[70]

German lobby efforts to introduce private commercial television heated up again in 1968 when two groups in the Saar region agitated for private licenses. Television in Germany then consisted of two state-run channels that did allow ads but rigidly controlled them as to content while limiting their airing to brief evening periods when ads were lumped together at the start and end of shows. There was a distinct difference between private commercial stations and state-run outlets that permitted ads. While U.S. interests preferred the latter over state-run television that allowed no ads at all, they were never satisfied until the former was initiated. As those two Saar groups pressured for private licenses U.S. ad agency branches and transnational merchandisers were busy getting acquainted with those groups, just in case. "If the Saar actually comes out with a profitable private enterprise locally, the other lands may follow suit and open the way for a whole series of enterprising businesses to get started with local private commercial stations here."[71]

Pointing to the popularity of U.S. series on Scandinavian television in 1967, reporter Fradley Garner explained that in the absence of commercially sponsored programs Scandinavia's budget-conscious state-run systems had neither the money nor the talent to fill more than a small part of their own needs for entertainment fare; and local independent production, "even if it existed, would be no profitable business." However, Garner had to admit there was no way of saying for sure how popular the foreign products were because there was "no such thing as regular ratings." Critics in the four nations took pains to criticize sharply most U.S. series with evaluations ranging from "imbecility" to "sinister catering to the worst type of U.S. small town conformity" (this was said of "I Love Lucy").[72]

American ad agency Foote, Cone & Belding held a 1966 gathering of its foreign managers to consider the coming of private commercial television to Europe. The group was optimistic about the prospects. Nonetheless a few warnings were sounded. The agency's Paris manager noted there was a lot of resistance to it in France, with people arguing that since they paid a tax for television (the annual license fee) why should they have to have commercial television? Foote's Copenhagen, Denmark, manager E. Helbech Hansen claimed that a lot of "illogical" things had been said against commercial television in Denmark. State television authorities had sent a study group to the U.S. to investigate and report back. When the group returned it told the Danish state television authority, said Hansen, that commercial television "interrupted everything" to bring in commercials. They said, that from a business standpoint, the big companies will be the dominating factor. They said it will help establish monopolies and that it will ruin the press. They also claimed that it will make us a nation of conformists." In general, ad agency branches thought it was "politics and fear" that kept commercial television out of much of Europe. However, they also argued that "the cost of color television developments and common market competition will hasten commercial television's day."[73]

BBC Secretary Charles Curran reiterated the BBC's reason for not accepting ads by saying that "advertising and public service broadcasting are incompatible." As to the argument that accepting commercials did not prove disastrous for the ITV commercial U.K. network so would not prove fatal to the BBC, Curran replied, "a service financed by advertising could safely be accepted because the BBC would still be there to set high standards. The existence of, and competition from, the BBC has no doubt helped to maintain the quality of the commercial television output." Once BBC depended on ad revenue it would have to plan its programming to attract the largest possible audience for the longest possible time. Once ads accounted for any part of BBC's revenues the public would have a ready-made reply to any request for an increase in license fees: take more ads. "Once advertising is accepted, there is no road back," warned Curran.[74]

Having embraced television completely Hollywood found the 1960s a tough period in which to sell its feature films to foreign television, for various reasons. At home the situation was the reverse as stations bought up more and more old Hollywood films. Since television consumed feature films at a much faster rate than Hollywood could produce them, the huge backlog was quickly whittled down. In time that lack of available feature films gave birth to a new species — the made-for-television movie. Back when television was just an infant and when Hollywood was busy boycotting the newcomer, one pioneer of the film industry expressed Hollywood's collective attitude when he remarked, "if we can keep our old pictures away from television we can destroy them." Yet the screening of old films allowed extended broadcast hours — more product sold in total — and helped kill live television, which created a bigger market for Hollywood's television series and even more features. During 1964 Los Angeles had seven television stations, which regularly aired a combined total of 200 to 240 films per week. Prices ranged from $1,200 to $23,000. For a package of 50 first-class films the cost worked out to $19,000 per title, with unlimited runs over a seven-year period. According to KHJ — TV program director Wally Sherman the average number of screenings per title per year in Los Angeles was three — a total of 20 over the contract's life. Despite the seeming high price it was a good deal for the station. Assuming a title cost $19,000, was screened 20 times over seven years, and filled a 90-minute time slot, the per-hour cost to the station was just $633.[75]

In San Francisco a feature film might go to a station in 1963 for $4,500 for, say, five runs. That worked out to $900 per screening, or $300 per half-hour. Such bargain prices tended to make it difficult for a syndicated series (one sold not to a network but outlet by outlet) to get time. An off-network series went for $800 per hour, $400 per half-hour. This concentrated power within the cartel, as it became harder to turn a series into a hit selling only through the syndication route.[76]

For the 1966-67 television season the three U.S. networks spent a combined $52.5 million for feature films. The average price paid by one of the networks was $350,000 for one title. At the time feature films accounted for 16 percent of the prime time on both NBC and CBS, 8 percent on ABC. A staple of U.S. television programming feature films garnered an average of 30 to 35 percent of the available audience over the course of a television season.[77]

Overseas the picture was much less rosy for U.S. features. One reason was that Hollywood had deliberately pursued a policy in a number of off-shore markets of holding back their pre–1948 features for so long that in certain major territories the post–1948s had caught up with them and depressed the value of the pre–1948s. In Australia, for example, in 1962 some of Fox's pre–1948s had not been sold with those movies forced into competition with the post–1948s. That go-slow release policy was partly adopted to placate local film exhibitors who didn't want newish releases on the home screen (actually they preferred no films at all). Hollywood was always loath at first to release films to television, as it feared this would hurt theater box offices and depress its theatrical business. Mostly, though, the holdback was due to financial concerns, to push up prices. As a report noted, "it's not a question of policy but of price, with the distributor holding out for higher prices and being caught up by newer pix hitting the market." While all the Hollywood majors were then marketing their features everywhere they did so with less vigor than that displayed by firms without major Hollywood ties trying to sell independent features abroad. Mixed emotions tended to check some of Hollywood's drive.[78]

Other reasons for the relatively slow spread of Hollywood features abroad had to do with local conditions and situation. The most lucrative markets for U.S. features were Canada and Australia because, observed *Variety*, "both countries developed TV commercial systems parallel to that of the U.S." Sales of features to the U.K. were blocked by FIDO, a group financed by the local motion picture industry, which was dedicated to keeping movies off television. Strong exhibitor pressure in both West Germany and Japan blocked any large-scale sale of movies in those key markets. With the issue as sensitive as it was in so many markets, the Hollywood majors were forced to treat the situation gingerly. They sympathized with foreign cinema interests in not wanting to jeopardize overseas box office revenues. Additionally, state-owned television systems for the most part were not on the air enough hours each day to need a large stockpile of movies. In Latin America the stations then averaged six hours a day of broadcasting. Subtitled movies did not work well on the small screen. Japanese television buyers and American suppliers had talked about movies, and price was the main reason few deals with struck.

Observers felt that when the price was deemed right Hollywood would risk the wrath of local film industries and sell to television. Australia paid $2,500 to $10,000 for a feature; Canada's CBC (English), $2,500 to $8,000; Canada's private CTV, $3,000 to $4,000; Canada's CBC (French), $2,000 to $4,000 for a dubbed feature. Occasionally movies sold in France, Italy and West Germany for, respectively, $1,200 to $2,000, $1,000 to $3,000, and $8,200. In the Philippines a feature sold for $500, $150 in Hong Kong. Theoretically a U.S. movie that sold everywhere could gross $50,000 offshore. Yet in 1963 one industry estimate was that the sale of movies to television abroad was less than 10 percent of the total foreign television revenue.[79]

France's second channel commenced operation in 1964. Together the two state-run networks broadcast about 200 features per year, all pre–1958s, due to exhibitor pressure. Almost half of them were American movies; 100 were French made. That country's national television organization, ORTF, wanted to "deAmericanize" the movies on television but found that alternative films that could be used, such as Italian and Spanish titles, were not dubbed. As the U.S. ones were dubbed it was much cheaper to use them. Also, many of those European films were considered too mature for television use.[80]

France was unable to accomplish its particular goal, as the sale of U.S. features abroad started to increase. For 1966 those sales were estimated at $15 million, up 20 percent over 1965. Countries that had significantly increased the use of U.S. movies were the U.K., Australia, West Germany, France and Italy. France used more U.S. movies than it did U.S. television series. Generally those foreign buyers were able to exercise more choice in what they selected, still having the luxury of avoiding the purchasing of wholesale U.S. cinema turkeys as so many American stations had to do. Prices were up considerably in just a couple of years, thanks to such events as the addition of a second network in both France and the U.K., state run though they were. Nonetheless the number of broadcast hours at least doubled when a second channel went on the air. CBC (English) paid $8,500 to $10,000 for post–1948 movies, for one play in one year; CBC (French), $4,500 to $5,000; Australia, $8,000 to $13,000 for five-year all-Australia rights; U.K., $12,000 to $14,000 for two plays over one year; Germany, $6,100 to $8,500 for two- to five-year deals; and France paid $1,600 to $3,500 for a one- to three-year license. Japan said it would go as high as $3,500 to purchase a U.S. movie, but MGM and several other of the majors refused to sell at that "low" price.[81]

Sales of other specialty material such as news and public affairs programs remained fairly low and spotty. CBS Films did sign deals with Australian, German and Philippine television for some material from that area. Germany's second network (ZDF) signed a deal that called for it to take a minimum of 20 hours per year of news and public affairs — from programs such as "CBS Reports" and "Chronicle" — while Australia's state-run ABC network signed a deal to take a minimum of 50 hours per year. Japan had a deal for the same amount of hours.[82]

Additionally, the selling of sports programs began in a limited way in the 1960s. CBS Films was peddling horse racing shows, yachting events, golf and auto racing. In 1967 CBS signed up Mexico for Dallas Cowboys pro football games. The deal provided for a Spanish-language commentator in the CBS booth. As part of that package Mexico also received NFL play-off and Super Bowl games. For some years NBC had been selling the World Series in Canada and the Caribbean. In 1967 that network sold a condensed presentation of the World Series to the BBC as a sort of test. Wrote a journalist, "the sport flunked. The British passed it up this time."[83]

Foreign television product still had a next-to-impossible time in breaking onto American home screens. While there were no government regulations preventing their entry, no quotas, the power of the cartel to exclude was greater than most government-imposed sanctions. In fact American distributors independent of the cartel had a hard time selling in the domestic syndication (rerun) market. Those distributors complained "there's no stricter 'quota law' than network option time, which limits the time availability of locally bought programs."[84]

Screen Gems executive Lloyd Burns agreed, saying, "U.S. television has given few foreign products a nod." The problem was, he said, "that foreign producers still work for their local markets, do not or cannot tailor-make shows for our tastes. U.S. sales are accident by accident, not by design." Sig Mickelson of Time-Life Broadcasting said, "It's hard to make foreign stations conform to U.S. practices and tastes."[85]

When Burns was in Japan on a 1963 selling trip he was pressured to export some Japanese television programs. Said Burns, "I think the worst thing that could happen at the present time is for the Japanese to export too early. We would be conservative in selecting programs for world distribution. We would want the programs to be right. Premature distribution would be a mistake. Tremendous harm can be done to the producing country if programs are exported before they are ready. Then you would be doing a disservice." Asked by a U.S. reporter about the export potential of Japanese fare Burns replied, "I would say that at the present time it's limited." A few years later Fox executive Alan Silverbach was in Japan on a selling trip. When he was asked about the possibility of exporting Japanese television material, he said, "The only production here of international interest at the moment is animation. While the U.S. market is fairly well saturated with animation, we have other markets to consider."[86]

What little penetration foreign product made on U.S. home screens was limited to a few U.K.-made programs such as "Robin Hood," "The Saint," "Secret Agent," and "The Avengers," which were mostly from producer Lew Grade, whose product was oriented from the start to American shores. British networks paid about $50,000 per episode for a domestically produced series compared to about $8,000 for an American import. While some in the U.S.

television industry had once worried about possible competition from serious penetration of U.S. television by British sales, that fear was dead toward the end of the 1960s. CBS-TV executive Mike Dann remarked, "There was a time when we really felt the English market would cut into Hollywood production but I do not believe that's going to happen." He explained that "up to this time there hasn't been a single successful series made in England for the U.S. market…. This makes it evident that England's contribution to the American television scene will be essentially for use of British product only on a low-budget hour or as a summer replacement." Over the previous several years he claimed much discussion and experimentation had taken place to determine whether British production groups could successfully turn out programs for the American market. Those attempts had failed, he flatly declared, "and as a result Hollywood is more dominant in the television film industry today than it ever has been." Dann concluded, "There seems to be no real competition at this point to the Hollywood industry from England, or any other place abroad."[87]

Anxious to enter into coproduction deals with American producers — to gain entry to the American market — London Weekend TV sent executive Stella Richman to the U.S. for a month to assess the situation before formulating production plans and inviting participation. Richman discovered, said *Variety*, that "apart from the obvious point that America isn't interested in extremes of British dialect, that scripts, in the opinion of U.S. TV men, don't always come up to a sufficiently high standard."[88]

Government assistance was extended to the television export industry in a variety of ways again. One program was the USIA's Informational Media Guarantee (IMG), which basically guaranteed American exporters of film, television and other media convertability guarantees; that is, a guarantee of dollars out of a country in the case of currency blockage, major currency devaluation, and so on. In such cases the U.S. government would assume the contract, paying the U.S. supplier in dollars at a favorable rate. Mainly the IMG applied to Soviet bloc nations. Such insurance was granted to material only if it showed the U.S. "in a positive favorable light." That meant, said *Variety*, it "prohibits the inclusion of most U.S. entertainment shows." TPEA head McCarthy complained about that IMG policy, arguing the Soviet bloc would be reluctant to buy television programming that showed America solely in a positive light. In fact, he said, such programs might not be bought at all. Thus U.S. fare might not be bought in, say, Poland and Yugoslavia, and the programming vacuum might be filled by anti–American shows coming from the Soviet camp. In response to McCarthy's complaints the IMG refused to back off from its policy but admitted it may have been too stringent in applying it. Henceforth it would review on a show-by-show basis. The first program to receive a reversed ruling was NBC's "Danger Is My Business," which was then covered under the IMG program.[89]

The U.S. State Department continued its program of hosting in America foreign television broadcasters from nations with fledgling industries. Working through the USIA that program had begun in 1957 as a one-way exchange to educate broadcasting visitors "as well as to further international relations." In 1962, a group of 21 broadcasters from Europe, Africa, Latin America, the Middle East and the Far East came to America on a four-month "learn and look" visit to the U.S. By 1964 the program was larger and more formal, with television personnel from other nations being placed in observer roles at U.S. television stations from coast to coast. Observers were allowed to spend 60 days at a station, followed by a two-week period for travel prior to returning to their homelands. Each station paid its observers a per diem rate of $12 with the State Department picking up the bill for all travel and living expenses, exclusive of the 60-day period.[90]

The USIA continued and expanded its program of sending television fare to foreign nations for their free use. In 1965 motion pictures and television were combined in a single service within the USIA. By then it was estimated that 2,600 television stations in 93 nations aired the USIA programs.[91]

Saudi Arabia initiated television service in 1965. King Saud had made the decision about two years earlier while he was in a Boston hospital, where he became "addicted to television." In May 1964 the U.S. State Department was asked to help the Saudis build a television system. The State Department handed the job over to the U.S. Army Corps of Engineers, which undertook to "manage" contracts for the country. RCA supplied the hardware, while NBC supplied personnel for operations and for training Saudis to take over the system. Arab personnel were trained in the U.S.[92]

In other ways the U.S. military helped push nations into starting television services. U.S. Armed Forces Radio and Television Service had started a television station in 1955 at their Keflavík, Iceland, air base. After they successfully lobbied the Iceland government to let them increase the station's power, the number of Icelandic black watchers increased. That U.S. station was on the air seven hours a day Monday through Friday and 18 hours on weekends. Iceland started its own television service in 1966, on air two hours a day. That start-up was a result of pressure from locals who were black-watching the U.S. outlet.[93]

Armed Forces Radio and Television Service operated eight channels in six nations, including Germany and France. Although German television sets could not receive American television shows without an expensive adaptor, and vice versa, there were still black watchers. In a tacit acknowledgment of that situation American channels in Germany did not broadcast "Combat" on the military channel, as it was on the German television banned list. Similarly "Big Valley" was not shown on military outlets in Germany because the rights to it had been bought by a German station and the U.S. military did not want any overlapping.[94]

Television came to South Vietnam in 1966 under the guidance of U.S.

broadcaster Loren Stone, then working for the U.S. AID program and in conjunction with the Vietnam ministry of psychological warfare. Transmissions were limited to one hour each night on one channel and two hours per night on a second channel. As ground stations were not then ready, both outlets used the facilities of specially equipped U.S. airplanes to send signals. Washington promised to supply a minimum of 2,500 television sets to the Vietnam government for community viewing. Some 500 of those sets had been distributed at the time service began. Each of those communal sets was watched by from 100 to 1,000 people each. Vietnamese television was said to have been established for educational reasons and "as an instrument of psychological warfare."[95]

When television came to Turkey in March 1968 an estimated 7,000 receivers there were picking up signals from Russia, Bulgaria, Romania and Syria. Initial programming was scheduled to be two hours per day. While the specific programs were not listed, *Variety* speculated that "the first shows may well consist of documentaries and newsreels supplied by the U.S. Information Service, which has served similar fodder to other embryonic television nations."[96]

Executives were still sent abroad as freelance television consultants. Former Kansas City broadcaster Donald Davis spent three months in Ecuador and then went to Manila for a similar six-month stint as a consultant. Robert Sweezy, an ex–New Orleans broadcaster, was sent to Iran on a similar job. All those 1960s assignments were paid for by the U.S. government through the International Executive Service Corp.[97]

Television was a very profitable business, at home and abroad. Domestically, in 1962, television profits, before federal income tax, passed $300 million for the first time, reaching $311 million in revenues for the three networks excluding their 15 owned and operated outlets and 539 other television stations; those outlets and stations made profits slightly under $1.5 billion. Revenues for the three networks and their 15 stations were $754 million (slightly over 50 percent of the total), with profits for the networks at $114 million (36 percent of the total). Those 15 outlets of the three networks had total profits of $135 million in 1969. Those stations were turning a profit after depreciation and before taxes of between 60 and 65 percent: NBC had $50 million in profits from its five owned and operated stations, CBS had $44 million and ABC had $40 million.[98]

Foreign earnings for U.S. exporters of television material were estimated at $15 million in 1958, $25 million in 1959, $30 million in 1960, $55 million in 1962, $66 million in 1963, $70 million in 1964, $76 million in 1965, $70 million in 1966 (the decrease due to an Australian dispute), $78 million in 1967 and $80 million in 1968. Estimates for these years vary in some accounts.[99]

If American firms took some $55 million in 1962 from exports of television fare, they took another $50 million from the export of broadcast equipment and receivers. Foreign gross for 1961 was about $44 million from program sales. Average prices paid per half-hour episode were as follows: Canada, $3,000 (English); Canada, $2,250 (French); U.K., $2,800; Germany, $3,000; Latin America, (in total, minus Brazil) $3,800; Australia, $1,300; Japan, $800; and Italy, $600. In Germany distributors had to pay about $1,500 to dub each segment; in Latin America the distributor bore $800 in dubbing costs. At the low end of the price scale Lebanon paid $30 to $35 for a half-hour segment, while Haiti paid $20. "But past experience has taught American distributors that a limited market can develop into a flourishing one as set distribution widens," explained *Broadcasting*. Some 55 nations were then considered active buyers of U.S. television fare. The consensus was that Canada, the U.K., Australia, Japan and Latin America were the most lucrative markets for American exporters: "It is noteworthy that these are the nations in which commercial television flourishes. In other areas, advertising either is extremely limited or does not exist." The leading distributor was thought to be Screen Gems, taking $12 million, followed closely by MCA.[100]

With a foreign gross estimated at $70 million in 1964, Canada, the U.K., Australia and New Zealand were responsible for $40 million; the Far East (Japan, Philippines, Hong Kong, and others), $14 million; Latin America and the Caribbean, $9 million; Western Europe (minus the U.K.), $5 million; and the Near East and Africa, $2 million. Sales of U.S. feature films were estimated at 20 percent of the total. Foreign receipts were thought to be 13 to 15 percent of America's world gross.[101]

At the start of the 1960s perhaps 30 to 35 percent of overseas programming was from America. By 1965 it was down to 15 to 20 percent. Foreign nations were doing more for themselves, producing more local fare. Offsetting that was the increase in the number of stations on air along with extended hours for all outlets — which kept U.S. export sales up. Manila's six commercial stations were almost entirely dependent on U.S. shows in 1960, but five years later half of their fare was local. Initial estimates of U.S. foreign gross for 1966 were $80 million, with the following nations being the major buyers: Canada, $20 million; Australia, $16 million; Japan, $12 million; Latin America and the Caribbean, $11 million; the U.K., $7 million; Western Europe (minus the U.K.), $7.5 million; the Near East and Africa, $3 million; the Far East (minus Japan), $3.5 million. However, an Australian dispute lowered the grand total and their contribution by $10 million for that year. Canada and the U.K. each paid $3,000 for a half-hour episode and $5,000 to $6,000 for a one-hour show (the U.K. had 14 million sets); Australia paid $5,500 for a one-hour program (2 million sets); Japan paid $4,000 to $5,000 for a one-hour segment (20 million receivers). One problem annoying foreign buyers was the ruthless cancellations that occurred in U.S. television. Those foreign buyers often spent a great deal of money in promoting the programs at home, which sometimes were bigger hits offshore than in the U.S. Those cancellations forced foreign broadcasters to buy replacement shows. Of 46 new programs scheduled domestically by the three U.S. networks for the 1965-66 season for their debuts or during their second season (starting early in 1966), 29 — almost 70 percent — were cancelled. Those cancellations were, of course, dictated by American response to the shows. One estimate for 1966 said that of the $70 million in foreign television revenue that year just $7 million came from the sale of feature films to television.[102]

Chapter 4

1960s:
"We Are Not Getting a Fair Price Here"

Within individual nations on the receiving end of U.S. television material responses varied. Not surprisingly resistance to American television was strongest in those countries most seriously affected: Japan, Canada, Australia and the U.K. In other nations resistance was lower due to the minimal amount of television available or the fact the country was financially forced to turn to the cheap U.S. product over locally produced material. In any case wherever resistance, however meager, arose Americans were on hand to try to crush it. Brazil passed a decree in 1963 to regulate television and radio programs. One of the articles in the decree banned from prime-time imported shows dealing with "police events of any nature, the Far West, or sex." Television Program Export Association (TPEA) leader John McCarthy complained to the State Department in Washington. The State Department then sent instructions to the U.S. embassy in Brazil to protest that decree as a violation of GATT and to "express our concern about the potential effects of this decree on our trade with Brazil in television programs." According to McCarthy, the State Department instructed its Brazilian embassy that the attitude of the disputed article seemed to be directed "specifically against United States product, rather than representing a serious attempt to apply standards of quality to films admitted for telecast in Brazil."[1]

During 1965 the four channels in Buenos Aires, Argentina, used a total of 230 hours weekly of foreign television material, most of it American. That total was expected to reach 300 hours weekly when a fifth channel went on air six months in the future. Virtually none of that material was dubbed into Spanish within Argentina. Dubbing of U.S. fare into Spanish was done mostly in Mexico, Puerto Rico and Miami. U.S. exporters sought the cheapest dubbing facilities, often playing one country off another. To remedy that the Argentinean Chamber of Deputies passed a bill in 1965 stating that foreign-language television material had to be dubbed in Argentina starting with 20 percent in 1966 and going up by 20 percent steps each year until 1970, when all material would be dubbed in Argentina. Since the bill needed Argentinean Senate approval senators were besieged by television executives who claimed that local dubbing on such a scale was not feasible "without prior experience in the field." Opponents of the bill had to admit that adequate dubbing facilities existed in Argentina, so they fell back on the argument that Argentinean dubbers were inexperienced. They also argued that if Argentina unilaterally imposed local dubbing other nations might follow the example. Television executives in Argentina had long argued to U.S. suppliers that dubbing work should be spread around more evenly, not only to speed up delivery but also to avoid problems with the government.[2]

Nigeria's second channel went permanently on air in 1963. As with the nation's first station this Lagos-based outlet featured an RCA installation along with NBC involvement from the beginning in training, management and consulting. With a price tag in Africa of from $25 to $30 for a half-hour American television series episode, Nigerian television bought programs such as "Lucy," "Perry Mason" and "Deputy Dawg."[3]

Taiwan's commercial television system went on air in 1962. Three years later it broadcast from 5:30 P.M. to 11:30 P.M. seven days a week, with 40 percent taped and 60 percent live material. Ninety percent of the filmed fare was U.S. made. When filmed product was aired subtitles were sometimes used; sometimes an off-screen voice gave a brief narration in Chinese.[4]

Television was introduced in Egypt in 1960 in the interests of education and to promote Egyptian president Gamal Nasser's Arab socialism. While those objectives were still pursued, U.S. series of all types and old, old movies were reported to dominate the home screen. The *New York Times* explained this thus: "American movies and television shows are imported here in bulk to keep Cairo's three television channels supplied." Some of that American product was dubbed into Arabic but some wasn't; it came in English only. Still, it was reported that children in Cairo were crazy about U.S. television Westerns and all of them wanted a cowboy suit.[5]

Korean television began in the late 1950s. By 1965 South Korea had two channels; one was government run, while the other was commercial. Both accepted commercials. The government channel, which was on air nine hours daily, was allowed to sell two hours and 42 minutes of that time for ads —18 minutes per hour. At that time the U.S. Armed Forces Korean Network, which began operations in the Seoul area in 1957, was completing a major microwave setup that would link Seoul with Pusan in the south and feed all U.S. military bases: "This will also mean that South Koreans will be able to pick up a complete diet of American television along with programs now being offered by two native outlets."[6]

Israel delayed starting a television service for a long time because of the expense and for other reasons. With television estimated to cost Israel some

$200 million over the first six years of operation it was considered a luxury the nation could not afford. A change in attitude came primarily because Israelis, with some 30,000 sets in Israel, were watching television anyway, tuning in broadcasts from neighboring Arab nations and Cyprus. When Israel decided to start its own television service it hired CBS in 1966 to advise, plan and train personnel for that first outlet. It was a contract worth an estimated $500,000 over two and one-half years.[7]

Television began in Israel in 1967, being on the air from 7 P.M. to 11 P.M., just three nights a week. Half the programs were imported. As Israel readied for an outlet, TPEA's McCarthy said product would be sold there at low prices, as "in any country that is just getting started and we help them build an audience and sell television sets."[8]

In Japan a battle over prices paid for U.S. television product had started in the late 1950s. Back in 1959 there was a blanket Japanese ceiling price on imported television shows of $300 per half-hour episode, a strict limit on the number of programs that could be imported and a maximum dollar allocation of $1.1 million for all foreign television imports. Pressure from U.S. and local lobbyists lifted both the ceiling, to $500 per half-hour for 1960-61, and the dollar total, to $2.05 million. MCA-TV was so upset by the Japanese prices of that period that they pulled out of the Japanese market in 1960, claiming prices were "rockbottom." For 1961-62 ceiling prices for each show and the limit on the number of programs were both eliminated, with the total dollar allocation moved to $3 million, then up to $3.3 million for fiscal 1962-63. However, those moves were not sufficient for U.S. exporters, who continued to apply pressure.[9]

With fiscal 1963-64 starting on April 1, 1963, American television interests applied heavy pressure in Japan in those early months of 1963. John McCarthy spent two weeks in Tokyo meeting with Finance Ministry officials to try to get Japan's television laws liberalized. If he could not get complete free trade, then he at least wanted to increase the dollar allocation. According to McCarthy a good half-hour program then fetched $1,000 in Japan, up from the ceiling of $300 just a few years earlier, but McCarthy called that higher price far from equitable: "We are not getting a fair price here. Based on a registered set count of over 12,000,000 the prices are out of line with those in other markets." As an example, McCarthy cited Australia, a nation with 1.2 million sets, which paid $1,125 for a 30-minute show and where no dubbing costs were involved. At the very least McCarthy wanted to see the dollar allocation doubled. Even if that happened McCarthy believed that extra money would go to paying higher prices for approximately the same amount of U.S. product. He rationalized this by claiming that price doubling would be necessary not because of greed but because the present amount of material on Japanese television was "almost all Japan can absorb, considering that many U.S. shows cannot hurdle the cultural barrier between the two countries."[10]

Somewhat surprisingly Japan announced that from the April 1, 1963, start of the fiscal year, the dollar allocation was lifted completely (for material up to one hour in length; feature films remained subject to some controls). All contracts for sales in which the unit price was $1,000 or less per 30-minute segment were automatically approved by the Bank of Japan. Contracts in which the unit price was higher had to be approved on application to the Finance Ministry — which had let the industry know that in no cases would approval be withheld. An enthusiastic McCarthy declared the Japanese television market "wide open.... I am very happy at the result." He added that the move had "tremendous implications" for other markets because "artificially depressed" prices in Japan due to the ceiling had tended to keep prices down in other comparable markets, particularly in the Far East. While other Far East nations didn't have ceilings, they pointed to Japan's ceilings as an argument for their not paying more.[11]

Just before the announcement that the ceiling would be removed Screen Gems vice president Lloyd Burns, expecting only a doubling of the allocation amount, commented, "You're never satisfied with it. You can't be. You never think you're getting enough for your product." As to any other liberalization of Japanese television, Burns remarked, "Words like liberalization have a great deal of appeal for us."[12]

On Tokyo's five commercial stations at the time 62 U.S. series could be seen weekly on television in the evenings. Immediately upon removal of the price limits U.S. suppliers doubled and tripled their price. One Japanese television executive complained, "Japanese TV stations will not ... cannot, afford to buy American TV films if the American producers continue to sell their merchandise at outrageous prices." Prior to abolishing the ceiling the price for a one-hour U.S. series rarely cost over $2,000, but after April 1, 1963, $2,000 became the going rate for a half-hour segment, $4,000 for a one-hour segment. Added on were air freight charges, duty, customs handling fees, dubbing and incidental costs. American exporters declared that foreign stations were getting a bargain, considering production costs in the U.S. ran from $50,000 to $60,000 per half-hour segment.[13]

That American greed came back to haunt the U.S. exporters in Japan. During a 1964 visit to America, Junzo Imamichi, vice president of the Tokyo Broadcasting System, said that U.S. programs on his network then occupied one-third of prime time, down from 50 percent two to three years earlier. That had happened because after the ceiling was lifted, prices had gone "up and up." An additional irritant was the fact that, according to Imamichi, in order for his network to secure the series it wanted, it had to also buy "scrap product" — meaning block-booking. Another factor was the growth of locally produced material. Imamichi was a commercial broadcaster who favored free enterprise broadcasting over government-sponsored television.[14]

Later that same year when NBC International president Joseph Klein was in Japan he noted that U.S. fare filled about 12 percent of Japanese air time, compared to 20 to 25 percent in the peak 1962-63 period. U.S. suppliers were then trying to extract $6,000 to $8,000 for a one-hour show. It led both Japanese stations and Japanese sponsors to immediately encourage local production. A one-hour Japanese program could be produced for from $4,000 to $10,000. Those domestic shows became popular with viewers. Of the 25 top-rated programs on Japanese television, 20 were domestic and 5 were American, whereas many of the top 10 shows had been American just a few years earlier, explained Klein.[15]

A year after that, in 1965, Klein was back in Tokyo, where he found that just 10 percent of Japanese television was of foreign origin, overwhelmingly U.S. Exporters were then asking a more "realistic" price for their product. When demands of $8,000 an hour were not met, the asking price was reduced to $4,000. When Independent Television Corporation president Abe Mandell made a 1967 visit to Tokyo — his first visit there in five years — he bemoaned the fact that on his previous visit 60 percent of Japanese prime-time television was foreign, primarily American — then it was only 15 percent.[16]

Canada remained the major market throughout the 1960s for U.S. television material. The quota that had been adopted was a lax one that didn't affect prime time. When the CBC conducted its own survey in 1964 it found that in five Canadian cities, in the prime-time period of 6 P.M. to midnight only 30 percent of the material was Canadian. CBC president Alphonse Ouimet complained about that situation publicly in a speech, arguing his CBC needed more money. A day later an editorial in the Montreal *Gazette* supported Ouimet's worries: "It is only necessary to examine the fare offered by the American networks to see the value of a public body (such as the CBC). As has been pointed out by many commentators, the quality of American television is being lowered as the years pass." All of that caused *Variety* to lash back: "The constant harping by VIP Canadians and editorialists on the importance of protecting Canadian culture from being overwhelmed by U.S. attractions and reading materials, has been described in some circles as the chronic Canadian weakness of blaming the U.S. cultural and showbiz milieu, for its own inadequacies." The trade journal went on to claim that because of these inadequacies U.S. television was being used as a "whipping boy."[17]

When the CBC issued its annual report in 1965 it again wanted more funding from the government to eliminate some of its commercials and to provide more Canadian fare. The report added that CBC prime-time hours on television had become highly inflexible for program planners due to "fixed commercial commitments" for various American shows. Calling U.S. product well-made, popular and escapist the CBC nevertheless declared such programs represented the daily importation of other standards, other speech habits, other dress and other viewpoints. If some of that was acceptable, "the present volume is too great." Responding to the conventional argument of private broadcasters that American shows were what the public wanted and watched, the CBC did its own survey of seven Canadian cities. Whereas the average CBC outlet in those cities devoted 57 percent of prime time to Canadian television and drew 53 percent of the audience, the average commercial outlet in those cities gathered 28 percent of the audience, with 34 percent of prime time being Canadian. It caused the CBC to conclude, "When the supply of U.S. programs is predominant, audience viewing of U.S. programs is also predominant.... Viewing of Canadian programs is predominant on stations [CBC] where such programs are predominant."[18]

Those barriers established by Canadian television had little effect. Sometimes it was easy to make a "Canadian" show. A cartoon series, "The Mighty Hercules," was entirely American with one exception. A spokesman for the producing company, Translux, explained, "We thought we might get in on the Canadian production quota if we had the show's sound track prepared in Canada. With that being done the Canadian government accepted the program giving it 100 percent credit for Canadian content."[19]

Even if the program remained American it had little trouble penetrating the northern border. CBS Films Canada executive Ken Page commented that in Canada his company "has little selling to do. There is a quota system in effect against foreign programming, but it's a generous one." Page added that "American product is welcomed because we live by it.... We have to have it. And the same shows are enjoyed." Those U.S. shows were very desirable north of the border, thought Page, "because in Canada the audiences can be heard. In other countries in the world, the audience's taste is not being considered. In Canada ratings are considered." Regarding the effect of the 55 percent Canadian content rule Page believed the private broadcasters used it to "seek to depress U.S. program prices in an effort to subsidize their own production costs."[20]

When a Canadian commission known as the Fowler Committee on Broadcasting made its 1965 report to the Canadian federal government it strongly attacked broadcasters and recommended drastic changes, including a reduction in the amount of foreign television material screened in Canada. As expected it was particularly critical of private broadcasting. *Variety* complained the report's recommendations were aimed basically at the U.S. orientation "even more than it is aimed at the lack of Canadian content." When the Canadian Association of Broadcasters (CAB), a lobby group for private telecasters, held its first annual meeting after the release of the Fowler report the somewhat nervous group had its fears put to rest when federal Transport Minister J. W. Pickersgill appeared before them to tell them there was no federal intention of a drastic shakeup in the television industry. Another speaker was CBS president Frank Stanton, who said of current Canadian programming, "I think it's first class." CBC executive Jean Poullot told delegates "Despite the efforts of pseudo-intellectuals who want to prevent it, the so-called

American culture will develop in all countries when the standard of living reaches a certain level." As the convention ended on a happy note, the *Montreal Star* editorialized, "The private broadcasters wound up their convention here in a very good mood. They have had a prosperous year in a prosperous Canada, and their hopes rise that nothing will come of the Fowler Committee report which was sharply critical of their performance. The government has had it in hand for many months now, and nothing has been done." Pickersgill expressed the hope publicly that private broadcasters would voluntarily do something substantial on their own to strengthen Canadian content. In reply to that, the *Star* editorial said, "Mr. Pickersgill (and the government) are going to wait a long time for that. The day has long since passed when any sensible person expects the huge majority of private broadcasters to do anything but make money."[21]

Less reassuring to private broadcasters was another Canadian federal politician. In 1967 Canadian state secretary Judy LaMarsh told Canadian Parliament's broadcasting committee, "I just don't think it's good enough to sit all evening and let the culture of another country pour into our ears and eyes." Private television had been left pretty much alone, she thought, partly because the BBG regulatory agency lacked adequate enforcement authority and party because of the BBG's worry that such enforcement might bring financial hardship to broadcasters in some cases. Soon, LaMarsh announced, private television would no longer be permitted to feed the public "whatever junk" private television wanted to. LaMarsh promised that private broadcasters would face regulations with real teeth in them. Later that year the BBG was replaced by the CRTC (Canadian Radio and Television Commission).[22]

Changing technology kept the Canadian government scrambling to retain what little control it chose to exercise. As Canada became rapidly cabled in the late 1960s new regulations had to be enacted bringing the new television delivery system under the appropriate ministry for control — Transport in this case, which was also charged with television oversight. Then regulations had to be passed limiting foreign ownership of cable systems to 20 percent of the voting stock and 40 percent of the total investment.[23]

In the face of strong demand, especially by cable television (CATV) outfits, for U.S. programs on cable in areas where they could not be picked up directly by aerial, CRTC chair Pierre Juneau stated CRTC "will not license broadcasting receiving undertakings based on the use of microwave or other technical systems for the wholesale importation of programs from distant U.S. stations and therefore the enlargement of the Canadian audience and market areas of U.S. networks or stations." He declared that such an "invasion" of Canadian airwaves would wreck Canadian broadcasters. Juneau noted that while both CBC and the private CTV network were observing the letter of the 55 percent Canadian quota rule both were flouting its spirit by loading mostly U.S. shows into prime-time hours. CATV was an additional worry in that it was not subject to the 55 percent rule, but Juneau declared it would soon become so.[24]

That CRTC ruling against microwave transmission from "distant" U.S. cities brought howls of protest and was unanimously denounced by cable operators. Canadian Cable Television Association president Claude Boucher called it "censorship" and an "infringement on basic Canadian rights." For a long time the Canadian government could do nothing about Canadian viewers who could pick up U.S. channels directly, so cable became the issue.[25]

Still, the audience for Canadian fare managed to improve, at least in some cities. In Toronto the share of the audience for Canadian shows moved from 30.6 percent in 1960 to 55.9 percent in 1968; in Vancouver the increase was from 35.9 percent to 51 percent. However, in Winnipeg it fell from 100 percent to 79.6 percent. That was because of the establishment of a U.S. outlet in Pembina, North Dakota, a village of about 200 people just south of the international border. Most of that station's viewers were Canadians. Said the CRTC, "it seems obvious that the Pembina station was established to tap the Canadian market.... It has succeeded in its mission." In his 1965 report Robert Fowler stated, "The Canadian broadcasting system must never become a mere agency for transmitting foreign programs.... A population of 20,000,000 people must surely have something of its own to say."[26]

If any market gave Canada a run for the position of being most open to U.S. television product in the 1960s, it was Australia. An article in 1962 summed up that country's television history by stating, "In the six years that it has had television, Australia has probably done less than any other country to present programs which reflect its own way of life.... The commercial stations have almost consistently offered viewers the ready-made products of American television." One reason cited was the cheapness of U.S. shows. An example was the Dinah Shore variety show, which in the late 1950s had a production budget in America of about $100,000 per show. Despite that, it was sold to Australia for $1,000 per episode, with that cost split between a Sydney station and one in Melbourne. Under such circumstances why would a sponsor choose to pay perhaps $5,000 to produce a local show? Another reason was that three stations in each of the two major cities all went on the air at the same time and had relatively long broadcast days, necessitating the need for a lot of programming. "Finally, and most importantly, there is no law placing a limit on the amount of foreign programming which may be used."[27]

A 1963 survey of Australian television schedules found only 10 percent of prime-time was held by local programs, while almost all of the remaining 90 percent was American fare. Politicians began making demands for more local fare. Quickly a government committee was struck, sneered at by *Variety* as "minus any show biz know-how," to investigate the issue. Proposals were discussed as to reducing the amount of U.S. programs on Australian television by introducing a quota, perhaps one of 40 percent minimum local content.

Angrily *Variety* replied, "There's undoubted proof here that the average Aussie viewer prefers imported shows to the locally-made. There's further proof that because of high demands made by Aussie Actors Equity, it is economically impossible to set up an Aussie production organization." Railing on, the journal declared, "Politicians here fail to realize the fact that the Aussie viewer pays in the vicinity of $350 for an average set, plus $10 per annum to the government for a license to view programs of his own choosing; not what the government compels him to look at."[28]

By this time a situation described as "comfortable" for Australian television buyers had settled in, with unofficial price ceilings at about $2,250 for a one-hour show, half that for a 30-minute episode. U.S. suppliers grumbled about those ceilings "and other characteristics of a cartel." That changed when Rupert Murdoch, through his News Ltd. corporation, was granted a new station license for Adelaide. Television was then expanding in Australia, with outlets opening in all other major cities plus a third commercial outlet opening in both Melbourne and Sydney. Once again there was a sudden need for much more product. Murdoch then had a tie with ABC International, "which serves as his buying agent and which has a minority interest in his operation." Feeling he could not go along with the gentlemen's agreement on prices Murdoch flew to the U.S. where he bought $2.5 million worth of television shows, reportedly paying more than those unofficial ceiling amounts. Media baron Frank Packer allowed Murdoch to buy a 23 percent interest in Packer's established Sydney station. Rumor had it that the deal was made in an effort to bring Murdoch back into line to honor the gentlemen's agreement.[29]

Late in 1963 *Variety* announced "for all practical purposes the buying cartel that existed in Australia for years has been broken." The price of $2,250 per hour was said to be then substantially higher. *Variety* credited the change to the addition of all those new stations. Having a different perspective was Charles Michelson, an American who acted as a buyer for one Australian commercial network. He said, "Pressures by American film suppliers to increase their Australian prices without regard to the local economy forced some Australian broadcasters to establish ceiling prices in certain instances. It is no cartel, just an association formed for a specific purpose…. It cannot afford some of the king-sized prices being asked." Michelson added, "The activities of the TV export associations and the U.S. distributors have been limited to trying to get more out of foreign stations than anything else…. They are only interested in getting as many dollars as possible without giving of themselves."[30]

In its annual report for the year ending June 30, 1963, the Australian Broadcasting Control Board reported that of imported television programs 83 percent were from the U.S. and 17 percent from the U.K. (compared to 84 percent and 15 percent respectively the prior year). For 1964 the figures were 76 percent from the U.S., 21 percent from the U.K. and 3 percent from all others. Pressure forced through a local content rule for Australian television with a 40 percent minimum local fare, beginning in 1963.[31]

Those new outlets helped push prices higher. Early in 1966 it was reported that U.S. exporters had raised prices to the "sky's-the-limit" range, with a resultant souring of relations with Australian broadcasters to the point where once again they had a gentlemen's agreement not to go "berserk" outbidding each other for U.S. product.[32]

Later in the year William Wells, a CBS Films executive stationed in Australia, complained that all the Australian commercial networks and the Australian Broadcasting Commission were involved in a "cartel." While he said the government-run ABC was not a part of the cartel, he claimed ABC went along with a number of conditions the cartel set on price. CBS executive Ralph Baruch explained that a group of Australian broadcasters came to New York declaring their costs were up and their profits down, therefore they would lower the price they paid for television product by one-third. While four to five years earlier exporters sold to just four or five cities in Australia, by this time many smaller centers had their own outlets. Grumbled Baruch, "Then the stations forced us — and I mean forced us — to sell all Australian rights. They in turn sold to the smaller markets at prices that destroyed the market. Now they want to pay one-third less and hand us back these rights. The prices are destroyed. This is a situation that is untenable from our point of view."[33]

Australia's buying of U.S. television product came to a halt as broadcasters in Sydney, Melbourne, Brisbane and Adelaide maintained a united front. They wanted price ceilings of $1,500 per half-hour show, $3,000 for one-hour and $10,000 for a feature film, and those prices were to be for rights to just those four cities for the shorter material and all-Australia rights for the film price. Australians argued that prices obtained there by U.S. exporters were comparable to the prices secured in England, which had a set count seven to eight times that of Australia. In reply the Americans said it was unfair to compare prices in a "restricted market" such as England with that of a "free market" in Australia. As one U.S. exporter put it regarding the U.K. quota, "we're being bled by the quota" resulting in prices being brought down to "ridiculous levels." Prior to the impasse U.S. distributors received $1,500 to $2,250 per half-hour (most prices leaned toward the high end), double that for one hour and $10,000 to $15,000 for movies. American exporters contended that Australian broadcasters could get some price relief "if they utilized reruns more effectively and in a more organized fashion." When sales halted in 1966, *Variety* preferred to label it a "boycott" by Australian broadcasters instead of a price dispute or a boycott by U.S. suppliers. Prior to the halt, Australia was the second largest market for U.S. television fare, taking $16 million worth of product annually (Canada was first at $19 million). In third place was Japan, at $10 million, followed by the U.K., at $7 million.[34]

Yet in another article *Variety* admitted that Motion Picture Association of America (MPAA) members, along with CBS and NBC, "have agreed not to sell their product at the ceilings offered by" the Australian broadcasters. Some independent U.S. suppliers were still selling in that market.[35]

Such arrogance on the part of U.S. exporters led to more pressure to reduce American presence on the Australian home screen. When Australian opposition senator McClelland rose in Parliament to ask the government how much was spent on imported television programs he was told that in fiscal 1964-65 the amount spent was $16.1 million. Of that total $2.8 million was spent in the sterling area (almost all from the U.K.) and $13.3 million was spent in the nonsterling area (virtually all of it for U.S. product).[36]

Later in 1967 the Australian Television Control Board introduced new rules intended to offset U.S. control and to provide additional employment for Australian talent. Under the new regulations commercial stations had to present Australian-made programs at least 50 percent of the time. Between 7 P.M. and 9:30 P.M. all commercial outlets had to televise not less than 12 hours of locally produced programs each month, including 2 hours of drama. Although the prime-time rules were modest it was an important step in that past quotas had had no specific regulations with regard to prime time, thus allowing U.S. shows to totally dominate the prime hours while Australian material was shunted to the least-desired time slots but still fulfilled quota percentages. The demand that a certain proportion of the domestic material be drama (which included sitcoms) was included to guard against the possibility that all locally produced fare would be from the cheapest-to-produce genres, such as game shows or talking heads panel discussions. As these measures were enacted U.S. exporters continued to refuse to reduce the cost of a one-hour show from $4,000 to the previous figure of $3,000.[37]

As the buying halt extended into 1967, Australia's commercial stations survived nicely by going to repeats and by turning to more local fare. Plenty of sponsors were found who were ready to back local shows, and local studios that had been long dormant become active overnight. Australian viewers began to switch allegiance to favor local programs.[38]

When the dispute had been ongoing for almost 18 months the U.S. exporters quietly decided to capitulate and accept the Australian ceilings. Reasons included a fear that local shows would indeed become too popular and that other foreign nations might use the opportunity to establish their own product in Australia thus preventing a full American return when the dispute ended. Also, the dispute cost U.S. suppliers some $10 million annually in lost revenue, dropping the total for U.S. exports to Austrialia from $16 million down to $6 million or less and total U.S. foreign gross from $80 million to $70 million for the year. In Australia, for the year ending June 30, 1969, of all imported television product, 75 percent of it was from the U.S., 19 percent from the U.K. and 6 percent from all others. American exporters quickly regained control of the import market, at least their percentage of it.[39]

That buying agreement had been entered into initially in March 1966 by six commercial stations (all the commercial outlets in Melbourne and Sydney). Before the agreement those outlets were in a mad scramble for U.S. product. They, and additional new country outlets, went overboard for a few years, buying a total of $50 million worth of U.S. fare. Hints were dropped by politicians at the time that unless stations got control over their spending the Treasury Department would step in to stem such a huge dollar drain. Station management then got together to set up a buying pool. While it was clearly effective, dissension arose, with some executives inferring that favored stations received product priority leaving only "leftovers" available to the less-favored station. It all came to a head in 1969 when two stations, ATN and HSV, left the pool and went to court to have the buying pool broken up. Australia's high court unanimously declared the pool null and void on antitrust grounds. U.S. suppliers were said to be "whooping it up" in Australia over the decision. ATN executive Bruce Gyngell declared "that now that there is a totally free market in which to buy programs, Aussie viewers must benefit from the increased competition between stations."[40]

Continental Europe remained a poor market for American television shows. The area stubbornly resisted the American call to commercialize the industry. Most countries got their second channel in the 1960s, but all operated on short broadcasting hours compared to U.S. outlets. What few commercials were allowed were limited severely as to number and placement. Hollywood had long ruled the film screens of continental Europe and the rest of the world but was frustrated in its efforts to do the same to the home screen. In this period Japan generated more revenue for U.S. television suppliers than did all of continental Europe.

Germany's second network went into operation in 1963; both were government-run. The first network, ARD, was on the air from 4:30 P.M. to 11 P.M. six days a week and 11 A.M. to midnight on Sundays, while the second network broadcast 5:30 P.M. to 10 P.M. Sundays, 6:30 P.M. to 11 P.M. on the other six days. Even though there wasn't much U.S. fare on German television what there was still drew flak. A current joke referred to German television as a "social office for helping foreigners" while someone asked if his monthly television license fee "is going to have to be paid in dollars instead of German marks."[41]

Frustrated by the slow growth and government control of television in France, *Variety* commented that complaints about the "lackluster look of government television" were getting louder all the time, adding that it "feels that in France today one could live without television but it would be impossible in other big countries, especially the U.S., where television teaches, reveals, instructs and has become a necessity."[42]

Pressure in Italy from actors unions and other television personnel kept American home screen presence fairly low there. Asked whether coproductions between Italians and Americans might help ease the situation, an American sales executive for a Hollywood major said he saw no basis for joint ventures because "Italians are not geared to the kind of highly organized technique employed by Americans to turn out two half-hour shows or an hourlong telepic per week." On the positive side was said to be the goodwill between U.S. distributors and Italian government-run RAI television staff where, said *Variety*, "The inclination there is to program more U.S. product, but politics, nationalism and social pressure prevent it."[43]

For some months in the late 1960s Spain refused to screen any U.S.-made one-hour material dubbed in Spanish by NBC in Mexico City. Spaniards mulled over the possibility of adding a different soundtrack in Madrid, but faced with additional cost they finally capitulated. They allowed the off-shore-dubbed material back on Spanish home screens.[44]

When Iceland announced it was starting its own television service due to pressure from citizens who picked up the U.S. military television channel there, Icelandic reporter Sigurd Lindal wrote that "a great foreign power has pushed its way into Icelandic society with the help of the most powerful propaganda instrument ever invented. I refer to the American television station in our country which has brought a more mischievous influence into our national life than we have ever experienced before." When Icelandic television arrived, more sets would be bought. However, as the national service was to broadcast only two hours a day (due to financial limits), more Iceland citizens would watch U.S. television, as the military channel was on air seven to fourteen hours a day. It all caused Lindal to remark, "The double talk of the Americans — when, for instance, they boast of being the protectors of a small nation and try at the same time to undermine its existence from within — is, to say the least, disgusting."[45]

The only decent market for U.S. television fare in Europe was the U.K. It too was slow in developing television along U.S. lines. As the dominant markets for Hollywood films had always been the rich Commonwealth nations — the U.K., Australia and Canada — Hollywood felt the same should be true for the small screen; the language was the same, and the cultures were not that far apart. Not only did the U.K. stubbornly resist an Americanized television service, but it also imposed a quota on foreign product, one that was effective. Australia and Canada both imposed quotas in the 1960s, but the quotas were loose and did little harm to the American position. Japan also had a strong quota into the very early 1960s, which Hollywood successfully broke. Hollywood offered resistance to quotas that didn't really hurt — as a general principal — but really went after quotas that did affect its position. For that reason the U.K. came under great American pressure to commercialize more and to admit more foreign product. As well, a third channel was set, to be awarded in Britain in the 1960s; Hollywood hoped it would be a private outlet. Additionally in operation was Hollywood's concept of the domino theory, by which if one European nation went commercial in the American-style, they all would. And conversely, if one country adopted a quota that successfully undercut the U.S. position, then other nations would adopt similar measures. All those factors led to the U.K.'s being the European land most pressured in the 1960s by the U.S. television industry.

When the Pilkington report was delivered in the U.K. at the beginning of the 1960s its criticism of the commercial ITV guaranteed that the third network in Britain would go to the noncommercial BBC. However, that report said nothing, made no recommendations, to safeguard the amount of British fare on television. As well, the report neglected even to say that the current arrangement of an unofficial 14 percent quota should continue, let alone be expanded. That oversight was protested by the Radio and TV Safeguards Committee, a body comprising sixteen trade unions that represented all radio and television creative and technical talent.[46]

BBC2 began operation early in 1964 in the London area, gradually extending its service across the nation as the years passed. By the end of the 1960s BBC1 was broadcasting 76 hours a week (about the same for ITV) as compared to the BBC2's 40 hours of weekly transmission. As BBC2 prepared to launch, U.S. exporters were delighted. However, BBC director Kenneth Adam announced the corporation would be using less U.S. product in the future because of viewer preference for local programs.[47]

Initially, though, the launch of the U.K.'s third network was good news for U.S. exporters. It was reported that with three networks competing for programs prices paid were increasing and that both BBC1 and ITV were also taking options for two and three years on shows, something they had not done in the past. Seldom in the past had BBC paid above $7,000 per hour, a figure that was then being regularly exceeded. It marked a change in a market that, said *Variety*, had been "hitherto very much a buyer's market." U.S. exporters were unhappy that the third network was not a commercial one, but even a noncommercial addition meant an increase in sales of U.S. product. Before BBC2 launched, BBC1 and ITV each programmed roughly eight hours a week of U.S. shows. Assuming the quota stayed the same, total U.S. exposure would go from 16 to 24 hours a week once BBC2 was on air as many hours as the other two. "Even better from the foreign telefilm salesman's point of view is the likelihood of a further commercial channel here within the next few years," concluded an optimist. It would come but not for many years.[48]

Some six months prior to the BBC2 start Hollywood made another assault on the U.K. quota. In a memorandum to the U.S. State Department, TPEA chief McCarthy filed a strong protest against the 14 percent rule. Calling for help from the State Department he claimed the quota was having a "disastrous effect on the sale of U.S. television programs in the United Kingdom." In addition he laid the same case before U.K. chancellor of the Exchequer Reginald Maudling, calling the quota a violation of "all precepts of commercial relations and foreign trade." McCarthy wanted the U.S. government to intercede to obtain "reasonable relief" from the 86 percent figure. He argued that the coming of BBC2 in a few months, with its resultant need for more programming, might mean "a greater receptivity on the part of British program contractors to buy foreign and particularly U.S. programs." However, that could not happen unless the British quota "is reasonably reduced." As McCarthy kept up his "strenuous efforts" to break the quota, critics in Britain regarded it as untimely. Trade union leaders in the U.K. continued to argue that 14 percent was too high a figure, lobbying to have it reduced to a 10 percent maximum of foreign product.[49]

Just before BBC2 debuted, U.S. reporter Roger Watkins admitted U.S. programs were in trouble; during 1963 the 20 top-rated shows in the U.K. did not include one U.S. show. Watkins acknowledged that it is "accurate to say that where once Yank shows dominated local top ten lists, nowadays it is unusual to get more than one U.S. telefilm in the same charts." Rather than admit people preferred their own programs Watkins tried to explain this popularity slippage in other ways. He claimed that U.S. programs were often used as troubleshooters, that is, put up against tough competition, which weakened the ratings of both; that on the commercial ITV, U.S. shows were no longer networked fully as often as in the past thus lowering potential audience size; that U.S. material was given poor time slots; that even if U.S. product was fully networked on the BBC that network was so weak in its share of the audience draw (compared to ITV) that all programs on the BBC started with a handicap. Yet he then went on to list top-rated U.K. shows in the top twenty on the BBC, showing that it could be done. While Watkins argued that his listed reasons explained the low popularity of U.S. shows, it is at least as logical to argue that a poorly rated show was given bad time slots, not fully networked, and so on, precisely *because* it was poorly rated. In reality the strong U.K. quota had been instrumental in causing the development of a strong U.K. domestic television industry. People in the U.K., and all other countries, preferred to watch their own programs, not, of course, exclusively. A strong quota allowed a domestic industry to be born, to take root and finally to thrive. American programming was still bought to the allowable quota limit because it was so cheap. However, more and more in the U.K. it got shunted to weak time periods, to less than full networking, and so on.[50]

Pressure from Hollywood led to a major breakthrough in 1964 when the British Cinematograph Exhibitors Association relaxed its ban on the sale of feature films to television provided those movies were at least five years old. The first major deal struck after that policy shift was the sale of 100 films by Warner to Associated British Picture Corporation's subsidiary ABC-TV, in which Warner had a 25 percent stake. Associated television's managing director Lew Grade was said to have offered an average $14,000 per title for an unlimited number of runs over seven years. The next year U.S. film exporters appealed to the State Department again to use its offices "to help ease stiff Brit television quota."[51]

During this period CBS executive Ralph Baruch reminisced about the early U.K. television situation by saying, "Time was when the only way a British television station could secure top American product was to pick it up in a package which contained plenty of mediocre material." Baruch denied that CBS had ever done that. He spoke of the U.K. then being a hard sell because of "the 14% limit on U.S. product" (note the jingoism involved: the quota applied to all foreign). British buyers were then asking for lower prices on older U.S. product. However, Baruch said there would be no cuts.[52]

In fact, U.S. suppliers were fighting for price increases. Fox won the first round when it secured $4,000 for a half-hour of "Batman," which caused other American distributors to go after more. Both CBS and NBC decided to go after a minimum of $7,000 an hour for new material for an all-U.K. sale. If a show was sold station by station, they wanted a proportionate market share price so that the sum total would not fall before the $7,000 minimum. Currently stations could pick up a U.S. series individually for about half what their audience share might indicate the price to be. Despite those increases one article grumbled "The 14% quota in Britain, though, makes it one of the most competition markets on the globe, and the prices are low compared to the U.K. set count."[53]

Another intensive effort by U.S. exporters to break the quota came in 1967, just prior to the final stages of a round of GATT negotiations to reduce world tariffs in cross-border trading deals. Motion Picture Export Association (MPEA) television executive William Fineshriber was in Geneva early that year serving as the industry executive to brief and support the American negotiators in bringing about an easing of the 14 percent quota. Afterward Fineshriber stopped in London for meetings with Lord Hill, chairman of the Independent Television Authority (ITA), officials of the British Board of Trade and leaders of the three main unions in the British television industry. This push was regarded as the culmination of a campaign that began more than a decade earlier when quotas were first introduced and which had "intensified during the past eight years since Fineshriber took over the v.p. chair at the MPAA." The initiative for the latest pressure was taken by MPAA president Jack Valenti, who outlined in detail the MPAA's thoughts on quota revision in letters to the parties concerned. *Variety* remarked that the U.K. quota had been a sore spot for U.S. suppliers not just because of its limiting the U.K. market "but because it also served as a model for other countries to introduce comparable protective measures. If the British quotas can be eased, so, probably, will the restrictions in many other countries in the Western world; and that, indeed, is its main significance." Fineshriber believed he had made some headway with union chiefs, "the original architects of the 14% quota." Some years earlier agreement was reached with ITA for the import of quality documentaries over and above the 14 percent limit. The MPEA was also working to widen the area of exclusion, especially in the area of feature films, a then-growing proportion of the 14 percent. The MPEA hope was that if the quota could be liberalized on the commercial network the BBC would follow suit.[54]

U.S. negotiators argued against the quota saying it had served its purpose in enabling the U.K. industry to get established but the time had come to stop "subsidizing" British stations with low-priced American product. Among other demands of the U.S. negotiators were the following: a new, looser definition of British content; a distinction between shows specifically made for television and feature films, with the latter taken out of the quota; in the non-prime period of 5 P.M. to 6 P.M. foreign fare should count only as 50 percent non-British; and an extension of total broadcast hours with the last hour exempt from the quota. At the same time U.K. unions lobbied to cut the amount of foreign fare from 14 percent to 10 percent. They argued the 14 percent was actually exceeded if foreign acts in domestic programs were included. As this battle came to a climax, *Variety* reported "The feeling here is that while the Americans may not get all they are asking for, there is confidence that a breakthrough will be achieved."[55]

In the end the American exporters got nothing at all. The U.K. quota was held at 14 percent with no new or widened exemptions. *Variety* lamented, "Seems now that the only factor that will up the U.S. content on the British airwaves is either the introduction of new video channels or the extension of broadcast hours. Either development is at least three years off."[56]

Hostility at home continued to swirl around the image and content of U.S. television fare exported abroad. Minow's "vast wasteland" remark irritated U.S. exporters for years after the speech was made. Said one U.S. supplier, "You hear the phrase 'vast wasteland' used against you over and over again.... If they get the idea firmly implanted that commercial systems like those of the U.S. produce junk, then second systems in developed TV countries and initial systems in emerging countries could be doomed for commercial TV." John McCarthy, a former State Department official, blasted Washington for its television attitude: "The repeated attacks by Washington on the U.S. television industry ... [in the form of] congressional hearings, FCC hearings, and the blanket indictment of the industry by the FCC, [have] had repercussions in foreign markets everywhere. In addition, the continual fomenting of popular discontent by Washington with the TV industry and the repeated indications that the only hope for better TV lies through the government is an inhibiting and discouraging factor in the growth of television in many markets." Among the benefits McCarthy listed accruing to the U.S. from exporting television programs was the millions of dollars produced in overseas earnings to meet domestic balance of payments difficulties along with assistance in a thousand different ways to U.S. exporters of all types of products "by portraying American products every day of the week to hundreds of millions of potential purchasers all over the world." In return for all that, McCarthy complained, "it just doesn't make sense to me to revile the programs of the industry and hold them up to international scorn and contempt.[57]

Continuing his argument McCarthy explained that the government often expressed concern over the image created abroad by U.S. television material; he felt it was those attacks that actually created a damaging image. Worried that continued attacks on U.S. television fare by U.S. government sources would shut down foreign markets even more, McCarthy urged Washington, for the good of the nation and the good of the industry, to adopt a course of "quiet and helpful cooperation."[58]

Fred Friendly quit his job as CBS News head in protest when his network screened a fifth rerun of an "I Love Lucy" show instead of a 1966 Senate Foreign Relations Committee hearing on Vietnam. Speaking in London shortly thereafter, Friendly warned British television not to fall into the same dollar-influenced trap U.S. television had and accused the U.S. industry of breach of promise. Talking of the perils to the BBC if it pursued ratings and popularity solely like its commercial rival, Friendly remarked, "Before you know it, mediocrity becomes the accepted order of the day. The climb back is difficult, if not impossible, not only because a high profit level cannot be suddenly depressed, but because you invariably depress the standards of your audience. You style their appetites and they in turn will reach a depth of tolerance where they will suddenly not accept your best, even when the time comes when you decide to improve your product."[59]

Grumbling about barriers against U.S. television product in general CBS's Ralph Baruch said in 1966, "We believe that American television is being sold short. We believe that our quality and balance of programs are as good, if not better, than anything shown in television anywhere. What we are looking forward to is reciprocity in unrestricted commerce in television programming without artificial barriers."[60]

Even a country as uncritically accepting of U.S. product as Canada felt compelled to react once in a while. In 1969 the public broadcaster CBC dropped both the "Hogan's Heroes" and "High Chaparral" series from its schedule due to violent content. As well, several new U.S. series had been rejected as possible pickups for the same reason. CBC president George Davidson told the Canadian federal Senate Finance Committee in Ottawa that most television violence problems stemmed from American rather than Canadian programs.[61]

Chapter 5

1970s:
"A One-way Street"

One 1970s dream had to do with global cable television, which would educate and uplift the masses worldwide. This rhetoric was used to rationalize a system whose real purpose was to blanket the globe with even more U.S. television material. Early in 1970 ad agency executive William Boulton wrote at length about the great and coming potential of cable television, then making rapid roads domestically: "The U.S. not only leads the world now in the quantity, quality and distribution of cable television, but it will undoubtedly emerge as leader in cable programming as well," he said. Domestically the problem was that the saturation point in channel allocation had long been passed. One could obtain a television channel only by buying an existing one, causing Boulton to comment, "Since there is Standing Room Only within the narrow network spectrum, the cost of free speech comes very high." As cable had only recently been domestically granted the right to produce its own programming, Boulton envisioned cable providing a forum for politicians to speak, specialty channels such as a United Nations (UN) channel, one devoted to the interest of seniors, and so on. "One of cable television's strengths is that it need not depend on advertising for its support," stated Boulton. "Satellites may soon make possible a virtual international network of cable systems, with unlimited range and boosted by microwave. The illiterate masses of Asia, Africa and South America may therefore eventually inherit the human right to an education and wide-ranging awareness of the world." Any scarcity of receivers in poor lands could be overcome through community viewing at social centers. "When there is a shortage of skilled teachers, the superlative teacher can be enabled to teach a class of 1,000,000 students," said Boulton enthusiastically. One thing that he thought would ease cable's penetration offshore was the fact that Europeans mostly paid a monthly license fee for a television set, which meant they were conditioned to paying. Boulton concluded, "The people of the world feel misunderstood. No one understands no one nowadays. In a world full of lonely people there is a hunger for other voices in other rooms."[1]

Satellite transmission made no real headway in the 1960s despite government encouragement in that direction. Telstar, Comsat, Early Bird and other such 1960s orbiters whose main use was for telephone and related transmission could be and were used for television transmissions. However, such use was minimal despite the estimate that network transmission fees paid to AT&T for land lines could be cut in half if networks broadcast to their affiliates through satellites. Networks shunned such satellites, arguing falsely that such orbiters were too costly. A more salient reason may have been the high degree of government involvement and regulation in those systems. Political desires could play havoc with the right to high, unregulated profits. All that changed dramatically in 1972 when the U.S. Federal Communications Commission (FCC) voted for a "multiple entry" policy for domestic communication satellites. It meant that anyone who was financially and technically qualified and "whose service would be in the public interest" could put up a satellite. "Public interest" came to be a phrase very loosely interpreted. It was consistent with the American ethos of free markets, an ideology that carefully overlooks the suspension of that policy of little or no government involvement when it comes to huge public expenditures on research, the results of which were then expropriated at little or no cost by private firms to make high private profits.[2]

That FCC ruling laid the groundwork for what would become worldwide television satellite transmission, both to cable systems and direct-to-the-home, or direct broadcast satellites, (DBS). Although DBS was nonexistent in 1972 nations of the world saw its potential to lead to even more U.S. domination of the home screen. In the UN the DBS issue was debated off and on during the 1970s. America's position remained unchanging: it held firm to the concept that any nation should be allowed to carry out global television broadcasting by satellites without the consent of nations receiving the television fare. However, in debate within the UN and its Outer Space Committee there was overwhelming opposition to the U.S. position, from countries including Canada, Sweden, and France, the Third World and the East Bloc. U.S. resolutions containing free transmission policies were regularly beaten by votes of 100 to 1, for example.[3]

Leading opposition in the UN was the Soviet Union, which proposed an international convention to prevent nations from directing television broadcasts from satellites to private homes in other nations without those countries' express consent. Such broadcasts, said Soviet foreign minister Andrei Gromyko, would represent "interference in a state's internal affairs" and should be banned.[4]

In a draft resolution introduced in the UN in 1972 by the Soviets, any nation would be authorized to destroy any satellite that was broadcasting to its citizens directly against the nation's government's desire. Within a couple of years the Soviets softened their stance with a new proposal only to take unspecified "measures" against such satellites. U.S. representatives continued to argue for free and open exchange of information. Writing in *Foreign Policy*, William Read complained that in UN debates over DBS "it's everybody against us, with the United States opposed to any restrictions on DBS, while all others prefer some controls." At a symposium on the international flow of television programs held at the University of Tampere in Finland, the attitude of many who were critical of "information (or cultural) imperialism" was summarized by Finnish president Urho Kekkonen, who said he had "read a calculation that two-thirds of the communications disseminated throughout the world originate in one way or another in the United States."[5]

That lack of interest in satellites by the U.S. industry ended quickly with the FCC's ruling. Starting in mid–1974, eight communication satellites, all privately financed and operated, were put into orbit over two years. They carried 8 to 24 "transponder" units of communications capacity, each equal to one color-television signal. Space aboard could, of course, be put to other uses besides television transmission, such as carrying phone conversations. Sending any kind of message — television, telephone, and so on — by land line or microwave required a "repeater" (amplifier) every 30 miles or so. But it took only one amplication to send a message from a transmitter anywhere within a satellite's coverage range to a receiving station at any other point. A color television channel on one of those satellites, RCA's, costs $41,000 per month, versus $97,720 for conventional land transmission. The first regular use of a satellite for television purposes was made when Time Inc.'s Home Box Office subsidiary used the RCA satellite Satcom I, launched in December 1975, to create a national cable television network covering 200 cable systems around the U.S. This was satellite to cable company transmission only. DBS satellites were yet to come.[6]

Occasional use was made of existing satellites to transmit television fare before this era. It was limited to events where the outcome would be known to the potential foreign viewers before the tape of the program arrived in that nation, thus possibly hurting audience size and commercial revenue. The 1970 Oscar ceremony was broadcast live to Mexico and a couple of other South American nations including Brazil. In the previous year some 140 million viewers in 39 foreign nations saw the Oscar awards live or via tape delay. Canada and Mexico received it live by way of ground transmission while most of the others viewed it on tape delay. For 1970 the telecast went from Hollywood over AT&T land lines to New York and then by ground to West Virginia. From there it was uplinked to a satellite, and then it went on to South America. Delay of conventional broadcasts varied from a 24-hour delay in London to up to a week in some countries. ABC sold the program for prices ranging from $10,000 in Australia to $10 in Liberia. For the Mexican telecast, actor Alejandro Rey (then costar of the ABC series "The Flying Nun") was brought in for Spanish commentary while Brazilian star Bibi Ferreira was slated for the Portuguese segment.[7]

Hollywood's major theatrical film producers tightened their hold on the television industry both at home and abroad. Their dumping of U.S. material on foreign markets at fire sale prices was a powerful inducement for buying American product, even to cash-short public broadcasters, indirectly crushing the local producers. By 1970 Columbia, Fox, MGM, Paramount, United Artists, Warner and Universal all had representatives based in Paris from where they covered Europe and sometimes the Middle East (for television sales only; they already had agents throughout the world to handle theatrical film business). Some of those agents covered England, some just continental Europe. London was the main European base for agents from Disney and all three U.S. television networks. French television then consisted of two networks, both under government control under an agency known as ORTF. One of those networks, the original one, was on the air 100 hours a week while the second one aired 32 hours a week. ORTF paid $2,000 for a single U.S. episode, whether it was 30 or 60 minutes long and whether it was color or black-and-white. American distributors paid the approximate $1,500 it cost to dub the segment into French but could then sell that French version in other French-speaking areas such as Canada, Switzerland, Belgium and parts of Africa. And, noted a journalist, those markets "do not pay as much, in most cases, as the French, but these sales can bring in a fair profit since the costs are already amortized." Of all foreign series bought for French television 75 percent were American and 20 percent were from the U.K. During 1969 some 170 U.S. feature films were screened on French television for prices ranging from $2,000 up to $10,000 for one showing. In contrast to the $2,000 price for a U.S. series episode, it cost ORTF $45,000 to make a domestic 60-minute black-and-white episode or $80,000 for a color segment.[8]

Profits from domestic television continued to be rich. For 1976 official FCC figures revealed the U.S. domestic television industry had revenues of $5.2 billion and pretax profits of $1.25 billion. Network profits were $295 million on revenue of $2.1 billion. Those 15 stations owned and operated by the three networks had pretax profits of $159 million on revenue of $486 million. The other 477 VHF outlets had revenue of $2.2 billion and profits of $730 million with the 177 UHF stations making pretax profits of $64 million on $363 million worth of revenue. Total advertising expenditure in the industry was $6 billion with $992 million going to agency commissions.[9]

For the 1971-72 domestic television season the Hollywood majors were the dominant force with 35 hours weekly of programming in prime time on the three U.S. networks. Independent producers who once briefly dominated the schedule in television's earliest years and then spent a few years more or less running even with the majors were then reduced to just eight weekly prime-time hours of network programming.[10]

In 1978 Paramount, MGM, Universal, Fox, Warner, Columbia, United Artists and Disney combined took 93.9 percent of domestic movie rental revenue from theatrical exhibition. That same year Universal, Fox, Paramount, Warner and Columbia accounted for one-third of the regularly scheduled prime-time series on the networks. Domination was actually higher, as the above figures refer to series only, omitting any network prime time devoted to feature film screening, which was dominated, of course, by those same majors. During the 1960s the average price of a theatrical movie rose from $100,000 for two U.S. network runs in 1960 to $800,000 by the end of 1967 as the stockpile of old features was depleted. Prices skyrocketed again in the mid–1970s as Hollywood cut back further in the number of features it produced yearly. Also, more of them were R rated, thus less acceptable for television screening. On average the lag time in 1972 to move a feature from cinema release to the home screen was six years; in 1979, it was down to 3.7 years. All of these factors caused the networks to turn more and more to a new genre, made-for-television feature films.[11]

As cable got off to a slow and hesitant start in Europe, American firms tried to buy in, always fearing government control of the new delivery mechanism. In 1974 America's Cox Cable Communications purchased a 30 percent stake in a CATV firm in Denmark with an option to increase its holdings up to 75 percent. Denmark had just one channel, but the cable company imported signals from Sweden and Germany, bringing the channel total to six. France's government announced that the state television network, ORTF, was joining forces with that country's postal and telephone authorities to enter cable television. Apparently that indicated government control, but a worried American reporter said hopefully, "Presumably the government's big monopoly is going to be vigorously challenged." Fledgling cable systems were operating in Belgium, Holland and Germany in the early 1970s, but it was unclear whether the approved systems would eventually be state-owned or privately held. In Britain the government announced it would soon invite bids from firms to launch an experimental cable service in the U.K. Still, it appeared the actual cable networks would, as in France, be owned and operated by the post office with rental fees to the government. As all of this unfolded *Variety* declared, "there is unquestionably going to be a struggle for power."[12]

By the early 1970s in the U.S. the FCC Prime Time Access rule was in effect, which forbade the three U.S. networks from selling offshore independently produced programming that was on their schedule. It was put in place because the networks had been in the habit of extracting harsh contract terms from the independents as a condition of getting their programs on one of the three U.S. networks in prime time. Networks were thus limited to selling abroad only programming they themselves produced, typically specials, sports, news and public affairs. It had the effect of concentrating power over offshore selling of U.S. television fare in the hands of the Hollywood majors. Those three networks were eliminated as major competitors. One of the first results of that ruling was that ABC sold its syndication arm, Worldvision, in 1973 to a group of its own executives, who then left the network. Kevin O'Sullivan, new president of Worldvision, said the company would concentrate "on becoming the biggest world distributor of independent shows."[13]

Selling its product cheap offshore continued to be an effective marketing tool for Hollywood. By 1972 a series produced in France cost the ORTF from $60,000 to $100,000 per hour, compared to an American one-hour series, which could be had for from $10,000 to $20,000 already dubbed. Explained *Variety*, "Budgetary problems have also made it necessary to get cheaper foreign fodder."[14]

Once in a while an American journalist would let slip the unreality of the myth that all foreigners just naturally loved U.S. movies and television fare, that Americans were the world's greatest storytellers, and so on. Noting that Spain was not a particularly good market for American product, Dave Kaufman stated, "Like most countries, it has an understandable preference for domestic material."[15]

Other selling techniques were disclosed when it was reported in 1976 that a U.S. series could then achieve a sale price of $10,000 to $12,000 per hour in the U.K., compared to $8,000 one year earlier. "Those averages are for single runs, the norm in this market. Second runs are an occasional 'sweetener,' sometimes thrown in as part of a package deal whereby the buyer also acquires a piece of distress merchandise."[16]

If those programs sold cheaply abroad they were expensive to make at home. NBC-TV president Robert Howard told the U.S. Senate Communication Subcommittee in 1977 that the average prime-time half-hour program cost a network $155,000 per episode for two showings; the average one-hour segment, $335,000; a made-for-television movie, $882,000.[17]

One method of keeping successful foreign shows out of America was to make a domestic copy. Both "All in the Family" and "Sanford and Son" were adapted from earlier popular U.K. sitcoms. Although they were both controversial series in the U.S., they were considerably diluted from the British originals. It sometimes made selling those series abroad more difficult. British viewers rejected "Family" apparently because they found it too tame compared to the U.K. original "Till Death Us Do Part." Regarding the general selling of U.S. television programs offshore, *New York Times* reporter John O'Connor commented, "For the most part, the American product makes no pretense to quality of content. If quality is involved at all, it is in the technical production values."[18]

Block-booking continued to be a major U.S. selling tool whenever and wherever it could be imposed. In Sydney, Australia, in 1970, not long after the three commercial networks' buying pool for U.S. programs had been canceled by a court decision, a spokesman for one of the three networks (TEN) complained that prices had increased greatly. He also complained about U.S. distributors' trying to impose "package deals" on all the Australian commercial networks. According to him in order for an Australian network to get program A, a top-rated series, the buyer would also have to purchase programs B, C and D. Program B would be a medium-rated show run near the prime-time hours of 6:30 to 10 P.M., program C would be a lower-rated show and would be aired in Australia late at night, while program D "would be so low-rated that it would not be shown at all." TEN told distributors it was not prepared any longer to make package deals but was ready to negotiate for individual product. It hoped the other two commercial networks would join it in refusing the package deal system. However, as a ratings battle was taking place between all three networks, observers felt TEN couldn't both buck the U.S. majors and stay in the ratings race.[19]

Keeping foreign sales especially lucrative was the fact that Hollywood still dodged residual payments from time to time. The American Federation of Television and Radio Artists (AFTRA) had been negotiating for years to get residual rights for the showing of U.S. fare overseas. Some 20 production companies were being chased by AFTRA. Writers had been in arbitration for more than a year against ABC and Zodiac Productions over unpaid residuals from the screening of the variety series "Hollywood Palace" in Canada and the Philippines. When a decision in favor of the writers was rendered, ABC appealed. Generally networks argued that a major issue was whether the show was authorized by the network or by the producer to be shown. In this particular case, ABC said, "there's no question that, if the union allegations are to be believed, certain shows aired in the Philippines were never authorized by the Networks. There is some question of piracy of shows."[20]

Growth in television set ownership abroad continued at a furious pace. By the end of 1975 there were 100 million color television sets in the world (57.7 million in the U.S., 19.8 million in Japan, 6.8 million in the U.K. and 4.3 million in West Germany). Some 364 million receivers were then in use worldwide. Of the 264 million black-and-white sets 63.4 million were in the United States. Despite that there was much doom and gloom within the U.S. television industry over offshore potential, with reporter Dave Kaufman declaring the "global market for American television films is shrinking." In response Screen Gems was said to be doing more indigenous product offshore and intensifying foreign sales of feature films. Their executives agreed the global market was "declining principally because as each nation progresses it becomes more interested in producing its own shows with the obvious result being less demand for U.S. product. Nationalism is a predominant fact in every country." Every country was devoting more time to local production. There were then no U.S. shows in the U.K. top ten. BBC bought 13 "All in the Family" segments but didn't even air all of them because of low ratings. Another major problem was state control of television systems. Wrote Kaufman, "Best market for U.S. is where a country is just developing.... Emerging countries will take anything from U.S., including comedy." Screen Gems' Canadian manager Bruce Ledger remarked that tastes in Canada and the U.S. were "identical." Ledger pointed out Screen Gems was the largest "independent" producer in Canada turning out "Canadian" shows. Company executives concluded that "the old days when almost any U.S. TV film would sell in the world marketplace are gone, that continued shrinkage is in store as each country continues to increase production for the medium. Only exception is movies, still in demand."[21]

At that time the U.S. majors were particularly disgruntled by the U.K. market's going rate for programs and especially feature films. While the Cinema Owners Association had erased its total ban on features being broadcast on the home screen, U.S. distributors were still unhappy with being allowed to sell to television only features that were over five years old. Prices for features then ranged from $40,000 to $60,000. If newer titles were allowed to be broadcast, U.S. exporters hoped to see a $100,000 price for at least a few of the newer titles. But they worried that the U.K. commercial buyers for television would not enter a price war for newer titles, as many also had financial involvement in cinema exhibition. So depressed were the U.S. distributors over the U.K. situation that rumor had it there was a suggestion that all Motion Picture Export Association (MPEA) member companies should be represented in Britain by a single individual who would negotiate on their behalf with both the BBC and ITV. A similar system then operated on the African continent and was said to be working satisfactorily. Nevertheless, that idea was rejected for the U.K. as not workable for unstated reasons.[22]

Notwithstanding the gloomy outlooks, U.S. television fare still held sway throughout the world. According to a 1977 Finnish study the world's single most common cultural experience was "Bonanza," the U.S. television western. Although new episodes were no longer being made, some 400 million people around the world — almost twice the U.S. population then — tuned in every week.[23]

If the percentage of American programs on offshore schedules disappointed U.S. suppliers, the percentage of American product in global television sales remained dominant. Figures released by UNESCO showed that in 1974 the U.S. exported 150,000 hours of television material. The closest competitors were the U.K. (20,000 hours), France (20,000) and West Germany (6,000). In other words U.S. suppliers exported more than three times as much material as the second-, third- and fourth-largest exporters did combined. America exported enough material that year to completely fill the broadcasting schedules of 22 networks (or stations) operating 18 hours a day for an entire year. Five years later the estimate was that U.S. distributors exported 200,000 hours of television programs.[24]

As always, the drive to commercialize television worldwide continued. Italy's RAI was a public monopoly created by Italian Parliament in 1954 and endorsed ten years later by Italy's Constitutional Court. Every ten years RAI had to get a new lease on life from Parliament. With the next renewal due in 1974 private interests had already gathered by 1970 to prevent parliamentary contract renewal of RAI as a two-channel monopoly. Journalist Hank Werba wondered, "How can these private industry potentates capture Italian television for private profit? The answer, as one strategically placed RAI-TV insider explained, is to destroy public and Parliamentary confidence in this vital public service ... the campaign to sour Parliament on extending another ten year contract to RAI-TV is now fully underway. Aside from the vital aim of private industry to wield a strong political voice on a television net in private hands, there is also the gold mine prospects of full-scale television commercials — now rigidly controlled by RAI-TV."[25]

Even when a European system did allow commercials they tended to be controlled. Finland had two stations operating in 1970 with air time limited to 70 hours a week. It was a state-run system that licensed some time, 17 hours a week, to a commercial setup. Both television setups used about 50 percent foreign material, mainly American. On the commercial setup one ad break was allowed every 30 minutes; no sponsored shows were allowed in the American sense. France's two government-run networks limited ads to 18 minutes per day each.[26]

Since advertisers generally could not place ads within specific shows in Europe, ratings had less power. In any case European scheduling was all quite strange from an American supplier's perspective. Most European buyers would take only 6, 8 or up to 13 episodes of a show at a time, no more. The series could be revived in that country the next year or several years later or never. A series could be pulled off the air when it was still highly popular, something Americans found inscrutable. In the U.K., ads were limited to six minutes per hour with advertisers unable to sponsor a program fully or to even buy spot ads around a particular program. When an advertiser bought spots on the commercial network those ads were rotated by the network schedulers through the allowable periods. Thus, in due course, each advertiser had its turn in the more desirable periods.[27]

Indian advertising executives were assembled in New Delhi in 1970 to watch two hours of American television commercials. That forum was essentially a lobby for commercial television in India, even though the country then had virtually no television at all (there was one very small educational station in India operating on limited power with limited hours). Those ads were brought over by the United States Information Agency (USIA) in New Delhi for a one-shot showing during a conference of the Indian Society of Advertisers. Said one of the Americans involved, "Like the Sears Roebuck and the Montgomery Ward catalogs, these television commercials show our bountiful way of life in America even though they were not made for that purpose."[28]

France's two networks carried just 18 minutes of ads per day each in 1979 (the cap was 6,570 minutes per year). Those ads were regulated by the Regie Francaise de Publicite (RFP), which allowed no ads from the entertainment industry, such as for films, theater and records, and none for tobacco or spirits. In all cases the RFP checked for morality and decency while also keeping an eye open for fraudulent claims. Adjectives such as "new" and "best" could not be used in those ads. Ratings of shows did exist but were not made public. Those ratings were done by the Centre d'Étude d'Opinions (CEO), which used them to divide up money from the set license fees paid by households. A private agency set up by 45 publicity agencies and twelve manufacturers, such as the French subsidiaries of Colgate and Proctor & Gamble, the Centre d'Étude des Supports Publicité, ran polls to service advertisers. A program on French television could never be interrupted by a commercial; all were placed at the end of one show, before another began. Reporter Joan Dupont concluded, "as a result, the public has to pretty much put up with the television it gets…. Gradually the public and the advertisers are bringing pressure to bear on the rigid system." No evidence was introduced to indicate the public wanted more ads. Commercials began on French television in 1968 when the second channel was born and television needed new financing sources. Regarding that time RFP executive Phillippe Green said, "Manufacturers and the industries were putting on the heat." Christine Berbudeau of RFP remarked, "The only real justification for commercials on television is that it keeps down the price of the set license money." CEO director Philippe Ragueneau commented, "There should be no relation between the nature of a program and money."[29]

Selling feature films to offshore television remained a major strong point for U.S. suppliers. As Hollywood had long dominated the world's theater screens it had a built-in advantage in that many of Hollywood's features were already dubbed or subtitled into various languages. Another advantage came from the Hollywood publicity machine, which promoted its entire output incessantly by way of star appearances, magazines, fan clubs, and so on, keeping Hollywood stars actively in the public mind.

In West Germany in 1970 the cheapest and most popular programming for the two networks was U.S. movies. There was much protest from German cinema owners who wanted to limit the number of films on television, the age of those films and so on. However, noted reporter Hazel Guild, the "Biggest bargain in German television is the old American Film — which can be bought here for as low as $6,000 with rates zooming up to $25,000 for a really exceptional product." In the eight years leading up to 1971, foreign films, mainly American, picked up around $50 million in sales to German television. Under an existing rule only full-length German features over five years old and foreign films unable to find a German theatrical distributor could obtain a screening on television, but that rule was loosely applied. As the 1970s began, that rule was more and more ignored.[30]

Protests continued in West Germany with actors, directors and producers complaining about the use of foreign films on television joining the angry
local cinema owners. Germany's First Network announced it had spent close
to $5 million on feature films for 1973 screening. It was cheaper than pro-
ducing their own or buying from the independent television filmmakers. The
protestors suggested Germany do more film buying and selling in the Common Market thus reducing their imports from the U.S. arguing that the U.S.
was not making any moves for a "fair exchange" of German television shows.
Of the films bought for German television for 1973, one-third were German.
A study done in that country of the first 20 years of German television revealed
that about 3,250 feature films had been telecast, with the highest number of
them being American. With regard to the German protests Guild concluded,
"Luckily, for the Yanks, the anti–American wave of the German film technicians isn't catching on with the television public who still prefer the U.S.
films and teleseries."[31]

Still, some restrictions of features broadcast on television remained in
Europe in the early 1970s. British television had a movie broadcast every night
except Mondays and Thursdays, France allowed no features on the home
screen on Tuesdays and Wednesdays while Germany telecast none on Tuesdays and Fridays. Belgium allowed features to be broadcast four nights per
week. All these restrictions were designed to keep cinema attendance up.
Generally the clearance time from the date of a movie's cinema release until
its allowed release to television was longer in Europe than in America. British
clearance time was five years, due to a sort of gentlemen's agreement between
distributors and cinema owners. For foreign language features in the U.K.
the clearance time was three years.[32]

For the year 1970 France's ORTF screened 370 feature films from the
following sources: U.S., 169; France, 130; U.K., 12; West Germany, 8; Italy,
7; Brazil, 4; Japan, 3; Hungary, 3; 2 each from Russia, Switzerland, Poland,
Yugoslavia and Sweden; 1 each from Denmark and Romania.[33]

Hollywood's lobby group kept up pressure in Europe to break all restrictions and to drive up the price received for features. Prices paid were often
described by MPAA/MPEA as "absurdly low." MPEA vice president Marc
Siegel brought to bear the full weight of Hollywood in Spain in 1973, finally
reaching agreement with Television Espanola (TVE) for a 40 percent increase
across the board for all U.S. product, films and series. Around the same time
MPEA reached an agreement with Italy's RAI, with the latter agreeing to
double the price paid for U.S. films in steps to reach the top level by mid–1975.
For many years Hollywood had received $6,000 per title, but under the new
agreement that amount moved to $12,000 in just 18 months. Speaking of
those Italian negotiators *Variety* remarked, "Siegel, backed by a hard-line
negotiating committee from MPAA's vice president for television, William
Fineshriber, had to choke off supply of U.S. product in initial Italo talk stages

early last summer." Italy was not a great market for Hollywood but still bought 50 to 60 American movies each year for television. A one-for-one rule applied at the time whereby one Italian film had to be telecast for each foreign movie aired. Each of the two RAI networks was limited to telecasting one feature film per week.[34]

Within America the price paid for Hollywood features also escalated in the syndication market. In Los Angeles in 1976 stations KNXT, KCOP and KTLA paid, respectively, $36,000, $60,000 and $85,000 for a title. The next year Los Angeles independent station KCOP paid $1.5 million for 15 titles, breaking the $100,000 per film barrier. Around that time Japanese television aired 1,077 movies in one year, 643 American, 220 Japanese, 163 Italian, 133 French, 79 British, 15 German and 64 from all other nations. Pressure from within France caused the government to initiate new rules in 1978 for the networks that mandated that films could not be shown on French television until at least three years after their theatrical career ended. On French television, both TF1 and A2 networks were limited to telecasting a maximum of 150 films a year, at least half of which had to be French. However, since the penalty was just a $3,000 fine for each foreign title broadcast in excess of that quota, it may have been still financially worthwhile for a network to ignore the quota.[35]

At the end of the decade U.S. distributors remained the biggest supplier of films to German television. During 1978, 436 features were sold to the First and Second Networks with 209 American, 78 West German, 40 British and 23 French. The seven German regional television outlets aired 749 features, 423 American, 85 German and 84 French.[36]

When countries were not "open" enough, Hollywood applied its muscle. Late in the 1970s the major distributors launched an unofficial boycott by refusing to sell feature films, whatever their age, to Israeli television. Although no official reason was ever given, a rumor was allowed to spread that an Israeli theater owners group had put pressure on distributors, warning them any deal with television would result in refusals by Israeli cinema owners to play American films. Privately though, Hollywood executives agreed they didn't "fear any measures the theatres may try against them, as without their product the theatres might as well close down." In private talks with *Variety*, Hollywood distributors "were quite willing to hint that the prices paid by Israeli TV (about $800 per feature film) are not appetizing enough to tempt them. When asked for product majors simply say no material is available at the moment."[37]

In the middle 1970s the MPEA launched what became a five-year boycott of feature films from Swedish television. That boycott was lifted in 1979 when the Swedish state broadcaster and the MPEA reached an agreement on a fixed price of $10,000 per title, double what the Swedes were paying when the MPEA boycott was imposed. The old per-title price was keyed to the number of television set licenses in Sweden — 3 million. However, the majors became disgruntled when they decided that was an unrealistic price because Sweden was a strong filmgoing market with a potential for big theatrical reissue revenue. Broadcasting a film on television would, of course, reduce that cinema reissue potential. During the boycott period the film famine on Swedish television was filled by fare from such countries as Bulgaria and Hungary.[38]

With television growing around the world in the 1970s more and more foreign producers tried to place their product on the large and rich American television market. As before, the appearance of foreign fare on U.S. television was minimal.

Articles continued to speak of breakthroughs — always illusory — by foreign fare into the U.S. market. *Variety*'s Jack Pitman declared in 1970 that prospects had never seemed more promising for British television product selling in offshore markets, particularly in the U.S. and Canada. One reason cited was the pending cutback in network programmed time of 30 minutes per day, supposedly leaving a little more room for independent and foreign product. Pitman declared, "At the moment the British are enjoying a new level of success in the U.S. market." Aside from a few items from U.S. producer Lew Grade with his "posh mid–Atlantic output for the networks," no other evidence was cited. Yet three months later an article in the same journal stated "With scattered exceptions, notably Lew Grade's cozy relationship with ABC-TV, the Yank market has always been a tough nut for the British: Ditto, to be sure, other foreign producers as well."[39]

Reporter Les Brown noted in 1971 that America, the richest of all world television markets, "remains one of the toughest for foreign producers to crack." He, too, believed that new ruling by the FCC limiting the three U.S. networks to three hours of daily prime-time programming might open up the U.S. domestic market. It could be a break especially for Canada, he thought, "which previously had exported only creative, production and performing talent to American television in the greatest brain drain in all show biz." Speculating further, Brown thought that cable television and the coming videocassette might also help outsiders crack the U.S. market, as the former promised many channels (20 to 40) while the latter did not need a huge market. Still, at that point "the networks remain a lean market for all but native product."[40]

Journalist Andrew Bailey pondered why it was that U.S. sitcoms succeeded in the U.K. while the reverse was not true. At the time not one sitcom series had been sold to U.S. television by either the BBC or any of the independent contractors who produced for the British commercial network. One explanation for U.S. sitcom success was "Because of its size and ethnic complexity, America tends to produce sitcoms that are as relevant to a hick as to a sophisticate." On the other hand, the BBC had no obligation to advertisers, as no commercials were screened; it was obligated only to the set license fee payers, "Therefore the broadcaster's only responsibility is toward the British viewer and programs are made without consideration of the export market. Result: unsalable comedy series." The independent British contractors producing sitcoms for the commercial network did have an obligation to their shareholders and therefore produced more internationally oriented fare, but the problem with making sitcoms with the U.S. market in mind was that comedy by its nature "has an unpredictable export potential," compared to, say, private eye/spy programs, "And one dare not take risks with shareholders' money," concluded Bailey.[41]

One item Bailey didn't mention was that on the rare occasion they displayed any interest, rather than import a U.K. sitcom, Americans would simply clone it, creating a domestic copycat version. Producers Norman Lear and Bud Yorkin had already turned the U.K. BBC hit "Till Death Us Do Part" into "All in the Family" and were then in the process of changing another U.K. hit, "Steptoe and Son" into the domestic series "Sanford and Son."[42]

The small amount of foreign material that did make its way to U.S. home screens was mainly British and that mostly on PBS, public television. France's ORTF was able to sell television product to American television for the year of 1971 that amounted to just $22,000, approximately five percent of France's total foreign television sales that year. In perspective it cost French television that much money to buy just two movies from American suppliers.[43]

Even that small amount of foreign fare that did get through was enough to incense some people. The AFL-CIO's executive council issued a 1973 resolution condemning the Corporation for Public Broadcasting for having a schedule "dominated by foreign produced programs" and urging PBS to increase the number of programs featuring more American talent. Continuing, the labor body explained that trade unions were increasingly concerned about taxpayers' money being used to support foreign programs imported for showing on public broadcasting. Due to that concern the resolution was passed.[44]

Mexico's Televisa network made part-time affiliates of nine U.S. outlets in 1976, providing them with 25 hours of Spanish-language fare per week. FCC chair Richard Wiley expressed concern about that. While it violated no FCC rules he felt the implication was "staggering" because "if Mexico could do it, why not also Canada?" He fretted Canada's private CTV network might imitate the arrangement and set up part-time affiliate U.S. outlets, and then "Canadian television would come spilling across the border."[45]

Les Brown offered advice to foreign producers in 1973, then said to be excited about the possibility of cracking that U.S. market. It wasn't whom you knew, wrote Brown, it "is knowing the American market — its conditions, its mentality, its limitations, the ever-changing needs — and how the American television system works. Someone who keeps coming around to sell the wrong thing at the wrong time is going to be dismissed." Regarding cracking the big prize of network prime time, Brown did admit that "the competitive stakes are far too high for any foreign operator to have realistic hopes of placing a full-fledged series there." As far as Brown was considered the best bet for foreign producers was to try to place something on the public broadcasting market, "although it stands to be the least lucrative." Even there, however, it was not easy: "In theory, there is a market for documentaries from abroad, because so few are being produced in American television these days, but it is a spotty market and in the main the sales have to be made to individual stations. This is because the public television network, answering to pressure from the Nixon Administration, is wary of controversial and issue-oriented programming."[46]

French television producer Philippe Baraduc complained about the American importers' unwillingness to accept dubbing, noting it forced European producers wanting to enter the potential export market to make two versions, one in the native tongue and one in English, if they had any hope of dealing in the U.S. market. Other limiting factors were that French television series, as was true for the series of most European nations, ran to 13 episodes or fewer and were 26 minutes in length. For America's purposes the number of episodes was too small (U.S. series were 22 to 24 segments per year) and the 30-minute segments were too long — more time than 4 minutes was needed for ads. Baraduc called U.S. series "slightly immature — the thrillers stylized, the plots barely believable, often to the dismay of European viewers." France's ORTF was putting its hopes on coproductions with other European countries as a way to crack the American market. With a third network in operation in France ORTF had even more product to sell.[47]

However, it wasn't going to matter at all. The only coproductions that interested Americans were those in which it was a partner — which meant U.S. control of the material. As reporter Bob Knight remarked in 1973, "the prime American network interest in overseas programming lies in the coproduction of mini-series and specials, rather than outright buys of existing programming."[48]

According to a UNESCO study released in 1974 traffic in television fare was a "one-way street," with only the U.S., U.K., France, Germany and Italy doing virtually all the exporting — and the U.S. dominating that. The UN agency predicted that the coming of satellites for television transmission would only confirm the concentration of power in the hands of those nations that already had international programming power. In the highly commercial Latin American markets about one-third of total programming came from the U.S. Worldwide total foreign sales of television product varied between 100,000 and 200,000 hours annually, with one-third of that going to Latin America and one-third to the Far East and East Asia with most of the remainder to western Europe. Those western European nations imported 30 to 40 percent of their programming, with 40 to 60 percent of that total supplied by the U.S. On dollar volume the best market for U.S. exporters was Canada (19 percent of the total) followed by Australia, Japan and the U.K., who took, respectively, 18 percent, 17 percent and 12 percent. U.K. producers sold 30,000 hours of television material offshore yearly; France, 15,000 to 30,000; Germany, 5,000; Italy, 4,000; and the U.S. about 150,000 hours. UNESCO found that in American television commercial outlets imported just 1 percent of their material, while on noncommercial U.S. television (public broadcasting) the amount of total broadcast time devoted to foreign material was 2 percent — the "domination" that so upset the AFL-CIO. Most of that imported fare was from the U.K. and much of that from Lew Grade, with variety material starring the likes of Tom Jones and Englebert Humperdinck, hardly foreign.[49]

Nothing had changed by 1978 when Larry Michi reported, "except on low-paying PBS, British product currently occupies less than 1% of U.S. airtime."[50]

Early in 1978, 35 top-level Japanese broadcast executives, all eager to export to the U.S., spent six days in Los Angeles and New York hoping to promote such deals. They got a warm welcome but no deals. Consistently they asked how to get their product on U.S. television. Consistently they were told, "It's difficult, it's very complicated. The timing may not be right. Eventually it will happen." Tactfully Shinso Takahushi said he welcomed the opportunity to exchange views with U.S. executives but had hoped more meaningful "fruits" could be achieved. American executive John Porter pointed out some major problems for the Japanese including language and cultural differences, the "problem of clearing residual rights" and "perhaps the major stumbling block, the costs involved in the post-production editing that includes the adding of subtitles or dubbing." Porter made it plain to the Japanese that "virtually all foreign TV product has great difficulty in finding acceptance in the U.S." Television Bureau of Advertising president Roger Rice emphasized the exchange of ideas more than program sales, although he expressed confidence that eventually there would be a "breakthrough" for the Japanese.[51]

Speaking to a 1979 meeting in Canada of domestic television producers broadcast executive Hillard Elkins told them the only way they could get foreign distribution of their product was by going to Hollywood and learning the system. The picture he gave Canadian producers seeking more than domestic distribution was described as "bleak." Noting that of all the worldwide trade in television product some 75 percent of it was done by U.S. suppliers, Elkins told the Canadians it was a fact they had to address if they wanted to crack the foreign market, as "It's a very closed system." In specific instructions he advised Canadian producers to "go to California and meet with network officials. You must work within the framework of their requirements. There is no other answer and no other way." Columbia executive Norman Horowitz told the group that the three U.S. networks "are the whole ballgame in television film distribution. There is no fourth network and anybody who tells you there is is either lying or naive." Regarding the Canadian government's attempts to help develop a stronger native television industry through the likes of quotas, Horowitz stated, "Legislating a TV industry in Canada is not going to happen. You can legislate it for Canada, but you cannot export it."[52]

Even major American firms who were outside the Hollywood cartel had a hard time placing foreign fare. U.S. distributor Time-Life Films tried to sell the BBC hit show "Fawlty Towers," starring John Cleese, in the 1970s. None of the three U.S. networks would buy it although all said they liked it. One problem was that there were only six episodes in the series (a couple years later another six would be produced). "Fawlty" went on to enjoy cult status on the PBS stations that aired it and still do. Another problem was that episodes were 29 to 31 minutes long, and Cleese would not allow any time editing. "Monty Python's Flying Circus" also doomed its chances in America — if it had any at all on commercial television — by also refusing to be content edited. Finally Time-Life was able to sell "Fawlty" to just six PBS stations, which paid about two-thirds less for material than did commercial outlets. Noted an account in the *New York Times*, "the percentage of British programs carried by ABC, CBS or NBC in any given year has been minuscule."[53]

One of the reasons the FCC imposed tougher rules on the three U.S. networks — such as reducing prime-time network programmed time to three hours from three and one-half per day and limiting their distribution rights to material produced in-house only — was the enormous profits received by the networks. Figures for 1969 from the FCC revealed that network pretax profits from broadcasting activity, not including owned and operated stations, climbed to $92.7 million for the three, a rise of 64 percent over 1968. The 15 owned and operated stations racked up a pretax profit of $133.4 million.[54]

For 1970 domestic U.S. television sales reached about $340 million with offshore sales adding another $100 million, about 22 percent of the world total — theatrical film revenue from offshore sales was still near 50 percent of the global total. For the first time that year Japan became the top dollar market for U.S. product followed by Australia and Canada. One year earlier Australia took the top spot for the first time from Canada. Top European markets were, in order, Britain, Germany and France.[55]

When Tapio Varis studied global traffic in television product in the early 1970s he declared an ideal system was one in which sovereign national networks screened the best programs from all over the world and balanced them with their own productions. He concluded, "This system, however, has never been shown to exist, in fact, evidence tends to show a quite different effect." During the mid–1960s the U.S. exported more than twice as many programs as all other countries combined. Within America there were 150 companies active in the producing and exporting of television programs, although the MPEA member companies accounted for some 80 percent of total U.S. sales offshore. Throughout western Europe U.S. fare accounted for half of all imported programs and from 15 to 20 percent of total transmission time. That underestimated impact, since it did not take into account items such as audience size. As Varis wrote, "studies about prime-time programming in various countries tend to show that the proportion of foreign material during these hours is considerably greater than at other times." During one sample week in the study, in the U.K. 90 percent of foreign programming used by the BBC was of U.S. origin and all of the imported material used by the commercial ITV was American. Data also suggested that Japanese and Australian commercial outlets purchased more of their programs from the U.S. than did their noncommercial counterparts.[56]

For 1973 U.S. offshore television sales came to $130 million, still representing about 22 percent of the world total. Top markets were, in order, Canada, Japan, Australia and the U.K. Analyzing the success of U.S. television abroad William Read wrote in *Foreign Policy*, "Television, a highly technical field, developed rapidly in the United States, and saturated the domestic market in a few years. Initial random sales of popular programs to stations abroad sparked interest and created markets, before there was significant competition." A sample of stations in some 60 nations in 1970-71 found only 3 stations that imported as little as 1 percent of their programs; tied at that level were Japan's educational station, the People's Republic of China Shanghai station and U.S. commercial stations 16 sampled). Next on the list of most insular was the U.S. noncommercial outlets (PBS, 18 sampled), which imported just 2 percent foreign product. Then came Japan's NHK (state-run) general network at 4 percent and the Soviet Union's Central system at 5 percent. At the other end was Saudi Arabia's Aramco TV, which imported 100 percent of programming; New Zealand, 75 percent; Zambia, 64 percent; Singapore, 78 percent. Read felt coproductions would increase in the future because "joint ventures undercut cries of imperialism, and they also require production of programs suitable for ['saleable to' is perhaps more apt] at least two countries." Still, he admitted coproductions led to blander fare and diminished the ability of a participating nation to control the social and cultural content of its programming. Read concluded, "Nations which have been politically and economically dependent on the United States have, perhaps unwittingly, become culturally dependent too. And we know even less about the impact of multinational mass media than we do about multinational businesses."[57]

U.S. offshore television sales in 1970 totaled $97 million, $85 million in 1971, $94 million in 1972, $136 million in 1973, $124 million in 1974, $160 million in 1975, $190 million in 1976, $240 million in 1977, $284 million in 1978, $350 million in 1979 and $365 million in 1980. The leading firm in 1976 was MCA-TV, with $37.2 million in offshore revenue ($63.5 million domestic). Britain then paid from $25,000 to $50,000 for movies; Japan, $20,000 to $60,000; Mexico, $10,000 to $50,000; Canada, $8,500 to $40,000; CBC French, $4,000 to $5,000; France, $14,000 to $20,000; Italy, $11,000 to $14,000. Seven of those nations paid $2,000 or more for half-hour series episodes, U.K., Australia, Germany, France, Japan, Canada, and Brazil. "The Mary Tyler Moore Show" was then seen in 50 nations, from Brazil to West Germany to Mexico to a number of Arab lands. Some quotas against foreign television product existed unofficially. Metromedia's Klaus Lehmann said that although it's not posted formally "everybody knows" that in West Germany it's 10 percent. Viacom's Fred Gilson stated that France's unions would scream "bloody murder" if the French networks allowed more than 20 percent foreign. Of nations that had developed television in the previous decade, such as Greece, Turkey and Spain, Worldvision's Colin Campbell declared, "These countries have finally begun to realize that they've got to pay more money to get the programs they require, that it's still cheaper for them to buy the slickness of American shows than to produce it themselves." Whereas in nations such as France, Britain and Germany, television buyers still tended to buy only six to thirteen episodes of a series at a time (instead of a full year's worth of 22 to 24 episodes), nations such as Australia and in Latin America bought in bulk, as did both public and private networks in Canada. North of the border Canadians bought in bulk because they were on air up to twenty hours a day "and they end up playing the bulk of the American series in primetime, with most of the 60% total of local production relegated to fringe-time periods."[58]

For 1977 U.S. offshore television sales amounted to some $240 million in 120 markets abroad. Over the previous decade, while the number of television sets abroad increased 62 percent U.S. total sales rose 120 percent. MPAA/MPEA head Jack Valenti said of that record, "It is not profit. It is the return of needed production capital…. this sales record is tribute to the excellence and quality of the U.S. production." While sales were made in 120 countries, the top five markets, in order, Canada, Japan, Australia, U.K. and Brazil, accounted for more than 65 percent of the total. The primarily English-language markets of Canada, Australia, U.K. and New Zealand made up 43 percent of overseas sales. Of the non-English-language markets, western Europe made up 18 percent of the market; Latin America and the Caribbean, 19 percent; the Far East, 16 percent; the Middle East, 2.5 percent; Africa, 1 percent; and Eastern Europe, .5 percent. Stubbornly the percentage of U.S. offshore television sales remained in the 22 to 23 percent of world gross range. Asked if U.S. offshore sales would even approach the elusive 50 percent mark, Valenti said, "It seems unlikely" because "In many countries television is not only subsidized but actually owned and operated by the government. It is an instrument of national policy, a principal means of communication, both cultural and political. The economic necessity which motivates theatrical exhibitors throughout the free world to buy the best and most popular entertainment available is absent in these government controlled TV systems." At that time the videocassette industry was just barely underway in America in any meaningful way, which caused Valenti to say that one of the greatest threats facing his industry then was "the cancerous growth of piracy."[59]

Discussing the idea of freedom of information UNESCO said, "The 'free flow' of TV material between nations means in actual fact that only those countries with considerable economic resources have ... the freedom to produce, while those with scarcer resources have the 'freedom' to choose whether or not to take advantage of the material made available to them." Or, as media writer Jeremy Tunstall put it, "a non–American way out of the media box is difficult to discover because it is an American-built box." In 1976, there were only five countries in the world that did not broadcast any U.S. television material, China, North Korea, North Vietnam, Albania and Mongolia.[60]

Chapter 6

1970s:
"Canada Has Nowhere
Else to Go for TV Fare"

In Latin America the fortunes of U.S. suppliers waxed and waned. In some nations local programs began to squeeze out U.S. shows; in others, financial troubles led to a greater reliance on cheaper U.S. material. In all countries any increase in stations and/or extension of on-air hours for existing ones meant more sales for U.S. distributors. In still others, regulations of ads and/or foreign programming were introduced or existing ones were strengthened. Direct ownership of Latin American outlets was no longer a penetration method of choice for Hollywood in the region. Fidel Castro's nationalization of Cuba's television industry remained fresh in their minds as to the pitfalls of such an approach. Also, increased nationalism in the 1960s and 1970s throughout the region made such methods of operation less and less acceptable to the region's inhabitants.

Nationalism especially worried Hollywood. In the *New York Times* in 1971, Malcolm Browne wrote that television in Latin America was becoming a major target of surging nationalist movements from both the left and the right of the political spectrum, all of whom increasingly regarded television as a potent menace from the imperialistic world, America in particular. It was the cheapness of the U.S. product that made even state-run outlets dependent to varying degrees upon it. A Chilean Communist publication described television as "the monster in the living room" and an "analgesic for making the masses forget their own pain, an agent for paralyzing action and promoting passivity in the face of great historic events." Paraguay's sole television station was largely an outlet for the nation's right-wing dictator, Alfredo Stroessner, while showing much U.S. fare at other times of the day. Station manager Ricardo Sanchez said he had tried to find alternatives to the U.S. product shown each day in Paraguay, "But let's face it. These shows are entertaining even to our Indians in the wilderness. Furthermore, we can get them from the United States at a much lower cost than shows we have been offered from Europe, especially France. The American producers can give us a sustained output at reasonable cost — something no one else can do." Impoverished Bolivia got television in 1969, determined to avoid that path. It placed heavy programming emphasis on televised literacy programs (the overwhelming majority of Bolivians were illiterate), public health instruction and agricultural advice. Pure entertainment, not counting sports, filled only about 24 percent of Bolivian air time. Bolivian television received and utilized film from the United States Information Agency (USIA) as well as from similar agencies in the Soviet Union, Italy and France. Many Hollywood observers of this period worried that in leftist-oriented nations in the region such as Chile, Peru and Bolivia, television ties with the U.S. would disappear.[1]

Journalist Dave Kaufman worried the Latin American market for U.S. fare was decreasing for another reason as well. Stations in the region were relying more and more on Latino-produced fare for their programming. Soap operas, called telenovelas, were produced mainly in Mexico at the time and were increasing in popularity throughout the whole region. The four main markets for U.S. shows were Mexico, Brazil, Venezuela and Argentina. Central America was a smaller market, which, due to its size, couldn't afford to produce its own programs, thus having a greater reliance on U.S. series and Latino soaps. While the popularity of U.S. series on some of the area's home screens declined, Hollywood movies remained a popular draw. Sitcoms from America did not do well here. "All in the Family" didn't sell well or attain any popularity where it was screened, as the prejudices expressed on the program were alien to most areas. Brazil had a large black population and was racially integrated; "Family" simply made little sense in Latin America.[2]

Argentina was one country that instituted measures to limit the amount of foreign product on television. As of 1971 a maximum of 20 percent foreign was allowed to be aired both throughout the day as a whole as well as within the prime-time period of 8:30 to 11:30 P.M. Thus the four stations of Buenos Aires broadcast just sixteen and a half hours weekly of foreign fare out of 84 total prime hours. Of the weekly total of 300 broadcasting hours by the four outlets, 59 hours were devoted to foreign fare, 49 hours to feature films, ten hours to series. Virtually all the foreign product was American. Movies figured heavily in the foreign component because, said reporter Domingo di Nubila, "they are somewhat cheaper than an ambitious locally-produced show." Other than movies, local programs were the viewers' favorites.[3]

Another lesson in the perils of media ownership came in November 1971, when Peru's military government placed all television and radio stations under what amounted to state control. Under the law the state was to acquire at least 51 percent of all television stations — nineteen at the time, one of which was government owned. Five or six families were said to own most of the television stations. One clause in the law put limits on ownership concentration while also barring foreigners from being either owners or employees of stations. Domestic content of programming was ordered raised to 60 percent from the prevailing rate of about 36 percent. Henceforth all television commercials had to be of Peruvian origin. Brigadier general Anibal Meza Cuadra said the Peruvian government "finds it imperative that mass communications be employed for the security, mass education, social, cultural and economic development of the people in whose name the military governs." He added, for too long "a few people have exercised inordinate control over the mass media." That government was not Marxist. At that time around 40 percent of Peruvian broadcast time was given over to commercials.[4]

Content of U.S. programming continued to be an irritant in offshore markets. In 1974 Mexico banned 37 imported television programs, mostly American, including "Ironside," "The Fugitive" and "The FBI" on the ground they were too violent. For the same reason Argentina banned U.S. programs "Kung Fu," "Mod Squad" and "Mannix."[5]

Chilean television began in the early 1960s with high hopes and ideals; it would focus on education and culture with no selling of the people to advertisers. There would be no commercials, with broadcasting left in the hands of the universities — which, in the mid–1970s, did run three of the four channels. The fourth was state run. As television grew and programming hours were extended, costs obviously increased, all covered by government subsidies. However, financial difficulties caused those subsidies to decline and then to be eliminated entirely. Broadcasters had to self-finance. As reporter Hans Ehrmann noted, "the necessity of self-financing will inevitably lead to more U.S. serials and commercial programming to attract viewers (and advertisers)." By late in the 1970s about 75 percent of Chilean air time was occupied by imported fare, mainly U.S.— it was much cheaper than local product. Then ads were allowed, and while theoretically those commercials were limited to six minutes an hour, in practice the "sky's the limit."[6]

Brazilian law limited broadcasters to a maximum of 50 percent imported material later in the 1970s. However, here also, that law was widely ignored; reporter Ira Lee observed that the limit on foreign fare "is not observed in practice." Finding the situation unacceptable Brazil's government threatened to slash the allowable foreign content down to 30 percent. Mostly it was just rhetoric, as was the response of Brazil's largest network, Globo, which cut a couple of U.S. series from its schedule while announcing it would air more local stuff. All of that was apparently in response to the government's threat. A typical television weekday of Globo's Rio outlet at the time aired 60 percent imported fare in a 16-hour broadcast day while Nicaragua's Sandinista government nationalized that nation's two television stations late in 1979. Government spokesman Jaime Brenes said that prior to the takeover "programming had consisted almost entirely of U.S. series." Brenes wanted to begin to "decolonize" television from the influence of U.S. video and to "place the home screen at the service of democracy." One of the two outlets had been owned by dictator Anastasio Somoza. Due to government austerity the Nicaraguan government was forced to broadcast the same programs over both channels. Weekdays the channels broadcast from 2 P.M. to midnight.[7]

Financial problems in the television industry in other countries always served the U.S. Singapore television was run as part of that country's Ministry of Culture and never conceived as a commercial enterprise, although ads paid for half the service's budget by 1975. Sixty percent of its schedule was imported programs. Said observer Edgar Koh, "The limited budget of U.S. $1,200,000 a year for program acquisition easily favors the American distributor seeking to market his wares here." He added that "With the introduction of pilot color transmission last August, the edge has become even better for U.S. products. They were among the first programs to be put out in color." Prime-time in Singapore then featured the likes of "I Love Lucy," "Rhoda" and "Gomer Pyle."[8]

One network in Turkey, TTV, broadcast 44 hours per week in 1979, with most of its imports being U.S. fare. By law 40 percent of broadcast time had to be occupied by domestic product. TTV program director Tarcan Gunenc explained, "In the early years, we paid $200–$250 for an hour of U.S. programming. Last year the cost increased to $600 and this year to $750. A feature film —$1,200 in 1978, now costs $1,600." As to the most recent price increases Gunenc complained they were "presented almost as an ultimatum without any prior consultation."[9]

Prior to its civil war Nigeria had a single national network. At war's end the industry was restructured into 18 regional stations, all in color, all accepting commercials, all broadcasting five to six hours per day. The going rate was then about $150 for a one-hour U.S. episode, per station, which meant a full pickup yielded over $2,500, a sum described as "all the sweeter because the Nigerians foot the cost of prints." On paper, Nigeria was called a "dream market." However, because of its severe financial problems one domestic exporter termed the country, in reality, the "all-time deadbeat," with debts to U.S. suppliers then estimated at $2 million for television fare. Still, exporters were loathe to write off the market since it could be lucrative if only Nigeria paid its bills. Product was shipped to Nigerian stations on videocassettes with the outlet instructed to erase the tape after telecasting. Some did but some did not, resulting in pirated tapes making the rounds.[10]

Although India had a small UNESCO-aided television outlet established in the late 1950s, television did not arrive in a meaningful sense until 1972 with the launch of a Bombay station; television came later to other cities. India's prime minister, Morarji Desai, warned broadcasters in 1978, "If you must ape what is happening on television in the West I'm afraid I will have to think several times before I agree to any extension of television in India." He wanted television not just to entertain but to uplift and spread India's culture and heritage. Desai and his supporters cited the UNESCO report that Western influence had overwhelmed television around the globe and that Western-oriented programs had an unfavorable impact on developing lands. There was much criticism in India about Indians who had been trained abroad in programming and technical aspects feeling they had "acquired a value system alien to our own. When they return to India they look to New York, Los Angeles or London for ideas and programs to respond to the small part of the television audience that is Western oriented." The fear of cultural imperialism had, said *Variety*, "kept almost all American television programs off the air." When "I Love Lucy" was not renewed for Indian television, officials said it was because the nation was trying to preserve its foreign exchange. *Variety* contended the real reason was the cry of cultural imperialism. Only the affluent in India could afford to own a set, but many sets were located in village community centers.[11]

Although Japan was served by five commercial networks and two state-run, non-commercial networks by the end of the 1970s, journalist Harold Myers noted, "the reluctance to screen U.S. vidseries is something of a common policy. They do, however, give air time to Yank series, though usually they're relegated to off-peak periods." However, Hollywood feature films were still popular on television, causing Myers to say, "it is the continuing popularity of these feature pix that gives the American distribs a degree of leverage in off-loading some of their more acceptable series." Even though more and more networks aired Japanese programs in prime time, American executives claimed "that with very few and notable exceptions, the Japanese dramatic programs are very much a no-no for export." The only reason given for that was "it is probably the tough content of many of their drama programs that have made them a tough sell in overseas markets."[12]

Throughout the 1970s Canada remained bedeviled by the onslaught of American television fare. The signal spillover problem of the late 1940s was replaced by that of cable spillover. Some two-thirds of all Canadians were close enough to the border to receive U.S. television signals over the air. As Canada became more highly cabled, cities too distant from the border to receive U.S. signals directly were able to receive them by way of microwave transmissions to their cable companies. To prevent that, the Canadian Radio and Television Commission (CRTC) passed a rule banning the import of U.S. programming on microwave CATV systems over "great distances." That set off howls of protest from people in cities like Calgary and Edmonton, who could receive U.S. signals only through cable. No matter what the ruling, people in cities such as Toronto could continue to receive the same amount of U.S. transmission, over the air or over their cable lines, since there were not "great distances" involved. To pacify those distant cities the CRTC backed off, declaring their recent ban had actually only been meant to forbid "wholesale and indiscriminate" importing of American programs.[13]

At the beginning of 1970 the CRTC announced its intent to raise the Canadian content quota from 55 percent to 60 percent. More important the regulatory body said it would also impose that quota on the prime-time hours of 6:30 P.M. to 11:30 P.M. National public broadcaster CBC would have to meet the new quota by September 1970, while the private commercial CTV network would be given an extra 12 months to meet the quota. Advertising time was to be set at a maximum of twelve minutes per hour.[14]

At hearings debating the 60 percent proposal, Canadian Association of Broadcasters (CAB), a lobby group for private broadcasters, executive Raymond Crepault thundered, "We should be thinking not of separating from the civilized world but joining it vigorously and forcefully…. We will not create an international presence by dissipating our funds and energies on a fragmented series of necessarily low-budget interviews or amateur movies…. In the league of the very near future, one superb and masterly 90-minute program will do more for Canada and the Canadian identity than 60 hours a week of homely mediocrity." U.S. reporter Paul Gardner liked that idea and noted "It may also leave a whole lot more room for imported sitcoms."[15]

American-based *Broadcaster* magazine, the commercial industry's trade journal, editorialized that "a Canadian is not free to decide what he will watch on television or listen to on radio." That Canadian content (called Cancon) rule was "a shaft pointed right at the heart of the democratic system which is our national life blood." The editor described the CRTC as a group of "fanatical idealists." Noting the use Adolph Hitler had made of German broadcasting as a propaganda tool, the next issue of the journal declared that what the CRTC "is really doing — perhaps unknowingly — is laying the foundations on which other less scrupulous authorities may readily build a fascistic machine, comparable to the one Hitler used to enslave most of Europe." It added the CRTC "rampage" must be stopped because it was a rampage "aimed at the total subjugation of the Canadian broadcast media."[16]

Both the CBC and CTV chiefs appeared at the hearings on the 60 percent proposal. CBC head George Davidson acknowledged that the need for commercial revenue had led to "over-commercialization and over-Americanization of the primetime schedules … it is merely to recognize that economic pressures have resulted in a situation … not entirely compatible with the CBC's mandate." The CBC then broadcast 57.4 percent Canadian content over the full broadcast day, 49 percent in prime time. Regarding the yearly CBC funding ritual, Davidson explained that "when I go before the Treasury Board I'm greeted with inquiries about our earnings from commercial sales. I said last year we'd succeeded in pushing our gross revenues beyond $40,000,000. I wasn't even congratulated. They asked why it wasn't still higher."[17]

CTV president Murray Chercover warned the CRTC at the hearing that CTV would lose $6.7 million if the 60 percent rule was implemented — $3.1 million in lost revenue and $3.6 million in increased program costs. Additionally, the eleven member stations of CTV would lose ad income of between $6.9 and $8.7 million. Those figures were based on an estimate that U.S. shows had a 99 percent ad sellout rate; Canadian programs, 50 percent. Chercover argued that in 1965, 55 percent of the Canadian audience chose the Toronto stations over the Buffalo outlets, while in 1969 the preference for the Toronto outlets rose to 67 percent, with 33 percent for Buffalo. From those figures the implication was drawn that things were all right the way they were. *Variety* speculated that CTV's point was "What's the need to step up Canadian content when most Canadian viewers prefer Canadian stations anyway?" However, CTV's figures were limited to the Toronto area. Also unsaid was that both CTV and CBC carried more U.S. shows in the latter year than in the former and more of those programs were broadcast a day or more ahead of the Buffalo outlets than in 1965.[18]

As could be expected politicians made themselves heard at the hearing. Opposition Conservative member of Parliament Walter Dinsdale thundered that the CRTC was setting up "an electronic curtain" to insulate all Canadians living a fair distance from the border against U.S. shows because of its cable rule. Questioned by CRTC head Pierre Juneau, Dinsdale admitted he hadn't understood some microwave transmission would be allowed — that is, the rule had been so watered down as to be essentially meaningless. Worried that the 60 percent quota would lead to more Cancon on the CBC, one M.P. stated, "We have no damned intention of listening to that CBC crap for another four hours." *Globe & Mail* reporter Blair Kirby chastised the M.P.s for "browbeating" Juneau over the proposals, blasting what he called "the degree of ignorance the MPs' inquiries revealed in many of them." An editorial in the Ottawa *Citizen* said "Considering they helped create it, a depressing number of parliamentarians demonstrated an astounding ignorance of what the act is all about. Even more appalling was their tacitly expressed contempt for Canada's future potential and past achievements in ... broadcasting."[19]

Pressures from private broadcasters pushed the quota implementation back one full year, with the CBC required to meet it by September 1971 while CTV was given a deadline of October 1972. As well, no more than three-quarters of the 40 percent foreign maximum could be filled by the product of a single nation. Thus, during the five hours of Canadian prime time a maximum of two hours could be foreign and no more than 90 minutes of that could be from one nation. Theoretically it meant U.S. programs would be held to a maximum of 90 minutes during the 6:30 P.M. to 11:30 P.M. period. Advertising remained limited to twelve minutes per hour. Grumbled CAB president William McGregor, "An acceptable service cannot be created by regulations, not by an industry whose financial resources and ingenuity are diluted by these rules." Just a few months later, before the deadlines neared, the CRTC began to backtrack even more, looking for a face-saving way to scrap its new rules. It spread the word it might allow the CTV to carry 45 percent U.S., 5 percent other foreign and 50 percent Canadian. The CRTC also said that it might allow Canadian content percentages to be calculated on an annual basis, instead of the quarterly basis then in force. An annual calculation would allow Canadian programs to be offloaded heavily in the slack summer period — mostly then reruns — allowing a greater concentration of U.S. material in prime-time hours during the important fall/winter/spring television season.[20]

Backtracking was completed in 1972 by the CRTC to the point that its 1970 "landmark" hearings were essentially rendered meaningless, except symbolically. The prime-time requirement for private television was reduced from 60 percent to 50 percent (the CBC continued to be held to 60 percent). At the same time the definition of prime time was enlarged to 6 P.M. to midnight, a half-hour extension in each direction that had always been Cancon since that was when local news was aired. Also, the requirement that a maximum of 75 percent of the foreign fare could be from any one nation was scrapped. Under this new formula all of the peak viewing hours of 7 P.M. to 10 P.M. could be filled with U.S. shows, rather than a maximum of 90 minutes, as was the case with the original rules. Moreover, the basis on which content averages were to be calculated was changed from a calendar quarter to a full year.[21]

When the CRTC brought cable under its authority in 1969 it enabled itself to regulate the industry. Another rule imposed by the CRTC in the early 1970s was a regulation that Canadian CATV systems had to delete commercials beamed from the U.S. channels they carried. Those ads had to be replaced by commercials produced and transmitted in Canada. An unnamed spokesman for the Canadian cable industry complained that it was "immoral" for the government of Canada to sanction deletion of U.S.-made commercials without providing for remuneration to those advertisers, adding, "We can expect that Ottawa will be telephoned rather quickly by the U.S. State Department complaining over this ruling. Legally the CRTC move is probably okay, but morally it stinks."[22]

In 1975 the Gallup polling organization asked Canadians, "Do you think Canadians' culture, or way of life, is or is not being influenced too much by American TV?" Responses were 59 percent yes, 35 percent no, 6 percent undecided; five years earlier the figures were, respectively, 49 percent, 40 percent, 11 percent. Most apprehensive were Canadians under the age of 30, with 61 percent of those respondents saying yes, 31 percent no.[23]

Cable companies in Canada did begin to delete commercials from U.S. stations around 1973. Those deletions were minimal but they were done, under CRTC encouragement, on a random basis in order to undermine the guaranteed delivery promised by U.S. stations. Three Buffalo stations took Rogers Cable TV of Toronto to court because it was deleting ads from those three stations for its Toronto customers. That policy was adopted to discourage Canadian advertisers from using U.S. outlets to advertise their wares.

Buffalo's three key stations, one from each of ABC, NBC and CBS, took in annually some $7 million in ad revenue from the Toronto market. The court ruled against the Buffalo outlets, declaring those stations had no legal right to their signals in Canadian airspace because they had never been licensed to broadcast north of the border.[24]

That random deletion rule caused Montreal's *Financial Times* to declare that the CRTC was "turning into a monster." CRTC chairman Harry Boyle explained that some Canadian production companies were going to New York and using American actors to sell Canadian products to Canadians. Boyle explained, "It's so hard to make people understand that U.S. stations have no legitimate right here. The Americans can't understand nor respect a sovereign nation which fails to resist their economic and political imperatives." According to Boyle, Canada then paid out $40 million a year for U.S. programs plus another $20 million per year going to U.S. border stations for ads. A station in Bellingham, Washington, took 90 percent of its $9 million yearly revenue from Vancouver, British Columbia, while a station in Pembina, North Dakota, took $1.4 million of its $1.6 million total revenue from Winnipeg.[25]

Despite the favorable court ruling the CRTC backed off on its random deletions. First it softened its order to cable operators from one to randomly delete to one simply requiring cable operators to have the technical capability to do so. Then the rule was dropped altogether. In its place the CRTC issued a new rule whereby if two stations carried the same show at the same time on both a Canadian and a U.S. station then the U.S. signal had to be blacked out, with the Canadian version telecast on that channel. That rule remains in effect today; however, not that many shows are simulcast. Most Canadian outlets have the right to broadcast a U.S. series episode slightly ahead of whenever U.S. outlets air it. That rule has the effect of placing the Canadian ads (from the Canadian outlets) on the U.S. channel even if the viewer picked the U.S. outlet over the Canadian station for the simulcast.[26]

Another push came from the Canadian government, legislation designed to discourage Canadian ads on U.S. stations. Under Bill C58, which took effect in January 1976, Parliament disallowed income tax deductions for commercials for Canadian firms who advertised on U.S. television stations — effectively doubling the cost of such ads. In response to that, some U.S. stations slashed their rate cards while others undertook to compensate Canadian advertisers directly for any losses suffered when C58 took effect. At a more official level America was said to be considering two retaliatory steps. One was a ban on the U.S. importation of Canadian films, television fare and recordings — not too powerful considering the negligible amount of such material that went south of the border. A second item was a proposed 50 percent excise tax (on the selling price) of U.S. material bound for Canadian television. Although that would increase the cost to Canada for U.S. television fare, a U.S. State Department spokesperson said he doubted if Hollywood would suffer any sales decline since "Canada has nowhere else to go for TV fare." Writing from the U.S. perspective, reporter Paul Harris said Canadians were being "ungrateful since the viability of their broadcast system results from U.S. subsidization at a fraction of the cost of producing shows themselves." Thus, exporters were not dumping their material in offshore markets; they were subsidizing those offshore television industries. Why weren't all foreigners more grateful? Even then pressure was working as the implementation of C58 was almost delayed, supposedly to allow Parliament to verify that enough air time existed in Canada for those advertisers.[27]

During 1975 CRTC license renewal hearings for CTV, network president Murray Chercover predicted the "collapse" of Canada's broadcasting system if U.S.-made police shows were removed from Canadian prime time. CTV said it aired 31.5 percent Cancon in prime time, 61.3 percent over the full day. Of that latter total some one-third was made up of news, public affairs and game shows. Of the drama (including sitcoms) shows on CTV prime time, 92.8 percent were American. Jack Gray, executive of the 4,900-member Association of Canadian Television and Radio Artists (ACTRA) said CTV preferred to buy U.S. programs because "they can sell them more easily to advertisers, especially in prime-time" and "they're cheap." A one-hour episode of the program "Kojak" then cost about $250,000 to produce but cost CTV just $4,000 per episode to buy. Nonetheless, ACTRA favored license renewal for CTV but wanted more conditions attached to force CTV to produce more Canadian shows to replace some of the U.S. programs.[28]

In the middle 1970s a third network started up in Canada. Global was regional, limited to the rich Ontario market, although much later it would become more or less national in coverage. During its early years Global president Allan Slaight pleaded with the CRTC for a reduction in Cancon, down to 33.3 percent in prime time, 40 percent at other times. He argued that foreign shows cost Global 34 percent of its direct programming costs but produced 75 percent of total revenue, while Canadian shows cost 66 percent while producing 25 percent of revenue. Said Slaight, "We can't force an advertiser to take a package, including Canadian shows, as Toronto's big CFTO can, so we can't prop up Canadian content that way." Attending that hearing was ACTRA's Gray who said, "What saddens us is that we're reluctant to face up to the brutal truth. I don't think I've ever seen a colony as dependent as we are. The Americans want us to survive, but when we impinge even slightly on them they strike back."[29]

CBC president Al Johnson announced in 1977 that starting with the coming fall television season foreign programming in the 8 P.M. to 10 P.M. period would be reduced by 30 minutes per season until 1981 when it would be all Canadian. That portion of prime time (the most heavily viewed) was then all American on the CBC. Although Canadian content on CBC prime time was at 60 percent, all of it was in the 6:30 P.M. to 8 P.M. and 10 P.M. to

11:30 P.M. periods. Johnson hoped to move Cancon up to 80 percent in prime time over the coming few years.[30]

Battles over C58 ended, for a time, in 1976 with a truce. The U.S. agreed to drop its official governmental opposition to that bill. In return Canada promised to instruct cable companies to stop randomly deleting ads on U.S. stations from their feeds — something they were drifting toward in any case. The simulcast rule stood. Within two years of the implementation of C58 the amount of money going from Canadian companies and their ad agencies to buy commercials in the U.S. had dropped from $20 million yearly to $9 million. If the U.S. government had reached a truce, the stations had not. In September of 1978, 15 of the most-affected outlets (some 70 U.S. border stations had their programs viewed by Canadians to some extent) filed a complaint under the U.S. Trade Act, besides consistently lobbying Canadian advertisers, for relief. Those stations were located in communities such as Detroit, Buffalo, Spokane, Washington and Great Falls, Montana. Canadian minister of communications Jeanne Sauve pointed out that the $20 million lost annually before C58 was less than one-half of 1 percent of total U.S. television ad revenues but represented 10 percent of the Canadian total. She also noted that those U.S. stations were not licensed to broadcast in Canada (thus were not meeting the 60 percent Cancon rule). Those comments were in response to charges by those U.S. outlets that C58 was a "discriminatory and unreasonable barrier restricting U.S. commerce." One lawyer for some of those stations was Bart Fisher, who complained, "They're taking our service and not paying for it." Some U.S. outlets continued to try to lure Canadian advertisers by offering air time at rates 50 percent cheaper than that charged to U.S. advertisers. Buffalo's WKBW sold $2.3 million worth of commercial time to Canadian advertisers before C58 but sold only $500,000 in the first year after C58 implementation. On the other hand, ad revenue for Toronto's CITY-TV soared 43 percent in the first year after C58 took effect.[31]

Continuing to fiddle with cable regulations the CRTC came out with a new one in 1978 when it decreed that no more than four U.S. signals, one of them to be noncommercial, could be carried on any Canadian CATV system, "as a general rule." T. J. Allard, head of the CAB during some of this period, declared that any government could have severely limited the number of cable operations and their areas of operation. He wrote that the "primary reason for the existence of cable is to make available to Canadians (who obviously want them) more and more American programs…. government policy has encouraged easy availability to American programming." As an apologist for the CAB, Allard argued that despite the amount of U.S. entertainment material available over the years "the Canadian culture and speech remains untouched … the Canadian culture, lifestyle and value base remain clearly identifiable; clearly distinct from the American."[32]

A report issued in 1977 by the Ontario Royal Commission on Violence in the Communications Industries received a great deal of media coverage when it leveled heavy criticism at the violence in U.S. television series on Canadian channels. That report declared, "We find that Canadians generally are watching more and more U.S.-made television with much higher levels of violence than that produced here (in Canada) or anywhere else." Due to its heavy reliance on American series the commission went on to state that the private network CTV was "the most violent major network in the world."[33]

CRTC (the regulatory body was by now known as the Canadian Radio and Television Telecommunications Commission, although it kept its old initials from when it was the Canadian Radio and Television Commission) chairman Pierre Camu suddenly resigned in 1979 after serving only two years of his seven-year term. Depressed about the proliferation of U.S.-based cable systems sending new channels into Canada and the coming of satellite transmission in the near future, he said, "It's not possible to hold back such choices from the people here. We have to be realistic about that." He added, "If you get the right equipment in your home, you can have the world at your fingertips, and no one really can interfere with you." Basically he resigned in the face of what he saw as an impossible task, stemming the flood of U.S. television shows into Canada.[34]

While the value of U.S. television exports in 1977 was estimated at $240 million in offshore revenue, Canada remained the top dollar market, accounting for about 19 percent of that total. Generally Canada paid more for U.S. product than any other nation, on a per capita basis. Only Australia came close. Ultimately, pricing had little to do with size of population. Whatever bargaining clout Canada had in setting prices was further eroded in the 1970s when the Global network started in 1974 and a couple of large independent stations in the large southern Ontario market became more aggressively active in the buying market. Those developments dramatically pushed up the cost of U.S. shows. Additionally, Bill C58 pumped a lot of extra money into the Canadian television marketplace, also helping to boost prices. Global president Slaight admitted in 1975, "Global is costing everybody money." CTV was sometimes paying $20,000 for a one-hour segment, whereas five years earlier it had paid $2,500 per hour. Back only in 1975, CBC bought seven and a half hours of U.S. fare for a total of $30,000, while at the same time CTV purchased twenty and a half hours of U.S. prime-time fare for $78,000 total. One Canadian-made series popular domestically in 1975 was "King of Kensington," which cost $60,000 per episode to produce. Columbia executive Michael Horowitz summed up the situation when he observed "Certainly the best American customer today, the easiest customer, the best payer, is Canada."[35]

In another part of the world Australia struggled with the same problems as Canada. Australian Broadcasting Control Board chairman Miles Wright announced increases in Australian content rules effective in 1971 and 1972.

Under existing rules television stations had to show at least 18 hours of Australian product between 7 P.M. and 9:30 P.M. every 28 days (25 percent). New regulations required 50.4 hours of Australian shows every 28 days between 6 P.M. and 10 P.M., 45 percent, starting in 1971. From July 1972, the amount had to be increased to 56 hours every 28 days, 50 percent. Current requirement of two hours of Australian-made drama each month was increased to six hours, all to be first-run. Commercial stations argued the local content rise would cost them an additional $1 million. Federation of Australian Commercial Television Stations general manager Arthur Cowan grumbled that while his group would comply he doubted whether or not it could financially meet the new conditions. Screen Gems executives arrived in Australia for talks with industry executives looking to make product "by Australians for Australians." They thought that U.S. stars would have to be brought in from time to time to accomplish that. It was an obvious move to try to circumvent the new quotas.[36]

More local pressure was applied when the Australian commercial networks and the national Australian public broadcaster ABC were asked in 1973 not to buy any more foreign programs until they discussed the cost with the Federal Minister for the Media Senator Doug McClelland. He said that on a "receiver basis" the cost of imported programs in Australia was at least twice the cost it was in other countries. Brisbane Channel 0 manager Ron Archer said that a common practice was for U.S. distributors to force Australian networks to buy inferior programs as a condition of their taking the ones they wanted. Murray Norris, manager of Brisbane's Channel 7, noted that Americans were taking advantage of Australian networks' trying to outbid each other for programs.[37]

To solve the problem Australia's Tariff Board issued a proposal to establish a statutory authority to buy all overseas programs for local television. The aim was to reduce prices paid for overseas product. Behind it was the theory that intense competition between television stations resulted in exorbitant prices' being paid. Quickly that proposal was rejected by Arthur Cowan's group on the grounds that a buying authority would have a problem in passing on any savings and that it would be unable to judge which films to buy for the stations. Also working against the proposal was the stations' previous failure to cooperate in buying pools. Freedom of choice was also mentioned. Still upset by quotas Cowan claimed that stations could expect a profit of $1,767 from the first run of an hour-long foreign drama series compared to the loss of $3,523 from the first run of an hour-long local drama. That Tariff Board proposal died when the federal cabinet rejected it.[38]

In 1973 Media Minister McClelland announced a new point system for Australian television aimed mainly at increasing the local content in Australian television and its quality. Under the complex point system broadcasters had to telecast local programs in sufficient quantity to meet a point total from a scale of points for different types of programs. For example, an indigenous one-hour drama was awarded ten points for a first-run prime time and five points for a first-run off-peak, while the airing of a local major sports event would be worth one point for a first run in prime time.[39]

Within three years of the introduction of the point system, which replaced the 50 percent quota, Australian Broadcasting Control Board chairman Miles Wright stated that "this broad, blunt instrument failed completely, since it was possible to meet the target with infantile game shows, endless table tennis matches and all sorts of other simple and inexpensive ploys to fill the less popular viewing times."[40]

Throughout it all the American share of offshore product remained constant. For the year ending June 30, 1974, 73 percent of all foreign television product broadcast was from America with 24 percent from the U.K.; the next year it was 74 percent U.S., 23 percent British. For 1976 the U.S. share of imports stood at 79.7 percent, with 17.8 percent from the U.K.[41]

When it was clear the point system had not been successful, representatives of five television-related unions urged the Australian Broadcasting Control Board to increase local content, claiming it was at a lower point in 1975 then it had been over the past ten years. At the same time television stations in Australia were very profitable, notwithstanding their constant plea of being too poor to increase locally made production. For 1974 the seven existing television stations in Los Angeles (with a population reach about equal to that of Australia) had total revenue of $122 million while the 48 Australian commercial outlets had revenues of $135 million. Each group had a profit of $24 million.[42]

American distributors sold perhaps $25 million worth of television product to Australia in 1976 and, wrote reporter Frank Beerman, "there was very little traffic the other way. In fact, for the last five years, give or take a few million dollars, the ratio has been the same." He concluded that "Somehow that doesn't seem to bother the Australians.... They seem to have a rosy confidence that there is room for change in the future if only they can overcome some problems." Chief among them was a lack of stars and the "problem" of the Australian accent. Local television writer Elizabeth Riddell believed Australia imported a lot of programs for two reasons. One was the lengthy broadcasting day, which stretched from 7 A.M. to midnight and even longer on one or two days a week. Also, it was usually cheaper to import programming than to produce locally. While there was some agitation for a shorter broadcast day (this was favored by ABC) many opposed it, including all the commercial networks.[43]

Figures released by the governmental agency the Australian Broadcasting Tribunal for fiscal 1977-78 showed Australian television stations spent $157.6 million on programs and $43.2 million of that was spent on offshore product, "mostly in the U.S." The remaining $114.4 was spent locally. For that period the 50 commercial outlets had total revenue of $369 million. Melbourne station ATVO screened the first and second series of "Gilligan's Island" fifteen times each, nine times each for the final series. By the end of the 1970s there was a requirement in place to use 50 percent Australian content between 4 and 10 P.M.[44]

Late in 1979 New Zealand had a two-channel television service. An organization calling itself the Broadcasting Action Group wanted, among other things, a minimum quota of New Zealand–origin product, which they said then stood at "a pathetic 5.6 percent." They cited Australia where the introduction of a 10 percent local quota led to an increase in air time of local shows from 9.6 percent to 15.2 percent in 12 months, while the 20 percent quota imposed later led to a local content of 27 percent.[45]

Lack of adequate financial resources plagued even the relatively well off nations of continental Europe. Germany's two state-run networks each owed over $200 million in the mid–1970s. Revenue came from a $3.12 monthly television set license fee, with 70 percent going to the ARD network and 30 percent to the ZDF, and from severely limited ad time. Half of that license revenue was paid out by each network to the Deutsche Bundespost (post office), which owned and maintained the technical equipment. Lobby groups continued pressure for private television. The newest of such lobby groups had been formed by a Munich journalist who was said to be "idealistically" backed by journalists and publishers.[46]

A few years later ARD removed a few U.S. series such as "Kojak" and "Mission Impossible" from its schedule due to their violent content. The intent was to replace them with local shows but a lack of cash made that difficult. It was much cheaper to buy U.S. shows, particularly color ones, than to produce domestic alternatives. A one-hour episode of a U.S. crime series sold for $20,000 in Germany, while the cost of production for a comparable local program then on the air there was $250,000 per episode. *Variety* noted, "Hard-pressed German stations have obviously turned to the American series because of the lower costs and the audience appeal."[47]

Television came to Greece in 1966, a year before the Colonels' coup in 1967, a regime that lasted until 1974. According to reporter Margo Hammond, during that seven-year span "most of the air time was occupied by old U.S. series, commercial Greek films and government propaganda." By the end of the 1970s the two state-run networks ran 30 percent and 40 percent foreign fare respectively, mainly American. Both accepted ads to such an extent that up to half the air time was given over to commercials. After that situation was protested in a newspaper campaign both stations agreed to a maximum of 15 to 18 minutes of ad time per hour. According to Tassos Papadopoulos, director of programming for one of the networks, "A foreign program that costs us $800 would cost us twenty times that amount to produce ourselves. And we don't even have the technical means to make some programs — like the U.S. detective series — as good."[48]

Starting in 1975 France's television system was completely reorganized. Disbanded was the ORTF, replaced by a new setup of three semiautonomous networks, two of them, TF1 and A2, were national, and FR3 was a regional setup. All three remained controlled by the government; limited ads were accepted. French television directors complained later that year that while total air time had almost doubled in the preceding 12 months, television budgets had not increased. They said, "This means more foreign, especially U.S. sitcoms and skeins, with French TV losing its public service image and aiming more toward distracting than informing."[49]

Seeing that situation differently was American writer Ted Clark. He saw a new spirit of competition in France then, "and nationalistic resistance to U.S. shows has evaporated. U.S. program peddlers are cashing in." Sales included many old series such as "Peyton Place" that French television had refused to buy for years. "Peyton Place" went on the air in America in 1964 and had come and gone years ago in most European nations. Vice president of Fox William Saunders exclaimed, "Since the three independent channels were set up, the French market has really come to life." Columbia executive Jean-Pierre Barrot agreed, noting his company would take twice as much money out of France that year compared to a year earlier: "The new competitiveness between the three channels has stimulated our increased sales."[50]

Eighteen months after being reorganized, French television found itself in difficulty. French president Valery Giscard d'Estaing, the man responsible for the reorganization, ordered Prime Minister Jacques Chirac to come up with a formula to stimulate more domestic television production. The three networks had to order local production from the state-owned production company SFP. However, they had been ordering few programs, preferring to buy a higher proportion of imports because they were cheaper. The networks claimed they couldn't afford to buy through the SFP. The result was that 1,000 of SFP's employees were effectively without work.[51]

One measure adopted was a requirement that the two largest networks, TF1 and A2, increase their broadcasting of local fare of a fictional nature to a joint total of 300 hours a year from the current figure of 197 hours. FR3 had to increase its production to 60 hours a year. Additionally, a total of 150 hours of domestic documentaries had to be aired annually by TF1 and A2 and 60 hours by FR3. Regarding those measures, after a very prosperous eighteen months, Saunders said, "I expect sales to be more difficult during the next twelve months, but I am not pessimistic for the long term. The fact remains that local production is very expensive and the imported programs are an economical way of filling air time with first-class product. But for the next year we must be patient."[52]

Summing up the French situation in April 1977, 27 months after reorganization, *Variety* declared, "A feature of the first two post–ORTF years was the falling off of French television production. France has been fertile territory for foreign program salesmen, particularly those peddling U.S. product."[53]

One European market declared poor for U.S. product was Italy in 1971. RAI had a policy then of matching one Italian movie on television for each foreign film aired. Since only two features were allowed telecast per week, it set a maximum on Hollywood features of no more than 52 a year. Additionally, RAI sponsored more and more local production of material. Still, according to an American reporter, "Many RAI execs look upon American telefilms as a solution for the teleweb's financial stress," but "any breach of the trend to native shows would soon cause a parliamentary uproar. As a result, the small portion of U.S. telepix programmed almost goes unnoticed." RAI was said to pay "a mere $1,200" for an hour of imported programming. Equally annoying to American exporters was RAI's a habit of buying a maximum of six episodes from a series, giving no guarantee those six would run in consecutive weeks.[54]

All of that changed almost overnight in Italy following a 1976 court decision that upheld RAI's right to be a monopoly broadcaster in Italy on a national scale while at the same time allowing privately owned, regional broadcasters to start up. Through technicalities regional broadcasters would join together to form what amounted to national networks that competed with the state-run RAI yet were not quite in breach of the law. Some 50 private stations sprang up within months of the 1976 ruling; some 120 were in operation by mid–1977 (with about 80 of those providing "organized" daily programs); one year later around 400 private television stations were in operation in Italy, perhaps half of them broadcasting on a daily basis. Caught by surprise the government tried to prepare a draft bill that would require private broadcasters to produce a maximum of 50 percent of the programs they aired, but political infighting kept it from every becoming law. During that first chaotic year Motion Picture Export Association (MPEA) members took a public stand of loyalty to support RAI "in its hour of need." This included a refusal by MPEA companies to sell any of their material to the private stations if it had been purchased by RAI and had not completed its run on the government network. As *Variety* noted of that move, the real reason was because Hollywood cartel members would have had lean picking from the new outlets because they "do not yet have the coin to pay the MPEA companies what RAI pays." Hollywood wanted to keep its price scale up.[55]

Commercial television thus came to Italy suddenly and "without rules or regulations" and mushroom growth. Over time those private stations would consolidate and be controlled by a few large firms. Destined to become biggest was Silvio Berlusconi, operating through his publishing world conglomerate Fininvest. Early in 1980 his television network encompassed ten main Italian cities. On a trip to America that year to visit the Hollywood cartel to plead for cheaper prices for U.S. product he said, "The Seven Sisters (MPEA majors) could help us create a new and thriving market in Italy by making their recent quality programs available at softer prices. For this cooperation now they will not only have a new important source of revenue, but it is quite possible that our example will lead to the growth of private television in many other parts of Europe." In 1979, he said he spent some $6 million in program acquisitions while at the same time RAI spent $650,000 on acquiring U.S. product. Berlusconi said he would spend the same sum in 1980 on acquisition. Another argument he made to Hollywood for lower prices was that private television in Italy constituted a safeguard for democracy in general as well as a barrier against "irresponsible outlooks." Thus product should be made available in Italy more cheaply, "at below the MPEA scale in Italy — at least during the current period of early growth and consolidation for private television." He felt U.S. product was a "prime requisite" to build a fast national audience for his goal of parity with RAI.[56]

As the fourth biggest market for U.S. television fare, the U.K. remained resistant to any change in its structure. The 14 percent quota held through the 1970s, with the system still composed of two BBC networks and one commercial network. That system allowed a thriving local industry to develop and to become the second-largest exporting country of television product — albeit a very distant second to the U.S. Early in 1971 no U.S. series had made the local U.K. top twenty list for about six months. American writer Jack Pitman stated that "it's all the more understandable considering the range of ingenuity of British programming." Commercial network ITV also carried imports only on a syndication basis (sold station by station). It networked only domestic fare. "Bonanza" was then running in a Sunday afternoon time slot. In spite of all this Pitman felt compelled to find a supposed admiration of U.S. series by BBC executives; he wrote, "One suspects they'd go for a lot more American output were it not for domestic consideration and the quota."[57]

One bright note for U.S. exporters came in 1972 when the U.K. government proclaimed an end to the restricted hours for both television and radio. But it decided to veto a second commercial television network at that time. Although the 14 percent quota remained in place, it would be 14 percent of more hours. Hitherto both the BBC and ITV had been limited to programming a basic 53.5 hour week (some classroom material was allowed outside those hours). Those coming extra broadcast hours caused Pitman to state that "it has to be a reliable hunch that daytime will also hark to some staple cheapie entertainments, which development could open up a new market for American syndication schlock." Pitman did admit that "Britain, with three channels, yields more diversified programming in a night than New York with seven major outlets (including PTV), does in a week."[58]

For every ten hours of American programming that appeared on U.K. home screens, about six hours was devoted to old feature films, with only four hours left for American series. The prospect of more broadcast hours — to occur fairly slowly over time with no sudden open floodgates — made it likely that the imbalance between features and series would increase. Also in 1972, the Independent Broadcasting Authority (IBA, formerly the Independent Television Authority, ITA) abolished its concessionary "outer quota" under which the IBA allowed commercial stations to screen foreign product of educational, informational or cultural value without that product being counted against the formal 14 percent quota. U.S. suppliers were upset at this loss and by its "discriminatory" nature. "Sesame Street" had appeared under that outer quota, but under the new rule it had to be counted in calculating the 14 percent quota. The largest impact on U.S. suppliers was said to be against the three U.S. television networks, which sold most of that type of product to Britain. Thus the promise of more sales due to increased hours was undercut to some degree by the loss of the outer quota.[59]

The BBC then programmed about 15 percent foreign, 12 percent from the U.S. Those quotas were not set by the government directly but by the industry, the BBC and IBA in conjunction with the various industry trade unions. Among the rules imposed on the commercial outlets by the IBA was that a maximum of seven features could be aired per week, no more than five of which could be foreign, with no more than five films in the 7 to 11 P.M. period, and one of those five could not air before 10:30 P.M. Partly to maintain some balance on program forms, the IBA, for example, frowned on back-to-back comedy, drama, variety, and so forth, which was common in America where it was called "block programming." Additionally, there had to be two current affairs shows broadcast weekly in prime time, an arts program on weekends and documentaries regularly screened in prime time. The Broadcast Act kept advertisers away from program producers. If the content of a program irritated adjacent advertisers those ads were moved or lost altogether. Advertisers did not sponsor programs; they bought time. And commercials were limited to seven minutes per hour. In the middle 1970s ITV was composed of 15 separate stations, with each having the sole franchise in one part of the U.K. except in London, where that franchise was split between Thames TV (weekdays) and London Weekend Television.[60]

Those increased hours did help increase the price paid by U.K. buyers, as did the price setting practiced by the Hollywood cartel. Columbia executive Norman Horowitz stated the average price paid in the U.K. for a one-hour episode in 1976 was about $15,000, double the $7,000 to $8,000 of five to ten years earlier. During that earlier period the average price for a feature was $25,000, whereby it was $100,000 in 1976, occasionally as high as $200,000 for blockbusters. In Canada the average price for a series episode was then $12,000, compared to $3,000 some four to five years earlier.[61]

When the IBA announced in 1977 a reduction in the foreign quota from 14 percent to 12 percent it set off strong protests by the MPEA and by the Hollywood majors individually. Commonwealth material, such as from Canada and Australia, which was previously considered domestic, was redefined as foreign. As the U.K. was then a member of the European Union, material from member nations was classified as domestic. Pressure for the reduced quota was believed to have come from the unions who worried about an increased home screen penetration from other E.U. member nations that could no longer be controlled under the foreign quota figure. Such penetration was negligible at the time.[62]

Lobbying by Hollywood, described as "ferocious" with the MPEA hinting at retaliatory action if the lower quota was put in place, did delay the implementation for a time but ultimately failed. By the end of 1979 the U.K. network price for a top American series had moved up to $25,000 per hour, yet such series were not used as cornerstone pieces and sometimes were not used at all. *Variety* remarked that "U.S. programming here is becoming so much cosmetic fill-in material — attractive more because it is cheap to buy than for any substantive rating clout." Even some of the buying was forced on the U.K. networks through U.S. block-booking practices. "Often, in a market that basically has two customers, BBC and ITV, the only way certain shows and series can be sold is via a piggyback deal with a package of features. One major ITV station says it has more than 50 hours of American shows picked up this way that will never be aired," explained *Variety*. The popularity of Hollywood feature films — and the lack of alternatives (which was partly due to Hollywood's past cartel control of that industry) — allowed U.S. distributors to impose such deals from time to time. None of the ratings hungry U.K. commercial stations on the ITV network used its full quota of American programs in prime time. In London neither independent station Thames TV nor London Weekend TV came close to using the five hours of foreign fare allowed in primetime; one to two hours was the norm, excluding features.[63]

During the 1960s and 1970s Hollywood retained its dominant position in the exporting of television product around the world. Yet commercial television was slow in coming to Europe, nonexistent in the American meaning of the term. In areas such as Latin America that had adopted U.S.-format television the area was saturated and poor. U.S. revenue increased steadily, as sales did increase, due in part to extended broadcast hours and more channels. However, most of the increase was a result of imposing price increases and through block-booking. They had been exporting for decades but the world television market was not taking off as American exporters hoped it would. Years of lobbying in favor of private television had largely produced nothing in Europe. Domestic production always captured the audience to a greater extent than did U.S. imports. What American exporters had in their favor was that they sold cheap, really cheap in comparison with the cost of local production. At the end of the 1970s, three events would drastically change that situation and lead to a huge increase of U.S. television product abroad although not to any increase in its popularity or its percentage share in specific nations, at least not after the first few years. One development was the videocassette, which was just becoming significant as a moneymaker in

America in the late 1970s. Later it would spread all over the world, greatly favoring the Hollywood cartel, which had all those films ready for the new delivery system. A second major development was the coming of commercial television to all of Europe, more in the American style. Italy was the beginning. Typically, nations in financial trouble and right-wing regimes dedicated to destruction of public services pushed more commercial television onto the home screen.

The final major development was the coming of satellite delivery of television signals. It began in late 1975 with the launch of Time Inc.'s Home Box Office (HBO), the world's first satellite-delivered private television network. Within two years it brought its nightly package of films, sports and specials to more than 350 cable operators in 45 states covering over 700,000 subscribers. One year later, in December 1976, a small company owned by Ted Turner launched an obscure Atlanta-based local independent television outlet, WTCG, into orbit to become the first superstation (later renamed WTBS, called TBS). Within a year, TBS reached some 787,000 subscribers. The station received no income or direct compensation from the cable systems carrying it or from the subscribers. Southern Satellite charged cable systems 10¢ per subscriber per month to carry TBS. Once the Federal Communications Commission (FCC) okayed the resale carriers that fed local stations to cable television systems, other stations followed. Soon WGN (Chicago) and KTLA (Los Angeles) were launched as superstations; more followed. The day after the FCC okayed the superstation concept Ted Turner announced TBS would revise its advertising rates upward to reflect its larger audience, which it said was 2 million viewers in late 1978. At that time Turner appeared before a select group of major advertisers in New York to introduce the superstation concept to executives from firms such as General Foods and Johnson and Johnson. "This is going to be a wired nation in the next ten years," Turner said enthusiastically. He told his audience that TBS's cost per thousand was two-thirds that of the three U.S. networks and that the station delivered to an audience with twice the per capita income.[64]

All of these events affected only the domestic television situation, but they laid the groundwork for the coming world satellite delivery of television signals. After so many people had dreamed for so many decades of a coming global satellite system, its actual arrival, the first concrete steps, passed largely unnoticed. While the trade press printed a few perfunctory accounts of those launches, no one commented at all on their implications. In fact, the Motion Picture Association of America (MPAA) actually fought the arrival of the superstations. It petitioned the FCC to halt the superstation launches. MPAA argued that superstations would be bidding for national advertising and offering expensive programming, against which most local stations would not be able to compete. At the heart of the MPAA fear was the potential loss of syndication income for its members. It told FCC officials, "The producers of high-cost television programming must rely upon multiple outlets to recoup their production costs. If superstations are allowed to develop at the cost of local television outlets, the economic base necessary to support program production will shrink and ultimately fewer programs will be produced." Hollywood's lobby group also asked the FCC if superstations, which catered exclusively to national advertisers, would reduce the access of purely local advertisers to the television medium and if carriage of those superstations would discourage cable companies from originating their own programming. When the FCC asked MPAA petitioners if they had looked at the income they would receive from satellite distribution versus the potential without it, a MPAA staffer admitted it had not but was then working on it. Fortunately for Hollywood, it lost this particular fight. Satellite transmission would become the mainstay of Hollywood's future forays into trying to control the world's home screens. It was a system that, of course, favored significantly the very rich firms that already dominated the market.[65]

Chapter 7

1980s:
"Hollywood
Owns the World"

Worldwide, television changed dramatically in the 1980s. At the start of the decade there was little or no cable or satellite transmission of signals outside of North America. By the end of the decade those methods were pervasive around the globe. Europe had little commercial television in 1980 anywhere close to U.S.-style private and ad-laden television. By the end of the 1980s that style more and more came to dominate. From having a relatively small number of stations the globe moved to the saturation point and beyond in many areas. All of these developments favored the Hollywood cartel and its product; they had long promoted such developments.

Dreamers saw the future of worldwide television more and more simply in terms of advertising possibilities. Gone was the lip service paid so often in the past to global television's potential to educate, instruct, inform, and so forth. In a lecture delivered in Tokyo in 1985, CBS vice president John Eger noted that pressures from an increase in the number of stations and climbing cost of television production meant "The force of global marketing — including economies of scale — is irresistible." The U.S., he thought, depended on unified, transnational advertising and marketing and "The same television commercial can sell Coca-Cola in Liverpool and Kuala Lumpur. It is a world-class commercial. I believe that it's not a question of 'if' but 'when' it becomes a standard option for a program-production source to fund production from global advertisers and distribute that production throughout the world with two or three commercial announcements included. Product-hungry electronic media will contract for that programming, perhaps receiving it free of charge in return for carrying the commercials. Local or regional media thus will have the programs they need, without straining their budgets." To get there Eger believed Hollywood might have to change its production somewhat since "Until now, the major communications forces in the U.S. have always treated the universe as bordered on the west by Los Angeles and on the east by New

York ... we can no longer afford to regard the rest of the world as an ancillary market to be considered only incidentally after the creative decisions have been made."[1]

In a 1985 speech at Hofstra University, another CBS vice president, James Rosenfield, declared the coming of satellite television "clearly stimulated an age of abundance in broadcasting. No more is the television viewer a passive participant, but a consumer king, with an enormous range of choices to command by tapping a remote switch.... In fact, this age of abundance has also dawned throughout the developed world, and is also emerging in the developing world." In that age of abundance he predicted "those who hold the rights of the most popular and enduring television programming will be best able to enjoy the benefits of the mixed distribution system. Increasingly, the same programming can be successfully distributed through all forms, including pay television, advertiser-supported television, and government-supported television." The largest single economic force driving television into that age of abundance was advertising, worldwide. An example he cited was Italy where the increase in television advertising was 39 percent after private television arrived compared to an overall advertising increase of 9 percent in the same period. Rosenfield cited an August 1985 editorial in the *Wall Street Journal* that said, "We've long felt that one thing that could really get Europe's economic engine to turn over again is, quite honestly, TV commercials. That's right. Miller Lite, Chevy trucks, The Whopper. Even here in the U.S. we probably don't fully appreciate how much worthwhile drive and adrenaline all that TV selling instills in the American enterprise."[2]

More predictions came from John Eger in 1987. By that time the former director of the White House Office of Telecommunications Policy (1973–76) had left CBS and was president of Worldwide Media Group, a firm specializing in international communications. Talking about the globalization of markets, he said, "These developments, coupled with overlapping buying behaviors among global consumers, set the stage for the emergence of national, regional and global television systems used in the service of global marketing campaigns." One reason the concept of global television was moving swiftly from concept to reality was "The convergence of wants and needs, tastes and interests of demographic groups the world over; marketing companies can now devise truly global campaigns based upon these 'commonalities' rather than the differences which distinguish cultures, classes and nations." Another reason Eger cited was "the needs of global marketing companies to increase the level of their communications across a broad spectrum and to develop corporate and brand awareness in order to achieve the penetration and acceptability they must have to be competitive in an increasingly competitive world arena." While traditionally international marketing had been based on the differences between peoples, global marketing "seeks out, stresses, even insists on, 'similarities' among people." Cited was Harvard Business School scholar

Theodore Levitt, who believed the modern global corporation "will seek sensibly to force suitably standardized products and practices on the entire globe. They are exactly what the world will take, if they come also with low prices, high quality and blessed reliability." Levitt continued, "Almost everyone everywhere wants all the things they have heard about, seen, or experienced via the new technologies." Acknowledging cases where national or regional differences did resist homogenization, he conceded that "the global corporation accepts and adjusts to these differences only reluctantly, only after relentlessly testing their immutability, after trying in various ways to circumvent and reshape them." Robert James, president of advertising agency McCann–Erickson Worldwide, asked, "Why not use the same agency to sell the same brand in the same way to the same people around the world?" As to why global marketing was then considered so full of promise Eger stated, "Because television, that most efficient, effective and spectacularly profitable of all mass media, will soon be available to serve as global marketing's instrument of consumer access." It would soon be available because "The magical marketing tool of television has been bound with the chains of laws and regulations in much of the world, and it has not been free to exercise more than a tiny fraction of its potential as a conduit to the consumer. Those chains, at last, are being chiseled off. Irreversible forces are at work to vastly increase commercial television in Europe and around the world." Invoking historic myth, Eger called global television "Prometheus unbound" and said it brought "another revolutionary tool" to humankind.[3]

At that time West Germany limited television ads to 20 minutes a day in grouped time segments, while no commercials at all were allowed on Belgian or Swedish television. Norway and Denmark grouped and strictly limited ad time. In Europe, only in Austria and Italy could particular programs be fully sponsored, and there the advertiser had to be fully identified with that program. With private television then unregulated in Italy the private broadcasters "voluntarily" restricted advertising to 14 percent of air time. The arrival of new stations and new transmission systems meant it was more and more expensive to compete for viewers. Expanded advertising was one of the few "acceptable" ways to raise money. Addressing the idea that global marketing had to evolve alongside global programming to a degree, Eger suggested a starting point could be a barter system whereby stations received "free" programs in exchange for air time that would be sold by the programs' syndicators to product sponsors. Elaborating, he said, "Advertisers can underwrite programming of general appeal, and provide that programming free of charge to the financially struggling broadcasters of the world. The programming will include advertising for the world-class products of the advertisers." Barter might provide a framework, but even if it didn't "aggressive and creative manufacturers and their advertising agencies will find a way." Eger concluded, "Economically, there is a vast reservoir of money waiting to support global marketing and, at the same time, to reward handsomely the full range of participants — station owners, programmers, technologists and the like — who are building global television into the dominant medium of the 21st century."[4]

At a more practical level Ted Turner was starting to build a truly global network. Speaking at a 1982 television conference in Edinburgh, he announced his intention to extend Cable News Network (CNN) to Europe, claiming that satellite and cable television were "a positive force for good." Turner told his audience of broadcasters, "I intend to conquer the world, but instead of conquering with bombs, I intend to conquer with good ideas." Virtually all of those broadcasters believed that pay cable would need to win a mass audience to be profitable, that would require populist programming.[5]

Turner's CNN took a major step when it debuted in Japan in April 1984. Japan Cable TV initially televised seventeen and one-half hours of CNN live, distributing the English-language feed to 15,000 homes, 22 hotels and numerous foreign consulates in and around Tokyo. The Japanese signal was downlinked from CNN's Intelsat transmission to Australia's Seven Network, which had taken the CNN feed for around a year. Turner Program Services executive Sidney Pike said CNN feeds to Europe and Africa would start soon. Describing the actions to establish a global television news service Pike said Turner was not only looking at additional revenue sources but looking on the venture as a means "to create more understanding and ultimately contribute to overall peace" in the world. Japan Cable TV parent TV Asahi started using some of the CNN feed later in the year, abbreviated, tape-delayed and translated into Japanese. CNN was then also broadcast to some U.S. military installations in several lands via the Armed Forces Radio and Television Services.[6]

CNN finally broke into the major market of Europe with a feed commencing on September 15, 1985. Carried by the Intelsat V satellite, a special service generated by a 40-person team at Turner's Atlanta headquarters was beamed to all members of the European Broadcast Union (EBU) and to selected hotels. For the first 90 days the broadcasters could lift any hard news items they wanted from the feed free of charge. After that they had to start paying Turner Program Services, the London-based export arm of Turner Broadcasting System (TBS). For "soft" news, separate sales arrangements had to be made to get access to the daily roster of sports, entertainment and so on. A subcarrier on the CNN transponder supplied a regularly updated price list two to three hours in advance of the items' availability for broadcast to allow stations to decide what they wanted. Signed up from the beginning was the U.K.'s BBC and Independent Television News, France's Antenne-Z (A2) and Canal Plus, Germany's ZDF, Italy's RAI, and Portugal's RTP. The hotel feed kicked off that month in London's Dorchester Hotel with major chains taking the transmission including Hilton, Sheraton, Marriott, and Intercontinental. Extending the service beyond those two sets of receivers into European cable and satellite markets reaching potentially all homes was to take longer because of various regulatory setups across the region. Turner was an associate member of the Union, in which members were forbidden from encroaching on each other's territories. The hotel feed was allowed because the service was only in English and most viewers were not residents of the nations where the feed was seen. However, spilling into an EBU member's domestic arrangements was not allowed, so officially that was not on the Turner agenda. TBS was then opening offices all over Europe. As well as marketing the news feed, TBS was involved in the general sale of Turner programs — which included a vast library of old Hollywood films and an equally vast library of cartoons.[7]

One year later Turner claimed that CNN was available in 10,000 hotel rooms, all first-class, in nine countries across Europe. Additionally, newspapers, broadcasters, conference centers, embassies, consulates and VIPs — including two prime ministers' offices on the Continent — took the service. Noted *Variety*, "with daytime TV pretty much of a desert in Europe, Turner thinks it can persuade more of the public that CNN is a 'fresh' window on the world around the clock." Turner's method of gaining permission to make his feeds available to all the people of Europe — and the world — was simple and effective. Initially the feed went to the elite of the nation and to important business people who stayed in those high-price hotel rooms. It got them used to and dependent on CNN, particularly in the daytime hours, a period that was still dark in much of Europe due to financial constraints. It was those elite viewers who would either make the final decisions or influence those who did as to whether Turner programs would be allowed into all the homes of a nation. While CNN touted itself as an all-news station, it did break its feed down into two categories, hard and soft news. Much of the soft material, such as its entertainment segments, were little more than publicity for Hollywood films, television programs and so forth. Such material directly helped the Hollywood cartel (Turner would officially become a member of it some ten years later) and kept up the American publicity onslaught.[8]

First breakthrough in that area came in 1986 when CNN signed deals with Finland's public broadcaster YIE, Sweden's SVT, Austria's ORF network, and Holland's Veronica broadcaster. Those one-year pacts, with a total value of $380,000 to CNN, were standard in that the Europeans got access to the CNN 24-hour European news feed and were allowed to take what they wanted, within contractual limits. Still provided only in English and produced completely in Atlanta, Georgia, headquarters, the standard CNN 24-hour-a-day feed was adjusted to some degree and called a "European" news feed. More important for CNN in those four nations was that under the terms of the contracts "objections to the satellite-to-cable news service entering cable systems in the broadcaster's own country have been waived."[9]

Domestically, satellites dotted the sky. In 1981 nine domestic satellites were in orbit with most of them having 24 transponders (one transponder unit carried one television channel) and all of them occupied. Capacity on all satellites cleared for launch by the FCC through 1985 was 95 percent booked in 1981. Even then some firms accused others of warehousing transponders (that is, leasing but not using) in order to keep competitive programming off the air. Some firms rented space against a possible future need or as speculation, hoping they could sublease to another company for a profit. Monthly rental fees for one transponder were then in the $50,000 to $150,000 range. Robert Wold, who owned a company that sold transponder time to cable and television programmers, remarked, "It has become a business for companies with deep pockets" and in a deregulated environment "would concentrate even more power in the hands of a few companies."[10]

Rupert Murdoch launched his Sky Channel in 1982, beaming his satellite-to-cable service to several nations including Norway and Finland. However, some nations, like Holland (heavily cabled by European standards), refused to permit the transmission to Dutch cable operators. In 1984 Sky Channel started beaming its signal to cable head ends in the U.K., making it something considered unthinkable only a few years earlier, an unlicensed commercial telecaster. Sky Channel carried lots of American programming and lots of commercials.[11]

Sky Channel could be received by more than 5 million European households across 11 nations by early 1986. Through audience research the outlet found it did much better at drawing audiences in northern European countries such as Norway and Sweden than it did in southern European lands such as France, where it drew in the poor-to-low range. One major reason for that result, thought Bruce Roberts, head of research for Sky, was culture: "People in Sweden have more in common with people in Minnesota than with people in Switzerland. They have similar religion, similar attitudes and like similar things." Of Sky's programming, American reporter Bill Grantham remarked, "Sky's program bias is toward U.S. imports — movies of the week, sitcoms and adventure series, in particular."[12]

Tiny Luxembourg had its own orbiter when a private broadcaster there, CLT, began satellite transmission. Complete with ads, it was principally a delivery system for American programming, as it had been when solely a terrestrially based telecaster in that nation with signal spillover into other more populous nations. A French government minister condemned Luxembourg's broadcast satellite as a "Coca-Cola satellite attacking our artistic and cultural integrity."[13]

Some European broadcasters voiced a different complaint in 1988 when 120 European television representatives held a meeting to discuss European cooperation in coproductions and other things. It was partly to help stem the American onslaught, but they also protested a decision of the Motion Picture Export Association (MPEA) to withhold multination movie rights from European satellite operators. Hollywood preferred to sell film rights country by country rather than to a satellite operator whose footprint (broadcast range) covered more than one country — there was more money in the former method. Once the price was raised the MPEA dropped its opposition. Young and Rubicam ad agency vice president Charles Dawson believed that even if the European Union (E.U.) adopted area-wide regulations limiting imports from outside the common market, it would have to exempt movie channels from such a quota because if they had to rely mainly on European features such channels could not be profitable. One estimate was that by 1990 there would be over 100 satellites parked over Europe, and the need for television programming would move from 180,000 hours in 1985 to 470,000 hours in 1990.[14]

Murdoch's Sky Channel was in trouble by the end of the 1980s, with losses estimated at $65 million from its launch until 1988 even though it was then available in 13 million households across Europe. Sky had counted on a rapid cabling occurring in the U.K., something that did not materialize as citizens stubbornly resisted the lure of cable. Thus in 1989 News Corp. chief executive Murdoch relaunched his service as Sky Television, with a crucial difference: it was now a DBS (direct broadcast satellite) that could be picked up directly by any home that had a dish; no cable company or connection was necessary. Start-up costs for Sky TV were estimated at $50 to $60 million for the relaunch, with first year losses expected to add another $50 million to that total. That single channel was restructured into four new ones; three were advertiser supported (free to dish owners) and were modeled after the likes of superstation TBS in America. The commercially oriented programming to be carried would see "about half of it supplied by American producers." The fourth channel was a pay-movie outlet. Launched the very same year, 1989, was a rival three-channel system, British Satellite Broadcasting (BSB), backed by a consortium of European media firms. BSB announced it planned to spend $500 million in acquiring product. One deal with MGM/ UA was valued at over $100 million alone.[15]

Murdoch's one pay channel, Sky Movies, was available free for a few months then encrypted and sold as a pay outlet for $20 a month. It was actually a joint channel shared between Sky Movies and the Disney Channel; Disney was a joint stakeholder in that particular enterprise. That this rivalry was destined to be a fight to the death was preordained by one single fact; Sky and BSB could be received by households only on separate, incompatible dishes. Moving satellite service from satellite-to-cable to satellite-to-home took even more control of the television situation away from a nation's government. As long as cable companies based within a country were the sole or major receivers of satellite transmission, governments could still take measures to curtail real or perceived abuses. Once the satellite signal beamed directly to homes, that was gone. It was politically unwise for governments to take punitive action against its citizens merely for owning a receiving dish.[16]

Another network going global was the music channel. After a countdown by Elton John, MTV Europe launched in August 1987. It was a basic (no-pay) cable service on systems reaching 1.6 million television sets with an estimated potential of 17 million viewers. One news account described the service as encompassing video clips and other features designed to reflect "the diversity and uniqueness of the many European cultures it represents." MTV Europe was available only in the English language.[17]

In 1981 with the home-video market still in its infancy journalist Steven Knoll was confident that the role of America in the home-video market would develop according to the pattern set by other U.S. software industries such as the motion picture business: "While local licensers in many cases will handle distribution, U.S. feature product is expected to dominate the still embryonic though fast-growing market." One difference was thought to be a greater measure of freedom in terms of what could be introduced into foreign territories as there would not be the same amount of government restrictions as had been erected in the spheres of feature film and television exhibition. Problems for Hollywood were expected to be limited to issues such as piracy of tapes and the length of the releasing window, that is, clearance time that had to elapse between the time a feature had its theatrical release and the time it appeared on videocassette. In America there were no regulations covering that period, but the U.S. industry had then settled into a pattern of six to nine months' clearance before releasing product to the nontheatrical arena. The U.K. had already established a regulation for the industry that kept the window at two years. Knoll concluded, "But undoubtedly it's the American motion picture libraries that will lend the basic momentum to the international home video market."[18]

In some of the poorer European markets Hollywood held back from the home-video market until the numbers were right. Late in 1981 Spain had 40,000 videocassette recorders (VCRs) in the whole country. Hollywood's majors were not entering the market then but waiting until the number of VCRs reached the 100,000 mark. At the same time those majors were getting ready to enter the Italian market for a reason that was true for all countries. Reporting on the Italian entry, Hank Werba said, "This move is attributed to the number of distrib-sponsored films by the American companies that are judged inappropriate for the Italian theatrical market"—that is, really bad movies. Video was beloved by Hollywood for many reasons, one being the possibility of flogging material so bad that theaters generally would not screen it. Television had always been used somewhat for that purpose, but it was limited in that television always censored what went into the home. A really bad film shunned by exhibitors but rated General might make it onto the home screen, but a really bad film rated Adult Only had no place to go — until the arrival of home video.[19]

The amount of money that could be extracted in richer markets — and the ability of the home-video industry to drive up prices paid by television — could be seen in Scandinavia in 1981. In some cases the price for video cassette distribution rights in the region exceeded that for the broadcast rights to the same property. American distribution executive Stuart Graber explained that in Scandinavia the average guarantee for the acquisition of home-video rights to a two-hour made-for-television movie was $12,000 paid against a 20 percent royalty. Comparable figures for a sale to broadcast television was $10,000 for one run over a one or two year period. All American distributors knew that only a limited amount of material could be sold to Scandinavian television, but now they had another outlet. The miniseries "Alcatraz: The Whole Shocking Story" starring Telly Savalas was refused by all Scandinavian broadcasters, but two dozen home-video firms in the region wanted to buy it.[20]

Even though the Hollywood majors had no problems and little competition in the international home-video industry, embryonic as it then was, Motion Picture Association of America (MPAA) president Jack Valenti found much to complain about. In a speech to the International Tape–Disk Association Valenti grumbled about piracy and how home video was also being burdened by "import duties, turnover taxes, added value taxes, sales taxes, income taxes, remittance taxes, and the list is endless." Unless a set of reasonable taxing principles was fashioned for home video, Valenti warned, "we will pay under a tax credo whose sole criterion is, how much money can we get out of these bastards."[21]

By 1985 the U.S. release time window was down to four to six months and was usually dictated by how a film did at the box office. A movie that did poorly at cinemas was released to home video more quickly, to take advantage of whatever value its publicity might still have in the public consciousness. France imposed a one-year window between theatrical and home-video release. That regulation was challenged in court by MCA Home Video, which released in France under the name CIC Video. (This was a joint venture involving MCA, Paramount and MGM/UA — a sort of minicartel within the cartel.) Most U.S. distributors had been releasing product to home video in France six months after the theatrical release. When the European Court of Justice upheld the legality of France's one-year window, MCA executive Gene Giaquinto said, "We're obviously not happy about it ... the one year window favors pirates, and they'll get copies out faster knowing that we're precluded" from doing the same. He added, "I'm wondering what this does, putting such constraints on the industry ... especially when a film is not successful. In that case it's imperative to release a film into home video before the ad campaign and public awareness fade into oblivion." More ominous, in his mind, was that West Germany had a representative argue before the court in favor of the French law. Giaquinto concluded, "it's going to be counterproductive."[22]

One brief experiment tried to blend television and home video in Scandinavia. Describing the scheme, journalist Tom Bierbaum said enthusiastically that Scandinavia television viewers "who've seen only limited amounts of U.S. TV on their high-brow, government-run television services, will have a shot at a regular diet of U.S. series programming, thanks to an innovative video cassette scheme." It was a joint venture between Swedish video distributor Transworld Communications and Televentures, which was a joint venture involving several U.S. distributors, including Tristar. Video stores would rent two-hour cassettes supplied by Transworld that featured two to three U.S. television series episodes plus up to twelve minutes of commercials and wrappers and inserts produced in the native language of each country. Programs themselves were subtitled in the appropriate language. U.S. series included were the likes of "21 Jump Street," "My Two Dads," "Werewolf" and "Buck James." An initial strategy was to present on each tape one series appealing to kids, one to females and one to males. Scandinavia was thought to be a good market for such a venture since it had a high standard of living and a high amount of leisure time yet minimal television; Norway was limited to one state-run network and Sweden, just two. Tristar executive Arnold Messer complained, "None of the public broadcasting services in those countries tend to emphasize general entertainment." To attract the attention of consumers in the region Transworld planned to take out newspaper ads next to the television listings showing viewers the alternatives available through the videocassettes. Tristar executives programmed the series, added on any commercials sold in America, and sent the tape to Transworld, which handled subtitling, the adding on of ads sold in Scandinavia and distribution. Messer called his group's endeavor an attempt "to kick start a market that never existed before." Nothing more was ever heard of this venture.[23]

At the end of the 1980s Hollywood looked at the proposal to unite the 12 members of European Community (E.C.) into a single market in 1992 with both hope and fear — more of the former. One observer said of the one-market E.U., "an important, lucrative market for U.S. video cassette programming can only get bigger and better." It was hoped that various regulations in different countries would disappear and that with the dropping of tariffs between those nations companies would be "free to find the most advantageous locations in Europe to make their tapes, without having to figure in all the tariffs they'd face shipping from those locations into the rest of Europe." One nagging fear for some was that the E.C. lands would band together and require a quota of European programming. U.S. distributor Gary Barber thought that was unlikely because "They'd have a tough time going up against the U.S. We will continue to be the predominant force in top-budget pictures. Hollywood is Hollywood." Over the short term the single E.U. market might bring only modest changes, but over the longer term some executives believed "European audiences eventually will begin to align their tastes. The dominant language will no doubt be English, and the dominant source of entertainment programming can be the U.S." The European market then accounted for half the foreign business generated by U.S. videocassettes.[24]

The area ignored the longest for home videos was Latin America, where only Cinema International Corporation (CIC; Paramount and MCA) was doing business late in 1984. Other majors were, however, then planning to enter that market. They had delayed entering the Latin market, they said, because of piracy problems in the region. Yet it was that rampant piracy that ultimately motivated them to enter the arena. Hollywood no longer wished to let the pirates make off with a market the MPAA estimated at $100 million annually. The MPAA had worked with local governments to crack down on pirates as well as badgering South American businesses to cooperate. One example of the changing climate was when the Brazilian Video Union, a group of some 300 dealers, signed a gentlemen's agreement to freeze pirate product levels and then begin withdrawing pirate product from their shelves as licensed product became available. Reportedly the retailers took the initiative in the arrangement. Those dealers didn't want to remove all pirate material at once since it would have left little or nothing on their shelves. Another problem for Hollywood was a Brazilian law requiring 25 percent of a foreign company's home-video sales to be from domestic product.[25]

One of those reluctant entries into the Latin American home-video market was CBS/Fox (another joint venture), which by 1988 was active only in Argentina, Mexico, and Venezuela (using local middlemen in all cases). CBS/Fox executive Ele Juarez complained about falling currency rates in Venezuela, "endless taxes and an 80% piracy scene," business that was either falling or barely holding its own in the three markets in which they were active, and he also grumbled about Brazil's 25 percent rule, although CBS/Fox was not then even in that market. Asked why, in light of all the problems he had mentioned, CBS/Fox was planning to enter more Latin markets Juarez replied, "we want to maintain a presence in Latin America, and as long as there's any business to be done, we'll be doing it."[26]

Buying into foreign television operations found more favor in Hollywood in the 1980s, as did management "consultancy" pacts, supposedly for the benefit of both sides. To decrease the possibility of protest from those foreign nations worried about foreign control of indigenous media, friendly local firms were usually sought out to become partners with the American concerns. In the middle 1980s ABC had a small ownership position in Japan's TV Asahi, one of four major commercial networks in Japan. From its flagship Tokyo station JOEX-TV, it fed 19 affiliates around the country. About the same time Viacom, the tenth largest cable television operator in the U.S., announced it would be an equity partner in the cabling of Japan, joining domestic firms Mitsui and Toshiba, among others. Viacom also then had a foothold in British cable plans.[27]

When the pay cable operation called Filmnet started in Holland in 1984, a 20 percent ownership stake was held by United International Pictures (UIP; composed of Universal, Paramount and MGM/UA). One other pay service just then getting underway there was Screen Sports, a British-based satellite channel in which ABC and U.S. sports channel ESPN held stakes (ESPN was owned by ABC). Dutch cable systems were municipally owned and governed by must-carry rules for the two Dutch networks. Additionally, they usually offered the three German terrestrial channels, the Flemish service of the Belgian national network and up to four British networks. An upgrading program was then underway in Holland to increase cable system capacity from the current nine to eleven channels up to eighteen to twenty.[28]

Most of the majors moved early to get a piece of the U.K. cable system industry, an industry they hoped would grow rapidly. One enterprise had MGM/UA, Paramount and Universal, through their UIP foreign partnership, moving into the British pay-cable market in a challenge to another U.S.-dominated consortium. Columbia, 20th Century–Fox, CBS and HBO were teaming up with the British Goldcrest Films in another pay U.K. service. British partners were involved in both ventures. At that time, 1983, cable penetration stood at 14 percent of U.K. homes, just one-third of the penetration rate in America.[29]

Initially those four U.S. firms and Goldcrest were to provide cable programming overseas, with those five owning 49 percent of the venture and the unspecified U.K. firms owning the remainder. What started as a straight deal for just cable programming in Britain became much broader in scope. The "Big Four" tried to negotiate a deal "to lock up Direct Broadcast Satellite rights on a global scale," wrote Roger Watkins. Advertising executives saw a potential for an annual $200 million in ad revenue from such a venture. Supposedly the Big Four felt "vulnerable" because they were only program suppliers with their right of cable access not guaranteed as the government had the power to pull the plug at any time. Therefore the Big Four were trying to lease satellite transponders from many of the smaller nations, just a few of which would combine for a DBS footprint that would initially cover most of Europe, the Caribbean and Latin America. Discussions took place with Ireland, Liechtenstein, the Benelux nations, Bermuda and Israel. Those countries all had their own orbital slots courtesy of the 1977 World Administrative Radio Conference, which felt it was politically necessary then to give smaller countries their slots with the understanding they would neither want nor be ready to launch for decades, if ever. Ongoing satellite development made the slots of enormous value to entertainment conglomerates "all anxious to carve up the world for themselves." Small impoverished lands were hard pressed to pay the estimated $300 million necessary to build, launch and maintain a satellite system, but "the multinationals would gladly pay and in the trade-off get a big piece of the bird." Advancing satellite technology meant footprints got bigger and covered more territory than ever envisioned by the Administrative Radio Conference. Most Western lands had long since agreed to take no action against such spillover. CBS and Fox started the whole thing around

1980 when they hoped to link up for a broad range of television, film and home-video distribution, a deal later modified to include just home video. Then came Tristar, the CBS–Columbia–Fox–HBO venture for motion picture production and distribution. That later led to the Big Four hookup with Goldcrest in the U.K.[30]

Regarding that potential DBS venture *Variety* concluded, "Clearly the partners envisioned a global DBS network, providing program services to high-power DBS satellites now being built to cover Europe, and, much later, possibly the world. While the partnership agreement talked only about program services, the partners were contemplating some ownership of channels as well. That's not a bad way to make money." However, the deal died when CBS backed out of it for unspecified reasons saying only that it liked the idea in concept but in practice there were problems.[31]

By 1984 the UIP trio were partnered with U.K. firm Rank and Rediffusion (cable owners) to launch a pay-cable service The Entertainment Network. Meanwhile, HBO, Fox, and Columbia joined with Showtime/The Movie Channel and Warner to partner with U.K. firms Goldcrest and Thorn EMI (cable owners) to launch their pay-cable outlet, Premiere. Thorn then had only a few thousand homes wired in Britain, making profits seem many years away. Thorn thought it was better to have the big American firms with you than against you and, more important, "Thorn wants in on the majors' plans for becoming global narrowcasters." British firms held just over 50 percent of Premiere, Thorn owned 41.2 percent and the other six each held 9.9 percent. Fox executive Steve Roberts remarked that Premiere's partners were confident their venture would not trigger any U.S. government concern since the overseas competition by "two major forces" proved there was "by no means a monopoly." Premiere was a satellite-to-cable service.[32]

That British cable market never really materialized, as Britons were slow to sign up. At the end of the 1980s, a new blitz was underway; this time North American telephone companies lead the way in trying to develop a big cable presence in the U.K. According to Jon Davey, head of the regulatory Cable Authority, North American firms accounted for more than 90 percent of money pledged to build cable systems in Britain — some $5 to $6 billion over the next few years. American phone companies such as Pacific Telesis and U.S. West were then barred at home from carrying television signals; there were less restrictions in the U.K. While British regulations barred non-European countries from owning cable companies, those regulations were finally dropped after the Cable Authority turned a blind eye to the decoy offshore companies shielding U.S. firms.[33]

As Italian television went private and commercial in a big way the three U.S. television networks were all heavily involved. Each of the networks had a "special relationship" with one or more Italian broadcasting organizations; ABC, with Rete4; CBS, with Canale5 and Italia1; NBC, with the three state networks run by RAI (two national, one regional). Executives from all three U.S. networks agreed "the U.S. government has restricted American network opportunities abroad by refusing, for the time being, to lift restrictions against network ownership of programming." As well they also agreed that "Italy currently has the most wide-open, competitive commercial television system in Europe, and that it may be setting important precedents for the rest of the continent." In its deal with Rete4, ABC assigned Steve Carlin as its consultant. Carlin said his input went beyond consulting to direct involvement. ABC also advised on program scheduling, program promotion spots, advertising and the acquisition of U.S. product. While the deal talked of coproductions none, of course, ever happened. Programming offered by ABC to the Italian private network included movies of the week, soft news, sports and "lots of races" of all kinds. ABC also lent its expertise to Rete4 on game shows, advised the network on its on-air look and even "helps them by sharing promotion tips on programs it once carried and were bought by Rete4."[34]

NBC's pact with RAI called for program exchanges (which also never took place) and "information swapping." Several times a year executives met from the two partners to discuss technical details and new developments. The U.S. network shared its expertise in program strategy and U.S. program trends. Of RAI, NBC Enterprises vice president Mike Perez said, "Regardless of how big you are you can't produce 24 hours a day for three networks. You have to acquire programs." In its deal with two large, private Italian networks, CBS engaged in the same activities as the other U.S. networks and helped its partners develop their ad rates. CBS executive John Eger was also disappointed in setbacks in loosening restrictions against network ownership: "It's a big blow. It's far more serious than we've demonstrated." CBS needed to own more programs so "CBS can extend its network in effect." The coming of global marketing could be assisted by the U.S. networks. Said Eger, "We could do that with programming from the majors. But if we don't have some control over program rights, we won't be able to expand." He felt then that European commercial television was inevitable.[35]

When CBS Broadcast International (CBI) signed its first Italian pact in 1982, with Italia-1, CBS's Arthur Kane called the deal "the first media pact with Italy for coproduction, program exchange and broadcasting consultancy." However, *Variety* wrote, "It was in effect a lucrative unidirectional agreement for CBI." Kane called the consultancy aspect a key part of the deal with the CBI pipeline cluing Italian "programmers to the art and commerce of game shows."[36]

In 1989, NBC International created a separate division, NBC Europe, to develop activities in that area, including the sale of NBC television shows and the exploration of possible joint ventures. NBC Europe executive Patrick Cox remarked, "Setting up such a company clearly means that NBC is looking to do more business, and more different kinds of business, with Europeans.

The days of symbolic goodwill gestures are over. NBC Europe will be in the business of scouting for opportunities which will yield commercial results." ABC had just announced a bridgehead into Germany through a 49 percent financial stake in the Munich-based satellite-delivered program service company, Telemunchen, which was part owner of Tele-5.[37]

That mid–1980s rush into the U.K. cable industry involved almost all of the U.S. Hollywood majors, aligned into two camps. When the satellite and cable distribution stabilized, the Hollywood majors planned to own part of the worldwide pay television profits. Ownership was a dream for Hollywood. Many continued to nurse grudges against the three U.S. networks, believing those Hollywood majors turned ABC, NBC and CBS into giant money-makers by licensing their libraries to them in the 1950s and beyond with no ownership stake for themselves. Similarly when HBO had arrived a decade earlier Hollywood again licensed only; HBO swelled into a rich giant. Hollywood was determined to have an ownership stake in future endeavors. That Premiere partnership had been joined in Germany with the Beta giant (minus Goldcrest) while UIP was partnered with the Bettlesmann publishing group in Germany; it also had deals with local firms in both Norway and, as previously mentioned, Holland. As to the possibility that such merging could set off monopoly alarm bells, U.S. reporter Larry Michie said, "The antitrust laws in the U.S. are such that the overseas partners are wary of even nodding to each other on their home turf. As long as they're making money together offshore, antitrust laws allow them to cooperate; but at home it's verboten." It had been suggested that UIP and Premiere merge into one, making a true monopoly and one that would potentially generate more profits. More and more, Hollywood was then trying to sell product on nonexclusive licenses, which generated more profit. (When a station bought product on an exclusive license it meant the distributor could not sell it to other broadcasters within a specified area over a specified period of time. A nonexclusive license meant a cheaper product for the broadcaster but also the worry the distributor would sell to a competitor at the same time.) Thus the two competing groups in the U.K. planned on nonexclusive selling, even to themselves, meaning the two channels would be essentially the same. Since they would be so similar, why not join together? Yet, with one eye out for cries of monopoly Larry Michie noted that it was not likely to happen, for with nominal competition from two firms it was "safer this way."[38]

When it came to selling their product offshore American distributors continued the fiction that their material sold because it was popular, ignoring the realities of cartel-control of the arena and the cheapness of their fare. American suppliers had many problems with the Latin American market in the 1980s including various currency crises, slow payments and sometimes no payment at all. Expressing confidence that market would pull out of its problems, Telepictures president Michael Jay Solomon explained, "Meanwhile, we won't stop shipments. We're giving credit.... As a continuous supplier we should help them in their hour of need. At the end we'll get 100% of our money out, albeit late and without interest, but it's my responsibility to help out."[39]

Syd Silverman, publisher of *Variety* and grandson of that publication's 1905 founder, Sime Silverman, boasted that "Hollywood owns the world," meaning the growth of the Los Angeles creative community "has made American motion pictures and television programs overwhelmingly popular in virtually every country where they are exhibited." No matter what developments technology held in store, the "software, or the show, is still the essence of show business." Americans didn't understand foreign charges of cultural imperialism leveled at Hollywood because "we in America were inclined to take a breezy, open-market, let-the-people-decide approach to popular entertainment." Silverman added, "Our show business entrepreneurs stumble over each other in the rush to supply what the public demands."[40]

U.S. exporters played off region against region and delivery mechanism against delivery mechanism in sales strategy. Early U.S. sales to French pay-cable outlet Canal Plus, Murdoch's Sky Channel and a consortium of German publishers eager to lock up rights for what they hoped would be an emerging cable market in Germany put pressure on terrestrial television networks to bid higher for American product. Typically rights were sold by language, instead of country by country. Worldvision, for example, sold the German-language rights for "Love Boat" to the German publishers while selling the English-language rights to that program to a satellite feed that covered Germany. U.S. exporters gave Canal Plus a six-month window before selling the same product to the terrestrial outlets in competition. Some firms sold nothing at all to these newcomers. Explaining why Telepictures avoided deals with Sky Channel and Canal Plus, president Michael Solomon said, "I just don't think the market is ready yet," meaning the prices were not high enough.[41]

With so many people, China always beckoned Hollywood as a potentially huge market. However, the nation had little money to spend on foreign television programming. To the rescue came CBS with a barter deal; no hard currency had to be expended by the Chinese. In the works for two years, a deal was finally signed between CBI and state-run China Central Television (CCTV) in 1983 that called for CBS to provide 64 hours of regularly scheduled CBS-owned American programming, complete with commercials. That concept was developed by CBI midway though the protracted bargaining. CBS's John Eger saw it all as part of an "evolving relationship" with CCTV that would come to include coproductions, networking and marketing advice. CCTV got to choose the 64 hours from 700 hours work of news, entertainment and sports. Chosen material was to run on Chinese television from 8 to 9 P.M. each Friday, after the Chinese news. At the time of the deal,

CCTV had at least two channels in each province, with signals reaching over one-third of its population. An estimated 16 million sets were then in use in China, with as many as 30 viewers per set. The Chinese network broadcast about 30 hours of material a week, mostly news, instruction and drama. CBI was in charge of selling ad time, keeping part of the income from those sales. It was the price CCTV agreed to pay in order to receive those 64 hours of programming for "free." Eger called the deal "a milestone in international broadcasting."[42]

Asked about the type of programs the Chinese selected Eger said, "their goals are very different—first to inform and educate." As to the barter deal in general, Eger remarked, "We don't call it a barter arrangement for several reasons. One, that has a lot of connotations. We call it a sponsorship program arrangement by which we give them the 64 hours, which they will run on Friday after the news.... That was more important than anything else: that it be regularly scheduled programming and that we have five minutes in each hour that we could sell [commercial] time." He added that CBS wanted to make the deal work because informing consumers "is what advertising really is about."[43]

In the deal China got to keep half of the ad revenue generated. When CBS vice president Arthur Kane was asked if China might worry about Western influences and eventually cancel the deal, he said, "But the thing about TV is that once people start watching certain kinds of programs they get used to them. And when they reach that point you can do almost anything to them except take those programs away." In its first year of operation, 1984, the deal was not as successful as CBS hoped. Revenue was well short of the expected $3 million. CBS offered mainly U.S. transnationals a full-year package on a take-it-or-leave-it basis. Hoping for the maximum twelve advertisers, it got only six. For the second year a more flexible CBS offered advertisers a choice of three-, six-, and twelve-month packages.[44]

CBS was happy with the barter arrangement because in exchange for those hours of programming "CCTV has provided United States advertisers with what amounts to enormous audiences on mainland China." One result was that a developing nation was exposed to Western marketing techniques and U.S. advertisers were able to "communicate" with consumers who, although they could not buy products directly, could influence buying decisions made in a highly centralized economy. As a CBS executive related in a speech, "For example, one of the advertisers, Stauffer Chemical, told a reporter that its advertising campaign in China was designed to interest farmers in a brand name for a rice herbicide that would be eventually bought through a central purchasing office."[45]

A year's worth of ads, 52 minutes, cost each sponsor $300,000. When CCTV bought a second batch of CBS reruns for 1986 screening, CBS signed up four advertisers from the 1984 broadcasting of the first batch of shows:

Boeing, Kodak, Weyerhauser and Stauffer Chemical. IBM declined to renew. New sponsors for 1986 included Philips Electronics and Colgate-Palmolive. American firms could buy commercial time from CCTV for programs other than the CBS reruns, but they couldn't specify when they would appear. The Chinese network aired commercials on randomly selected shows with all ads, regardless of national origin, rotated through the slots. U.S. advertisers preferred the CBS arrangement because it gave them control. According to the *New York Times*, "Unlike Americans, the Chinese do not tune commercials out — or off. People sit still for advertising because they are not saturated with it." Still, some firms were worried due to the absence of television polling organizations. A Kodak spokesperson wailed that "We don't know who is watching, when they are watching, where they are watching from."[46]

CBS Broadcast International executive Donald Wear stated the television industry should not be trapped into thinking a barter deal was a panacea; it was merely a "good alternative when license fees are small." The primary goal was to make an international television broadcasting sale, and all methods would be considered. Because there was no television polling in China, CBS commissioned its own "audience recall" studies for advertisers. NBC International executive Eric Stanley called barter "just another arrow in the quiver of the international distributor." Higher transaction and incidental expenses made it less attractive to some distributors.[47]

Nonetheless, barter quickly became the method of choice for Chinese television in this period. Disney signed a 1986 deal with CCTV for 104 30-minute episodes of Disney cartoons to be aired over a two-year period. Two minutes of ads were allowed per episode, with Disney having the right to sell that time. What drew Disney to China, explained company president Frank Wells, was "the allure of hundreds of millions of potential consumers for Disney products" — particularly those bearing the likeness of Donald Duck and Mickey Mouse. Throughout China at the time one could purchase items ranging from coffee cups to pens to thermometers to children's books, all bearing the likeness of the duck and the mouse but all unauthorized and unlicensed — meaning no royalties to Disney. Stating he had won a commitment from the Chinese that they would begin enforcing Disney's trademark rights in China, Wells added, "We decided the first move should be to bring the characters to national television."[48]

One year later CCTV struck a deal with Paramount/MCA (Universal) to screen 100 hours of programs, two hours each week on a fixed night in prime time. According to MCA at that time 90 percent of China's population had access to a television, although for many that access was through some sort of communal viewing situation, not at home. Some 65 million sets in the country were viewed by 370 million viewers who watched regularly. Series to be screened included "Columbo" and "Marcus Welby, M.D." (both from Universal) and "Family Affair" and "Star Trek" (both from Paramount). This barter deal allowed the U.S. firms a maximum of five minutes of time to sell each hour to advertisers. As this marked the debut of U.S. drama shows in Chinese prime time, *Variety* reported that China had finally "a chance to sink its teeth into American programs." The Chinese agreed to do all the dubbing themselves.[49]

At a 1987 television symposium in France in 1987, allegations surfaced that French networks got certain U.S. programs for little or no money or were even paid to program certain shows — the toy-driven U.S. shows. At that time in America there were 24 male action toys, 17 of which had their own television shows. Allegations were that toy groups were selling cheap television programs to broadcasters with the sole purpose of marketing associated merchandise. One unnamed U.S. executive said producers never offered to pay French network A2 to have shows programmed but the network had received proposals for a supply of programs at zero cost. Said A2 spokesman Laurence Kaufmann, "We have always refused these offers. We have always paid, though in some cases it has been very little." Kaufmann declared that program selection was always on a quality basis, never on the basis of sharing in merchandising income. An American senior licensing executive, also unidentified, stated it was widely known offers "are being made to networks in France of payment in return for programming toy-driven television shows." A2 did admit it sometimes shared in merchandising income related to shows it aired but said it set a top limit of 20 percent on the share of licensing income it demanded from programs it broadcast.[50]

Licensing Corporation of America (a Warner subsidiary) had a major "prize" on its hands in the late 1980s in the person of game show "Wheel of Fortune" letter turner Vanna White. The company introduced a Vanna White line of clothing, hoping to generate $50 million in retail sales in the first years because the show was seen all over the world and White had an "appeal to women overseas as well as stateside." According to Daniel Simon of Carolco Licensing, by the summer of 1988 worldwide revenues generated by toys, T-shirts and other items bearing the likeness of the Sylvester Stallone action hero had gone over $200 million. Concluded *Variety*, "the licensers and merchandisers seem to have one sure card to play — the insatiable consumer appetite of kids."[51]

If foreign income from television product was incidental in the 1950s, it was integral in the 1980s. Lorimar TV executive Michael Jay Solomon remarked "We don't produce anything until we've mixed the international revenues into the formula. And if the international dollars are not going to soak up the production deficits, the program shouldn't get made." Phil Howort, president of LBS Telecommunications, observed, "The linkage between the domestic and international marketplaces has become absolutely essential. Projected international revenues are an integral part of the financing of American-produced programs." A slick action show like "Miami Vice" could rack up $375,000 in offshore sales. A miniseries could gross $3 million in foreign revenue, and a made-for-television movie could gross up to $600,000. There was no big money in domestic syndication of those genres "because minis and television movies don't rerun well." Noting that Italy was glutted with American product, Solomon said, "But American product tends not to do well in Italy anyway. A slickly produced local show will do better in Italy than an American product. Come to think of it, that's true not only of Italy but of all other countries as well." But, pointed out reporter John Dempsey, "broadcasters in these countries find it cheaper to buy glossy American product than to pony up the big bucks it would take to produce equivalent programs locally." Even if offshore revenue was crucial domestic revenue remained the key because "if revenue projections from U.S. sales are not substantial, the program will never get beyond the idea stage."[52]

The 1980s was a crucial decade for offshore television as private, commercial television arrived in country after country. Even where state-run networks held their ground the amount of commercials aired tended to increase. Initially on French television there were no commercials at all; then a number were allowed but only between programs, with no actual program interruption allowed. Then spot ads were allowed to break into shows. By 1987 one of France's three state-owned networks, TF1, had been sold to a private consortium. The maximum of commercials on French television allowed had moved from 18 minutes per day in 1985 to 12 minutes per hour in 1987. All this took place under a Socialist government. It was all driven by advertisers, many of whom focused increasingly on global advertising.[53]

When the International Advertising Association formed its Global Media Commission (GMC) in 1984, one of the first acts of that commission was to release a position paper, "Global Marketing," which talked about the concept of "world-class products being sold by uniform advertising campaigns on commercial television around the world." That paper spoke also of "a new age of television abundance." Commission chairman was CBS executive John Eger, who saw his company as a supplier of programming for advertisers: "We see the possibility of CBS playing a significant role in all ad-supported media around the world.... TV is changing abroad. The government has no money," explained Eger. Under a consent decree signed in 1980 with the U.S. Justice Department the network was allowed to produce two and one-half hours a week of entertainment programming for prime time, eight hours weekly for daytime and eleven hours for early fringe time. CBS had long complained that Hollywood producers blocked CBS's financial participation in network programming.[54]

During 1985 the GMC, "the high priests of global marketing," met in London, England, where it passed a resolution calling for the "universal right to advertise legitimate goods and services in all media in all countries" and to "seek such rights for those involved in transborder transmission of information and advertising." Among the 60 members of that lobby group were Coca-Cola, Pepsi-Cola, ITT, Time Inc., ABC, CBS, Eastman Kodak, Canon, Boeing, Gillette, Mitsubishi and Matsushita plus leading ad agencies and other commercial broadcasters. Additionally, the GMC demanded the "lifting of arbitrary, artificial and unnecessary restrictions" on advertising and their replacement by "responsible freedom." Since its formation the GMC had adopted an "educational" role in an effort to persuade governments and broadcasters that if given free rein advertising got economies moving, created jobs, funded broadcasting and stimulated prosperity in the print media. A theme stressed by the group was that advertising would pay the bill for the new media — the coming of pervasive satellite television. One of the group's hopes was that the barter system being used then by U.S. exporters in China might be adopted in Europe, with advertisers intent on global marketing picking up the tab for the programs "that are given to broadcasters. These barter shows would have some commercials in place with some unsold spots left as sweeteners for the buying station." With television advertising in the top ten European markets then estimated to total $3.9 billion annually the GMC estimated that if commercial television were "liberated" from its current restrictions that television ad total could double by the end of the century.[55]

As global advertising grew along with global television it favored world brands such as Coca-Cola and McDonald's, which used the same trademarks and packaging around the world. Advertising agencies merged into bigger and bigger entities. Saatchi & Saatchi became the world's largest ad agency through a series of mergers climaxing in 1986 with the $400 million purchase of the Ted Bates Agency. McCann–Erickson Worldwide chairman Robert James explained his company's interest in a global approach: "It's a shrinking world, and we tend to have [similar] attitudes about products, and therefore we can be approached the same way. And you can sell ... the same shirts all around the world, the same shoes, the same toothpaste and the same soft drinks. Those are the things that we all have in common and, sure as rain, they're growing, there's more of them. So there's going to be more global advertising as well." John Eger remarked, "It's a global business. Production, distribution and those who support it [advertisers] are global." He saw the role of those ads as "providing consumers with more product information through competitive commercials ... helping develop 'world class' programming."[56]

Worldwide advertising expenditures were estimated at $200 billion in 1986 while worldwide television advertising that same year was estimated at only $30 billion — there was much room for growth. Earl Jones, who owned his own U.S.-based international ad agency believed that as more programs and commercials from America penetrated newly privatized offshore airwaves those initial cries of "cultural imperialism" in the new era of global television would "give way to the realities of satisfied viewers who appreciate the expanded range of program viewing choices."[57]

Block-booking continued to be a powerful selling tool for Hollywood through the 1980s. Known in the past by such names as "tie-ins" and "packaging," *Variety* noted in 1981 that the practice was then called "sales by volume." It was a familiar way of doing business in the American film and television distribution business. "In order to get what you want you have to buy the rest of the pack — turkeys and all." Although it was illegal in the U.S., "distributors try it all the time." Offshore it was a different story, as it was perfectly legal for U.S. exporters to use the practice as long as they didn't block-book at home. "In exchange for a popular series or theatrical, an Arab country, for example, may be forced to take repeats as well as a slew of ne'er-do-well movies of the week." In larger countries with increasing domestic production "the majors have trouble ramming home any package deal. But in the secondary markets — the Arab states, Asia, Africa, and even in some larger markets like Latin America and Australia — the majors are in the driver's seat and packaging is a way of life." When asked if the U.S. distributors imposed block-booking, one Arab broadcasting executive replied, "Sure, they do it all the time." Was he forced to take the package? "Sure.... They sort of have you over a barrel." Generally, the majors denied the practice existed. One executive said, "Nobody packages anymore. The market's become too sophisticated." Another said, "Oh no, we don't do that." However, one executive for a major did say, "We don't call it packaging any more. We call it sales by volume. We just can't afford to let some of this product go for those prices." That is, since smaller, poorer markets didn't pay much for the product they *did* want, it was alright to offload material they did *not* want on them at the same time. Concluded *Variety*, "But whether it's called packaging, tie-ins or sales by volume, it may soon become more widespread as the worldwide demand for programming becomes insatiable — fueled by the growth of broadcasting, networks, satellites, cable, homevideo and all the rest."[58]

Midway through the 1980s when U.S. exporters had over 20 miniseries on display for potential purchase at an annual television sales fair in Cannes, France, reporter Jack Loftus declared, "look for the U.S. distributors to rewrite the book on block booking — packaging the desirable with the not so desirable. In the U.S. block booking is illegal. But overseas ... block booking is both common and legal."[59]

Coproductions continued to be touted as the wave of the future but in fact took place only rarely. For coproductions most U.S. producers insisted on three criteria, wrote Jack Loftus, "a U.S. presale, artistic control and worldwide rights." Going further, Lorimar Telepictures' Michael Jay Solomon emphasized it was essential that coproductions be in English and that those coproductions have writers, actors and distributors capable of producing in English since Americans would not accept dubbing into English.[60]

While Hollywood enjoyed cartel control over the market it became extremely upset at any sign of similar activity offshore. By the late 1980s foreigners such as Robert Maxwell of Britain and Silvio Berlusconi of Italy owned or had plans to own television outlets in two or more nations. Luxembourg-based CLT then owned stations in Belgium, France, Luxembourg and West Germany. Hollywood worried these programmers intended to combine their stations or their cross-border reach to give them more clout when buying programs. U.S. suppliers preferred to sell market by market. Both Berlusconi and CLT had tried in the past to buy for their combined holdings on a one-deal basis, but Columbia International president Nicholas Bingham told them, "No…. We don't do that type of selling." Another spokesman for a Hollywood major explained, "If the combined price from all markets equals what I can get if I negotiate separately with each country, then I might look at it." MCA International president Colin Davis noted that sellers found the going more profitable by playing the channels against each other. Another annoyance for Hollywood was signal spillover. Signals from French network A2 spilled over into Italy. Complained Bingham, "Governments aren't sympathetic with rights owners. Why is A-2 available in Italy? It isn't easy for program owners to stomach that type of uncompensated crossover." The coming of DBS promised, of course, much more signal spillover. However, said Bingham, "There will be no problem selling DBS to programmers provided you get the justified price." At that time Sky Channel, despite its cross-border reach — picked up mainly by homes in Holland, Belgium, West Germany and Scandinavia — paid what was considered by the majors a very low price of $3,000 for a one-hour program. As a result, Sky, like CLT, "has difficulties obtaining top shows," reported Bruce Alderman.[61]

In terms of market potential the American television exporters turned to Europe in the 1980s; it was finally becoming the promised land. Said CBS International vice president Don Weir, "In France you've got new channels coming in and privatization of state-run networks; Italy has been a pathfinder and continues to expand; the U.K. is re-examining its private and public television channels, and Scandinavia is taking a look at satellites." NBC International executive Jerry Wexler said that "many U.S. programs can't get placed in foreign markets because there isn't enough room for them," but satellites "will give them an additional outlet." Another reason for a more intense focus on Europe was a decline in other areas. Robert Bramson, president of MCA International, remarked that in Japan there was then only one U.S. series running in Japanese prime time, and "Australia is really no different. They're not taking as much as they used to."[62]

When European television executives met in Italy for a three-day conference in 1983 on television a primary topic discussed was the "Global Success of U.S. TV Series — Why?" At the time U.S. series such as "Dallas," "Dynasty," and "Starsky and Hutch" were seen throughout much of the world. Nobody at the conference had an answer to the question. American media writer Erik Barnouw reportedly came closest to pinpointing the reasons when he said American series "Constitute carefully constructed popular entertainment involving the common run of emotions, situations, conflicts, etc., and each series can be acquired for a lot less that a similar series produced in each given country." Barnouw added that America produced "a homogenized product that represents no one culture. It is formula fiction that endlessly recycles a mythology of its own, a mythology that can be understood anywhere but is really nowhere." Hollywood favored the unending series in which continuing characters were seen in endless variations of a standard plot formula which lent itself to endless foreign syndication in any order a specific telecaster desired.[63]

Looking at that rapidly expanding market in Europe reporter Morrie Gelman wondered if new European outlets would have to buy second-rate U.S. product because their limited capital in the beginning precluded their buying much else. Lorimar Telepictures' Michael Jay Solomon said that rather than becoming a "dumping" ground for such material those new television services in the beginning "perhaps because they don't have the advertising revenues as yet — will tend to buy ... 'quality' reruns." One example he cited was Sky Channel: "The money they pay us does not enable us to sell them our new series. So we will only sell them older series." Thus, in 1987, Lorimar sold Sky the CBS series which ran from 1963 to 1965, "My Favorite Martian." Solomon admitted his company would not be able to sell it to the BBC or any other major European networks. Westerworld Television executive Matthew Ody declared that for firms such as his, an independent television distributor, there was then an opportunity to "off-load a lot of catalog which previously was not acceptable or was sold and shown, but no longer is rerun" but that "the money offered for product is going to be disappointing" for those four to five years of new commercial television ventures. If it meant "very low dollars" for each individual series sold (from $500 for a half-hour episode up to $4,000 for a feature film) it was still attractive because "it's bulk, quantity, that is attractive to an American distribution company because it looks like big figures for old catalog." Solomon stated Lorimar would not make its new programs available at reduced license fees to the new European television services to gain a foothold. What distributors like Lorimar and others were doing was designing programs for the new services within their program budgets. Said Solomon, "Any station that gives me a budget and tells me this is all I have to spend I can design up a schedule for them of reruns and older theatrical feature films, plus television features."[64]

By 1987 the top eight markets for American television product accounted for 80 percent of U.S. total offshore sales; five of them were in Europe — Britain, France, Germany, Italy and Scandinavia (considered a group) — with the others being Australia, Canada and Japan. Latin America's share of U.S. business stood at 15 percent of the total, down considerably from years earlier. Jack Healy of ABC remarked, "These are good times to be selling programs overseas," and Worldvision's Bert Cohen said enthusiastically, "I anticipate the continued rebirth of evergreens (in Europe) where they've been on the shelf for several years." "Evergreen" is a euphemism for "oldie."[65]

One example of the effect of new, commercialized television on U.S. sales in Europe could be seen in France where, in 1986, Lorimar sold its long-running hit series "Knot's Landing"—thirteen episodes at $12,000 to $15,000 each. One year later, with one state-run channel privatized and new commercial networks in operation Lorimar sold 150 episodes of "Knot's" for around $50,000 each. Remarked Lorimar's Solomon, "In markets where you've had only one or two stations, you now have four or five or six. It's had an enormous economic impact." Producing a one-hour drama in Europe cost $500,000; buying a U.S. hit cost one-tenth of that. World export value of television product in 1986 was estimated at $1 billion, 79 percent of it was American. Western Europe was then the biggest customer for U.S. television product taking about 56 percent of the total. From time to time the point was made that U.S. television product was popular offshore because, among other things, U.S. producers always had the international market in mind. As to that international aspect of U.S. shows Paramount Pictures president for international television Bruce Gordon admitted, "American production is still going to produce what the American networks want and discount what international wants."[66]

According to a survey conducted by Prognos, a media research firm based in Basel, Switzerland, the number of television channels in western Europe grew from 37 in 1983 to 61 in 1986; at the same time programming hours more than doubled, from 110,000 to 230,000 hours. In its survey Prognos predicted that by the end of the 1980s the volume of imported television programming in western Europe would be more than 50 percent, compared to 30 percent in 1983, and "Producers in the U.S. will profit most by the growing demand."[67]

In a 1987 speech Lorimar chairman Merv Adelson wondered what kind of product the consumer wanted to see in all those new offshore markets. He favored more international coproductions, primarily to head off foreign criticisms of cultural imperialism. He believed that "high-quality but low-cost" U.S. shows would make it possible for many of those foreign stations to stay on the air "as they develop their own local production process." That would lead to more coproductions, and an eventual two-way street in television product flow would further reduce charges of cultural imperialism. Adelson also was hopeful about the use of barter. "But achieving the full potential of barter will require a company to align itself closely with multinational advertising agencies and advertisers." A key factor in satisfying global audiences was to keep in mind it was dominated by a youth audience. "It only makes sense that a young person in Europe would have more in common with a young person in the United States or Australia than with his own parents—and research bears this out," said Adelson. He concluded, "It seems to me the trick to meeting the demands of this brave new world of international entertainment is not entirely different from satisfying our own audiences."[68]

That the new television scene was limited to the big money players could be seen in the costs involved. Annual rental for one satellite transponder (one station) ran from $6 to $11 million on satellites launched in Europe in the late 1980s. When the U.K. government approved a franchise for DBS service by British Satellite Broadcasting, the start-up costs for the system (four services on three channels) were estimated at $1 billion to $1.25 billion. Denmark's government provided $43 million for the start-up of a commercial, second channel in that country. Ad revenues were estimated at $58 million yearly.[69]

For 20th Century–Fox the foreign market was a good place to sell its miniseries and made-for-television movies particularly because there was a poor domestic market for the syndication (reruns) of such product. Reporter John Dempsey remarked, "With a steady flow of highly saleable theatrical movies funneled through its worldwide distribution operation, Fox can boost the revenues of television movies and minis by packaging them with the theatricals for foreign sales." As one executive put it, "Theatricals can serve as very powerful locomotives to pull all sorts of other product."[70]

As the 1980s began, the cost of maintaining public television in European nations such as France, Germany, Italy and the U.K. was becoming a bigger burden to state treasuries. While the cost of the annual television license fee — the main source of television financing in those countries — could always be raised it was very much a political issue, with politicians often loathe to impose a license fee increase. As early as 1980 there were hundreds of private television stations throughout Italy, and according to MPEA research "They have become a potent new program buying force and while they do not offer big prices, combined they represent the biggest syndication market outside the U.S." Ad hoc networks were then being formed from among those outlets by syndications, and "These are often linked by ad agencies which buy shows, implant commercials and distribute them on an exclusive regional basis to 25–30 stations covering most of the country." Part of such deals was that each station involved agreed to show each program at the same time as all the other outlets, effectively creating national networks to compete against the RAI's three networks. If the laws of the marketplace did not apply to France and Germany in 1980 it was hoped they soon would. One push in that direction would be the arrival of satellite television, which would give recipient nations little or no control. Wrote reporter Roger Watkins, "Nations may be getting commercial services beamed in from outside sources — without restriction and against their will.... One form of protection against outside commercialism, politicians figure, is to establish internally the means for advertisers to reach the video audience. It's an argument that's bound to gain sway in a decade when the falling economic barometer and ailing domestic economies make the cost of state-television a vote-getting issue." It was believed that some countries gave official backing and blessing to cable television systems in their territory — offering the potential for more U.S. product being available — as a way of blunting the effects of satellite television. If viewers took the satellite signals through an intermediary cable company — in lieu of direct-from-satellite reception — some measure of control could still be exercised since the cable systems were locally based. In the direct-reception scenario a government's only action was against individual dish owners, which was often politically unacceptable.[71]

Scandinavian countries faced the same budgetary restraints. For political reasons license fees could be raised only by small increments, often not enough to cover increasing costs, which went even higher if more domestic production was attempted. Home video was then starting to be able to outbid the state broadcasters for some product, raising costs still higher. If a state telecaster didn't increase its bidding and lost product to home video it ran the risk of losing viewers. When viewership declined it became harder for the state broadcaster to justify the money it currently received, let alone any increase. Nevertheless with much public hostility to commercial television there was no easy answer. In Norway a minority Conservative government tried to slip commercial television in by way of the back door. It announced it would establish an experimental television operation as a test. Behind that lay the theory that once the public had sampled something it would be hooked and not let the government take it away.[72]

One critic of the rapid spread of commercialized, private television in Italy was Milan University communications professor Carlo Sartori: "The American economic system could not exist as it does without television as it is. The three networks are in business to produce viewers, not programs." He held out little hope for any significant changes in commercial television programming. Responding to the idea that networks gave people what they wanted, Sartori declared, "Audiences may want certain kinds of programs because they get those kinds of programs from the beginning." If audiences were not aware of alternatives because they had not been given them then it set up a sort of limiting vicious circle. At the time some hailed the coming of pay television, cable television, satellite television, and so on, as all these new outlets would increase television's diversity, somehow democratize it more. To that idea, Sartori said, "No, the programs will still come from the same sources and only the big corporations will be able to afford to jump on the new wave."[73]

By the middle of the 1980s when reporter Jack Loftus surveyed the commercial television situation in western Europe, he said, "it does appear that European parliaments wrestling with the controversial issues of commercial broadcasting probably will yield one day to the onslaught from big business, especially the media giants, eager to carve out a stake in the new media." As to France, which had just approved no fewer than three new commercial networks, that was done, wrote Loftus, by a "Socialist government gone bonkers for commercial broadcasting." One of those was owned by Frenchman Jerome Seydoux, in partnership with Italy's Silvio Berlusconi. All of those new networks meant the price for U.S. product would increase. A Lorimar spokesman commented "Berlusconi whets the appetite of the European audience. He's going to do the same thing in France that he's done in Italy, and he's going to be looking for a lot of American product."[74]

Once commercial television became fully private not only would ads be accepted, but all restrictions would also be removed. In America the old advertising guidelines of the National Association of Broadcasters, which allowed 268.5 advertising minutes for an 18-hour broadcast day (14.9 minutes per hour), were voided by court order in the 1980s. Lobbying for that move were, of course, the large advertisers. At the same time commercial broadcasters in the U.K. were permitted no more than 70 minutes of commercials daily (they had a shorter broadcast day). And those regulations, harsh for advertisers by U.S. standards, were among the loosest in all of Europe. Estimates were that if restrictions on advertising in Europe were "liberalized" to a point comparable with U.K. standards an additional $2 billion in ad expenditures could be expected annually. Writing about the privatization of European television in the *Columbia Journal of World Business* in 1987, Steven Wildman declared, "To date the biggest beneficiaries of the demand for more programming and heightened broadcaster competition have been established program suppliers especially those from the U.S." As the number of outlets increased "there is a sizeable lag between the opening of new distributor channels and the full response of domestic program industries. As a result, the short-term outlook is for increasing sales and profits for suppliers of American programming as privatization takes hold in other countries on the continent. Over the longer run, however, ... evidence from other markets suggest that European program industries may satisfy much of the demand for programming that is being unleashed by privatization." Still, a smaller share of a much larger market would translate into significantly increased European earnings compared to levels prior to privatization. When it all played out Wildman was confident "the position of the U.S. as the dominant source of internationally traded films and programs" would be maintained.[75]

Holland still had just two networks in 1987, both state run. The Dutch public preferred local product, as the approximately 70 percent of transmission time devoted to Dutch programs drew some 85 percent of the total viewership. Most households received 15 cable services. Any commercial service initiated in Holland would find local programming costs too high to feed a viable commercial service, leaving only foreign product (mostly U.S.)—and thus less popular—available in volume at the "right price."[76]

In the wake of Italy's booming private television situation, France's granting new licenses for commercial outlets and privatizing the most popular of the three state-run networks and Spain's licensing of two private channels, one account stated, "Once a vast wasteland for viewers, advertisers and investors, European television is turning into a go-go business…. The revolution's most immediate beneficiaries are viewers…. With viewers getting more riveting fare, advertisers see vast opportunity." Beneficiaries were not limited to a few broadcasters who would become wealthy, but would encompass all because the explosion of private television "could boost whole economies. TV advertising is the world's most powerful sales tool." Even then, in 1987, restrictions on advertising abounded on European television. Most Scandinavian stations banned most ads; the three state-run German stations banned commercials in prime time and all day Sunday. Television ad revenues in Europe were expected to increase from $5 billion in 1986 to $7.5 billion in 1990; by contrast U.S. television ad spending was about $22 billion in 1986. About 20 satellite-delivered services were then in operation over Europe, all trying to attract customers, all losing money. Europe was expected to need 473,000 hours of programs a year, double the 1987 volume, and "The big winner will be the U.S., which already supplies more than half of Europe's imported programming." After being privatized, France's TF1 bought 160 episodes of "Knot's Landing" in 1986 for $43,750 per one-hour episode. Just a year earlier, before privatization and the licensing of other new private outlets, the situation was radically different. Said Michael Jay Solomon, president of distributor Lorimar Telepictures, "Before competition, we would have sold the episodes for $25,000 a piece. It would have taken them six months to decide, and we would have had to pay the $12,000-an-hour dubbing costs." Concluded the article, "Advertisers will learn — some better than others — the astonishing effectiveness of heavy mass TV advertising. On the tube or off, television in Europe is going to be a lot more fun to watch."[77]

By 1989 the surge to commercial television in Europe, deregulations, the selling of state monopolies, new commercial channels, cable and satellite delivery was well underway. In *Forbes* magazine John Marcom declared, "Throughout Western Europe, state monopolies on television broadcasting are crumbling. The winner: Hollywood." According to Disney executive Etienne de Villiers, a few years back a half-hour episode of a U.S. sitcom such as "Cheers" might have earned $25,000 Europe-wide, whereas in 1989 it could pull $75,000 or even $100,000. For Disney it wasn't just the money, as the company "is gaining better scheduling and a greater say in packaging and promotion." With the new EuroDisney then under construction outside Paris, "The company wants to use TV shows to drum up theme-park business as it long has in the U.S. The goal is three hours weekly of Disney-brand programming, a target it has met in Italy and France and is nearing in the U.K." According to Marcom, for 30 years the BBC and a commercial monopoly — "a group of sixteen companies that together form what's known as independent TV — tacitly decided which Hollywood products would air in the U.K. and kept prices for broadcasting rights to U.S. films or TV shows low." The two new satellite services promised to deliver an additional nine stations to British homes, upping the total received to thirteen stations. To compete with Sky Television (reincarnated from Sky Channel) British Broadcast Satellite (BSB) went on a shopping spree, with some deals stretching six years. It paid Columbia Pictures $160 million over several years for the rights to 175 films. In total, BSB lined up 1,800 movies involving up-front payments of around $175 million of the $1.2 billion total cost. Additionally BSB had to buy and launch its own satellite, with another $50 million budgeted for initial promotion. BSB's principal backers were U.K. media figures plus the local firm Granada TV and Australian media baron Alan Bond. Marcom stated, "It begins to look as if the owners of the entertainment software — the movies and filmed programs — will be the big winners as the broadcasters throw money into the competitive fight." Western Europe spent an estimated $675 million on U.S. television fare in 1987, a figure forecast to increase to $2.6 billion in 1992. As government control over television in Europe was being loosened, said Marcom, "entrepreneurs are being freed to feed the public what the public wants rather than what the governments think they should view." What Marcom failed to mention was what many others, including Rod Serling, had observed: commercial television presented what the advertiser wanted, not what the public desired. Nor did those advertisers take a backseat to governments in terms of censoring, controlling, reshaping, interfering with, and so forth the material appearing on the tube. If Marcom saw a 16-member monopoly in the U.K. he neglected to see a much lower number of members in an American cartel that had greater control in its home market and no competition from local or foreign fare, as commercial television did from the BBC in the U.K.[78]

All of the new outlets and delivery systems in Europe helped to drive up the cost of buying feature films. To protect his firm, Degeto, a Frankfurt-based company that bought for Germany's nine-station, state-run ARD network — one of two in Germany then — Franz Everschor explained that Degeto tried to buy cable and satellite rights along with terrestrial rights, but the U.S. suppliers resisted. He bought around 180 movies a year in 1984 and for years had been able to maintain prices at around $45,000 for an average title, but that was in the days when there was only competition between the two state networks. Home-video companies in Germany were then starting to offer more for a film than the networks. Nonetheless the two networks aired more than 800 films a year in total; some 50 percent were American.[79]

Prices for films shot up so much in Italy that the government financial committee began to delay approving the contracts for some of the more expensive acquisitions made by public telecaster RAI — such contract approvals were always necessary but had always been swift and virtually automatic before. RAI executive Giuseppe Cereda commented that what RAI paid in 1983 was the market value that year and the days when RAI paid $25,000 for a feature film "are over and the ministerial committee should understand that this scale ended when RAI's monopoly position ended."[80]

Twentieth Century–Fox owner Rupert Murdoch went to China to meet with television officials in 1985. That meeting began negotiations regarding Fox's showing its films on Chinese television. Agreement was finally reached, and the first Chinese nationally televised broadcast of U.S. movies began in October 1987 with "The Sound of Music." In the one-year deal, Fox got the same time slot over a 52-week period. Although Fox received no money it was allowed to have three minutes at the beginning of the broadcast and three minutes at the end for advertising. Films broadcast were selected by Chinese officials, who reportedly had access to all 2,000-plus titles in the Fox library from which to choose. Others selected included "How Green Was My Valley," "Broken Arrow," "The Grapes of Wrath," "The Day the Earth Stood Still," and most of Shirley Temple's movies. The most recent title selected was "Patton," released in 1970.[81]

Fox made a multimillion-dollar deal with Britain's commercial ITV network in 1989 for a film package of 80-plus titles. Block-booking formed part of the deal, for, as reporter Elizabeth Guider wrote, "As in most major deals in Britain each year, final package will also include some reruns … and some television movies and series." Helping to push up feature film prices in Britain was the additional competition from Sky TV and BSB. In the case of the former it was Murdoch's Sky TV buying films from Murdoch's Fox producer. Some British broadcasters responded by trying to buy collectively. In 1988 MGM/UA signed a deal with BSB and BBC providing for a package of films to be played first on BSB's Movie Channel (to be launched in 1989 as a pay-television service) and then 18 months later to be available on the BBC. Head of Fox TV in London Malcolm Vaughn said, "Our films are in constant circulation now. Rights are beginning to bounce from pay to free television, then back to free satellite."[82]

With the expansion of European outlets the three U.S. networks tried harder to sell their news programs offshore. By early in the 1980s CBS had formed CBS Broadcast International (CBI) to "go global." It then supplied news to Australia's Nine Network; to Italy's private Italia Uno; to the BBC and the U.K.'s new fourth network, the commercial Channel Four; to Germany's ARD network; and to all four Japanese networks. ABC was distributing "Good Morning America" to the Australian Nine Network. Optimistic about CBS's plans for some sort of global network was company executive John Eger who said, "the best chance for selling advertising world wide is by letting the networks into the international business. By extending the network you extend the advertising. The network doesn't just sell programming. It puts the audience and the advertiser together." For 1983, CBI projected news sales alone offshore would reach $4 million, more than half of which would be profit. The full affiliation packages CBI had with Italian Uno and Nine were each for five years and would each bring CBI $15 million — for news, sports and entertainment fare.[83]

By 1987 CBS had many deals around the world whereby CBS supplied a package of news items or an intact newscast from which the receiving nation selected the items it wanted to telecast. That year further inroads were made when France's private, pay-television service Canal Plus began broadcasting an intact, subtitled "CBS Evening News with Dan Rather" from CBS to 1.7 million households. Those newscasts, which aired in America Monday through Friday evenings, were telecast on a tape-delay basis the next day in France — Tuesday through Saturday from 7 to 8 A.M. That hour was one of three times per day when the pay service was offered free, as a teaser to attract subscribers. Although the subtitles were physically added by Canal Plus in France they came from CBS's own translations "because we want editorial control." U.S. advertising was deleted so that Canal Plus could sell the time for its own market. Two advertisers who signed on were American Express and Mobil Oil. The two partners shared equally in the profits after their individual costs were taken off the top. Government approval for the arrangement was necessary and given for a subtitled newscast as Canal Plus' charter otherwise required it to broadcast only in French.[84]

Within a couple of years the "CBS Evening News" had been sold in the intact version in Italy, Belgium, Japan and Monte Carlo in addition to France. Additionally CBS sold the program "60 Minutes" in full, intact original form or in segments, and also sold the format of the program. NBC made its first sale of the intact "NBC Nightly News with Tom Brokaw" to Italy's RAI in 1989. It aired in English with Italian subtitles at 7 A.M. the following day in Italy. As part of the deal NBC accepted RAI's terms of no commercials. As to why foreign networks would broadcast an intact American news show CBS executive Don Wear thought it was because offshore broadcasters are "generally interested in our perspective." ABC took a different approach to marketing its news shows, preferring to distribute that material through the London-based World TV News — 42.5 percent owned by Capital Cities/ABC. Subscribers could pick up individual news stories, in some cases using the video with the audio soundtrack.[85]

Meanwhile CNN had expanded itself to the point where it could be seen in 90 nations by the end of 1989. However, in most of those it could only be seen in hotels. Since the hotels were reluctant to pay for the CNN service and since the audience size was too small to attract many ads, CNN International was losing big money. In sports broadcasting America's best-known exclusive sports channel ESPN (owned by Capital Cities/ABC) was on view in some 60 countries where it allowed offshore broadcasters to customize sports events from raw footage rather than giving them nothing but the intact

U.S. cablecast. Those ESPN foreign feeds leaned toward more obscure sports events such as cycling races, Davis Cup matches, supercross racing, surfing and truck/tractor pulls. The network claimed there was a "great deal of interest" in the latter overseas since tractor pulls were new and different to foreigners. In reality those events were cheaper for ESPN. In any case the sports channel had no offshore rights to pro football or to pro baseball.[86]

As in the past offshore producers continued to try to sell their television material to American stations. As in the past they had virtually no success. When a number of French officials complained that the French saw so many U.S. films and television materials that the U.S. should respond by showing proportionately as many French shows at home, *Variety*'s publisher Syd Silverman responded by saying, "An American is unlikely to understand such reasoning because we're not accustomed to extensive government intervention in cultural affairs." He did admit that "it is all but impossible for a European television show to get exposure on a commercial network in this country." Silverman did not explain why that was so except to declare that most European programming "is slow-paced and dull."[87]

A television selling market called A–MIP took place in Miami in 1983. Ostensibly it was for foreigners to present their wares for possible purchase by American television. Reporter Roger Watkins commented, "Given the differing philosophical bases of American and most other television systems, particularly the state-run networks of Europe, there would seem to be little off-the-shelf programming from abroad that would slip easily into American skeds." Europeans who had come to America over the years had learned that. For Watkins the usual reasons were involved: "Slow pacing, unfamiliar language (or dubbed product), unknown talent and the lack of a Hollywood gloss will render much of what's on display a pain-in-the-eye for local syndicators looking for pickups." Still, many arrived from Europe and came year after year in hope because the U.S. market was so big and so rich. Actually such events as A–MIP were often used for reverse purposes. Said Horst Schering, a German television executive, "If the Americans attempt to turn the tables on us and instead of turning up to buy our programs they try to use the market as another chance to sell their programs to us — then it will be the last time we show up." Some new arrivals from eastern Europe were puzzled by the fact their buying of American shows did not promote a reciprocal reaction from the Americans. As Watkins observed, "Along with the rest of the Europeans, they'll have a lot of learning to do at A–MIP." While a country, say Poland, bought U.S. product, the idea that the U.S. would buy anything for television from Film Polski for domestic telecasting struck Watkins as "almost ludicrous."[88]

At a session of the National Association of TV Programming Executives (NATPE) a panel of American television executives picked apart a sampling of foreign programming hopeful of making U.S. station deals and, said *Variety*, "sent the bulk of the offshore product packing." Those executives reiterated a long-heard rationale to the foreigners: "To succeed with placing product in the U.S. market you have to produce programming with U.S. viewer taste in mind, not as an afterthought." That panel agreed unanimously that the bulk of the offshore product would "be relegated to the narrow-casting wastelands within the U.S. market, and at best could be repackaged to work for the PBS web, cable or homevideo." Although the panelists all agreed the production values of the programs presented were top-notch "and in some cases superior to U.S. standards," it didn't matter. One executive admonished off-shore producers to "do their homework" researching the subject's potential, format and placement.[89]

German network ZDF head of sales Rainer Regensburger admitted that despite forays to U.S. trade fairs sales to the U.S. remain "very difficult for us." He added, "We talk to PBS a lot, but the results are small." ZDF sold around 1,200 hours of programming to foreign markets in 1984, 75 percent of it going to European stations with Italy the main customer.[90]

Reporter John Dempsey stated in 1987 that "distributors of foreign television programs need not apply for a time-period berth on commercial television stations in the U.S.," with rare exceptions. As to why that was so MCA TV International president, Colin Davis said, "American product tends to be faster-paced and have better production values" than television shows produced abroad. Explained Lorimar's Michael Jay Solomon, "The magic word is pace. Foreign programming is too parochial. Their programmers don't think enough in terms of attracting a mass audience." Observed MGM/UA executive Norm Horowitz, "Foreign shows are not produced in either the tempo or the style of American programs. The foreign stars are not familiar to American audiences, the settings are not familiar — you've gotta reinvent the wheel to get these shows on television in the U.S." New World TV's international division president John McNamara added that foreign television programs "don't factor in peaks and crescendos throughout their show to build up to the commercial breaks. Their crescendos come at the end because they don't have all those commercial breaks." He continued, "And the subject matter of foreign shows tends to be more serious — American stations are looking for action adventure and fluff. And the social problems are different. Hospital strikes are a common occurrence in Europe, so they crop up as drama in a foreign show much more than in an American show." What little foreign fare did appear on U.S. television came mainly from English-speaking countries such as the U.K. or Canada. Any product from non–English-speaking nations had even less chance. All American TV president George Beck commented that most foreign product that did screen in America did so on PBS, which left a stigma that distributors of foreign programs had to shake before getting a shot at the U.S. commercial market. Yet that material appeared on PBS precisely because it couldn't find any other spot. Another stigma, noted Fox TV executive Michael Lambert, was that foreign shows were "perceived as talky and slow and thoughtful with very little action." Another reason for a tight American market, according to Horowitz, was "the huge inventory of American shows that never goes away — everything from 'I Love Lucy' and 'The Honeymooners' to the thousands of feature films. Stations would rather buy 'Get Smart' than 'Get Schwartz!'" Solomon felt a breakthrough would come for offshore property, but the "right property" hadn't come along yet. When it did, he believed it would be a coproduction between a European entity and an American firm.[91]

At a meeting held in America in the late 1980s between foreign distributors and U.S. broadcasters, several U.S. executives, including MCA's Larry Fraiberg, HBO's Jim Warner and Disney Channel's Bruce Rider, warned the offshore people that foreign shows would need to feature a "big celebrity." The brightest note for offshore distributors was a description of competition among U.S. buyers as "slight" — apparently this was a bright spot, as it was greater than zero. Britain's Granada TV head David Plowright accused the panel of being parochial, dismissing as patronizing the panelists' finding of a bright spot. "There must be something between PBS and what's on commercial television," exclaimed Plowright. Apparently he had abandoned hope of selling to the commercial networks. Responded Fraiberg, "You come here with ready-made products. Why don't you come here before you make them?"[92]

Larry Gersham, a former president of the MGM/UA Television Group and then head of the World International Network — aiming for international coproductions — worried about a growing anger on the part of European producers if America continued to refuse to buy their television shows. One solution he suggested was for the Europeans to allow American input during the production phase in exchange for assurances that their projects would remain under European control. And, Americans should seek provisions that allow for a second shooting or a modified version of the project.[93]

Various European producers sometimes spoke of two or more of their countries combining to do coproductions, without the Americans. Reporter Richard Melcher regarded the hopes of creating a pan–European production that sold across borders as "fanciful." U.S. movies and series "are still the only ones that regularly appeal to viewers everywhere." Melcher concluded, "A growing number of European programmers realize that they'll only succeed in the world market once they learn what works in America."[94]

According to the Anglo-American media research firm Booz–Allen & Hamilton in 1989 America produced 95 percent of its own network programming and 98 percent of its own network drama (basically all fiction fare) while at the same time the European Community imported 24 percent of all its programming and 40 percent of its drama material from the U.S.[95]

In 1980 U.S. producers exported about $350 million of television programs; in second place was the U.K. at $22 million. That same year U.S. producers exported $450 million worth of movies for cinemas; France was in second place, although it exported just $15 million worth of features. The OECD area then had 350 million sets out of a world total of 500 million receivers.[96]

Total U.S. television program sales worldwide stood at $1.3 billion in 1987 with about $800 million of that total coming from western Europe. Observers expected those totals to increase to $3.6 billion and $2.7 billion, respectively, in 1992.[97]

At that time, according to Lorimar's Michael Jay Solomon, a half-hour series would gross $50,000 to $100,000 per episode in foreign sales; a one-hour series, $100,000 to $150,000 per episode; a two-hour movie, $200,000 to $400,000; and a miniseries, $300,000 to $400,000 per hour. Domestically for a U.S. network the cost of a first year half-hour sitcom started at $350,000, a one-hour series at $850,000, a two-hour made-for-television movie at $2.7 million and a one-hour variety special at a $600,000 license fee. First-run syndication for a two-hour made-for-television movie brought $250,000 to $500,000. According to Paramount Television Group executive Vance Van Patten, normal projects worked on a budget of $500,000 to $700,000 per one-hour episode. On the high end was Paramount's "Star Trek: The Next Generation," which cost $1.2 to $1.3 million per one-hour episode. Speaking as a representative for basic cable, Turner Network Television's Scott Saysa said the budget for a first-run telefilm was $1.5 to $3 million per hour. For pay cable, HBO's Chris Albrecht reported that original programming such as the half-hour series "Hitchhiker" cost $450,000 to $600,000 per episode while an original HBO Pictures feature cost $2 to $5 million.[98]

A major study of world television trade was conducted in 1983 for UNESCO by researcher Tapio Varis. When he studied the same issue for UNESCO in 1972-73 his team of researchers concluded there were two indisputable trends: a one-way traffic flow from the big exporting nations to the rest of the world and the dominance of entertainment material (as opposed to news, educational, cultural, and so on) in the flow. Globally, in 1973, the average of imported programs was about one-third or more of total programming time. Comparing the 1983 results with the earlier ones Varis found the earlier pattern repeated. The difference between prime time and total time was not great with the exception of Latin America, where foreign programs tended to be more dominant in prime time. With Italian private television at its peak at the time of the study, estimates were that 80 to 85 percent of their total transmission time was devoted to imported fare (they were not included in the study itself). Imported programs on American television amounted to 2 percent in 1983, little changed from the 1 percent on commercial networks and 2 percent on public broadcasting in 1973. Of that total, 25 percent came from the U.K. and 25 percent from SIN (a Spanish-language network that distributed a full broadcast schedule each week to broadcast outlets in 21 U.S. markets; SIN was owned by Mexico's Televisa). Nationally PBS and SIN accounted for 90 percent of all time allotted to imports on U.S. television.[99]

One trend Varis noted was that "as soon as a television station increases its transmission time, there will automatically be an increase in imported programmes." Looking at Canadian television he found 40 percent of all programming to be foreign, 29 percent from the U.S.; thus 70 percent of all imports were American. Varis found the publicly owned networks showed more Canadian fare than did the private networks. Also confirmed was the private sector trend toward the displacement of Canadian programming during prime-time hours. Private network CTV's schedule was 99 percent imports during prime time and, wrote Varis, "indicates a considerable disregard for Canadian programming." Publicly owned Canadian networks not only had more Canadian content than did the private networks but also had more varied programs. As to higher viewership for U.S. fare, Varis remarked, "This is partly because Canadian programming tends not to benefit from the supporting web of publicity and star-recognition which surrounds American programming" and a relative lack of funds for Canadian production. Within Latin America the amount of imported material varied from 24 percent in Cuba to 66 percent in Ecuador with, on average, about half of all material telecast in the area being imported. U.S. transnational firms dominated, with 75 percent of all imports in the region. In the earlier study U.S. firms accounted for 75 percent of all Argentinean imports; in 1983 the figure was 89 percent. Western Europe contributed 5 to 6 percent of area imports in 1973; it was down to 2 percent in 1983. Of Brazil's television imports 93 percent came from America, 2 percent from Mexico and 5 percent from western Europe. Russia supplied Cuba with 23 percent of its television imports; the U.S., 22 percent.[100]

Looking at western Europe, Varis found the pattern of imports very similar in 1973 and 1983. There were heavy importing nations such as Iceland and Ireland in which about two-thirds of programming came from offshore, and there were nations importing relatively little. Differences among countries were notable. Overall about 30 percent of programs were imported, and 44 percent of those came from the U.S., giving America about 13 percent of total west European television transmission time. The U.K. was second at about 4.8 percent (16 percent of all imports). The U.S. share of total transmission time had been slightly higher in 1973, at 15 to 20 percent. However, cable television and "certain private stations which are heavy importers" (the new private Italian outlets) were not included in the study. American share of imports did fall in some nations, to 29 percent in Finland from 40 percent of all imports in 1973, in the U.K. from around 85 percent to 70 percent; in Germany the U.S. share remained the same at 60 percent. For feature films most European nations devoted 5 to 10 percent of transmission time to that genre, with the U.S. providing 62 percent of imports in that category and France providing 8 percent. Television drama took 10 to 20 percent of air time, with the U.S. providing 51 percent of those imports, the U.K. 19 percent. Overall entertainment fare made up 30 to 60 percent of western European material, with the main sources being the U.S. at 46 percent, U.K. at 15 percent and Germany at 7 percent. In Asia and the Pacific overall, averages for domestically produced material were 64 percent of total transmission time and 64 percent of prime time with a wide range, from 25 percent on New Zealand's Channel 2 to 97 percent for a station in Calcutta, India.[101]

Varis concluded that no major changes in the international flow of television programs had taken place since 1973. Globally, the average volume of imported fare remained at one-third or more of total air time. "On a global level, the majority of imported programmes originate in the United States.... The flow consists mainly of programmes of a recreational nature such as entertainment, films, sports, etc. In some regions such as Latin America, as much as three-quarters of the imported materials originate in the United States," he wrote. Owing to technological changes such as the new medium of videocassettes and the coming of satellites, Varis warned, "The pattern of the international flow in these fields is largely unknown but it may be even more concentrated in a few sources than the traditional pattern ... there is a trend towards transnational concentration."[102]

By value, for the year 1983, one researcher estimated that American product controlled 75 percent of the total television export market. Looking at the low level of foreign material on U.S. stations Colin Hoskins concluded, "We believe the evidence suggests that U.S. viewers are relatively insular and unusually intolerant of foreign programming." They would not accept dubbing or subtitles and didn't much care for British accents. Granada TV of the U.K. once offered its very successful long-running soap opera "Coronation Street" free to any U.S. commercial network that agreed to give it a reasonable trial by keeping it on the air for several months; none of the networks accepted the offer.[103]

For UNESCO Peter Larsen studied fiction programming in 15 nations in 1980 and in 1984 (encompassing all series, serials, plays, feature films, made-for-television movies and cartoons). Larsen wrote "research demonstrates that indigenous productions are usually more popular in a domestic market than the globally successfully distributed products. However, when importing foreign products, American programmes invariably predominate. It is strongly recommended, therefore, that governments and other cultural agencies give support to domestic productions." For 1984 U.S. offshore television sales were about $500 million; 90 percent of those programs were entertainment, nearly all of them fiction. Within that category the export ratio of series to feature films was about 60:40 in value and 70:30 in hours. Approximately 85 percent of U.S. television exports were accounted for by the members of the MPEA. Larsen determined, "An examination of American export prices indicates that the average export price is less than 1 percent of American production costs. Sales and distribution networks are well-developed, and viewers are acclimatized to the American product, including the stars, through past exposure to American feature films and television series."[104]

Chapter 8

1980s:
"The American Poison"

Latin America received little attention in the 1980s from U.S. television exporters since it was by then dominated by American product, American-style broadcasting systems and American-style commercial operations. A study conducted in 1984 revealed that three small nations in the region, Panama, Costa Rica, and El Salvador, had five, six and four outlets, respectively, in operation. Each had one government-run station, included in those totals. All followed the North American model of private ownership with minimal government oversight. Programming was heavily oriented toward entertainment and relied heavily on U.S. imports. Realistically such small nations could not be expected to produce much of their own programming. During the study period in 1984 those nations imported 78 to 88 percent of their programming, 65 to 75 percent of it from the U.S. Domestically produced were news, education, music, variety shows and, to a lesser extent, sports. Entertainment shows were almost all imports. Even religious shows were mainly imports. Although the countries were heavily Roman Catholic imports of religious shows were mainly Fundamentalist Christian programs from the U.S. Panama imported 80 percent of its material, 65 percent of it from America; in El Salvador those figures were 88 percent and 75 percent; and Costa Rica imported 78 percent, 74 percent from the U.S. Study leader Maria Wert found that most of the experts contacted in the course of the project "agreed that the international distributors remain the key gatekeepers; the only foreign programs available to the small, language-specific countries in Latin America are those selected and dubbed by regional distributors."[1]

Another study around the same time of six larger nations in the region found some had reduced the percentage of imported programs over a ten-year period. Venezuela imported 50 percent of its television fare in 1972, 33 percent in 1982; for Brazil those figures were 60 percent, 39 percent; Argentina, 20 percent, 40 percent; Chile, 56 percent, 44 percent; Mexico, 50 percent, 50 percent; and Peru, 60 percent, 70 percent. Livia Antola's study looked at audience hours of viewing in four of those countries as compared to just percentage of hours imported. In Argentina 63 percent of the audience hours went to domestic fare, 28 percent U.S. and 9 percent other Latin American. Domestic production took 60 percent of transmission hours but 63 percent of audience hours; 19 percent of Brazilian audience time went to U.S. material with 78 percent domestic. While domestic shows occupied 61 percent of air time they captured 78 percent of the audience hours. Mexico's audience split was 66 percent local, 33 percent U.S. fare. Occupying 50 percent of on-air time those local programs took 66 percent of the audience. Peru's schedule featured 34 percent of the audience watching local fare, 33 percent U.S. and 25 percent to other Latin imports. Thirty percent of Peruvian broadcast hours went to domestic fare, capturing 34 percent of the audience. Of the 50 top-rated shows in total (10 from each of 5 lands) only 4 were American, none higher than seventh place. In Chile a regulation existed whereby only one hour of foreign television from Mexico, Brazil or Venezuela could be shown per channel per day, but American programs were not so limited.[2]

One of the main reasons that Latin American television followed the American model so closely was because of heavy U.S. financial involvement in the early years. Brazil's large Globo network began through an association with Time-Life Corporation; in Peru NBC and CBS originally owned 20 percent shares in the first two stations. Throughout the region the U.S. networks provided capital and technical assistance to start television systems. While such direct influence ended a decade earlier, what was still true, said Antola, was "The initial transfer of hardware technology created a continuous demand for more television equipment and for U.S.-type television programs. This early U.S. influence is reflected still in Latin American television programming, administration and commercialization." Even though the U.S. networks sold their stakes to national interests "they left behind a pattern of professional and business values that are clearly North American." One such pattern was long broadcast hours. In Latin America that meant that in a nation with three channels and fifteen hours of broadcasting per day each channel was faced with a minimum of 100 hours of programming time to fill per week, or a total for the country each year of 16,000 hours. The cost of production per hour for a "telenovela" series (one of the least expensive genres) was $3,000 to $10,000, depending on the country. To fill an average of 100 hours per week a station would need a budget of $16 to $52 million per year, just for production costs. Since no Latin American station could handle that, the logical choice was to turn to cheap imports, American. In Peru the price of "Dallas" per episode was $1,000 (which included the right to broadcast each episode twice) while the cost of the cheapest local production was $3,000 to $5,000 per hour. Thus, concluded Antola, once Latin countries "accepted the idea of filling each day with television programming, they became committed to the heavy importation of foreign programs."[3]

When researcher Noreene Janus looked at the Latin television scene early in the 1980s she concluded that while U.S. direct ownership of broadcast facilities had ended, "foreign domination over these media did not come to an end; only the form of transnational control changed." Whereas network-affiliated stations inside the U.S. then limited advertising to around nine minutes per prime-time hour, Mexico permitted ads to 18 percent of total transmission time. An extreme case was Guatemala, with no regulations concerning the number of broadcast minutes that could be sold to advertisers. Thus a 60-minute imported show from the U.S. could run as long as 90 minutes to accommodate an extra 30 minutes of ads. During the 1960s and 1970s American ad agencies expanded all over the globe, by opening branch offices and purchasing local firms. In Belgium, Italy and the U.K. at least seven of the top ten largest agencies were U.S. owned or affiliated; it was nine of ten in West Germany. Central American advertising was dominated by a single U.S. transnational, McCann-Erickson. In Mexico, Argentina and Venezuela at least eight of the ten largest agencies were controlled by foreign capital. Worldwide 23 of the 25 largest agencies were U.S. owned. U.S. ad agencies had expanded internationally to serve their transnational clients. In many Third World nations the rapid growth of advertising was associated with the expansion of transnational manufacturing firms.[4]

Advertising, argued Janus, "is increasingly used to legitimize the presence of transnational corporations — to justify their existence — especially in countries where nationalists and revolutionary movements are struggling to regulate or expel such firms.... To promote specific products, corporations and even the free enterprise system, the transnationals rely heavily on and in fact promote certain types of media, especially television. Television is of fundamental importance to the global firms both because it is the best marketing device to reach illiterate groups and because it is one of the few successful means of advertising in countries, such as Israel, that have multiethnic and multilingual populations." In Mexico and Peru about 60 percent of all advertising placed in the mass media went to television and 30 percent went to television in the U.S. This difference was due to a difference in illiteracy rates. As advertising budgets expanded they gave rise to more media, or to the expansion of existing media. What got advertised the most in the U.S. and worldwide were prepared foods, soft drinks, beer, drugs and cosmetics, tobacco and soaps — industries generally controlled by transnational firms. "The primary use of the mass media in Latin America is not the preservation of Latin American cultures and national independence. Instead, they are used as marketing tools by global operators building world markets," wrote Janus. Nations that banned broadcast advertising found their borders assaulted anyway from signal spillover from nearby nations that did allow commercials. Advertising represented a vast amount of money — some $70 billion annually worldwide then — spent selling deodorants and cigarettes in the face of so many basic needs going unmet globally. "Equally important, the transnationalization of advertising is creating an international consumer culture whose members eat, drink, and smoke the same products," Janus concluded.[5]

Toward the end of the 1980s cable television firms in Argentina, Chile, Brazil, Venezuela and other areas of South America had created more business for themselves by pirating the programs the major U.S. networks provided for American military personnel abroad via satellite. The Pentagon, which put together the service, denounced the pirates and stated it would take steps to stop the pirating. But nobody much believed it. Said Jose Manuel Larrain of TV Cable in Santiago, Chile, "The United States would be crazy to give up this opportunity for cultural and political penetration. The value of this to the United States is immeasurable." Since the material was broadcast in English only, Latin viewers were believed to be only the well-educated and relatively affluent. Pirates picked up the signal from the Intelsat orbiter aimed at Europe, where most U.S. troops were based. Privately many U.S. embassy officials in South America were said to be pleased with the situation as it stood.[6]

Egyptian Television (ETV) spent around $2 million a year for foreign product in 1982, most of it from America. ETV scheduled about 900 hours of U.S. series and specials a year, at an average cost of $500 per one-hour, and 300 U.S. feature films, at an average cost of $1,000 per title. All foreign product was screened with subtitles. The value of the entire Arab television world, with its twenty separate markets, was valued at $10 million annually for foreign television traders.[7]

In Japan TV Asahi Channel 10 acquired 50 episodes of "Dallas," but the show bombed big time even though Victoria Principal—who played Pam Ewing on the series—was brought to Japan for a five-day whirlwind of interviews and other publicity ploys. TV Asahi manager Fujio Nakamura speculated, "it's just that the Japanese public these days much prefers to view homegrown entertainment shows. American shows were popular up until about fifteen years ago." Viacom Japan Inc. president Jiro Sugiyama said "Dallas" needed a 15 percent share of the audience to be successful, but it got only 4 percent. He estimated that about 4 percent of network programs were imported, with most of those being feature films. Sugiyama declared, "Television is a reflection of a society. When people are adequately served with their own entertainment, as in the U.S., they are satisfied." He added, "I hope that someday the Japanese get so bored with their own programs that they look for foreign shows," but held out little hope that would actually happen. Japanese television then paid $15,000 for a one-hour episode of foreign product, but dubbing costs had escalated rapidly. The program "60 Minutes" cost $6,000 to $7,000 to dub. U.S. movies that had played cinemas in Japan, and consequently had publicity, sold to the networks for $120,000 to $200,000 on average, with blockbusters going for up to $1 million.[8]

Generally Asian and Far East markets, once brisk for U.S. television product, were reported as having softened by the mid–1980s due to a strong U.S. dollar, a rise in local production and some stiff local content quotas. MCA Australian executive Paul Cleary said "U.S. product is not made for anywhere but the U.S. The fact that we sell it elsewhere is fantastic." In some of those markets Paramount and other distributors sold programs to an ad agency or sponsor that then supplied them to the stations. That way the distributor avoided many of the economic problems of currency repatriation or nonpaying outlets. Taiwan had a local content quota of 85 percent. Indonesia's state-run noncommercial service ran on a strict 80 percent local content rule. Overall in the area, prices ranged from a low of $150 per hour up to $4,000. Programs that did well in the area were ones with little spoken English but lots of action. Also popular were the likes of "Entertainment This Week," "That's Hollywood" and sports.[9]

Australia's market was also less welcoming for U.S. fare. Nine network vice president Ron Naynes said in 1984, "It's now true to say that Australian audiences are more interested in Australian material."[10]

Late in the 1980s Television New Zealand still consisted of two state-run networks. While TVNZ remained a big buyer of U.S. product, distributors grumbled that it was "pennypinching," as it imposed a flat fee of $25 per minute ($1,500 per hour) on what it paid for imports. That fee had not changed for three years, but as the local currency had declined from almost par with the U.S. dollar down to 45¢, TVNZ paid twice as much as it used to pay. TVNZ executive Des Monaghan said that U.S. product is "important, but not as important as it used to be…. In common with other countries New Zealand audiences are increasingly showing a preference for local product." However, the year before he had entered TVNZ into a three-year deal with CBS for all the material it originated, primarily news but also some entertainment fare. When a third station started there in 1989 (a commercial outlet) programming president of the new outlet Kel Geddes declared that the "bulk of programs, say 50%, will be American." Twenty-five percent would be local with the rest split between product from the U.K. and Australia. Hollywood distributors hoped that TVNZ's first-ever competitor would put on pressure, leading to higher prices for foreign material and breaking TVNZ's price ceiling.[11]

Within Canada during the 1980s much debate and attention was devoted to the issue of American television product in Canadian homes. Canada's minister of culture and communications, Francis Fox, got the period off to an odd start when he floated a suggestion before a Canadian Association of Broadcasters (CAB) convention that in the future private stations in Canada might be allowed to broadcast as much U.S. product as they wanted. At the time both public and private broadcasters had to adhere to a 60 percent local content (Cancon) over the broadcast day, 50 percent in prime time for the private outlets and 55 percent for the CBC. Fox told the CAB delegates regarding the Cancon quota, "I am not convinced this is the most desirable approach.... The preservation of cultural independence has governed the regulation of broadcasting in Canada almost from the beginning. Nevertheless, Canadians are no closer to this elusive autonomy." Protectionism had not worked in the past, and he felt it was even less likely to succeed in an era of satellite transmission. Fox's idea, which also featured a mostly Cancon role for the CBC, quietly died.[12]

Once again the Canadian Radio and Television Commission (CRTC) began looking for ways to tighten the rules to force broadcasters to use domestic material. In a speech CRTC chairman John Meisel said, "Any country which values what it is ... must ensure that television reflects its own concerns." Noting the overwhelming pressure in Canada by U.S. programs he declared the market could not be allowed to decide what was seen on Canadian television because "the market has no value other than economic values." During five days of hearings both the CBC and the Ontario government protested against a tactic used by private stations whereby some of them loaded all their U.S. prime-time allowance into the 8 P.M. to 10:30 P.M. prime-time peak hours, putting the Cancon in the fringe part of prime time. Yet that was itself a function of a CRTC decision taken a decade earlier that expanded the definition of prime time to run from 6 P.M. to 12 midnight, far too long a period. That step was taken back then as a face-saving measure by the CRTC. It established a 50 percent Cancon prime-time requirement while making the period so long that it didn't disturb the status quo at all. CBC president Al Johnson advocated a change in which at least 40 percent Cancon was required in the 7 to 11 P.M. period (a more appropriate definition of prime time). At the time Johnson said Cancon in that period was just 23 percent. However, to reach that level Johnson estimated that more money would be needed by the network to replace U.S. fare. No new Cancon rules were introduced."[13]

When American superstations such as TBS Atlanta and WGN Chicago began satellite transmission Canadian cable operators agitated to be allowed to carry them. Eventually the Canadian federal government allowed cable operators to carry them on a "controlled access" basis. This meant when Canadian cable systems were allowed to carry more U.S. services they had to add a certain number of Canadian channels to their system at the same time. The reasoning behind the decision was that if Canadian cable systems satisfied their viewers Canadians would not be tempted down the road to turn to service from American DBS systems, which could be picked up by Canadians with a dish and would not, of course, carry any Canadian channels. U.S. journalist Patricia Green wrote "The fear is that viewers taking this route would be lost to the Canadian system forever because Canada has no plans for similar powerful satellites. The programs they would watch would be purely American, of course, and so the question of Canadian cultural survival surfaces if segments of the population ingest only American attitudes, values and information 24 hours a day." An unnamed Canadian federal government source said that a controlled influx of U.S. channels might actually help Canadian programming "if we can just keep people hooked to cable, where Canadian stations and Canadian non-broadcast services (such as coverage of Parliament) will still get priority spots on the dial, then we can look at ways of beefiing up the appeal of the Canadian shows on those channels."[14]

During another round of parliamentary hearings into Canadian television in 1983 a group of 450 producers and directors who did freelance work for the CBC urged that network to drop all U.S. material and go to an all–Canadian schedule. Critics argued such a move would initially cost the CBC $57.6 million in advertising revenue and cost an additional $52.6 million to replace the 1,200 hours a year of U.S. programs with Canadian fare while saving just $25 million a year in U.S. license fees for those programs. Although CBC president Pierre Juneau agreed with the proposal for an all–Canadian schedule it didn't happen. Hearing chairman Marv Terhoch noted, "We think it's very difficult for Parliament to grant [the CBC] more money when it's presented with a service dominated by American programming."[15]

Covering the hearings was American reporter Douglas Martin, who noted that two out of every three programs available on Canadian screens was American and that Canadians spent three out of every four viewing hours watching those shows. As to why that was so, Martin wrote, "There is an added American lure. It is less expensive for the network to buy United States programs than to make Canadian ones; the CBC can purchase a network series for $30,000 per one-hour episode, one-tenth what it would cost to produce it."[16]

Calling the CRTC "the moral conscience" of Canadian broadcasting former CRTC chairman John Meisel added, "there is no such thing as a free-market in Canadian broadcasting, only markets where the most powerful players arrange matters in their favor."[17]

In 1985 the CRTC approved the application to allow some Canadian superstations. One was the Hamilton, Ontario-based CHCH independent outlet. When researcher Joyce Nelson checked its prime-time schedule she found that for the 7 to 11 P.M. period CHCH programmed just 2½ hours Cancon out of 28 hours in total — the remainder was U.S. fare. And those Canadian shows were mostly the cheapest genre to produce, talk shows. CHCH had been a highly profitable independent station for well over a decade but had done little to reinvest in Canadian productions. What it had done was to play a role in a bidding war that drove up prices paid for U.S. fare. Both the CBC and CTV opposed CHCH's superstation application on that ground, arguing higher prices for U.S. shows, paid by all, cut into money they used for local production. In awarding CHCH superstation status the CRTC said its decision "will improve the choice offered to Canadian viewers" and would contribute to "the critical struggle for a distinctive and strong Canadian broadcasting system."[18]

Lobbying continued by the Canadian Cable Association (CCA), a lobby group composed of the owners of Canada's 853 cable systems. The CCA wanted to import a wider range of U.S. series and to be freed from the existing government oversight of their prices charged to consumers. It argued more U.S. services were needed because of "public demand for increased quality and variety of programming" and subscribers' desire "to exercise more control over entertainment options."[19]

According to Joyce Nelson, as of 1984, of 17,500 hours of dramatic television fare aired across English-speaking Canada networks and stations only 1.5 percent of it was Canadian made. Canada then paid about $150 million annually for U.S. television product. Between 1975 and 1985 the average price paid by Canada for each half-hour of U.S. product rose fivefold, thanks to more outlets' bidding up the prices. Even at that much higher price it was still cheaper to buy American product than to produce locally, $20,000 compared to $100,000. "And that's how American dumping of TV shows works. By peddling its TV product around the globe, the U.S. entertainment industry undercuts the impulse to build a country's own indigenous programming."[20]

When a federal government task force on broadcasting issued a 1986 report, one of its key findings undermined the idea that Canadians preferred to watch U.S. shows instead of their own. That report showed that viewers watched Canadian programming in almost direct proportion to its availability. During an average week of English-language television 28 percent of programming was Canadian, watched by 29 percent of the audience; 2 percent of available material was Canadian drama, and Canadians devoted 2 percent of their viewing hours to Canadian drama. Canadian news fare was watched by viewers in almost double proportion to its availability. While the task force urged more Cancon on the air the CRTC was backpeddling. That regulatory body lowered Cancon requirements for the recently licensed pay-television movie channels from 50 percent to 30 percent. It also reduced the share of gross revenues they were required to invest in Canadian production from 45 percent to 20 percent.[21]

When Al Johnson looked at the situation in 1988 for a Canadian political journal he found that 75 percent of all programs on prime-time English-language television were American and almost that much on French-language outlets. Close to 95 percent of television drama on English-language outlets was American; over 70 percent of all general entertainment fare was American; over 50 percent of all news and current affairs shows were American. Johnson put the blame for that situation on many factors. One factor was the CRTC's licensing of the cable importation of whole U.S. services with the cost being limited to the cost of delivery plus a profit for the cable firms. That is, no extra charge for Canadian production was added on, but Canadian services delivered to the same screens had to pay for the production of those Canadian programs, their shows, crippling Canadian television production. Other factors included the following: the growth of private television and its mostly showing U.S. fare, with at the same time a near freezing of the capacity of the CBC to expand its Canadian programming; the CRTC's decision to deny the CBC a license for a second, genuinely Canadian channel; Americanization by fiscal deprivation by which a financially deprived CBC was unable even to replace the U.S. fare aired in prime time let alone compensate for the huge increases of U.S. product shown on private outlets.[22]

Toward the end of the 1980s Canada and the U.S. discussed, negotiated and finally signed a free trade deal. Negotiators for Canada managed to have cultural industries exempted from the pact, over strong U.S. protests. But U.S. domination of that sector was complete before the free trade deal took effect. In 1988 Canada paid an estimated Can$180 million for imported television product, mainly from the U.S. Canada paid Can$160–$170 million (wholesale) to U.S. sources for home video product. Estimated cinema box office receipts were Can$380 million, of which 80 percent went to the Hollywood cartel members (in English-language Canada the figure was 92 to 93 percent; 70 percent in French Canada). Estimated sales of records, tapes and CDs in 1988 were Can$675 million; 90 percent was for U.S. product.[23]

During 1987 a nationwide television debate was suggested on the issue of the free trade deal. Cable companies and the two private networks all attended a meeting with both sides of the issue to discuss the prospect. The only major Canadian television player that did not attend was the public broadcaster, the CBC. The CBC stated it could not consider cutting off any of its American programming for a debate because of ad revenue loss. The CBC was in an even greater financial bind because of government cuts to its budget, which would become even worse under the free trade deal favored by that government. In the end, for various other reasons, no nationally televised debate on free trade took place.[24]

Europe was where the real battle over U.S. television material took place in the 1980s. Holland had two channels in operation at the start of the decade. Air time on them was divided between a dozen stations including a Catholic one, a Socialist one, some Protestant outfits, and so forth. In an attempt to warn Dutch viewers of the horrors of American-style commercial television, the Socialist station, VARA-TV, aired a "typical day" of American television fare. It was meant to expose the "crass commercialism" that could become more prevalent in Holland in the future with more stations, more signal spillover, more privatization, and so on. Dutch stations were then partly financed by spot ads, but those commercials were severely limited compared to the U.S. Included in the marathon 3 P.M. to 4 A.M. run were "Tic Tac Dough," "Batman," "Gilligan's Island," "Love Boat," "PTL Club," the CBS news with Walter Cronkite, the feature film *Klute*, and lots of ads. Research on that day's experiment reportedly did show strong opposition to American television's liberal use of commercials.[25]

A couple of years later a special commission struck by the Dutch government wanted the amount of U.S. material on Dutch home screens reduced. It called on the government to start "de–Americanizing" the two national channels, warning the situation could only get worse as new delivery systems such as cable and satellites held out the possibility of more U.S. penetration. With no fixed minimum for domestic content there was a tendency to play "as much Yank material as the traffic will bear." One reason was it "cost far less than in-house programs at a time when, in the case of most Euro chains, government or public tax funding isn't keeping pace with inflation rates."[26]

In 1986 Spanish television broadcast 816 hours of U.S. series, up sharply from the 398 hours of the previous year. One reason for that jump was the Spanish service initiated morning telecasting in 1986. Of the 443 feature films broadcast that year, 204 were American (46 percent) 200 were E.C. (45.1 percent), and 39 were Spanish (8.9 percent). Of all imported telefilms 74 percent were American. In Turkey 70 percent of all foreign television material screened was from the U.S., 25 percent from Europe. The Motion Picture Export Association (MPEA) had, as in all foreign areas, fixed prices for that market. As of July 1, 1986, the MPEA price list for Turkey set a one-hour episode at $1,700 and a movie at $3,500. As in all lands those prices varied with the status of the title but usually constituted a minimum price.[27]

Germany's second network, ZDF, declared in 1981 that U.S. series were losing favor with viewers. Dietrich Leisching, a Munich program supplier, said one reason Yank series were "less useful and harder to see" was resistance in the U.S. market to foreign shows; "If they [the U.S.] don't buy, the Europeans can't afford to buy U.S. product." He added, "Americans don't think in terms of the international market." However, economics intervened. Budget considerations a year later required ZDF to reduce its contracts for independent local production to $90 million from $100 million. Factoring in inflation made the situation worse. Noted *Variety*, "It's expected that the station will fill air time with more reruns and with more feature films and series purchased from the U.S." They were cheaper. When ZDF announced a multimillion-dollar purchase of 1,264 U.S. films from twelve different sources in 1984, ZDF executive Dieter Stolte defended the purchase by stating that ZDF could not get along without U.S. television production because American films and series were inexpensive, professionally made and loved by the German television audience. German television authorities then limited commercials on ZDF to 20 minutes per day.[28]

By late in the 1980s commercial broadcasting had arrived in much of Europe, including Germany. That general proliferation had upped the demand for product all over Europe. Germany's two state networks, ZDF and ARD (the first network) remained financed 60 percent by monthly television set license fees and 40 percent by limited advertising. These stations oriented their programming, said reporter Jack Kindred, "along European standards of information, culture and sophisticated entertainment." However, three private, commercial networks were also then in operation in West Germany. One, Tele-5, operated around the clock, including airing a CBS newscast at 7 A.M.; the other two started at 6 A.M. and continued until well past midnight. In contrast both ARD and ZDF commenced at 9:45 A.M. weekdays and went dark around midnight. Those private broadcasters, said Kindred, had experimented "with American-style programming, including breakfast shows, stock market reports, tele-shopping; U.S.-style sitcoms and feature films as well as sports." Such an increase in broadcasters could only lead to price increases and in fact what ZDF had paid for a one-hour U.S. episode in 1981, $15,000, cost $50,000 in 1989. Still, it was cheaper than local productions. Acknowledging that German viewers preferred their own programs over imports Kindred said nonetheless "the reported average of $50,000 for U.S. primetime programming is an offer German execs can't refuse," in light of local costs. The success of those new commercial networks, wrote Kindred, "with their policy of showing light, consumer-oriented programs will, if anything, increase America's dominant position in the West German market."[29]

In the fall of 1981 in France the Committee for National Identity took out an ad in the newspaper *Le Monde* lashing out at the dominance of U.S. material in cinemas and on television. Signed by 49 personalities in the fields of entertainment, literature, science, education, the press, and so on, including actor Jean-Louis Barrault and playwright Eugene Ionesco, the ad called for a quota of French films on television to go from 50 percent to 60 percent and giving other foreign nations a chance by limiting U.S. films to a maximum of 20 percent — with some of that set aside for American independents, that is, those outside the cartel. According to the ad U.S. films then accounted for 40 percent of films shown on French television and 35 percent in cinemas. Calling the Motion Picture Association of America (MPAA) cartel a "powerful lobby that set a cultural imperialism whose objective was to maintain by diverse methods, the quasi-monopoly of the cinema in all non-socialist countries and particularly in developing nations," signers of the ad accused the MPAA of using "publicity bludgeoning subordination and various forms of pay-offs when its strongarm diplomacy came up against resistance." The committee went on to observe that the cinema "is one of the true images of national identity and that if abandoned to foreign interests inevitably leads to a certain deculturalization, particularly of young people." In a different article in *Le Monde* around the same time French film director Gerard Blain condemned "the American poison." Arguing that France was being invaded by the American way of life Blain said, "The American cinema powerfully carried from one end of the planet to the other by gigantic distribution networks, is the conclusive instrument of this undertaking of deculturalization. It is by films made in Hollywood that America infuses its venom into the spirits of people, that it insidiously but deeply imposes its stereotypes and literally saps their life force."[30]

France's newly elected government of Francois Mitterand did change the ratio of television material from 50:50 to 60:40 in favor of local over foreign material. As well, it slapped a temporary moratorium on the purchase of foreign programming for the government-run television system. One angry reaction in Hollywood called that move so provocative as to warrant consideration of a retaliatory anti–French boycott. However, as reporter Will Tusher commented, "U.S. TV ... buys little, if any French-produced television programming, so countermoves are not likely to be effective."[31]

As the French government wrestled with the problem of setting regulations for the new cable television industry they initially set a rule limiting imported production to 30 percent of programming. Some 128 communities had formally applied for a cable operation by the mid–1980s. Although the Mitterand government declared it would not invest heavily in cable for the benefit of foreign producers, journalist Jack Monet noted, "The government will bear the brunt of cable startup costs." In its final word on the issue the government provided considerable flexibility during cable start-up years, notably for the import of foreign networks. Local systems were still held to the standard of not turning over more than 30 percent of total capacity to foreign channels. But the rule did not apply in the beginning, with the quota being based on "final capacity." Thus a cable system with ten planned channels would be allowed to launch with six channels, composed of the obligatory three state networks and three foreign stations. Cable regulations also banned the interruption of programs by commercials, as was the case on the three state channels.[32]

When the French government announced its decision in 1985 to allow private television stations for the first time it was a move attacked by critics from the Left and the Right. Those on the Left said the plan gave too much to the private sector, while opponents on the Right called it liberalization on a leash with too much left in the hands of the state in terms of control over broadcasting. Those coming new channels were to be monitored by the National Council for Audiovisual Communications (in French, CNCL), which would, among other things, enforce limitations on imported programs. Defending the imposition of controls George Fillioud, Minister of Communications, said they were necessary to prevent "kilometers and kilometers of American and Japanese imports."[33]

By the end of 1986 it was reported that television production in France had dropped 30 percent over the previous five years while the transmission of foreign programs has grown 75 percent, much of that due to some of the private outlets' coming into service. Production costs in Europe for an hour-long drama were then around $4 million; the average cost of an hour-long U.S. episode was $350,000.[34]

One of the new private networks in France was TF-1, the former state-run network that was privatized. By 1987 it was described as the "darling" of certain American distributors, including MCA and Lorimar, because of the amount of U.S. product bought and the prices paid. Although the CNCL supposedly monitored the channels' foreign product, ensuring a maximum of 40 percent (60 percent minimum for E.C. product. Half of all transmission had to be French; the E.C. portion was French plus all other E.C.), one account remarked, "True, the CNCL has proved ineffective to date, but that situation can't last forever."[35]

But the CNCL did continue to be ineffective. For one thing it had no power to levy fines. Two private networks, TF-1 and LA-5, broadcast 24 hours a day, getting around the quotas by the overnight broadcasting of old French series and new low-budget productions. Not included in the quotas were news, sports, game shows and variety shows. By 1989 the CNCL was abolished, replaced by a new watchdog body, the CSA, which did have the power to levy fines. As well the court set a deadline for the networks to meet the quotas in a realistic fashion; it ordered the outlets to calculate the quota only from 6 P.M. to 1 A.M. In response TF-1 announced it was suspending overnight broadcasting. It also decided to drop certain U.S. series then being screened to make room for local product. TF-1 executive Etienne Mougeotte said his channel would "accelerate" acquisition of European programs "even though such changes will cost more money." His channel was trying to obtain a delay in the application of the court order and a more liberal definition of a French-made program.[36]

In 1989 the French government took over the function of defining prime time, as they had always done for the state networks. Initially prime time was set at 6:30 P.M. to 1 A.M. with plans to define it in the future as a five-hour period, set according to each national network's particular audience. The government threatened to reduce the amount of U.S. product on French television. Worldvision Enterprises vice president Bert Cohen declared, "This is a step backwards for French broadcasting." Fox executive Bill Saunders exclaimed, "The French always want to be the big boys of Europe. If the Government de–Americanizes the French broadcasting companies my question is: Where will they get the product to replace American TV series?... Once the French realize what these quotas will cost them in lost viewers they'll come back." LBS Telecommunications president Phil Howort stated, "Quotas will diminish the quality of the programming and the quality of the choice of French TV viewers. These viewers will seek other alternatives if what they find on their television sets is not up to quality standards." Some believed that as long as those quotas lasted there might be more coproductions. Regarding that possibility American reporter Bruce Alderman said, "the more pronounced the French content, the less chance the program will have of getting shown in the U.S. America is still the make or break market for expensively produced series and television movies."[37]

Britain saw the launch of a fourth network in the early 1980s, Channel 4, a sister commercial station to the ITV. Under pressure from Commonwealth nations such as Australia, the Independent Broadcasting Authority (IBA)— the agency that regulated commercial television — raised the foreign programming quota for the ITV network. It was a 1.5 percent special exemption, covering British Commonwealth nations. Until then those countries had to compete with U.S. producers for the broad 14 percent foreign quota, which was, said reporter Jack Pitman, "anything but a competition, of course,— more like a virtual Yank monopoly of the quota." While the domestic minimum for ITV was theoretically 86 percent there were some exemptions for fare such as news, sports, educational fare certain cultural fare and even "classic" movies, meaning pre–1945 cinema release.[38]

When the British government considered the issue of cable television regulations it issued a white paper that recommended what amounted to an open door for programs. That was a signal for major U.S. firms such as Fox, Viacom and CBS to quickly jump into the British cable industry with local partners. It also set off strong lobbying by British unionists from actors to stagehands to musicians to songwriters to journalists for the government to impose tight quotas on foreign programming allowed on cable television. Under the umbrella banner of the Radio and Television Safeguards Committee the group warned of American-made "shlock" swamping British tubes unless quotas were imposed. One thousand U.K. film and television directors and producers lobbied for a quota of a maximum of 14 percent foreign programming on cable television.[39]

The existing quotas remained self-imposed, as a result of agreements between broadcasters and unions. The 1981 Broadcasting Act specified only that "the proper proportion of recorded and other matter in the programs are of British origin and British performance." Some 30 hours of British prime time was then given over to U.S. material. Station HTV executive Patrick Dromgoole remarked, "Why do we pay the Americans to show their TV schlock when they could be asked to pay to air ours?... That's what our audiences are asked to see by BBC-TV and by us, independent TV." In discussing cable television proposals British home secretary William Whitelaw stated that while U.K. cablers should have an objective of relaying the maximum of British product "at first they would have no choice, on the grounds of both cost and availability, but to rely on a high level of readymade material, much of which will be American." BBC acquisitions head Alan Howden admitted the economic benefits of buying U.S. product: "it will be impossible to substitute economically local product for such material ... overall, as a package, American programs are still a fairly modest cost." In 1982 the BBC imported 14 percent of its programming. Thirty-one percent of the BBC's prime-time television was foreign; 26 percent was American.[40]

When Home Secretary Douglas Hurd released a white paper on television in 1988 he announced more deregulation, aimed at the commercial outfits. Those firms would be encouraged to seek revenue from sponsorship while the BBC would be encouraged to diversify its sources of funding — to explore the possibility of subscription fees as opposed to the set license fee system of funding, which then provided nearly all of the BBC's revenue. Reporter Elizabeth Guider wrote that if such proposals were adopted it would "mean British broadcasting is certain to look more American, feel more commercial and be more advertiser-led rather than program-led by the mid–'90s." Admitting that the U.S. was one of the models that inspired the "liberalization" in the white paper, Hurd agreed it would mean "more rubbish around" on the home screen.[41]

With the added channel and satellite services such as Sky Television and British Satellite Broadcasting it meant all British program buyers had to "pay a little more" for U.S. fare. Still, few, if any, American shows made it into the top ten in Britain, or even the top 50. The real boom came from a new lease on life for reruns and secondary material in the distributors' catalogs. Wrote *Variety*, "Bulk or volume buying is becoming routine for newcomers to broadcasting, as it is to some extent for established stations who for the first time are engaged in around-the-clock broadcasting." Watching the general entertainment Sky Channel "is like growing up in the '60s in America: everything from 'I Love Lucy' to 'General Hospital' to 'Dennis the Menace' to 'As the World turns.'"[42]

The situation in Italy was chaotic by the start of 1980, with public broadcaster RAI's three channels in competition with a private, commercial television sector that featured some 400 outlets in 21 regional operations, all after television product. With two rating services then in operation — one of them A. C. Nielsen — the private outlets were after more American programs, which they hoped would lead to big audiences, which would allow them to increase their advertising revenue, which would allow them to pay more money for American material. This situation tended to bid up the prices, which made it harder for RAI and increased its money problems. For their part the Hollywood cartel, the MPEA, declared it would use the MPEA–RAI price scale when it dealt with the private outlets; that is, it would not sell more cheaply to the newcomers. Paramount TV vice president Bruce Gordon explained the MPEA decided to hold the price line because the MPEA believed that even in the RAI scale, acquisitions were underpriced. Noting there were then no rules or regulations in the television industry and that "Anyone can open a private television station in Italy" Gordon hoped some regulations would be established to leave the field clear to the leading broadcasters. However, some U.S. independents such as Worldvision and Viacom — not MPEA members — reportedly were selling product to the new outlets at prices below scale. In the past those independents had complained that RAI discriminated against them by paying them less than MPEA scale for their product.[43]

Italian commercial television growth strengthened the hand of the MPEA in dealing with RAI. In negotiations with RAI the MPEA set a new price structure for a feature film at $28,100 and $7,000 for a one-hour episode, effective in 1980. For the following year the prices were, respectively, $33,600 and $8,400. Hollywood claimed that those increases merely brought Italian prices in line with what the rest of Europe paid. RAI was said to have offered much less resistance to the increases than it had in the past, prior to the arrival of commercial television. A new feature of the agreement eliminated the past obligation of MPEA members to ship an entire series to RAI from which the network buyers would pick only those segments that they felt appropriate for their audience — typically no more than 13 episodes from the entire run. As of 1980 suppliers shipped in only one or two segments for inspection, and RAI was forced to take a minimum of 13 segments or nothing. RAI asked for and was refused the right of first refusal on all MPEA product. Although Hollywood publicly had stated it would hold the private outlets to the RAI scale, when that network asked for a written confirmation of that MPEA policy it was refused. The promise was to be verbal only.[44]

One of the buyers for the private outlets was Sergio Barbesta, who made the "happy" discovery that U.S. shows that had remained unmarketed in Italy had a ready audience, regardless of age. "For all those programs RAI never got around to acquiring, our private television audiences accept as solid entertainment even those shows 20 to 25 years old." Another Italian buyer was Vittorio Balini who remarked in 1980, "In two years commercial television has consumed about ten years of American and foreign film features." Balini and others took advantage of the RAI policy of buying just 12 or 13 episodes of a series. RAI had acquired 13 episodes of "Dallas" but declined the producer's request to acquire the remaining 64 episodes. "It was a golden opportunity for our company to step in without procrastination and acquire the 64 segments. We will wait for RAI to launch the series and we will pick up where they leave off," Balini explained. Asked about prices he said the MPEA was holding to RAI scale on small purchases but was making "considerable allowances where bulk deals are signed." Italian television bought so much American product in 1980 that it moved into second place as an import market, trailing only Canada. In theatrical releases Italy stood seventh or eighth as a market for U.S. features. One deal had Paramount sell 300 of its movies from the 1950s and 1960s to private Italian television for a rumored $5 million — roughly $17,000 per title, half the MPEA scale even though Paramount was, of course, a member. Reporter Hank Werba said that private outfits acquired "massive quantities" of U.S. product below MPEA scale.[45]

In mid–1981 one report had it that over the previous year Italian television had spent a total of $50 million for product from the MPAA suppliers alone. If the MPEA scale was often undercut, so was it often exceeded. *Variety* noted, "Limited supply and keen competition — since the beginning of

1981—have tended to skirt ceiling figures and go to the highest bidder at much fancier prices." RAI acquired the upcoming MGM series "Fame" at $12,000 per hour but picked up Fox's "Fall Guys" at scale. Private television outlets could have regularly acquired hour segments at $4,000 to $5,000 just a few months or a year previously; by late 1981 they more and more often had to pay scale.[46]

When the MPEA negotiated a new price scale with RAI it featured another large two-step increase, with the price for 1984 being $12,100 for a one-hour segment and $48,400 for a feature film (dubbed or $32,100 for a movie not already dubbed). Half-hour episodes went for $6,000 each. Yet reportedly some series sales even exceeded those prices, with many episodes going for from $12,000 to $18,000 each with the odd one running up to $25,000. Werba speculated that it was an RAI strategy to encourage peak prices as a means to subdue the commercial outlets. On the other hand some U.S. suppliers worried that such high prices "could kill the goose that laid the golden egg." Indeed there were more and more public complaints in Italy; that it should turn more to domestic production because of the high cost of imports and that the RAI was becoming a "colonial" feed for American television product.[47]

Italy imported a total of 1,827 feature films and made-for-television movies in 1982, 1,418 of them from the U.S. with the next biggest supplier being the U.K. at 133. Total paid for that material was $36.6 million, $31.4 million to the U.S., $3.1 million to the U.K. Also imported that year were 18,928 television episodes, 12,865 from America, 1,565 from second-place Britain. Total paid for episodes was $98.9 million, $82.1 million to the U.S., $5 million to the U.K. In total the money paid for all television imports in 1982 was $135.6 million, $113.5 million from the U.S., $8.2 million from the U.K. and $2.9 million from third-place Japan. Such figures caused Remo Gaspari, Italian minister of communications, to declare his ministry would once again try to present a law to regulate commercial broadcasting. He wanted to end what he called "broadcasting anarchy" with a bill calling for a hefty domestic quota and a ceiling on advertising time, among other things. Emphasizing that almost all involved wanted to see regulations he admitted the problem lay in the fact everybody had different ideas on what regulations were necessary. Past attempts to regulate the industry had never gotten off the ground due to the political differences involved. Gaspari wanted curbs on imports to defend "the outstanding characteristics of our culture, our traditions, our way of life to avoid cultural colonization prevalent in massive programming of product from other countries so different in social structure and cultural outlook from ours." Another reason for curbs was the skyrocketing cost to outlets for television fare. Private television had by then developed into three major commercial, more-or-less national networks, all owned by Italian publishers, two of them by Silvio Berlusconi. Smaller independent commercial stations grumbled about having to compete for product against RAI and the major commercial networks. In rooting for the private networks, one U.S. supplier executive said, "We must support them. If they go down in competition with public broadcaster RAI, we will return to a non-competitive monopoly situation and again be at the mercy of RAI." Everyone was consuming American product at a "fever pitch." Berlusconi was said to have reached the point of acquiring some U.S. product "even in advance of a production start."[48]

Attempts to regulate private television failed again. But one thing the Ministry of Foreign Commerce did was slow down or refuse to give its necessary approval for the acquisition of television fare — it was a hard currency exchange. Political pressures from various angles tended to negate a major impact. Whereas in the early 1980s the ministry had approved the $1 million purchase of a single film — *Gone with the Wind* to RAI — it was less likely to do so a couple of years later. That was where the MPEA's bulk selling — block-booking — came in handy. MGM sold RAI 100 films for $8 million, an $80,000 per-title average, "and simply included a lot of features that were such dogs you could hear them bark." Unfounded rumors had it that the major private networks might work together with RAI to keep prices from rising any faster than they already had. RAI executive Leonard Breccia reported that in 1983 Italian television in total had spent about $150 million on foreign television product, 80 percent of it from America. RAI sold $15 million worth of television product abroad, "selling virtually everywhere except the U.S., where TV sales are infrequent."[49]

Many Italians and other Europeans hoped for more coproductions with American producers as a way of making more sales in the U.S. But *Variety* observed that the "point was made that the networks and American producers are first and foremost concerned about their own market and insist on full artistic control, regardless of the foreign partners participating. European coproducers are frustrated in getting even a small percentage of script control to protect European markets and ratings."[50]

For 1987 Italian television imported over $300 million of foreign television product with 80 percent of it coming from U.S. suppliers. That was despite the fact that more hours were allocated to local material and there was less audience favor for U.S. product; escalating prices kept the totals increasing. That was due to the continuing intense rivalry between RAI and the unregulated commercial outlets. By then most of the major U.S. distributors had an exclusive or near-exclusive deal with one or another Italian network, usually going through domestic middlemen. Observed Werba, "With U.S. supply lines hardening into preferential patterns, the pressure on television reps had dwindled. As costs mount for choice homescreen fare, sales execs can make more money with less effort. They know that this very competitive market will take everything available. Only remaining pressure is the scramble to option film titles in the preproduction stage, bargaining for the top dollar and blending peak priced pics into an ultimate package for approval of the per pic average for import clearance. Within the supply patterns now set, Yank sales execs are no longer in competition with each other in a market where public and private broadcasters are in a daily, deadly contest."[51]

Italy was the most extreme case of the invasion of private, commercial television in western Europe, but it was not alone. Particularly from 1985 until the end of the 1980s its effects were felt in many other nations. France saw the prices it paid for foreign product increase sharply; suddenly ads were all over the screen, even to the point of interrupting the programs, long a European taboo. The arrival of new television delivery systems such as cable and satellites held out new threats that the European home screens would be overrun by American television material. More and more Europeans felt they needed to take a unified, cohesive stand to stem the tide of U.S. imports; the scare term was "the Italian experience." Regarding the perils of non–European television, the European Communities Commission stated in 1986, "There is already a certain uniformity in the range of films screened on television in the Community. Programmes such as 'Dallas' are carried by almost every television channel in the member states. The creation of a common market for television production is thus one essential step if the dominance of the big American media corporations is to be counterbalanced."[52]

What further unnerved the Europeans were predictions like the one made by U.S.-based market research company Front & Sullivan. They found that in 1987 U.S. television exports to Europe totaled $675 million, 56 percent of the total export volume. Of the 250,000 program hours aired in the 12 E.C. nations, at least 25 percent came from U.S. suppliers. Front & Sullivan predicted a yearly airing of 400,000 program hours in the early 1990s with about 40 percent of that total being American product. If that prediction came true it would mean U.S. product on European sets would move in five years from 62,500 hours to 160,000 hours annually.[53]

As sentiment for European television quotas grew British press baron Robert Maxwell predicted in 1988 that Europe would impose program quotas, and "Americans should not get alarmed about this. The market will grow and when it does the quotas should regress progressively." He predicted a quota of about 50 percent minimum for European-made product. At the time France had a 60 percent quota for E.C. fare, with the U.K. maintaining its 86 percent level; no other European nation had a similar quota. In Italy, Berlusconi's stations broadcast about 62 percent U.S. product. "I think Berlusconi will accept a quota because he's interested in being an acceptable European," said Maxwell. The press lord further warned, "Americans should take it seriously that quotas are on the agenda. The European governments are serious about it and the European Commission is serious about it. There will be a quota system soon on a European basis, before 1990." He added he thought it would not be permanent because "Self-imposed quotas wouldn't work. No matter how honorable the station owner is, competition would drive them to the lowest denominator."[54]

Top European politicians and broadcast officials met in West Germany in June to call for European-wide program quotas and other incentives for European programming. In regard to quotas a report issued by the group noted, "the fact that the U.S. has a natural advantage by virtue of the size of the home market, gives authorities in Europe the right to demand specific exemptions without thereby creating obstacles which might endanger the free movement of ideas." A directive was issued calling for stations to air a minimum of 60 percent European product. Said the report "quotas might help protect [television services, private and public] from the tough competition" coming from new "transnational or national television channels whose main concern is commercial profit." The new stations, the report continued, are tempted to program "by the systematic use of low-priced non–European productions, which had already recouped their costs in other markets."[55]

Within the E.C. the 60 percent proposal was backed by France, Italy, Greece, Belgium and Spain but was opposed by the U.K., Denmark, the Netherlands and West Germany. Opponents of the proposal wanted to avoid precise quotas making sure that instead a "proper proportion" of material was E.C.-made.[56]

When the Internal Market ministers from the 12 E.C. countries met in March 1989, they compromised on the original E.C. proposal to force broadcasters to devote 60 percent of their air time to European product. As adopted the new proposal called only for a majority of air time to be devoted to E.C. programs "where applicable" and excluded certain programs such as sports, news and game shows. "Most observers agree that such language would soften the law considerably, if not kill it altogether, considering no real watchdog board will be established."[57]

Leading the fight for tough quotas was France. Culture Minister Jack Lang said of the E.C. proposal — known as the Television Without Frontiers (TWF) directive —"We are not doing this in order to be hostile toward the United States. We are in favor of competition, but it must be fair." Unhappy that TWF had been watered down, Lang nonetheless defended it saying, "This is only one step, and a timid one at that. To say that the directive responds totally to our wishes is stupid, absurd and a lie."[58]

A committee of leading European cinema figures, including David Puttnam, Wim Wenders and Ettore Scola, lobbied the E.C. to adopt strong quotas and to drop the vague phrase "when applicable" from the directive. With regard to U.S. anger over the TWF proposals, one unnamed E.C. spokesman said, "We're so surprised that Americans get upset over the directive. The commission has done everything in its power to make sure that it doesn't contain obligatory quotas." When American journalist Fred Hift assessed the E.C. campaign he declared the quota issue "has in fact little to do with any 'idealism,' cultural or otherwise. It seems firmly rooted in cold-blooded business considerations." Still, Hift added that even if a 50 percent quota was adopted it would not seriously affect the scale of U.S. programs in a rapidly expanding market in which U.S. material rarely occupied more than 45 percent of any network's schedule. In fact, he added, "in most countries, local shows grab the top ratings." Pleased that private networks in Europe took a more American-style approach to television he said, "What matters today in Europe is how many viewers a show can attract, not the measure of culture it conveys." Europeans who favored quotas, observed Hift, "are projecting themselves as guardians of culture, though the realities — perhaps inevitably — are commercial." MPAA president Jack Valenti warned that the adoption of a quota system could lead to a commercial war between Europe and America.[59]

U.S. trade representative Carla Hills lobbied hard against TWF, calling it "in effect, censorship of the fine programs developed in this country" and said it was "simply unacceptable." She added, "We have registered very sharp and strong opposition to local content in broadcasting." E.C. officials countered that the quotas had already been watered down to meet U.S. concerns. According to the MPAA its members recorded sales of $630 million of television product in the E.C. countries in 1988, roughly two-thirds of their offshore totals. European sales in 1980 were $100 million. In a position paper the MPAA likened the quota proposal to a "quietly growing malignancy" that put the industry's future in western Europe "to extreme hazard."[60]

In favor of tough quotas was French actor Claude Plieplu who said, "We need some limits to keep this from getting out of control. We see 'Starsky and Hutch,' this police show and that one. A faucet of banal stuff is filling our broadcasting space." Observed Nicolas Seydoux, French studio Gaumont chairman, "When you realize that children pass more time in front of television than at schools, how could one not be alarmed if television makes them lose all relationship with the culture of their parents and grandparents?" Europe's commercial broadcasters lobbied against any quotas because, said the *New York Times*, "European television stations can buy rights to an hour-long American show for less than one-tenth the cost of financing an hour-long domestic production."[61]

During the fall of 1989 Jack Lang was visited separately by both Valenti and Hills. In response to Lang's comments that the TWF proposals were very mild, Valenti told the minister, "I fought for over 20 years to keep our government out of our business and any change from any government is unacceptable to us." The Lang–Hills meeting was said by a Lang aide to contain "veiled threats." Although France was a major force in getting the quota proposals initiated, Lang was then opposed to TWF, threatening to vote against it as being too weak.[62]

According to a Paris research firm, Bipe, only 11 E.C. channels fell below the 50 percent mark; most of those were Italian, and the rest were pay-television channels. The TWF directive pertained to all channels; broadcast, cable and satellite. The relevant part of TWF, Article 4, paragraph 1 said, "The member states shall ensure, where practicable and by appropriate means, that broadcasters reserve for European works, within the meaning of Article 6, a majority proportion of their transmission time, excluding news, sports events, games, advertising and telecast services. This proportion, having regard to the broadcaster's informational, educational, cultural and entertainment responsibilities to its viewing public, should be achieved progressively, on the basis of suitable criteria." When *Variety* analyzed that clause it thought a liberal interpretation would exempt something like the Disney Channel, because how could you have a channel called Disney if it was not allowed to play Disney product? The Bipe report found the averages in all 12 E.C. nations were above 50 percent European content.[63]

The E.C. adopted the TWF directive in October 1989 with the clause noted above. The final vote was ten to two with only Belgium and Denmark opposed. The lobbying effort by Valenti, Hills and other Americans may have backfired, for one E.C. spokesperson said, "We have a directive today, thanks to the Americans." A last-minute compromise was worked out to get the votes of both Germany and the U.K. Under that compromise, which further weakened TWF, the E.C. declared Article 4 should be a political obligation, not a legal one. That meant that violators would not be taken to court. Said European Commission (the E.C.'s administrative branch) vice president Martin Bangemann, "I will not go to court. But a directive is a directive, and it is obligatory. If the quotas haven't been met, the Commission will report to the council and the Parliament." A spokesman for the British delegation stated, "We did not want to vote for a straitjacket. This text won't have any impact on television; you'll still be able to see 'L.A. Law.'" Thus, nations against the directive could argue it was only politically binding, not legally binding, while those in favor of TWF could argue it was both legally and politically binding. In any case TWF did not take effect for 18 months.[64]

President of the European Commission Jacques Delors said of U.S. complaints, "To the Americans I have only one question. Don't we have the right to exist?" Rumor had it that in addition to other lobbying, U.S. president George Bush directly contacted British prime minister Margaret Thatcher about the issue. Top government officials in other European countries were described as having been "pushed too hard" or "insulted" by Hills' lobbying. Former BBC director David Webster remarked, "The American pressure has been of such a nature that it has irritated most European countries." Privately, several Hollywood television executives admitted that TWF wouldn't be a bad thing as, for foreign product, "It sets 49.9% as the top level, and currently we're way under that."[65]

London's *Times* newspaper was against the directive, noting in an editorial, "The most cheering prognosis is that it will prove unpoliceable.... They have nonetheless set a precedent for the regulation of cultural choice which is at odds with the freedoms which are essential for the healthy development of European culture."[66]

Explaining why U.S. interests had fought so hard to oppose a regulation that probably would have no effect on U.S. television sales in Europe, one broadcast executive explained, "If it's just rhetoric this time, it might not be next time. We think it's better to fight now, because if you say it's all right as they move down the road toward quotas, then reversing that trend will be difficult." In its editorial the *New York Times* called TWF "an absurd effort to regulate public taste." At the start of the 1980s there were 28 major commercial channels in the E.U., 56 when TWF passed, with that number expected to double by 1995.[67]

In the aftermath of TWF's passage, Warner Television International president Michael Solomon slammed Lang, calling him "ignorant" about the entertainment industry, and said he and others in Europe had never "even really learned what the business is all about." He maintained there was no need for the directive. Somewhat earlier, when lobbying in Brussels, Jack Valenti declared, "I came here to see whether there's peace or war. You people just threw a grenade into our area, and the pin's pulled out."[68]

In its analysis *Forbes* magazine stated, "The directive represents a left-leaning, pull-the-drawbridge and social-engineering tendency within the E.C." The U.S. protest and case "has more than fairness going for it: For better or more, the U.S. has a knack for producing common-denominator entertainment that no other country can match." The magazine argued that in Europe locally produced material did best locally but didn't travel from say, Italy to Sweden, and so forth, while "U.S.-produced shows pull well almost everywhere." Explaining why there was no European material on U.S. stations *Forbes* reported, "European series typically have little appeal outside their home markets." Admitting the U.S. resistance to dubbed product the magazine added, "but beyond language is the subtler matter of having the common touch." Carla Hills condemned the final TWF passage as "Deplorable ... blatantly protectionist ... unjustifiable."[69]

At the end of 1989 Jack Lang continued to favor a harder line but admitted, "I wish there were others. I feel alone." He called the measure that finally passed "timid." As to coproductions with Americans Lang said fine if "we're not considered as a colony but as a real partner." U.S. reporter Bruce Alderman commented that Lang's "reputation for Gallic cultural snootiness is well deserved."[70]

Chapter 9

1990s:
"There Is No Stopping
the U.S. Tide"

With the arrival of the 1990s those old dreams of a global network were no longer being heard. That is perhaps because it was starting to become a reality as the Hollywood majors engaged in their own star wars, jockeying to beam their product to all of the world from satellites. It was the era of the branded channel as the majors pushed heavily into the new trend of exporting entire channels, all preprogrammed by them, of course, to foreign nations. Compare this to the old way of selling programs, singly or in bulk to foreign-owned stations that then broadcast them in whatever fashion they liked. Between 1980 and 1992 the number of television sets worldwide tripled, reaching 1 billion, and the number of satellite television stations moved from a handful to 300 during the same period. In 1980 there were 40-something television channels in what would become the European Union; in 1992, there were 150, with over 50 of them delivered by satellite. Worldwide spending on television programming reached $80 billion in 1992. For that same year the *Economist* magazine calculated that every American home paid $30 a month for its "free" television.[1]

Noted American journalist Carl Bernstein did a piece for *Time* magazine in late 1990 in which he discussed the pervasive influence of U.S. entertainment abroad, attributing its success to the usual reasons trotted out: its quality, its appeal to fantasy, and so forth. No mention was made of the monopoly power of the cartel, its distribution control and its block-booking practices or to the advertising function of U.S. mass entertainment. In the wake of the recent disintegration of the Eastern bloc, Bernstein declared, "The Evil Empire has fallen. The Leisure Empire strikes back." Motion Picture Association of America (MPAA) president Jack Valenti went so far as to argue U.S. entertainment — particularly movies, television and rock music — was primary catalyst in the collapse of communism in Europe and the Soviet Union. Italian foreign minister Gianni de Michelis declared, "The most important megatrend of the century is the availability of free time." Presumably much of that would be devoted to the consumption of U.S. mass entertainment. Bernstein argued that in today's entertainment industry the lines between entertainment, communications, education and information were increasingly blurred, with the U.S. entertainment industry uniquely positioned to provide software in all four areas. Undoubtedly Bernstein was right about the lines being blurred. Only toward the end of a long article, however, did Bernstein approach the heart of the matter, when he observed that the U.S. entertainment industry was a driving force behind other key segments of the nation's economy — fast food, sportswear, toys and games, sporting goods, advertising, travel, consumer electronics, and so on. Seeing the situation more clearly was France's culture minister, Jack Lang, who said, "Our destiny is not to become the vassals of an immense empire of profit."[2]

Media critic Ithiel de Sola Pool considered the issue of satellite television transmission back in 1975, long before it was a reality. He concluded that most of that transmitted material, in the absence of planned action, "will be the same one-way flow from the United States and a few other advanced countries as it is now."[3]

A decade later BBC Board of Management member David Webster pondered the problems of DBS satellite television. He concluded that even if a government was successful in turning its people away from the temptation of direct reception there was a catch: "The alternative, the cable system, has an insatiable and undiscriminating appetite for product. Few nations have the production base to feed the multi-channeled monster. The only source of popular entertainment at the right price is the United States ... but as the volume of transmissions increases, the cumulative effect will be more profound." Webster predicted, in 1984, that as technology brought more channels, market forces would come to dominate and most forms of government control would be eroded: "Technology and the market impetus will crash against the old barriers of supposed public good, and these eventually, will fall." He added that the U.S. "already shows every sign of expanding capacity to transmit far beyond its capacity to provide an economic base for anything worth watching. Another danger is that aspiring nations may invest in an infrastructure for communications far beyond their real needs." For Webster the idea that the more international communications, the better may have been true in theory, "But this will be so only if there is a real choice, enriching to the consumer, rather than a false choice between economic modules labelled as programs, manufactured for the largest audience at lowest cost."[4]

Speaking in 1990 Lord Rees-Mogg, chairman of the U.K. Broadcasting Standards Council, said regarding the proliferation of new satellite channels, "There is a concern I feel about the nature of the cultural impact of these channels. The cultural impact is predominantly American in character.... Where is the European dimension?" When Sky TV (in its revamped format) and BSB each launched satellite services in the late 1980s both companies said there would be only one winner — and one loser. Less than a year later they publicly agreed that both ventures could flourish in the 1990s. Less than a year after that they merged into one satellite service, BSkyB.[5]

When Sky and BSB merged at the end of 1990 they were reportedly losing a combined $15.7 million a week. By the end of 1992 BSkyB claimed to be making $1.1 million in operating profits per week from the six-channel service. It reached 3.6 million households by satellite, cable and satellite master antenna: 2.6 million on satellite dishes, 380,000 from cable. BSkyB had three movie channels, Sky Sports, Sky News and Sky One — a mix of soaps, dramas and game shows, the most popular of the six channels and featuring Fox's "The Simpsons."[6]

Prior to 1988 all European satellite television was beamed via Eutelsat orbiters, a Paris-based consortium of telecom firms. Principal owners were the national firms in France (19.4 percent), Spain (19.1 percent), U.K. (15.8 percent) and Germany (14.5 percent). It was at that time the privately owned Luxembourg-based company SES pioneered DBS satellite television in Europe with its Astra series of satellites. Late in 1992 Astra 1A and Astra 1B were both in orbit, each with a fully rented capacity of 16 television channels. Astra 1C, with space for another 16 channels, was launched in 1993; Astra 1D was set to go one year after that. SES expected that by mid–1995 its investments in satellites would be $813 million. Annual rental of an Astra transponder (one channel) was $4.9 million. As of 1992 Astra channels were received by 38 million homes, 28 million of those by cable, the rest direct. Eutelsat series II — which started to launch in 1990 — then had four orbiters in space, with all but 2 of its 64 total transponders rented. A fifth was launched in 1993 and the sixth the following year, for a total of 32 more transponders. On Eutelsat II satellites the annual rent for one transponder for television usage was $2.8 million. Eutelsat carried more European-oriented services, while Astra carried more "high-profile" services. When its sixth satellite was launched Eutelsat estimated its total investment would be some $730 million. That explosion of new programming services in Europe was good news for the U.S. majors. Columbia–Tristar Television International president Nicholas Bingham commented, "As new players they won't have very much money. That means they won't be so heavily involved in their own production, and they're likely to buy more U.S. product than less." Bingham saw the advent of new services such as the rerun channel U.K. Gold as "the beginnings of the secondary market, and that's good news for us."[7]

Pay television began to expand offshore in the 1990s. Before that, subscribers to cable paid a flat monthly rate for whatever services were offered. Dish owners also generally paid a flat rate for the basic services; but at the end of the 1980s a few premium channels — usually movies — were available for an extra fee. Time Warner (TW) expanded its Home Box Office (HBO) pay cable channel into Hungary in 1991 in a partnership with U.S. West and United International Holdings to become that nation's first pay entertainment channel. Additionally at that time TW entered Latin America in a 50-50 joint venture with Omnivision Latinamerican Entertainment. The Spanish-language service, HBO Ole, aired throughout Latin America and the Caribbean. TW had been investigating foreign markets for years, said HBO executive June Winters, and "The world has changed, and that has helped to open up some doors." Hungary's regulatory environment was described as "more hospitable" than that of other Eastern European nations.[8]

International pay television business had reportedly tripled its subscriber base by the end of 1993. The acquisition of Asian satellite broadcaster Star TV by Fox owner Rupert Murdoch suggested that it would increase further. Said reporter Don Groves, "That's why the producers of the big movies that drive the pay TV business are looking to get much more closely involved as partners in the launch of new services, after seeing their product used to make a fortune for pioneers such as Canal Plus in France." Outside of North America the number of people paying directly for television channels went from 4 million in 1990 to 12.5 million in 1993. Drew Kaza, president of United International Pictures (a Paramount, Universal and MGM venture) forecasted the subscriber base could go to 18 million to 20 million within three to five years. It was then estimated that Motion Picture Export Association (MPEA) companies pulled in from $600 million to $750 million per year from offshore pay television. The cost of a movie to pay television varied considerably, with hits costing much more. What constituted a hit depended on box office take, usually domestic (that is, U.S.) box office, sometimes regional or global.[9]

Although Murdoch had purchased a potentially lucrative platform for product, the political backlash along with the variety of languages and cultures in the region left the door open to problems. Malaysia's prime minister Mahathir Mohamad warned of the growing influence of Western media in the region. Lined up against Star TV was the so-called Gang of Five — the band of international programmers then using Indonesia's Palapa satellite. Included in the Gang were HBO Asia (a joint venture between TW and Paramount), Turner Broadcasting, Capital Cities/ABC's ESPN, Discovery Channel and Hong Kong network TVB. Meanwhile the UIP group was looking for more equity stakes in pay television systems such as Cine Canal, a new Latin American service in which United International Pictures (UIP) had a 37 percent interest. Kaza remarked, "UIP is interested in developing partnerships with people who have ground distribution. That's the strategy of the '90s, and our way of combating our competitors. We have seen the upside of operators like Canal Plus and BSkyB. We missed the boat in not having a piece of the successful pay services that are out there now." Hollywood's majors had conflicting views about the viability of "the next step" — pay-per-view. They were nervous because of the threat it could pose to video and skeptical because of the lack of development of pay-per-view in America.[10]

As the 1990s began, the U.K.'s fledgling cable television industry was 90 percent owned by North American cable and telephone companies. New legislation in the form of the Broadcasting Bill — which allowed for 100 percent foreign (non–E.U.) ownership of the cable industry — ensured the door would remain wide open. Under that bill the U.K. limited non–E.U. ownership and voting control of new television licenses, on the other hand, to 20 percent and 1 percent respectively. A major stakeholder was U.S. West, which had significant interests in eleven different, awarded U.K. cable franchises covering more than 3 million homes. Other big players were United Artists and Southwestern Bell.[11]

CNN and MTV were the pioneers of branded stations into Europe; many soon followed. Launched onto U.K. cable systems in 1993 were the Family Channel, Nickelodeon and TNT/Cartoon Network. Family and Nick were saying they were planning to adapt programming somewhat to become more British. Family European executive Mike Quintans remarked, "We always had this fear of being the ugly American, trying to do things our way and then finding we'd done it wrong, so we've all been very sensitive and open to the way the British do things. But we found that families in the U.K. are concerned about pretty much the same things as families in the States.... We came to the U.K. thinking we would have to do a major rewrite of our ideas and philosophies, but we've been pleasantly surprised." Also arriving were the USA Network, the Sci-Fi Channel, and the Disney Channel. Discovery Channel, Bravo and the Country Music Channel were all managed by cable giant TCI's London-based United Artists programming division. Family Channel's move to go British was limited to a plan to add one hour a night of locally produced quiz shows. Regarding Nick's plans to go local, Gerry Laybourne, executive with parent company MTV, stated, "Nickelodeon has always been about creating a global culture reflecting the expanding diversity of the American population. Now instead of just dealing with diversity on a national level, we can go up a notch and look at it internationally." In contrast TNT/Cartoon Europe (one channel split between movies and cartoons — a hybrid of the two separate channels operating in America), which was programmed by remote control from Atlanta, planned to remain "100% pure American" for the foreseeable future. Its TNT portion would focus exclusively on movies from its own library with, said *Variety*, "a particular emphasis on the older black-and-white films, which American audiences resist without colorization, but which Europeans love."[12]

It was believed that the four major niche markets in television were news, music, sports and documentaries, with those categories dominated in America by CNN, MTV, ESPN and Discovery, respectively. All were attempting to dominate those niche markets offshore in the early 1990s. One reason was that large cable networks were close to the saturation point at home and so had to go offshore for major expansion. Often the biggest expense was the rental of satellite time, which could run anywhere from $1 million a year to $7 million. Overseas, TNT was stripped of its domestic content of sports and rerun series. TNT Entertainment Networks International executive Ross Portugeis (TNT and the Cartoon Network were transmitted as two separate channels to Latin America) explained that in the Latin American region TNT "is a movie-driven service. We want to establish a worldwide brand that says TNT is the place to go if you want to see a classic movie." TNT amassed a huge collection of around 3,500 films encompassing the MGM and RKO libraries and all of the Warner pre–1948 titles. Although the USA Network, a general entertainment channel, was not a niche channel, company vice president Rafael Pastor felt a network like USA could succeed offshore because "the single most attractive programming throughout the world is American movies and one-hour TV dramas and action-adventure series. The vaults of USA's parent companies MCA/Universal and Paramount, are well stocked with this kind of TV fare." ESPN was all over the globe by 1993 with company executive Mark Reilly saying, "Our goal is to globalize ESPN as a brand name." Reporter John Dempsey concluded, "Discovery, CNN, MTV and ESPN, which are striving to thrust their brand into every country on the receiving end of a satellite signal, have one overriding goal; to corner the market in their programming category so that future competitors will think twice before challenging them."[13]

Another area of huge growth potential for Hollywood was in offshore video. As of 1991, VCR penetration in America was 71 percent of households; in France, 31 percent; in Italy, 51 percent. Some 35 to 40 percent of all Italian video sales were said to be pirate copies. The home-video market in the twelve E.C. lands generated about $4.3 billion in revenue, with U.S. producers taking "the lion's share." In every European nation the fastest moving videos, for sale or rent, were products from Hollywood. In the year ending June 30, 1992, the top 50 rental videos were all American. Blockbuster Entertainment was a huge chain in the U.K. Videocassette recorder (VCR) penetration in Brazil was just 6 percent, with 90 percent of all rentals being U.S. product. Of the 50 most-rented videos in Brazil in 1992, 49 were American. In Mexico VCR penetration stood at 35 percent, with 90 percent of all videos rented coming from Hollywood.[14]

As business expanded companies merged. Worldvision was acquired by Blockbuster. Viacom acquired Paramount and then merged with Blockbuster. Prior to its acquisition, Worldvision had purchased independent Spelling Entertainment (whose catalog included "Beverly Hills 90210" and "Melrose Place"). Then Capital Cities/ABC merged with Disney; CBS and Westinghouse merged; and TW united with Turner. As to what those mergers into a smaller number of bigger and bigger companies portended, James Marrinan, an international television executive, saw "a growing entrenchment of American product around the world." He and others pointed out "The muscle which these media conglomerates will be able to flex in determining what is produced, what is aired, and how and to whom it is distributed will be awesome." As of 1995 the largest media companies in the world were, in terms of annual revenues, Time Warner/Turner, $18.714 billion; Walt Disney/Capital Cities/ABC, $16.434 billion; Bertelsmann AG (German), $14.571 billion; News Corp (Murdoch's Fox empire), $8.862 billion; and Japan's Fujisankel, $8.210 billion.[15]

By 1995, the distinction between the Hollywood majors as separate entities began to blur a little as the studios sometimes got together to split the ever-increasing cost of film production. *Braveheart* (1995) cost $57 million; Paramount put up 40 percent and Fox 60 percent (Paramount held domestic rights and Fox held offshore rights). *The Indian in the Cupboard* (1995) was cofinanced by Paramount and Columbia (Sony), and Fox and MCA split the cost of 1994's *True Lies*. Fox and Disney split the cost of 1995 *Die Hard with a Vengeance*—Disney bought the foreign rights from Fox.[16]

Around the world major U.S. companies continued to buy into the world television scene. Capital Cities/ABC took equity stakes in three European television companies, Germany's Telemunchen, Spain's Tesauro and France's Hamster. Paramount bought 49 percent of the U.K.'s Zenith Production's and Fox partnered with the U.K.'s Witzend, Disney with Scottish TV. Said New World International executive Jim McNamara with respect to these moves in new directions and the supposed trend to more co-productions, the days of "rape and pillage," or of just "dumping product" and returning home are gone forever from the international television business. Generally, U.S. television executives were reported to be pleased by European moves "to incorporate American scriptwriting and production techniques."[17]

Other examples were equity stakes taken in Yorkshire TV by NBC and in the Initial Group by Time Warner. One studio executive remarked, "Cofinancing or spreading the risk, is perfectly understandable but I can't imagine that the U.S. TV industry will ever, in any way, evaluate its television pilot projects on the basis of whether they'll travel or not."[18]

Just 18 days after the fledgling German news network N-TV went on the air in 1992, CNN acquired the single largest stake in the operation, 27.5 percent. TW was the second largest stockholder, at 19.1 percent. It was a move that relieved CNN of its long-proposed German-language version of its international feed—decided to be too expensive. N-TV founder and CEO Karl-Ulrich Kuhlo announced N-TV was Germany's only private station without involvement of German conglomerates Kirch, CLT or Bertelsmann: "We'll be independent from Germany's giants." Until that announcement CNN had been in negotiations with public broadcaster ZDF about a possible similar deal.[19]

One of the reasons for U.S. firms to rush into the U.K. cable television industry was that as late as 1993 just 2 percent of television households subscribed to cable. Programmers from America rushed in, and, said an account, "Some even give away this service initially in order to cultivate an audience." By then U.S. cable giant Tele-Communications Inc. (TCI) was involved in cable operations in the U.K., Ireland, Israel, Hungary, Norway and Sweden; Comsat Corporation, in the U.K.; and Cox Cable, in Denmark and the U.K. Time Warner held cable stakes in Sweden and Hungary; Southwestern Bell, in Israel and the U.K.; U.S. West, in France, Hungary, Norway, Sweden and the U.K. Offshore United International Holdings (UCI), a partnership between TCI and U.S. West, was involved in many coventures.[20]

Through its ESPN subsidiary, Capital Cities/ABC owned one-third of Eurosport, the largest sports network in Europe. As well, it acquired a 21 percent stake in the Luxembourg-based Scandinavian Broadcasting Systems (SBS), one of the region's first commercial broadcasters. SBS owned four television outlets in Scandinavia and provided programming for Kanal Denmark, which operated five television stations in Denmark. Late in 1993 NBC bought Super Channel, Europe's largest general entertainment channel, then available in 30 million homes in Europe and most hotels via cable and satellite. Its reach extended throughout continental Europe and into Russia. Combined with NBC's recent launch of Canal de Noticas, a Spanish-language, Latin American 24-hour cable news channel, NBC then had the greatest worldwide presence of any U.S. broadcasting network, reaching 56 million television households. Commenting on the expansion NBC executive Tom Rogers said, "Between the acquisition internationally of Super Channel and the establishment and strengthening of our cable channels domestically, we have made huge strides in terms of the distribution of NBC programming." He added, "NBC's plan is to develop a global network TV brand that will create multinational and advertising opportunities." Since many of NBC's domestic shows such as "Today" and "The Tonight Show with Jay Leno" would also be carried by Super Channel, Rogers explained that it was likely global ad buys would be developed. Ultimately, Rogers hoped to extend NBC's brand globally into a variety of new and existing media.[21]

A year after acquiring the outlet Rogers elaborated, "We acquired Super Channel at a point where it looked like we better have a distribution system in the European market or we might get closed out ... NBC hopes to create the kind of brand identity that encourages viewers worldwide to seek it out for news, sports and entertainment." That was considered important in a multichannel universe where viewers might receive dozens of stations but usually watched the same half-dozen or so: "It works for Disney." All of this expansion did carry some risk. MTV Networks CEO Tom Freston explained, "Americans are going to lose tons of money. Most people still want to watch programming in their own language, about their own countries." Still, Freston conceded, "In the end, however, there is probably no stopping the U.S. tide from washing over the world. Viewers want more and more TV, and U.S. companies are ready to fill the void."[22]

In 1996 digital television was touted as ready to arrive in Europe in a big way. All the Hollywood studios were interested in grabbing an equity stake in European pay television; they had had no such thing in the first round of pay television for outlets such as France's Canal Plus. Commented MCA's Jim McNamara, "Digital means the producers will be able to participate, to stick our hands past the gatekeeper and get some of the revenues ourselves, whether from subscriptions or advertising." McNamara spoke of plans for "a Universal branded channel in every country of the world as the digital revolution spreads." New digital platforms suddenly made European pay television leader Canal Plus feel vulnerable. Reporter Adam Dawtrey said, "Canal Plus never has previously had to bother with Hollywood output deals, preferring to cherry-pick the best movies and making the studios increasingly frustrated in the process" ("output deal" was a '90s euphemism for "block-booking"). Aware of the new competitive potential and pressure, Canal Plus was said to be then talking output deals with program suppliers. At that time Warner was preparing to launch its branded general entertainment service, the Warner Channel, in the U.K. late in 1996; planning was said to be advanced for a later launch of the new channel into four other European nations.[23]

Aware that U.S. television material often did not draw well offshore or was shunted to off-peak hours, Hollywood producers put more effort into foreign promotion, or at least discussed the possibilities. Warner Brothers International television prepared local promotion campaigns aimed at boosting ratings for its programs in Italy and other nations on the Continent. Warner Rome office manager Rosario Ponzio explained Warner "wants to promote our series in Italy and other markets not because we are having any problem selling them, but because we want American product to again become as popular as it once was." Ponzio claimed that lack of promotion in European markets was the reason many U.S. television series regularly got beaten in the ratings by local programming, stating that most European broadcasters, while spending little or nothing to stir up audience interest for U.S. material, spent heavily promoting their own programs against them. Recalled were the good old days of the early 1980s when Silvio Berlusconi was building his private television empire, relying "almost entirely on the drawing power of American films, sitcoms and series such as 'Dallas' and 'Dynasty.'" Ratings for U.S. movies remained high on both private and public Italian networks, but audience levels for most American series had been falling steadily for the past five years in 1990. Most were then used as filler in the morning, afternoon or late night, but not in prime time. Buyer for Italian public broadcaster channel RAI-2 Claudio Fava thought such promotion would not work because, for example, how could an Italian relate to Los Angeles police officers who were always stopping to eat tacos on the street? Warner planned to ask local tele-casters to split the cost of such promotions 50-50; the state-run RAI network reportedly agreed to do so, at least on some product. A good promotion cam-paign in Italy (on television itself and in print media) for a television program was estimated to cost $100,000 by Ponzio, and for certain series Warner might also do some product merchandising "which will call for bigger spending." As to the possibility of other U.S. majors' launching similar campaigns for their own series, Ponzio declared, "We'll be happy. It doesn't matter if Italian audiences are watching Paramount, MGM or Warner Bros. product. What is important is to have them watching American product."[24]

Explaining why U.S. television suppliers were stepping up marketing efforts offshore one unnamed industry figure said that in a more ratings-con-scious, advertiser-led international television landscape U.S. shows would have to pull their own weight or else they "won't command high license fees, or won't be bought at all." A number of U.S. distributors including Warner, Columbia, Worldvision and Group W set up an informal marketing group around 1991 to exchange promotion ideas and discuss common problems. One idea that emerged was that "Stars, for example, will have to become much more attuned to the need to make an appearance in Cologne as well as in Cleve-land. Maybe it should be written into their contracts."[25]

One selling method used by U.S. producers was in selling format rights — as opposed to the actual tape of U.S. series — to programs, typically game shows. Thus "Wheel of Fortune" was being telecast in a local format version in many countries, including Belgium, Denmark, Italy, Spain, Greece, Portu-gal, France, Germany and Sweden. More than 300 million television house-holds were said to have access to a format or original episodes of "Wheel." Each format version featured a local Vanna White letter turner, local lan-guage, and so on. Specializing in game shows was Fremantle International, with about 80 percent of game show business. Standard drama and sitcoms cost five to six times more to produce than a game show. Fremantle started selling format rights to programs back in the mid–1970s. Another format seller was MTV Networks, whose executive Linda Kahn noted, "We can pro-vide a turnkey operation and give advice and shortcuts that can save produc-ers money." When an offshore broadcaster bought format rights — for a flat rate or a fee plus a percentage — that broadcaster received a "bible" that dic-tated everything from how to pick the hosts to the colors of the sets to what type of questions to ask. Most countries followed the bible closely. Some U.S. sellers viewed tapes of those format shows from time to time "to ensure qual-ity of product." Fremantle president Paul Talbot likened the process of fran-chising formats to the franchising system of McDonalds. By the 1990s Fremantle preferred to offer a package rather than sell the format and was then producing formats of some of its shows in its own studios for Spain. Many of those deals for game shows involved barter. Distributor King World sometimes worked with multinational Unilever in such deals. Molding a format for a game show in a new country was said to be easy because "What we've seen with game shows is that there aren't many changes. Success travels well." One difference was that big prizes couldn't be given away since, for example, there was a price limit in the U.K. And those prizes given away "must actually be purchased" by the game show.[26]

To try to get its foot in the door Warner engaged in a giveaway. For eight days at the end of January 1992 Russian television viewers were treated to Warner Week on their screens, 18 hours of free prime-time television shows donated to Russia, from Bugs Bunny cartoons to "Murphy Brown." Critics complained that Warner Week was as appropriate to the needs of post–Soviet broadcasting as giving ice cream to a starving child. For Warner executive Michael Jay Solomon, "The important thing is to expose the people of [Russia] to Western programming." As Warner gave away major movies to Russian television the MPEA was imposing a boycott on the theatrical release of Hollywood films in Russia until a solution to the widespread piracy problem was found. Warner hoped its free week would stimulate demand for its shows, which would in the long run encourage broadcasters to find the money to buy the shows. Disney reportedly offered a ten-year deal to Russian television (RTR) that was to include four to five hours a week of Disney programming plus some minor Disney investment in local production and training for free. In return, Disney would get exclusive rights to sell RTR's commercial time, splitting all RTR's domestic and foreign revenue after covering its own costs for the length of the deal. In effect RTR would be left with only about 25 percent of its own revenues and would have to force all would-be advertisers to deal through Disney. Another part of the deal required RTR to pay for Disney programming and services as soon as it had enough hard currency. RTR rejected the deal.[27]

Giveaways were rare; a more usual method of selling was through the still-pervasive block-booking system. Late in 1993 some of the earlier block-booking deals between Hollywood and the three Australian commercial networks were beginning to expire. In the heady days of the 1980s those networks had "locked themselves into expensive output deals with the U.S. majors … to guarantee product flow," Warner and Columbia with network Nine, MCA and Fox with network Ten, Disney with network Seven, for example.[28]

Belgium's VT4, owned by Scandinavian broadcaster SBS signed an output deal with Paramount in 1995. SBS was 24 percent owned by Capital Cities/ABC, and Viacom owned 6 percent (the latter owned Paramount). In 1994-95 Warner signed several multiyear "primary deals"—yet another euphemism — with networks in Italy, France, Spain, Germany and with Australia's network Nine again. At that time Warner was the largest single U.S. supplier of material to the world, taking an estimated 30 percent of the majors' offshore total revenue, upwards of $675 million out of a $2.5 billion total. In later 1995 Warner Brothers international television head Jeffrey Schlesinger said, "Two years ago we were primarily in the distribution business, with no foreign-based channels, no investments (abroad) and no co-productions. Now we have a more efficient distribution system, we are setting up thematic channels around the world and we are undertaking clearly defined local and co-production opportunities." As for those co-productions Schlesinger admitted they were only to create "Euro-quota qualifying product."[29]

Germany's media company, the Kirch Group, signed a 1996 output deal with Columbia TriStar for a staggering $1.1 billion for five years worth of television and film output. At the same time German bidding for Paramount output had then also passed the $1 billion plateau.[30]

Advertising on television grew tremendously in some areas. For the period 1993 to 1994 the increase was just 1 percent in North America and 2 percent in Japan. However, in India that increase was 10 percent, 17 percent in Indonesia, 23 percent in Venezuela and 43 percent in China.[31]

Speaking for the Ayer advertising agency in 1990 executive Marcella Rosen said she thought advertisers would be regularly sponsoring television programs for much or all of Europe by the end of the decade. She predicted that viewing tastes in Europe would become more similar, with that leading to the sponsorship of programs in individual nations and ultimately pan-European. Rosen was referring to U.S.-style sponsorship, whereby a marketer pays for the development of a show and owns all the commercial time during its telecast. This gave sponsors greater flexibility in choosing shows and in choosing audience. With 70 offices in 41 countries the agency had just formed a venture, Win Ayer, with a consortium of European broadcast companies to produce and distribute original programming around the world. Ayer would develop the programs on behalf of its clients. Rosen agreed that some of those broadcasters were hesitant about program sponsorship because they worried it implied "cultural control." Rosen explained to them that it wouldn't happen: "In the United States, you sponsor, but you don't have editorial control, because the marketplace won't let it work. All you want is a program good enough to get the audience."[32]

Despite U.S. dominance of the international television scene there were still pessimistic reports about U.S. prospects from time to time. Reporter Elizabeth Guider noted that in 1992 there were few U.S. shows that aired in prime time internationally: "In fact, Canada is the only major territory in the world which still runs a substantial amount of U.S. programming in prime-time." Most of it aired during off-peak hours. When major deals were struck they tended to be made quietly with as little publicity as possible, and "Talking about prices is definitely taboo." That was because it "would irritate our customers, it would tip off our competitors, it might make foreign governments cry foul play."[33]

Guider observed, in a different account, that while sales growth was expected in some European countries the saturation point had already been reached in the U.K. and Italy. Faster growth was then expected in South America and the Far East than in western Europe. At the time the U.S. accounted for 71 percent of the total world traffic in television material, taking $1.7 billion of the world total of $2.4 billion in world television exports (1989 figures). U.S. program exports were estimated at $1.9 billion for 1990 and predicted to reach the $3 billion mark in 1995. Those figures represented sales of all television material to all television outlets whether delivered over the air, through cable or by satellite but excluded video revenue. Perhaps irritating Americans the most was that world exports were a small portion of the world television industry. While world television exports were $2.4 billion in 1989, world total television production was estimated at $70 billion that year.[34]

Mostly, though, reports were optimistic about U.S. prospects in the 1990s. With the E.U.'s single market set to kick off officially on January 1, 1993, journalist Terry Ilott observed that the single market "may be designed as a gigantic fortress to defend Euro producers. But, as far as film and TV are concerned, Hollywood is already on the inside." Italian producers association Anica estimated a huge European audiovisual deficit of $2.5 billion with the U.S. for 1992, with film and television being the major culprits. Giuseppe Proietti, an Italian television executive, commented, "I'm sure these aggregate statistics don't fully explain the situation of European TV. For one thing, when an important film is sold to Europe, a whole package of TV product is attached which doesn't reflect real programming or market interest." According to Anica when European networks aired 100,000 hours of programming a year in the early 1980s, 22 percent was American; by the end of 1992 Europeans broadcast over 400,000 hours of material, 35 percent of which was American. Roughly a quarter of European broadcasting was devoted to drama, but more than 70 percent of that was American, some 70,000 hours of programming. At the low end were the BBC and Italy's RAI, broadcasting 15 to 16 percent foreign content, while at the other end were movie channels such as Sky Movies, 75 percent of which was foreign content. Many within the E.U. didn't see the deficit decreasing but hoped it would not get bigger. Said E.C. external relations spokesman Jonathan Scheele, "It is not that this is even an economic or commercial issue. We look at it culturally and socio-economically."[35]

For some, Latin America stood as the new El Dorado in the early 1990s as it had decades earlier. Specifically the boom was to come from a growth in satellite-delivered channels to the region's cable systems. Catalyst for renewed activity was the 1990 entry of HBO Olé, a joint venture between Time Warner and Venezuela's Omnivision Latinamerican Entertainment (OLE or Ole). Mexico's Multivision cable system had as part owners Fox and UIP. By 1993 other satellite services available included CNN, ESPN, Fox, MTV, NBC News, the Cartoon Network, USA Network and Cinemax-Olé. By the end of 1993 some 24 satellite channels were available, with others on a waiting list to rent satellite space. There were then an estimated 3.5 million cable homes in Latin America. Illustrating that the game was only for very rich players was the estimated start-up cost of a new service in Latin America — $20 to $50 million, including a year's rent on Panamsat 1. At an average charge of 50¢ per month per subscriber (paid by the cable system to the channel), annual revenue would be $21 million a year. At $2 per month, which was the amount charged by HBO Ole, revenue would be $84 million a year. Problems included piracy by cable systems with no payment at all and subscribing cable operators who under-reported the number of subscribers they had.[36]

Prices for product weren't expected to skyrocket, but, said a Hollywood studio executive, "It's that an impressive array of newcomer services need product of all sorts and every U.S. company worth its salt is finding new ways to make money out of the shows it controls." Whatever expansion took place was expected to be controlled, said *Variety*, by the six Hollywood majors plus a handful of "mini majors" like Viacom, Worldvision and Turner. Within a couple of years of that being written, the three named mini companies had become part of the six majors. Viacom and Worldvision became part of Paramount, and Turner merged with Warner. MCA TV International president Colin Davis observed, "The more we go to these markets the more it hits home that the key to success in this business is owning the negative."[37]

Private television outlets continued to surface everywhere in the 1990s, always a benefit to U.S. suppliers. Spain had three private networks launch in 1990, causing a big boom in sales, and "The deals of the decade have been made over the past half year, mostly with the majors." Those deals totaled well over $1 billion in purchase of television material. Holland saw the launch of its first commercial network in 1995, followed by others, leading to more demand for U.S. product. On Holland's public network, up to 50 percent of programming came from American suppliers. When Portugal licensed its first private television outlet in 1992 the license winner announced he would not be caught in a bidding war for material. Instead, SIC company executive Luis Silva announced that SIC had reached a gentlemen's agreement with the state-run RTP whereby each agreed only to pay the "going price" for material.[38]

Following deregulation the European television landscape was served by more than 80 primary channels in 1994 and as many as 900 regional and local services. On top of that, over 120 channels were delivered by satellite to approximately one-third of western Europe's 140 million television households. Outside the U.K., commercial, ad-driven "free" television hardly existed in Europe until the mid–1980s. In Spain and Scandinavia commercial television didn't arrive at all until 1990.[39]

With the collapse of Communism the television landscape also changed dramatically in eastern Europe. Bulgarian state-run television executive Vladimir Kobakov was looking for both sponsors and programs in 1990 for his nation's two formerly ad-free channels. Particularly appealing were 13 years worth of episodes of "Dallas" and similar U.S. series. However, Bulgarian television could not come up with the $400 or so per episode it would take to buy such material. "Maybe we will be the last country in the world to see 'Dallas,'" wailed Kobakov. Worldvision ("Dallas" distributor) executive William Peck said, "I'm not a believer in rushing in to make the first deal and I'll certainly never give a program away for free." Czech television executive Jaroslav Bazant said that in his nation the proportion of foreign programming aired on the state-run network would increase from 24 percent in 1989 to 30 percent in 1990 to 40 percent in 1991. As of late 1990 Russians could watch Western music videos on an hour-long show on Friday nights produced by MTV Europe. Sponsors included Benetton (knitwear), L.A. Gear (shoes), Wrangler (jeans) and Renault (automobiles). Writing in *Forbes* magazine John Marcom said, "Perhaps the shows will take the Russians' minds off the fact that they can't afford the sponsors' products while winning Gorbachev a little extra time to get the economy going." As to the possibility of Bulgaria's airing "Dallas," Marcom said, "With 13 years' worth of episodes available, the show could go a long way toward dulling the average Bulgarian's mind to the mess the country's economy presently faces."[40]

An American company called StoryFirst got licenses, with local partners, for two Russian television stations, the first legitimate over-the-air commercial television outlets in Russia (Saint Petersburg) and Ukraine (Kiev). Programming included "CBS This Morning," "CBS Evening News with Dan Rather" and the "Geraldo" talk show. Cash investment by StoryFirst totalled just $1 million. Programming was supplied for no cash advance with payments to be made out of ad revenue. Initially the two stations planned to run 80 percent foreign programming. Worried that might lead to a backlash, StoryFirst was considering bringing a full-time program executive in from the U.S. to train local program makers.[41]

Vladimir Zelezny was awarded the license to start Nova (to launch early in 1993), one of the first private television networks in Czechoslovakia. Other global players after that license were Rupert Murdoch, Ted Turner and Silvio Berlusconi. According to reporter J. Robins, "When Nova launches on February 4, the network's programming will look a lot like a major American market independent." Zelezny had a huge capital investment from American investors and "is doing nothing less than setting up the model for other private networks in the former Eastern bloc." Major bankroller was the Central European Development Corporation (CEDC), which was investing over $35 million. CEDC was financed in part by cosmetics billionaire Ronald Lauder and run by former U.S. ambassador to Hungary Mark Palmer. CEDC was then fighting for licenses in other parts of eastern Europe with Nova to become the linchpin. Robins wrote, "Zelezny's cheering section includes Hollywood studios such as Disney, Columbia and Paramount, who are major program suppliers, along with multinational advertisers such as Procter & Gamble and Unilever." Investors believed that if Nova succeeded, that success would speed up the move toward privatization throughout the region. The only competition was from the state-run network Czech TV (CTV). Nova was then paying the equivalent of only around $1,000 per hour for U.S. programming, much of that done in barter deals for ad time. CTV was funded mainly by a set license fee of $60 per year paid by each television household. While CTV was limited to 12 minutes of commercials per broadcast day Nova was allowed 12 minutes of ads per hour.[42]

American feature films continued to be a major item for U.S. sellers. For 1991 Germany's two state-run networks and four major commercial networks combined to broadcast over 6,000 feature films, and about 60 percent of them were U.S. titles. Italy passed a law in 1990 limiting the number of U.S. films that could be broadcast by the country's national telecasters. For the following three years 40 percent of all films telecast had to be produced by E.U. nations, half of that, 20 percent, had to be reserved for Italian titles. As well, broadcasters were limited to three ad breaks per film, compared to the previous six or seven on some private channels. Films lasting more than 110 minutes were allowed four ad breaks. Overall all national private networks were limited to 11 minutes and 48 seconds of commercials per hour.[43]

If American news programs made minor gains abroad, others declined. Back in 1991 BBC news went on the Star TV satellite in Asia beaming into China among other countries. That contract gave BBC editorial control over its all-news service to prevent political meddling. All that took place before Fox's Rupert Murdoch bought Star TV. Quietly Murdoch developed a Chinese-language movie channel that was launched in 1994. To free up satellite space for the new channel, Star dropped the BBC news service from the outlet's northern satellite beam, which covered China, Taiwan and Hong Kong. Substituting movies for news satisfied Star's political and commercial objectives, which was to placate Beijing, which accused western news organizations of bias. Star allowed the BBC to continue airing on the southern satellite feed that covered India. Being dropped from the northern feed reduced the BBC's Asian exposure and reduced its revenues when it needed cash. Murdoch anticipated more advertising revenue as a result of replacing the news service with a movie channel.[44]

The selling of game shows increased offshore as the number of channels increased. They were the cheapest genre to produce, by far. Prior to the mid–1970s most game shows were franchised to foreign producers who televised their own version of the games at a fixed price. Said Mark Goodson Productions vice president Jerry Chester, "Unfortunately, these shows were often unsatisfactory and there was very little money in terms of fees." As time passed U.S. producers tried more and more to cut co-production deals for their shows, preferring to retain control over their shows and "to get significantly more money in fees." Major player in the game show genre was New York–based Fremantle Inc., which controlled shows such as "I've Got a Secret," "What's My Line?" "Concentration," and "The Match Game." Fremantle president Paul Talbot said in 1992 that fifteen years earlier the international production of game shows was a "nothing business," adding, "Many foreign producers would simply steal shows from the American market and air them in their own countries. Now we produce about 80 percent of all game shows in Europe encompassing 76 individual shows." When a small U.S. distributor signed a deal for Fremantle to sell "You Bet Your Life" offshore, company executive Bob Jacobs said of Talbot "He handles all of these shows which foreign networks need, then brings in producers and supervisors from the U.S. and sets everything up as a one-stop show." Fremantle was 80 percent owned by Interpublic, a consortium of American, Canadian and British advertising agencies.[45]

National Basketball Association Commissioner David Stern boasted in 1990 that NBA games were seen in 75 lands. That year the NBA expected to gross around $500 million, $5 million of that from offshore. Stern believed that with the explosion of program delivery sources all U.S. sports would expand rapidly on offshore television sets, saying, "There's going to be a high acceptance of things American." Five years later the NBA had some 90 offshore television deals signed worth about $15 million annually. And that led to the league's getting a yearly take of around $400 million in the foreign market from the sale of everything from T-shirts to coffee mugs. The NBA's annual package of 46 games plus a weekly half-hour highlights program offered, said NBA vice president Michael Dresner, "compelling characters like Shaquille O'Neal and Charles Barkley." Those basketball games were beamed to about 170 different nations through, in some cases, a barter system whereby Nike and Sprite bought ad time thus allowing the games to go to certain impoverished broadcasters for "free." Sprite's main on-air pitchman was Detroit Piston Grant Hill, who toured in 1995 some of the nations that carried NBA games. Dresner commented that the NBA made sure that Hill did a round of interviews not only on sports shows but also on programming that appealed to teens.[46]

Domestically ESPN was America's major sports network. Back in the mid–1980s it was providing service by tape to various Latin American broadcasters, moving to satellite delivery to the entire region starting in 1989. ESPN International executive Richard Stone declared, "The concept is right for us and for our programmers, either cable or broadcast. It's also right for advertisers, either those looking for upscale or for general public." Note that viewers were not mentioned here. In 1991 most of the ESPN feed was still in English, although in 1990 ESPN did carry the World Series in both English and Spanish. All programming originated from ESPN headquarters in Connecticut. There the feed was separated into international and domestic signals, sent up by the GTE Spacenet, downlinked in Miami, and then uplinked again onto the PanAmSat orbiter covering the Latin region. Stone explained, "As we put the international service together we did it in consultation with our previous clients and ad agencies. We asked them how we should approach the market.... We're not here just to pump American sports but international sports." The two feeds were different, with, for example, more soccer on the offshore feed. As to the advertising, which could be carried throughout Latin America or region by region, ESPN International executive Andrew Brilliant said, "This is such a powerful idea that many multinational firms such as Visa, British Airways and Budweiser are already involved with the network, and virtually every multinational company has been calling us." ESPN launched the first 24-hour pay-cable sports network for the Indian subcontinent in 1995.[47]

As always foreign producers tried to place their product on U.S. home screens. As always success remained negligible. At a forum on international coproductions held in the U.S. in 1994 talk turned to why the television sales road remained a one-way street. Explained journalist Brian Lowry, "What remains a huge obstacle is the perceived reluctance to buy dubbed product or even programs where the performers are thickly accented." Lowry added, "Experts point out that history has as much to do with the matter as cultural bias. Europeans grew up watching American television shows and movies as the continent righted itself in the wake of World War II and became accustomed to watching subtitled programs while Americans did not."[48]

When the Canadian-made series "Due South" aired in 1995-96 it was the only foreign program running on U.S. prime-time network television. Made by Alliance Communications Corporation its chairman Robert Lantos remarked, "Five years ago, we embarked on a strategy that heavily targeted U.S. networks." Although a Canadian show presented no problems in terms of language or accent, locale did. Although the series was shot in Toronto the fictional locale was Chicago; it was believed the series would not succeed in America if the fictional setting was Toronto.[49]

In the wake of the merger of U.S. media companies in the mid-1990s, there was some merger activity as well abroad in Europe. When asked if those larger European entities would have an easier time in getting foreign product on U.S. home screens, TCI cable giant president Adam Singer said, "I don't think it changes the game at all, because I don't think they ever had a chance to start off with."[50]

With the exception of Ted Turner's channels the most aggressive channel in offshore expansion was MTV, owned by Viacom (which also owned Nickelodeon, Nick at Nite and Paramount studios). Early in 1990 Brazil became the 34th country to receive a version of MTV. The music video channel was then available in 60 million homes abroad, compared to 50 million at home. MTV, started in 1981, began exporting in 1984 when network Nine in Australia began broadcasting five hours of MTV under license. Six months later MTV Japan launched with four hours of programming. In 1987 MTV formed a partnership with Robert Maxwell for MTV Europe, a consortium of cable, satellite and broadcast firms that soon reached 23 nations on the Continent. MTV chairman Tom Freston said, "From the outset, our vision has been that this would be a worldwide rock-and-roll network." Company executive John Reardon added, "The idea so far has been to get a foothold everywhere we can."[51]

All programming for MTV was produced from London, in English. That, said the *New York Times*, "tends to reinforce the longstanding British-American hegemony over pop. But MTV research suggests that European teenagers like it that way: English is considered the international language of rock-and-roll." Despite that assertion, MTV went off the air in 1991 in Japan as imitators proved more successful than the original. That was despite MTV programmers' having tinkered with the formula in an attempt to make it more indigenous, using Japanese hosts and artists "but retaining the American focus." In Latin America the Spanish-language MTV Internacional was available. One of its hour-long segments, "Trax," featured a Spanish-speaking host, English-language videos, and one or two videos by local artists "at the bottom of the lineup."[52]

By 1991 Viacom had bought out its partners in MTV Europe. Its largest group of advertisers were the U.S. film producers, plugging their latest releases in Europe. Other major sponsors were Pepsi-Cola and Wrangler jeans. With a reach into 29 million households in 28 countries MTV was the closest thing to a pan–European network. "While the weekly playlist is dominated by Anglo-American sounds, MTV dedicates about 15% of air time to indigenous European talent.... Although transmitting in English, most of MTV Europe's veejays hail from Holland, Scandinavia and other countries," observed *Variety*.[53]

Reporting on MTV's supposed philosophy of producing locally, thinking globally, *Newsweek* commented that MTV Europe "creates unity by speaking English, both in news and music.... Such groups as Sweden's Ace of Base, which MTV helped propel to stardom, would get scant air time if they sang in their native tongue." The outlet's aim was seen as a desire to "leverage" its U.S. videos to create one musical taste, one common language.[54]

MTV was reported to reach 260 million households in 70 nations in 1996. But the channel was being overshadowed by local music video channels that were springing up. By showcasing local talent singing in the local languages they were building audiences as large as MTV's in a fraction of the time. Thanks to digital compression technology, which allowed more channels in the same space, MTV began to slice its satellite signal into several more narrow signals, allowing MTV to offer a Hindi channel for India and a Mandarin outlet for China in addition to MTV, which broadcast in English.

The rise of those indigenous music channels eroded the American-based myth that U.S. entertainment could travel anywhere and that cultural exporters could pursue a "one size fits all" policy. Trying to respond to those local pressures MTV announced in 1996 it would customize its service more. MTV Europe would be customized for various nations throughout the continent; in Latin America MTV would move to three services: MTV Brazil, a northern MTV for the northern region and a southern feed for the south. While the core of the service was to remain the same across the globe, as much as 50 percent of a service could be customized to appeal to viewers in specific regions, said MTV.[55]

Expanding more rapidly than any other branded service was Ted Turner's CNN. Starting domestically in 1980, it moved into Europe in 1985, by making itself available there in major hotels. During 1989, CNN completed its around-the-world network of satellite agreements, being available in 110,000 hotel rooms, to some 4 million cable subscribers, to 43 newspaper offices, to 25 broadcasters, to 25 government agencies and in 17 airport lounges. Reporting on its effect, Elizabeth Guider wrote "Diplomats and bankers, politicians, businessmen and journalists, from Strasbourg to Singapore, regularly monitor and rely on its reports. If they can't, they are now regularly complaining or soliciting the local authorities to remove remaining restrictions and let the service in." The penetration by CNN helped open the door for other Turner services and Hollywood material in general.[56]

Turner Broadcasting System (TBS) had two services in Latin America in 1991. Early in 1988 TBS signed with indigenous company Telemundo to produce a Spanish-language nightly newscast with that Spanish news bureau established at CNN's Atlanta headquarters. The next year CNN expanded when it launched its CNN feed on PanAmSat (Pan American Satellite) to beam its 24-hour-a-day feed to Latin America. When CNN International launched in the region, the 24-hour feed was entirely in English, with the exception of two 30-minute Spanish-language newscasts. Sister service TNT Latin America launched in early 1991 in English, Spanish and Portuguese. Primarily it was a movie service showing material from the vast Turner holding of MGM, RKO and pre–1948 Warner product. In the beginning those two feeds were "clean"—that is, contained no ads—but TBS planned to reserve spots for commercials: "In the future, we will generate funds from the service and ads, as in the U.S.," said company executive Mary Ann Passante.[57]

Turner's next move in Europe came in 1993 when TBS announced it would bring in a service offering a mix of cartoons and old movies. It also announced the dedicated Cartoon Network would be launched in Latin America. The single European channel would be split; 14 hours a day of the Cartoon Network and 10 hours of the TNT service offering old films. Turner owned an animation library of over 8,500 cartoons (including the characters Yogi Bear, the Flintstones, the Jetsons and Tom and Jerry) and would draw on that. That service was broadcast in English with translations into French, Swedish, Norwegian and other languages "in some time periods."[58]

As Turner prepared to launch TNT/Cartoon in Europe later that year he faced an assault of legal and cultural challenges from countries led by France. French media minister Alain Carignon attacked the service for failing to ensure a majority of its programming was European as required under the European Television Without Frontiers (TWF) directive. He criticized the British government for giving the Turner channel a license to broadcast; nominally TNT/Cartoon was U.K. based. Turner's European executives insisted the channel operated within the directive, which said quotas applied only "where applicable." British authorities backed a further Turner argument claiming that as a start-up network with a tight budget it could not afford a lot of European programming. Moreover, it was by definition a channel of American cartoons and films and thus should be exempt for "cultural reasons." Nevertheless TBS gave vague assurances that it would increase European content over time. Another argument the service made was that it would be spending $5 million a year dubbing in France (most other languages were to be subtitled). TNT/Cartoon was to be a free channel, not pay television, free to satellite dish owners — then estimated at some 15 million in Europe — and also to be available on basic cable once a fee was negotiated with cable systems.[59]

A few days before the launch of the service in September 1993, Joao de Deus Pinheiro, the European culture commissioner, sent U.K. heritage minister Peter Brooke a letter of complaint demanding to know why Britain had granted Turner a satellite broadcasting license for TNT/Cartoon as, he said, it could be in breach of the E.C.'s TWF directive requiring 51 percent minimum European programming. E.C. rules allowed any channel licensed in one nation automatic access to the other E.C. nations. *Times* of London reporter Alexandra Frean thought the complaint was not likely to receive a sympathetic hearing in Britain, which had become the satellite capital of Europe, where, at the time, 50 "non-domestic" satellite channels had been set up in London.[60]

France's Carignon declared that the French television regulatory body, CSA, had indicated that it would not sign the "convention" Turner would need before French cable operators were legally permitted to carry the Turner channel unless TBS agreed "to give the necessary guarantees." Those guarantees would include a commitment to immediately screen European programming. Europe's indigenous movie channels, such as France's Cine-Cinema and Cine-Cinefil, were mostly pay channels and resented going against TNT/Cartoon, which was to be free and unhampered by content rules. Those indigenous channels did, of course, observe the 51 percent rule. But it looked like several years could pass before the E.C. handed down a firm, final decision in the Turner case and, noted one account, "if Turner's team can make a go of pan–European satellite broadcasting, other American companies, armed with giant catalogs that have largely been amortized, will be tempted to follow suit."[61]

As legal maneuvers continued, the government of Belgium issued a ban on the distribution of TNT/Cartoon network in Brussels, on the grounds it contravened the E.C.'s quota provisions. At that point, 1994, the Belgian distributor had ignored the ban saying it would fight all the way to the highest court. France's Audiovisual Council carried out an investigation and found that the Cartoon and TNT segments of the channel broadcast 100 percent and 97 percent U.S. content, respectively.[62]

In mid–1994, Ted Turner made an eight-city Asian tour, "downfield-blocking" foreign governments as he scoured the world for opportunities on the road to globalization. Said Turner vice president Bob Ross, "Over the next ten years, international is where long-term growth has to come from: the U.S. market is saturated." Instead of making money by selling its products to established broadcasters, the company was creating its own satellite-delivered channels around the world. Start-up costs for such channels were then estimated at $25 million. Added Ross, "The company's conscious strategy is simply to exploit what we've already paid for: CNN already had [international] bureaus; we owned the MGM and Hanna-Barbera libraries.... We could either let these assets sit in the vault or take them into new markets as full services. Our incremental costs are lower than someone without such cross-elasticity. In the short run, syndication revenues will be higher than [establishing international] networks, but in time, that will switch." At that time CNN was estimated to be available in 78 million households in over 200 offshore nations. Despite its continuing problems in Europe, TNT/Cartoon was beaming into 18.8 million homes in 1994, via the Astra 1C satellite; some 3 million households received those two separate channels in Latin America. Around the end of 1992 CNN International began to change its focus, creating more original programs for offshore markets with, reportedly, most of its weekday news shows custom made and not shown in the U.S. by mid–1994 — although they were still produced in Atlanta. CNN International then had ten satellite transponders leased, 29 international bureaus and revenues of $93 million annually but still reported a loss.[63]

While the percentage of foreign programs on television stations globally may not have been high enough to please U.S. producers, it remained true that what international trade in television material did take place was dominated and controlled by Hollywood. The reasons were almost always economic. Gianni Pasquarelli, an executive with Italy's RAI network, stated that in 1990 the U.S. produced 70 percent of the 300,000 hours of television fiction telecast on European networks. He added that 50 percent of program schedules in Germany, 45 percent in France, 42 percent in Spain and 25 percent in the U.K. were American. For European broadcasters to buy a prime-time drama series from the U.S. it cost 5 to 10 percent of what it would cost to produce a similar show domestically. A prime-time drama made in the U.S. cost between $900,000 and $2 million to produce while the same type of fare from America cost $30,000 to $60,000 to buy. Similar ratios existed throughout Europe. Still, it was noted that "Nationally produced programming is consistently favoured by European audiences, over American programming."[64]

In Denmark a programmer could buy an hour-long episode of "Dallas" or "Miami Vice" for under $5,000, less than the cost of producing one original minute of Danish drama. Todd Gitlin commented, "There is evidence that if Europeans had a choice, they would prefer programs produced in their own countries. But in the end, no one is forcing the Danes to watch American shows. In 'Dallas' and its ilk they must be attracted by a range of pleasure comparable to those Americans find." Also noted, in 1992, was that barely 1 percent of American prime-time television came from abroad.[65]

Speaking to the myth that U.S. fare was produced with international appeal in mind, Dick Zimmerman, Group W Production president, gave his definition of universal appeal: "Car goes down the street, car makes the wrong turn, car blows up. Guy jumps out of the car, guy grabs somebody, everybody understands that." Another executive, unnamed, said, "Lust-greed-sex-power. That's translatable anywhere." On the other hand David Plowright, head of the U.K.'s Granada Television, said, "I've always called money spent on acquiring programs dead money. It does nothing toward building a production capacity or a thriving creative community." Recalling the Italian market a decade earlier when Silvio Berlusconi and others were loading up their schedules with up to 95 percent cheap U.S. imports, Warner executive Michael Jay Solomon said, "We could sell them things they didn't really want, because they were hungry to fill up time periods."[66]

Data from a U.K. market research firm, AGB, collected in 1990 from 15 nations showed that U.S. programs occupied just over 20 percent of transmission time; Malaysia, New Zealand, Italy, Hong Kong and the Philippines broadcast the highest percentages, and Thailand, the U.K. and the Netherlands broadcast the lowest. However, in all cases, noted AGB executive Stephan Buck, "their ratings are surprisingly low." In a typical week in 1990 just over 800 U.S. programs were aired in those 15 countries. Of those, only 70 were watched by more than 10 percent of viewers; most had ratings of under 5 percent. A program with a 10 percent audience in the U.K. would not make the weekly top-100 list, and a show drawing 5 percent would not make the top 200. Buck added, "while American programs may dominate the airwaves in many countries, they certainly do not dominate the ratings." Most U.S. shows tended to be telecast at off-peak hours on minor channels.[67]

Britain's commercial independent Channel 4 paid £10,000 for a U.S. one-hour show, compared with an average acquisition cost for the channel for all programs of £26,000. With a new network then coming to the U.K., a report from the National Economic Research Associates concluded the new Channel 3 companies could collectively increase their profits by £200 million by reducing their home-produced fare to 60 percent. The Independent Television Commission had stipulated that at least 65 percent of the hours telecast should be local during the start-up phase.[68]

ABC split itself into five divisions in 1993, one of which was ABC Cable and International Broadcast Group. That division produced five times as much profit as the entire ABC network. British viewers had access to four television channels around 1988; five years later the number was about 30, thanks mainly to satellite delivery either direct through DBS or satellite-to-cable systems. France had gone from 3 channels to 22. Warner's Solomon observed that his company sold $100 million worth of television fare offshore in 1988 and $600 million in 1993. CBS was then selling about $100 million worth of entertainment and news programs abroad. It then produced and owned 4 of the 22 hours of CBS prime-time programming — which it was allowed to sell offshore. When Japan's Nippon Television wanted to buy the Steven Spielberg film *E.T.* from Universal, that outlet was compelled to take a package of 19 other titles and pay a total of $1 million. Faced with the cultural imperialism issue, Solomon said, "The cultural argument is bullshit. All that people in television care about is ratings and profits." As for the notion Americans were resented because of insensitive and aggressive business practices he stated, "You can't say this is the general feeling abroad. The general feeling abroad is that people totally welcome the Americans." Discussing strategy of offshore expansion ABC executive Herb Granath said, "Americans running anything poses problems" so "we always keep a low profile." That is, they took a minority position rather than majority control. Granath concluded, "It's all very much like a club. If you are a member, you get to play. If you are not a member, you get what's left over."[69]

Also expanding offshore was NBC, whose pan–European Super Channel was available in 60 million households, in 32 countries in 1994. Added to the outlet's schedule in 1995 were, among others, "Entertainment X-Press," the "McLaughlin Group" and live Notre Dame football. Its fledgling Asian operation, ANBC, was launched in 1994 into 15 nations in the region, with plans to expand to all of Asia. NBC then also reached 3 million households in Latin America.[70]

As U.S. producers increased their penetration of Europe, U.K. consultant Nick Lovegrove was worried: "There's a real prospect of American companies being the gatekeepers of entertainment distribution in large parts of Europe and indeed around the world." Although both France and Belgium had bans in force then prohibiting their national cable systems from distributing TNT/Cartoon, that Turner service was still available to viewers in those nations who owned their own satellite dish — some 100,000 households in France. Referring to satellites beaming down U.S. programs from the skies over Europe, the French called them "a genuine war machine ... Audiovisual is the major strategic prize of the next century and the European market the principal target of the big American communications groups." Denver-based cable giant TCI (to merge with Bell Atlantic) had invested $450 million in cable systems and cable programming networks by the end of 1993, with plans to spend another $100 million. Disney produced children's programs in conjunction with major networks in several European nations. Viacom, through MTV, was all over Europe. When Viacom introduced the channel Nickelodeon across Europe it did so in partnership with British Sky Broadcasting, a satellite firm that was half owned by Fox empire head Rupert Murdoch. NBC renamed its European service "NBC Superchannel." In a promo spot for that network, talk show host Jay Leno said jokingly, "We're going to ruin your culture just like we ruined our own." NBC chose to fill much of the pan–European network's schedule with NBC's shows from the United States, as opposed to trying to make their operation a little more European.[71]

Nepal introduced television in 1986, but it could only afford a low-power transmitter in Katmandu with a broadcast range of 15 miles. In 1992 Nepal's per capita gross national product was estimated at $170 with the nation's 20 million people having only 80,000 phones and fewer televisions. Nevertheless Nepal businessman Prazwoi Pradhan launched his private Space Time Network in 1994, piping 16 satellite-delivered channels into some 1,000 homes in the nation's capital. The cable system cost consumers $40 to install, $3 per month. U.S. television industry veteran Robert Button spent two months in Nepal helping Space Time develop a business strategy. He was a volunteer in the International Executive Service Corps funded by the U.S. government. With its liberal foreign-investment environment, Nepal, said Button, "is worthy of interest by U.S. companies."[72]

Offshore a race was developing to be the leader in kids' programming between the Fox Children's Network (reaching 6.8 million households in Latin America and Australia in late 1995), Turner's Cartoon Network (reaching 28 million homes in Europe, 2 million in Asia and 4.5 million in Latin America) and Viacom's Nickelodeon (available in 12.5 million households in Britain, Germany and Australia). Internationally, Fox and Nickelodeon tried to create new shows with offshore partners, and the Cartoon Network relied on its own library. Said Turner executive David Levy, "Kids are kids and a blue dog is a blue dog. Nobody's going to say Huckleberry Hound is too American." Marketing of the Turner channel was in full swing in Mexico and South America, with a Cartoon Network magazine and candy, clothing and toy lines. As well, Toon Tours brought performers in the costumes of characters like Yogi Bear to malls or arenas where they performed and often signed up families for cable service.[73]

Murdoch's Sky Movies had, by 1990, acquired 3,000 films (many, of course, from Fox itself), paying $150,000 to $1.5 million per title in 175 separate deals. Additionally it also screened, wrote reporter Don Groves, "a weekly average of eight hours of programming including film reviews, upcoming theatrical releases and 'Entertainment Tonight,'" all of which were little more than advertising promotion for U.S. television and cinema product.[74]

American suppliers wanted an open-skies policy by which they could beam down their own product, and they wanted those open skies only under their own conditions. The MPEA lobbied the European Commission regarding the overlapping of satellite footprints, which allowed programs to be received in territories in which they were not licensed. It wanted European copyright changes so its entertainment business would be protected by nation-to-nation sequential distribution. Malaysia's television networks also came under pressure from U.S. suppliers to limit their reception outside of Malaysia. Principally the move was to prevent Malaysian programming from being viewed in Indonesia, where the use of satellite dishes was reported to be widespread. Malaysia's three networks used two satellites to convey programs to East Malaysian states. However, signals were also picked up as far afield as the Philippines and Vietnam. U.S. companies invoked a clause under the Berne Copyright Convention stating that television signals picked up outside the country to which material had been sold must be coded. According to Information Minister Datuk Mohamad Rahmat U.S. distributors gave the networks a deadline to encode their signals or face the possibility of a cutoff in supply of American product. Around 80 percent of the material used on two of the three networks (one government run, one private) was foreign, mainly American. Publicly Malaysia's response was a threat to buy less U.S. material, with Rahmat also arguing in favor of the "free flow" of information. Privately, though, Malaysia quickly conceded to the U.S. threat, asking only for more time to organize the coding operation. Within a few months Malaysia encrypted its television signals.[75]

Offshore revenue from television exports continued to increase dramatically for U.S. suppliers through the 1990s. But the Americans tended to celebrate those figures quietly because, said *Variety*, "While the European market provides a healthy revenue stream to U.S. companies, no one wants to break out figures. This reticence stems partly from hypersensitivity to European criticism of American cultural imperialism, product dumping and the lack of reciprocity in opening up the U.S. market to Euro programming." For the year 1989, U.S. producers accounted for 71 percent of the total world trade in television material, taking $1.7 billion of the world total of $2.4 billion. The world total was expected to reach $5 billion in 1995, but America's share was predicted to drop from 71 percent to 69 percent in 1990 and to 60 percent in 1995. Europe imported $1.6 billion worth of product in 1989, $1.8 billion in 1990.[76]

America's three major television networks, CBS, NBC and ABC, had annual revenues of around $175 million in total from foreign sales, just 7 percent of the $2.3 billion U.S. suppliers then took offshore. Recent FCC rule changes had just reversed a 20-year ban on the ability of the three networks to distribute anything other than the few in-house programs they produced each year. Theoretically it meant they could become bigger players, but it may have been too late, as the Hollywood majors controlled 80 percent or more of the revenue from U.S. offshore television sales. For the year ending June 30, 1988, the American Film Marketing Association (the main independent trade group, with 93 members) reported its revenue from foreign television sales was $224 million.[77]

For 1994, U.S. major exporters of television material took in $2.25 billion from overseas, $1.7 billion in revenue from free television outlets and $550 million from pay television outlets. American independent distributors accounted for another $300 to $400 million in revenue from abroad that year.[78]

Worldwide for 1995 (including the U.S.), revenue for the major U.S. producers from sales of filmed entertainment was about $8.6 billion, with home video accounting for 53 percent (the first year it topped the 50 percent mark); theatrical rentals, 27 percent; television sales, 18 percent; other sources, 2 percent. Home video was just as important offshore as at home. For example, the Buena Vista (Disney) 1995 animated film *The Lion King* sold about 25 million units offshore, compared to 30 million domestically. Based on an average wholesale price of $12 that film generated $300 million in offshore revenue for Disney.[79]

Figures leaked from the MPAA for 1995 indicated U.S. majors took $1.94 billion in 1995 from overseas sales to free television outlets. This combined with their $700 million in receipts from pay television outlets and the MPAA's "conservative" estimate of $300 million in revenue for the independents meant U.S. exporters took in a total of around $3 billion in television revenue in 1995. Those major producers were Warner, MCA, Paramount, Columbia TriStar, Disney, Fox, MGM and, as of 1994, Ted Turner's empire. Since then the Warner and Turner entities have merged. In individual markets (free outlets) Europe paid out $1.27 billion for U.S. fare (over 50 percent of the $1.94 billion total — up 14 percent on 1994). Far East revenue was $272 million (up 11 percent); Latin America, $129 million (up 2 percent); Canada, $157 million ($134 million in 1994); Australia, $82 million ($66 million in 1994); India, $967,000 ($2 million in 1994). Top European markets were Germany, $396 million ($302 million in 1994); France, $196 million ($145 million); U.K., $195 million ($168 million); Italy, $191 million ($142 million); and Spain, $100 million worth of Hollywood majors' television product in 1995, a decrease from the $258 million purchased in 1994. China took $3 million worth of product in 1995.[80]

Chapter 10

1990s:
"We Want Total
Access to Culture"

At the start of the 1990s U.S. suppliers going into Latin America on PanAmSat 1 were targeting an estimated 2.5 million households served by cable operators. Services such as CNN, ESPN, TNT, MTV and HBO Ole (a 50-50 joint venture between HBO parent Warner and Venezuela's largest cable system, Omnivision) roamed the skies. They expected to receive no more than $1 a month from subscribers, making total revenue a maximum of $30 million a year or more likely half of that. Thus they expected to lose money at first. In 1992 none of those services were talking publicly about numbers or income. Argentina then had an estimated 1,000 cable systems — only half of which were legal — ranging from a tiny operator with 300 subscribers up to Cablevision with 100,000 subscribers and VCC with 75,000 (both of those were in Buenos Aires). Argentina's capital had just 7 percent of its homes cabled. Cablevision charged subscribers $39 a month; VCC, $51. HBO Ole charged cable operators between $1.75 and $2.20 per month per subscriber; TNT, $1.50; ESPN, 68¢; but ECO (a latin service showing Mexican films, news, and so on from Mexico's Televisa) charged 20¢ per subscriber per month.[1]

Mainly those U.S. cable services in Latin America filled their air time with American programs dubbed in Spanish. As to the issue of whether or not those suppliers would invest in local production, reporter Meredith Amdur commented, "Because U.S. programs always have been extremely popular in Latin America, major producers and distributors see little need to spend much on production." Warner executive Michael Jay Solomon added, "The revenue generated in Latin America is too little, for the time being, to justify huge production budgets." Warner had then partnered with Venezuela's Marte TV, and Fox joined Mexico's Grupo Televisa.[2]

About 100 satellite-delivered channels roamed the Latin American skies by mid–1995, feeding a pay television market that generated an estimated $2.5

241

billion in 1994. Except for MTV Latino and MTV Brasil (which employed Spanish- and Portuguese-speaking veejays from their inception), "U.S. programmers began by creating regional channels that were basically dubbed or subtitled versions of a domestic signal. Scheduling changes and colorful promos helped create a distinctively Latin feel," said *Variety*. More channels arrived as both Warner and Sony (Columbia) announced new outlets for the region. Over the longer term two major U.S. satellite companies, PanAmSat and Hughes Communications (a satellite builder), announced they were committed to direct broadcast satellite (DBS) projects budgeted at several hundred million dollars each over the coming few years. Some of those existing U.S. services were said to be moving to more original programming, under pressure from Latin satellite-delivered services. ESPN then had 4.9 million Latin subscribers, and MTV Latino had 5 million. As to that original programming, ESPN reportedly had 35 to 40 percent of its programming created specifically for the service, while, wrote reporter Andrew Paxman, MTV was "screening interviews with U.S. and British acts conducted not by Anglos but by Latinos, who translate to camera." For its part TNT introduced a Sunday night film slot, "Passaporte Internacional," which featured mainly Latin American films while CNN International increased its daily count of half-hour Spanish-language newscasts from four to six. Fox also had its own branded Latin channel but was resisting the idea of the extra expense that original programming required.[3]

Those two new services, Warner Channel and Sony Entertainment Television, were both joint projects with HBO Ole in which the latter handled distribution. When HBO Ole launched in 1991 it was one of only four U.S. services in Latin America. By mid–1995 about 20 of those 100 channels were American outlets.[4]

Grandiose plans to dominate the satellite television market in Latin America were announced in 1995-96. Rupert Murdoch's News Corp said it would launch a DBS service with three partners: America's largest cable operator, TCI (Tele-Communications Inc); Brazil's leading media group, Globo; and Mexico's biggest broadcaster, Grupo Televisa. With a total investment of $500 million the service planned to transmit 150 channels and to have 1 million subscribers at the time of startup. With a potential of 400 million viewers (80 million households) in the region, the consortium hoped eventually to reach 40 million viewers —10 percent. News Corp was to have a 30 percent stake, TCI 10 percent, and the other two partners 30 percent each. Around the same time a second consortium announced plans to offer a similar DBS service. Led by Hughes Communications (part of the Hughes Division of General Motors) this group contained three smaller Latin media groups, Venezuela media magnate Gustavo Cisneros, Brazil's TVA and Mexico's Multivision. Cisneros said that DBS "is going to unite all of Latin America." However, decoder boxes for either system would cost an estimated $700 to

$800 per box. To reach the kind of mass market those proposed services wanted, those boxes would have to be leased or subsidized. It remained to be seen whether either service would succeed or even get off the ground.[5]

In other parts of the world the skies were more fully opened to U.S. product, though sometimes efforts were made to close those skies. Qatar's government banned satellite dishes in 1993 so that residents who wanted to view foreign broadcasts were compelled to subscribe to a state cable system run by the government. The only alternative was state-run Qatar TV and such channels as could be picked up by regular antennae from other Persian Gulf broadcasters, all of which were government run. That Qatar cable system carried CNN, Egyptian broadcasters and selected European stations of "a respectable nature."[6]

Japan's government announced in 1995 that Rupert Murdoch's Star TV and Turner Entertainment Networks Asia would be the first foreign satellite broadcasters allowed to beam their programs to Japanese subscribers. It was a first step toward opening the skies to foreign broadcasters following deregulation initiatives. Some U.S. observers considered it just a small step in the right direction, pointing out that Star and Turner had won approval to distribute their programming in Japan via Japanese cable television firms only. A Turner spokesmen remarked, "It's still going to cost us a lot of money to distribute in Japan, but not as much as it did before." Until then CNN had been available less than eight hours a day through Japanese over-the-air telecasters. Star planned to launch four channels in Japan; Turner expected to enter with its cartoon/movie service. Only about 1 million households in Japan, a nation of 124 million people, were wired for cable.[7]

Discovery Channel signed an agreement with Malaysia's sole subscription television service, Mega TV, to start service in late 1995 by providing a 24-hour-a-day channel in English that the country's education minister hoped would help raise the standard and fluency of that language among Malaysians. The nation's government wanted to push wide use of English in the country but had run into considerable resistance. Mega TV was operated by Cablevision Services, itself a consortium of five entities, one of which was the Malaysian government itself. Other services to be offered included CNN and ESPN. As all those entertainment services were to be delivered in English, Mega TV became the only service in Malaysia not obliged to carry any Malay programming. Education Minister Mohd Najib Tun Razak commented, "The Discovery Channel's type of programming will provide another dimension to the (currently weak) English language environment in Malaysia." Regarding all those English-language outlets to be provided, Mega TV chairman Khalid Ahmad declared, "This would make Mega TV an important English-teaching tool in Malaysia via entertainment, unencumbered by political baggage." With tough local censoring laws, services such as HBO were likely to agree to censoring of their material by local authorities; HBO had already agreed to package programs to suit conservative audiences to meet a demand by the government of Singapore. Malaysia also announced it would lift its ban on owning private satellite dishes early in 1996, just ahead of that nation's own satellite launch.[8]

A breakthrough occurred in India in 1994 when the state-run television telecaster Doordarshan started to broadcast MTV's "Most Wanted" segment, a five-day-a-week request show, with sponsors that included Coca-Cola. Doordarshan had permitted advertising on television at all only in the mid–1980s. MTV's deal marked the first time ads were permitted on the programs of foreign origination. To mark the occasion a launch party was planned in India for October 3, 1994, with ten MTV executives flown into Bombay from the U.S. and various parts of Europe. But the whole celebration was canceled because of a local plague outbreak.[9]

China announced the most sweeping action when, in 1993, it barred private individuals from owning satellite dishes in addition to prohibiting television stations and cable systems from using foreign satellite-delivered television product, as Beijing Cable was then doing by carrying ESPN. As a result ESPN was pulled off the system but was back in two months with ESPN programs recorded on video cassettes by the cable system and then piped to viewers after a delay. That method was ruled acceptable by the Chinese government, which made no real effort to enforce its dish ban. As to the amount of foreign material allowed on local outlets Xu Xiongxiong of the China TV Program Agency stated flatly that China had a sort of unofficial television quota that provided for a maximum of 20 percent foreign content. But he acknowledged that Chinese stations rarely met that quota. Bartering remained a major way of dealing in television product, as no cash was involved and thus avoided government oversight to a large extent. A standard agreement was for a station to yield one minute of advertising time for each one hour of programming, 30 seconds in major cities.[10]

CNN was distributed in China in late 1995 only on a limited basis to certain hotels and government offices, in English. For the Turner company it was a market "waiting to happen" with 30 million cable subscribers, increasing by 5 million per year. To try to increase the Turner presence in China company executive Bob Ross explained, "We've sold branded blocks of programming to individual cable systems in China, and we've also sold programming directly to the Ministry of Radio, Film and Television for their networks."[11]

In 1993 Rupert Murdoch made the statement that the information revolution was "an indigenous threat to totalitarian regimes everywhere." That remark was widely believed to have led to China's banning of dish ownership by individuals. Ever since, Murdoch worked to get back into Chinese good graces. Finally, in 1996, Star TV received permission to broadcast a single Chinese-language channel into China, to be available free to satellite dish owners. A company was set up in Hong Kong with two Chinese firms as partners with Star. While their identity was never revealed, rumor had it that both entities were linked to the government, one to the Chinese military and one to the Ministry of Radio, Film and Television. The deal circumvented China Central Television, which opposed the venture. Originally Star wanted permission for three Chinese-language channels but settled on an agreement for one service to get its foot in the door. One step Murdoch took along his road to redemption occurred in 1994, when he pulled the BBC World Service off his Star TV northern beam for supposed economic reasons. He later conceded he did so to placate Beijing officials who were unhappy with the content of certain BBC programs. Of course, Star TV didn't need any approval from China at all, as it could have uplinked as many Chinese-language or other services it wanted and beamed into China. But that was not practical at the time because Star wanted to link up with China's 1,000-plus cable systems to get that subscriber revenue. Beijing did have some control over that, since those cable systems were all based locally, of course. A wholesale ignoring of any government's wishes was practical only if most of the population had its own household satellite dish and if a reliable method of collecting monthly revenue from remote, foreign subscribers existed. Otherwise it was best to deal with, and placate, governments.[12]

Private television networks in Indonesia came under fire for their propensity to telecast U.S. action films and series, which, said the critics, incited street violence. Public broadcaster TVR1, which was not allowed to run ads, also bought a lot of U.S. product. In both cases the main reason was economic — American material was cheap. An episode from the U.S. could be had in Indonesia for $2,500; the cost of a local episode ranged between $10,000 and $15,000.[13]

Before Indonesia scrambled the television signals beamed down from its Palapa satellite in 1994 at the insistence of the Hollywood MPAA lobby group, an estimated 1 million satellite dishes had been purchased by Indonesians to pick up the then free-to-dish transmission. The problem was that some nine months after encryption only about 10,000 households had signed up for the pay television service Indovision. Presumably the rest of those million dish owners were sticking to the terrestrial free-to-air telecasters. With the state-run TVR1 service plus five commercial networks Indonesians were not thought to be starved for program choices. Indovision then handled a package consisting of CNN, ESPN, HBO Asia, the Discovery Channel and TNT/ Cartoon Network. It also planned to distribute Star TV's 16 to 20 channels when Star launched later on. Indovision's parent company was part of a conglomerate headed by Bambang Trinatmodjo, a son of Indonesian president Suharto.[14]

One of the new channels slated to debut in Indonesia and other parts of the region in 1996 was MGM Gold, Asia's first Hollywood-studio branded general entertainment channel. Featured were to be films from the UA catalog and post–1985 MGM titles (Ted Turner owned the earlier MGM titles, having acquired them earlier when he very briefly owned MGM). MGM/UA had merged into a single entity in the past. Also to be screened on MGM Gold were series ranging from "evergreens" such as "Highway Patrol" to modern ones. That channel was a joint venture of MGM/UA and Indonesia's Asia Media Management Ltd. First to sign up for MGM Gold was Indovision. *Variety* reported that "MGM Gold is a concrete example of MGM's long-term aim of forming networks around the world through equity partnerships. It's in keeping with attempts by other U.S. majors — ranging from Ted Turner's TNT/Cartoon Network to Time Warner's various HBO payboxes — to lift their foreign program sales efforts to a new level. Instead of selling their shows piecemeal to local broadcasters, Hollywood increasingly is taking advantage of new technologies and media deregulation abroad to offer webs of U.S.-originated programming."[15]

Infighting by Hollywood's majors over world domination of television was evident in Asia. Late in 1995 Star engineered a management takeover of Indovision after which two Star employees were placed in top management positions — for consideration unreported. Since its early 1994 launch, Indovision had carried the above listed five stations, the so-called Gang of Five. However, it was then two years after launch and encryption, and still only 14,000 of those 1 million dish owners had signed up. The Gang was unhappy to learn their archrival was then in a position to control the marketing and distribution of their channels in Indonesia. Almost immediately Star imposed "harsh" but undisclosed financial terms on the Gang of Five. One of them said, "They're trying to stick it into us, which is what we would do if we were in the same boat."[16]

Around the mid–1990s Asia was seen by the U.S. television exporters as the new El Dorado, with a resultant renewal of energy to push more product into the area. With two-thirds of the world's population, a growing middle class, growing economies and a perception of limited program choice and pent-up demand, Asia was an appealing market. Negative aspects were (1) a proliferation of channels would dilute ad revenue, (2) subscription television required persuasion of the people to pay and (3) no highly developed way of collecting those fees existed. In the old days U.S. suppliers sold syndicated television material to existing indigenous broadcasters. In the new rush they continued to do so but turned more to marketing entire channels. Complaining about Western television influence Malaysian prime minister Datuk Seri Mahathir bin Mohamad declared, "Today they broadcast slanted news. Tomorrow they will broadcast raw pornography to corrupt our children and destroy our culture." Fox's Rupert Murdoch bought Star TV in 1993 (it was started in 1990 by an Asian entrepreneur) to penetrate the area; HBO International, a Warner subsidiary and the world's largest subscription movie-channel service was already established. Under pressure from Washington to halt copyright infringement Taipei legalized its cable industry in 1993. It existed in an illegal, unregulated fashion before that, as it did in other countries, with the result being much pirating of signals and, of course, no payments to U.S. suppliers. South Korea embarked on a crash program of cable expansion to try to win back DBS viewers. By embracing cable, some governments hoped viewers would receive enough "choice" without the governments' opening their closed skies. Murdoch's Star TV offered "government-friendly" programming, and HBO's Asian operation based in Singapore and carried there on cable edited profanity, sex and violence out of its Singapore feed. Asian broadcaster researcher Susan Schoenfeld found that U.S. exporters were planning to bring English-language product to Asia without any understanding of how little English fluency there was in the region. She also found some suppliers subtitling rather than dubbing (the latter was much more expensive) programs targeted at viewers who could hardly read. ESPN was then dubbing a Mandarin track for some of its shows from the network's studio in Bristol, Connecticut. Still, as one account noted, "The most popular shows in the region are overwhelmingly local."[17]

HBO International president Lee DeBoer declared, "Asia could be bigger for us than the U.S." Murdoch referred to Star TV as offering "Very basic stuff—very old American programming, plus their own version of MTV and a sports channel." Star beamed five channels via satellite at the start of 1994 free of charge to 39 nations in the region. Its main rival in the region was the Gang of Five (actually the number in the Gang was a changing one), a consortium led by CNN, ESPN, HBO, Time Warner, Viacom and the Disney Channel. HBO Asia was a joint venture between Warner and Paramount Communications, which then had some 300,000 subscribers in the region. It sent its movie channel to pay-television services in Singapore, Thailand, Taiwan and the Philippines. As *Fortune* magazine observed, "The battle for Asian eyeballs has just begun."[18]

Murdoch bought an Indian station, the Hindi Zee TV; thus his Star TV service introduced Indian audiences to U.S. culture in the form of "Santa Barbara" and "Dynasty." It was the same India that in 1992 paid the U.S. majors a paltry $70,000 for television product. Responding to the inclusion, Indian state broadcaster Doordarshan decided to launch three new channels and bought more U.S. product itself in the process. The price for a U.S. series moved from $800 to $1,800 per hour in India. Overall, U.S. movies sold well in Asia, but television series, with the exception of some action series, did not; they were scheduled mostly in fringe times. Hollywood grumbled that stations paid "peanuts for series," as little as $1,500 per hour in Malaysia and Indonesia. For the eight Asian markets of Korea, the Philippines, Taiwan, Hong Kong, Indonesia, Malaysia, Thailand and Singapore, the majors reaped a total of "only" $30 million in 1992, from a high of $6.8 million in Korea to a low of $1.1 million in Singapore. Fox was then the only major studio supplying movies to its sister agency Star TV's free-to-air Star Plus channel, the other majors were waiting for Star to encrypt its signals. As well, those other Hollywood majors complained that Star was offering only $3,000 per hour for series to be broadcast in 39 markets. HBO Asia chief William Hooks said his outlet was challenging "the idea that Asians only want to see Asian programming.... Asians, particularly the young, have become more affluent, more educated and more multilingual. It's clear that audiences and advertisers throughout Asia can sustain more outlets." Yet everywhere local shows dominated the ratings. Korea state broadcaster KBS's two channels captured 85 to 88 percent of the viewers. The launch of private outlet SBC there in 1991 had succeeded in increasing the price of an average U.S. movie from $12,000 to $35,000.[19]

When China announced its ban on the individual ownership of satellite dishes in 1993 — never really enforced — the government declared that controlling foreign television "is an important measure to exercise and safeguard our national sovereignty." In the summer of 1994 the Gang of Five began broadcasting to the region on a new Hughes satellite. Star TV's free-to-air (free to dish owners and cable systems) announced it would shortly encrypt. One of the Gang of Five was ESPN, whose executive Andrew Brilliant commented, "Unlike Murdoch's, our signal is encrypted. We don't impose ourselves on the marketplace. We go only where we are wanted. We're dealing only with cable and other forms of terrestrial distribution that are sanctioned."[20]

While HBO Asia was a co-venture between Warner and Paramount, the latter studio was also partnered with Universal and MGM/UA in United International Pictures Pay-TV, a venture whose policy was to pursue equity positions in offshore pay services. By the end of 1994, HBO entered the new territories of Bangladesh and Papua New Guinea. They were small territories, "but every bit helps," explained executive William Hooks.[21]

Star TV was avoided by the U.S. majors because of its stingy payment rates. The service managed to maintain a relatively low initial investment and operating cost through revenue-sharing joint ventures with program suppliers. According to one account Star secured cheap programming through arrangements with MTV, BBC and Prime Sports Network of Denver. Apart from a small downpayment Star would pay nothing for a program until it started making money. Asian observer Joseph Man Chan commented, "In Europe, the introduction of satellite and commercial television has weakened, if not shattered, the dominance of public broadcasters." Noting that television in most of Asia's developing nations was controlled by a national government, he added, "The advent of Star TV will increase the pressure toward the general trend of deregulation in broadcasting, thereby lessening the role of government broadcasters. Indeed, it will become very difficult, if not impossible, to police the reception of satellite television when technological advances further miniaturize the required dish. The national television system will be locked into direct competition in terms set by Star TV and other satellite services."[22]

Turner launched his single service TNT/Cartoon network in Asia late in 1994 with the same split as in Europe: 14 hours of cartoons, 10 of movies. Since some of the markets, such as Indonesia, were predominantly Muslim, Porky Pig cartoons were not on the schedule. Disney was in the region, as was NBC, with plans to start a 24-hour-a-day business channel, with 10 hours of that to be local Asian programming. Singapore had a law that prohibited private individuals from using satellite dishes. Conceding that the time could soon come when it could no longer enforce that law, the state started up Singapore Cable Vision in 1995, offering some 50 channels, hoping to thereby exercise some measure of control over television by forestalling people from buying dishes.[23]

One of the earliest U.S. services to enter the area was MTV, which was beamed down from the Star satellite in 1991. When Murdoch bought the system in 1993 relations soured between MTV and Star as Star imposed harsher financial conditions. Finally the pair broke off their relations, with MTV jettisoned from Star in May of 1994. It remained off the Asian airwaves until it re-entered in October on India's state telecaster Doordarshan. But MTV had to agree to a review of its programming by the Indian government and stood ready to make the same deal elsewhere. Murdoch quickly replaced MTV with another music outlet, Channel V, jointly owned by four major record firms: BMG Music, EMI Music, Sony Pictures Entertainment and Warner Music Group. In 1995, MTV and PolyGram announced they had joined forces to start two MTV channels in Asia. After investigating starting its own record company, MTV parent Viacom decided instead to join forces with PolyGram, which had the largest market share in Asia (excluding Japan) of any record company.[24]

When Australia announced in 1994 that pay television would be allowed to launch, two groups quickly formed to fight for the market. While both had Australian stakeholders, the dominant players were the U.S. majors. One company was Galaxy, which signed equity and long-term licensing deals with Sony Pictures Entertainment (Columbia), MCA (Universal) and Paramount. The other company was Optus, which had reached similar deals with Warner, Disney and MGM/UA.[25]

When Australian media writer Tom O'Regan looked at the Australian television situation in 1993 he wrote, "In Australia and Canada, U.S. producers have been able to organize forms of block-booking, whereby Australia and Canadian television buyers must acquire programs they do not want in order to secure programs they do. Such ongoing arrangements provided one of the means by which U.S. producers have tied up the Australian commercial television market to exclude English-language producers from Britain, Canada and New Zealand ... this Australian purchasing situation became even more distorted in the late 1980s by Australian networks entering output agreements with Hollywood studios and affiliation agreements with U.S. networks." By early in 1993 Australian networks were seeking adjustments in their favor including "less reliance on deals which required them to buy programs they did not want along with those they did."[26]

As negotiations for the North American Free Trade Agreement (NAFTA) between Canada, the U.S. and Mexico began in spring 1991 U.S. trade representative Carla Hills told Canadian reporters that culture had to be on the bargaining table. Canada's representative Michael Wilson declared culture would not be on the table. Canada had obtained a cultural exemption in the Free Trade Agreement (FTA) signed in the 1980s by the two northern nations. The cultural exemption perpetuated a familiar charade, the myth that Canada had succeeded in protecting its cultural sector during FTA negotiations. U.S. corporations were especially bothered by Cancon quotas on television, which "discriminated" against U.S. product; and Bill C58, which disallowed tax breaks for Canadian advertisers using U.S. airwaves; and simulcasting requirements, which interfered with the "relationship" between U.S. advertisers and their Canadian audience. They were also annoyed by public funding of film and television production and in general by the state broadcaster CBC. Observed Canadian reporter Colleen Fuller, "Americans have long understood that U.S. penetration of the international cultural sphere would enable them to better control and influence the political discourse in other countries." In the spring of 1991 Mexican, American and Canadian unions representing performers in film, television and radio agreed to oppose any free trade agreement. Fuller wrote, "Aggressive public, regulatory and tax policies are precisely what is required to sustain a Canadian film industry, and these are precisely what are being done away with by free trade." Although the FTA 1980s agreement exempted culture, the deal contained a "notwithstanding" clause that meant that any negative economic impact on U.S. communications or entertainment industries caused by Canadian regulatory, tax or fiscal policies in the cultural sector could be "countervailed" with the equivalent commercial effect in other sectors of the Canadian economy. During the 1980s negotiations, U.S. entertainment companies targeted Canadian nontariff barriers "imposed under the guise of political or cultural concerns" as major impediments to their international business activities, in part because Canada set a poor example to other nations that had or were contemplating similar regulatory measures to protect their own industries from U.S. penetration. Under the simulcast rule, when a program was running on both a Canadian and a U.S. station at the same time cable systems had to run the Canadian signals on both channels. That combined with Bill C58 generated an estimated $130 million in revenue in 1989 for Canadian broadcasters.[27]

As the NAFTA negotiations continued in 1991, MPAA president Jack Valenti, extremely upset when culture was excluded from FTA, vowed it would not happen again. Valenti wanted Cancon quotas abolished, among other demands, saying, "All we're asking is to have the right to compete without artificial barriers." A newly formed lobby group in Canada in favor of cultural protection had as one member Gordon Ritchie (a former ambassador, a free trade advocate and the Canadian architect of the FTA deal), who declared "When the world's biggest economic superpower comes to you and says, 'We want total access to culture,' the answer is and will be an absolute, categorical 'no.'" He added, "It's not a question of access; it's a question of total domination here. Jack Valenti and that crowd have incredible access to the Canadian market." Ritchie reported that at the time of NAFTA talks American product represented more than 90 percent of English-language television in Canada and more than 70 percent in publishing and music and U.S. movies accounted for 97 percent of screen time in Anglo Canada, 78 percent in Quebec. "We've already allowed a great deal of erosion of Canadian culture. So what we're saying now is we've allowed you to go that far and no further. Period. Absolutely, totally non-negotiable. What we're talking about is protecting the last 3 percent to 30 percent," explained Ritchie. Countered Valenti, "We don't think there should be quotas of any kind. We don't have quotas, we don't think there should be quotas anywhere in the world. Keep in mind who chooses what movies they see, Canadian citizens. It's a question of free choice." Southam publishing spokesman John Fisher said, "It's important that Canada stick up for this rather than taking the view that it's all free trade. It isn't. It's our culture."[28]

While culture was exempted from NAFTA Peter Mortimer, head of the Canadian Film and Television Producers Association, reported in 1992 that Canadian airwaves were still dominated by U.S. fiction. Price was considered to be the key reason, as Canadian broadcasters could acquire a U.S. one-hour episode for $75,000 against an average $200,000 per hour for original English-language programming. Mortimer explained, "The big issue is that the programming slots aren't there for Canuck shows because they're filled with American programs acquired for a lesser license fee."[29]

The coming of DBS television created worries in Canada in 1993, with the regulatory body CRTC holding hearings on satellite television. Huge satellite dishes had been owned by private individuals in Canada for some time. Their numbers were small, and while they were illegal the Canadian government had completely abandoned enforcement of that law. But the coming of those small, "pizza-size" satellite dishes caused more worries, as they were expected to be widely available and relatively cheap. They could be used easily in city homes with little or no yard space and in apartments. Also worried was the Canadian cable industry — 75 percent of Canadian homes were wired — which fretted those coming "deathstars" would kill them off, as viewers were expected to receive hundreds of channels on those 18-inch dishes. It would be simple, said Stanley Hubbard, a U.S. entrepreneur at the hearing who planned to start up another Canadian cable service, and would render the CRTC impotent if "you just call a 1-800 number in Utah to get your services."[30]

An imposing array of America's largest companies stood behind DirecTv, the "death star" then up and running and threatening Canada. Actually it was a satellite parked 22,000 miles over Kansas. DirecTv was part of the General Motors (GM)/Hughes Electronics conglomerate, itself the oldest and largest commercial satellite firm in the world. Decoders and dishes for DirecTv were manufactured by RCA, and its service center was run by Matrix Marketing Inc., America's largest telemarketer. Operating the DBS billing center was Digital Equipment Corp. (DEC), second only to IBM in the manufacture of U.S. computers; Sony corporation provided the equipment for uplink facilities; Sears was expected to be the principal retailer of the DBS dishes.[31]

At the CRTC hearings DirecTv vice president Jim Ramo admitted that his service would offer no more than 1 to 2 percent Canadian content (Cancon) in the first year. Cable companies continued to worry they would lose customers to DBS. Declaring it had the right to regulate foreign satellite services beaming into Canadian airspace, CRTC established a rule whereby if a foreign satellite service, authorized for cable distribution in Canada, was also an unlicensed U.S. DBS service it could be removed from the list of "eligible satellite signals" carried by Canadian cable systems. Effective January 1, 1995, cable systems were required to carry one Canadian channel for every U.S. service (the previous ratio was two U.S. services to one Canadian). Cable operators complained that too might drive Canadian consumers, who they said wanted more U.S. services, to move to DBS services. Worries about "death stars" was premature. By the end of 1996 no Canadian service had launched — several had been announced but all aborted — and Canadians had not rushed to sign up for such U.S. DBS services as DirecTv.[32]

In a separate decision the CRTC evicted the U.S. Country Music Television (CMT) channel from Canadian cable systems as of January 1, 1995, after ten years, to be replaced by a Canadian-owned and -operated country music channel. Immediately Washington complained. In a statement released by the U.S. Department of State, Washington declared the decision "amounts to nothing less than a confiscation of CMT's business and will reflect negatively on Canada as a safe and secure place to invest." Arguing CMT was a worldwide showcase for Canadian and other artists, the statement continued, "Unless the government acts quickly, Canadian artist's access to this global audience will be threatened." U.S. trade representative Mickey Kantor wrote to Canadian trade minister McLaren demanding the Canadian government reverse that decision to "eliminate this discriminatory CRTC policy."[33]

CMT was owned by Westinghouse's Group W and Nashville's Gaylord Entertainment. After being booted off Canadian cable, CMT banned from its programs all Canadian artists who lacked U.S. recording contracts. Protests from Washington continued with the result that a compromise was reached later in 1995. CMT was allowed to buy 20 percent of the Canadian replacement service New Country Network with an option to buy a further 13 percent (when and if Canadian law allowed; foreigners then were limited to a maximum 20 percent ownership in indigenous outlets) in a new entity to be called Country Music Television (Canada).[34]

Late in 1995 the CRTC issued a rule whereby as a condition of license any Canadian DBS service that did launch had to buy non-proprietary exhibition rights for feature films from Canadian distributors. American firms retained rights for films they had financed (50 percent or more) and for those for which they held worldwide distribution rights. According to Industry Canada hardly any movies fell in that category. The large U.S. distributor Viacom (Paramount) had only three movies that fell in that category over the previous three years. Still, the U.S. lobbied vigorously against the rule, mainly through the Canadian Motion Picture Distributors Association, which was made up solely of Hollywood majors like Warner, MGM, Columbia, Viacom and Fox. Valenti stormed against that rule and other efforts by Canada to protect its cultural sector as part of an "infection" sweeping the world.[35]

Canada's federal government Standing Committee on Canadian Heritage issued a 1996 report on the future of the CBC. Committee chair and Winnipeg member of Parliament John Harvard observed, "Commercial broadcasting can't do everything. The CBC has to be more than just an entertainer. It has to inform. It has to educate. And I would hope that in some cases it would also promote national unity. Its responsibility and mandate is entirely different." He complained CBC English-language television had become too much like its commercial counterparts. The report called the CBC the only viable instrument to ensure the vitality and perhaps the survival of a distinct Canadian identity. It recommended changes in the way the CBC was funded, including a proposal to eliminate commercial ads, except on sports programming, to be replaced by a tariff on public utilities such as telephone and cable companies. None of it happened. Early in 1996 CBC president Perrin Beatty announced that by the autumn of 1996 all regularly scheduled U.S. programming between 7 and 11 P.M. would have been removed from CBC English-language prime time. That did happen, and it was the first time in the CBC's history that its prime time schedule was U.S. content free. Starting in the fall of 1996 that time period was 100 percent Cancon. However, all of this unfolded as the Canadian government inflicted huge budget cuts on the public broadcaster. Fully one-third of the CBC's budget was eliminated over about three years in the mid–1990s. From a peak of 13,000 employees in 1988 the CBC was projected to employ about 7,000 in 1998. The effects of such massive cuts have yet to be played out but will be disastrous for the CBC, putting pressure on it to sell more and more ad time, to import more cheap U.S. product, to produce the cheapest possible Cancon shows of its own — talking heads, for example. All of this will draw smaller audiences, which will reduce ad revenue, which will lead to even cheaper programming, and so on. Ultimately the effects of such policies could be to destroy the CBC completely, perhaps to be sold off to private interests.[36]

Within Europe the battle to increase U.S. television presence continued to be waged, within individual nations and within the region as a whole. As 1989 ended, Romania's two-channel, state-run system aired only two hours a day. After the execution of dictator Nicolae Ceauşescu the television system was renamed Free Romanian TV, still state operated. By early in 1990 the first channel was telecasting a minimum of 16 hours a day and needed massive infusions of programming. Romanian TV's chief buyer Ioan Ionel pleaded with U.S. suppliers to lower the officially established floor on prices set by the Motion Picture Export Association (MPEA) for his territory. Ionel claimed that his system could afford to pay no more than $600 per hour of programming, but the MPEA floor had been set at $900 a few years earlier. A letter from Romanian TV president Rasvau Theodorescu to MPEA head Jack Valenti requesting the U.S. majors to lower the license fee went unanswered. Studio sources said a vote had been taken by the MPEA members, the result of which was to keep the floor at $900. U.S. television suppliers believed Romania had an extremely low foreign debt at the time and had more hard currency reserves than most of its neighbors. Leading the hard-line approach were MCA TV International president Colin Davis and Fox TV International head William Saunders, who believed that agreeing to such requests could set a bad precedent. Davis explained that failure to stick to agreed-upon minimum prices would "denigrate" the value of U.S. product in the eyes of other clients. He added, "U.S. companies have in many incidences subsidized foreign broadcasters for years by providing them with product at relatively low prices." Another studio executive explained that most U.S. suppliers would be looking at ways to provide programming to eastern European lands through cash/barter and sponsorship deals and said, "We have to walk a fine line between maintaining good will in some cases and not unduly underpricing ourselves."[37]

Turkey had a single, state-run channel broadcasting in black and white in 1982; in 1989 there were three state-run channels broadcasting in color; at the end of 1992 there were six state-run channels and six private outlets on the air, with more in the planning stages. The country's prime minister, Turgut Özal, signaled in 1989 that while it was unconstitutional to set up private television channels on Turkish soil there was nothing illegal about broadcasting into Turkey from outside the borders. Özal's party favored the changing of the constitution to allow private stations in Turkey, but it lacked the two-thirds parliamentary majority necessary to change the constitution. A few months later, in early 1990, after Özal's signal, a company called Magic Box began to broadcast into Turkey from its transmitter in Germany. One of the partners in that Swiss-based company was Ahmet Özal (Turgut's son). That opened the floodgates to private television in Turkey. Magic Box was directed specifically at Turks and financed by ad revenue collected in Turkey. Soon Turkish municipalities began to install local antennae to receive the satellite feed and redistribute the signals to more people over the air. Although that was a violation of the constitution, no action was taken. Sometimes Magic Box bribed municipalities to install antennae and sometimes citizens pressured those communities because, for one thing, Magic Box screened "new and glitzy American series." More private stations started up with the result that the price for U.S. television material doubled. Foreign programs accounted for over 50 percent of total transmission time. Media writer Haluk Sahin commented, "The global media were also instrumental in reshaping the format of programs produced in Turkey. The national media channels, whether public or private ... increasingly imitated global media channels. This resemblance went all the way—down to small detail like the way women presenters dressed or the way cameras zoomed in. The global media exercised a hegemonic power by being accepted as the norm."[38]

France actually took its television quotas seriously. The private network TF1 was slapped with a fine of over $5 million in 1992 for producing only 107 hours of prime-time French programming—13 hours less than necessary to meet the minimum quota figure.[39]

When licenses for new commercial terrestrial television outlets, to launch in 1993, were being awarded in the U.K. in 1990-91 the regulatory body Independent Television Commission (ITC) issued a draft proposal that new license holders would be allowed to telecast a maximum of 25 percent foreign (non–E.C.) material. Since the existing outlets were held to 14 percent this seemed like an improvement for U.S. suppliers; however, the ITC intended to throw out all existing exemptions from the 14 percent rule such as sports, documentaries and anything of a cultural nature. The ITC estimated that if all such exempted material were added in to existing station calculations, the amount of non–E.C. material actually stood at about 25 percent. Thus the ITC proposal was likely to be neither a gain nor a loss for U.S. suppliers.[40]

That set up a storm of protest by the American lobby that delayed the official invitation to apply for the new ITV licenses. Said an ITC spokesperson, "It really was a very serious holdup, which forced people here to try and come up with a constructive and creative new formula to satisfy the Americans." The compromise reached was a 35 percent maximum allowed for foreign material including sports.[41]

In an article about imported shows' performing poorly in the ratings the *Times* of London observed that local material dominated. In a typical week the top 50 BBC and ITV programs easily passed the 8 million mark, while only three foreign shows topped that figure in the selected week, one Australian series and two U.S. feature films. "The relative success of British television is no accident. Britain has the largest production base in Europe, and our terrestrial broadcasters invest £1.8 billion in original programming a year — more than any other European country," concluded the newspaper. Left unsaid was that that strong industry had developed at least partly because of the strong quota system imposed on the British television industry from its very beginnings.[42]

Early in the 1990s the General Agreement on Trade and Tariffs (GATT) negotiations were underway, involving most of the world's nations. Hollywood was still smarting from the cultural exemptions in both the FTA and NAFTA agreements when a 1992 published report suggested that U.S. negotiators might jettison the audiovisual sector in those world trade talks. Immediately the MPAA fired off protest letters to U.S. trade representative Carla Hills and White House Chief of Staff James Baker. Signed by Jack Valenti and its seven member studio heads that MPAA letter said, "Our industry has twice been swept aside by last-minute decisions by our governments to accept cultural exclusions, first in the Canada-U.S. Free Trade Agreement and then from the just negotiated North American Free Trade Agreement." That letter continued, "To again exclude the A–V sectors would place our industry in a position where we would have to export jobs, rather than creative product in order to compete in the global marketplace. It would be intolerable and unacceptable."[43]

As GATT negotiations continued in 1993 some European trade lawyers accused Valenti of "megaphone diplomacy." Replied Valenti, "I think the people of Europe, who have the right to choose their own leaders, should have the right to choose their own television. The audience is king. I want more competition in the market place, less man-made barriers. Let the market forces collide and something better will come out of it."[44]

With a self-imposed deadline of December 1993 to reach a GATT accord most issues were resolved by that fall with the exception of audiovisual and agriculture. Leading the forces for a cultural exemption were the French. European Community trade commissioner Leon Brittan (U.K.) argued European film/television production would be better served by a "cultural specificity" clause allowing nations to maintain their own various rules — that is, include audiovisual in GATT but with an opt-out condition. Brittan admitted his ideas on cultural specificity were vague. Spain backed the French position, with the latter's foreign minister Alain Juppe arguing only the exclusion of audiovisual would allow the E.C. to properly enforce the TWF directive. Stressing the need for protection, E.C. audiovisual commissioner Joao de Deus Pinheiro noted that in 1991 American films' share of European cinemas' box office averaged 81 percent, while in the same year 54 percent of all dramas and comedies broadcast on European television originated in the U.S. Europe's collective body for public broadcasters, the European Broadcasting Union (EBU), also strongly supported audiovisual exclusion from GATT.[45]

French culture minister Jacques Toubon reaffirmed France would refuse to sign any GATT pact if it included audiovisual and said, "We are not fighting to close the [European] market. We want to stop the market falling into a [Japanese/American] monopoly." Also strongly supporting the exclusion side was the European Directors Association, ARP, which included Claude Berri, Volker Schlondorf, Bertrand Tavernier and Roman Polanski.[46]

As the December 15 deadline neared, U.S. trade representative Mickey Kantor claimed the U.S. had shown "great flexibility" but had not seen a similar attitude from the Europeans. In return for an unspecified concession on culture — taken to mean some bending on the quota issues — Kantor asked that American companies be awarded a portion of the subsidies available to national European film industries. Reportedly he followed this with a demand the U.S. firms also be given a piece of the action on European blank tape levies (France raised about $120 million a year from a tax on blank tapes, with that money being rechanneled back into the national movie and music industries). When the Europeans refused all those demands, Kantor reportedly stormed out of the meeting. That last demand was seen by the Europeans as "adding insult to injury." According to MPAA figures for 1992 the U.S. film, television and home-video industries posted total revenues of $18 billion, with $4 billion of that coming from western Europe. The E.C. observed that American product accounted for 70,000 hours annually of European television time, 28 percent of the total transmission time, and pocketed 70 percent of European box office revenue.[47]

A last-minute deal was almost made when the E.C.'s chief GATT negotiator Leon Brittan offered to scrap E.C. television quotas. However, he was forced to retreat under pressure from E.C. head Jacques Delors, who said Brittan was offering to give too much ground to the U.S. Even some American observers worried about the tenor of the talks and "may not agree with Valenti's aggressive stance in these talks, but the MPAA does such a job for them inside the United States that they are not going to break ranks over GATT." Some of Hollywood's majors didn't care that much; mostly they maintained a discreet public silence. There was lots of room for growth in the European market with new outlets and new delivery technology. This coupled with a trend to mergers in the U.S. leading to bigger entities along with more direct investment abroad by those entities, meant Hollywood was not worried about losing anything. An E.C. report estimated the areas' audiovisual market was worth around $11 billion annually, half that of the U.S. market in an area where the population was 25 percent larger.[48]

During those negotiations the U.S. put considerable pressure on the Australians to allow total free trade there in audiovisual — Australia's television quota remained at a 50 percent local content minimum. The Australians resisted and stated they would continue to do so. Asians took no sides in the GATT battle between America and Europe. The GATT pact set out clear rules to protect intellectual property and obliged member nations to take effective actions against counterfeiters. Member nations would be expected to place curbs on rampant music, film and video piracy in parts of Asia, to the potential future benefit of Hollywood.[49]

When the GATT accord was reached audiovisual was excluded from the world trade deal. Reporter Michael Williams wrote that by choosing to use a strident approach "Valenti inadvertently rallied previously apathetic Euros behind the French banner, raising European political consciousness over U.S. market domination." London-based film observer Jonathan Olsberg said, "Politically it [GATT] has accentuated the focus on what the Americans are doing over here. More and more the issue of the American domination of this marketplace is on the agenda." British film producer Chris Auty remarked, "One of the paradoxical results, which the Americans don't yet fully appreciate, is that the GATT debate has brought the British [film] community closer to the French position that it was before."[50]

France's communication minister Alain Carignon hailed the exclusion as a "great and beautiful victory for Europe and for French culture." Mickey Kantor, who had threatened Europe with unspecified retaliatory trade measures during negotiations, declared, "They didn't win. In fact, the French people lost. They are going to be denied the right to their freedom of choice."[51]

The GATT battle between Europe and America was an offshoot from their battle over the E.C. TWF directive of the late 1980s. That dispute continued into the 1990s. After the passage of that directive Valenti declared those European countries justified quotas as protection of their culture but that U.S. product was "hospitality received" by the people who "like, admire and patronize what we offer them. What this confirms is the E.C. objection has nothing to do with culture. What it is really about is commerce. The only way to force citizens not to watch American programs is to keep those programs off the air." At the same time, during a 1990 Los Angeles speech he urged his government not to exclude culture from GATT or it "will have forfeited the future of one of the few U.S. products whose mastery in world markets is affirmed." Signing an exclusionary GATT, he added, "would deprive other nations' citizens of the right to choose freely what they want to watch. It would be a wrong that cries out to be set right. And we will fight to do just that."[52]

A London-based research firm, CIT, concluded that sales of television product to Europe would grow from $4.9 billion in 1990 to $5.5 billion by 2000—a significant slowdown in growth rate. Noting the bulk of those sales were accounted for by U.S. firms the CIT report went on to observe that type for type domestically produced shows usually received better ratings than U.S. imports. According to CIT, Europe's 133.5 million television homes were offered 573,000 hours of programming in 1990, a 20 percent rise over 1989, a massive 76 percent increase over 1988. Hours of programming were predicted to rise 9 percent by 1992 and 16 percent by 2000. CIT estimated that in 1990 the west European television market, encompassing the cost of producing and acquiring programs, was around $15.6 billion. Almost a third of that figure was accounted for by program acquisition, mainly from the U.S. One U.S. executive stated the demand for American movies would always remain strong because "Europe doesn't have a film industry to speak of and television stations here will continue to depend on Hollywood for movies."[53]

A different study conducted about the same time found that American programs accounted for 24 percent of all European programming. Western Europe, which did 66 percent of the worldwide importing in 1990 of television product, got 80 percent of that product from the U.S. One conclusion was that "most U.S. material is not suited to a European audience and has weaker ratings than similar domestic fare." Yet there was room for growth in certain areas. At the end of the 1980s, 2.4 percent of U.K. homes received DBS and 1.4 percent were cabled; France had 1.2 percent cabled; Spain had 0.3 percent of its households receiving DBS.[54]

In mid–1991, U.S. trade representative Carla Hills placed the 12 E.C. nations on a "priority watch list" because of its TWF quotas (Australia was placed on the list at the same time for its 50 percent local content rule, up from 40 percent through 1991). Valenti said that that action put his government on record as saying "it'll not stand for these kinds of restrictions to fair trade. In time, these quotas will bite, wound or bleed those that adopt them." He was hopeful those quotas would go, pointing to Britain, which was allowed 35 percent non–E.C. material, for some newly licensed outlets, as a step in the right direction that did not go far enough. Washington reserved the right to take action against countries on the watch list if things didn't improve.[55]

Within the E.C., France agreed to reduce its quota of a minimum of 50 percent French-language product to 40 percent — while keeping the total amount of E.C. product at a 60 percent minimum. In return, France was allowed to keep its strict definition of what television genres should be counted in the quotas: fiction, scripted documentaries and animation. By comparison some other E.C. nations also counted variety shows and talk shows in the quotas. The E.C. had wanted France to align with that looser definition. France worried such a rule would make it easier for broadcasters to adhere to the quotas by filling up air time with cheap-to-produce variety and talk shows.[56]

The U.S. National Association of Broadcasters commissioned a report by Kenneth Donow in which he concluded the E.C.'s 50 percent quota would have little impact on U.S. suppliers. Calling the quotas merely symbolic, the report stated the quotas would not limit the flow of U.S. material to the E.C., as American programming accounted for less than 20 percent of television time in many E.C. countries, including Britain, France and Italy. Valenti slammed that report as "regrettable" and said it "seriously damages the interests of U.S. program producers and television stations alike." He went on to complain the report "appears to be premised on the false impression that the E.C. quota is applied on a country-by-country basis and requires only 50 percent of total broadcast programming to be of E.C. origin. In fact, the quota is applied on a station-by-station basis and sets a floor of 50 percent, which can be increased." Valenti added Donow failed to see the fact that the E.C. quota "forces E.C. broadcasters to show U.S. programming in less lucrative, non-primetime day parts." That was false.[57]

During a speech in mid–1992 before the Commonwealth Club of San Francisco, he lashed out again at the E.C., declaring the U.S. was in a trade war: "It is a world both untidy and mean" in which "there is among the leaders of the E.C. an awful squinting toward 'fortress Europe.'" Citing the fact that the U.S. film and television industries created an annual $3.5 billion trade surplus for the domestic economy, Valenti declared that trade asset was under attack by a "new trade religion" in which the "high priests ... threaten us and coerce us to bend to their longterm objectives." He complained the E.C. quota "inhospitably consigns the American creative film and TV program to a new form of purgatory. In this new netherworld, either we submit to a joint venture owned by Europeans or we, like Banquo's ghost, haunt the edges of the marketplace, our clamors to enter unheeded and unheard."[58]

Late in 1984 the E.C.'s European Commission released a draft of a revised TWF directive that would allow channels to continue broadcasting if they failed the quota but only if they set their own investment quotas to be of "equivalent effect" to the quota provisions of the directive. In practice it would mean channels would have to invest more than half their budget in European programs. Such a rule would most strongly affect U.S.-owned satellite channels in the region. Also proposed was removal of the ambiguous and contentious "where practicable" clause. European culture chief Joao de Deus Pinheiro, who engineered the new draft, wanted to plug another loophole by not including game shows, sporting events, and so on in the quota count. On the other hand another rule proposed that new services be allowed a generous five-year grace period to meet the 50 percent European quota. Pinheiro's draft had to be approved by each nation's European commissioner before it could be debated by the E.U. ministers. As might be expected, public broadcasters in Europe strongly favored tightening the rules, while private broadcasters strongly opposed any such rule tightening.[59]

France led the battle in the E.C. group to impose stricter rules; the U.K. led those opposed. London's *Times* editorialized against removal of the "where practicable" clause and stated, "Mandatory quotas would only weaken the competitiveness of Europe's broadcasting industry.... They would also offend against the principles of free speech."[60]

Reporter Andy Stern declared in early 1995 that only France supported tougher rules along with Belgium and Greece, but some of the others such as Denmark and Sweden not only didn't agree but favored dismantling or weakening quotas and were supported in this by Britain and Germany. In a compromise draft proposal reached in March 1995, the "where practicable" clause would be removed and quotas would remain at the 50 percent level but guaranteed to be maintained for ten years only. New services to come, plus new delivery mechanisms, would have the option of not meeting the quota but instead could dedicate 25 percent of their program budgets to creating new European programs. Additionally, those new outlets would be given three years to reach the 25 percent level. That compromise proposal was passed by a margin of 11 to 4 with 2 absent (U.K., Germany, Austria and the Netherlands were opposed) by E.U. negotiators and could then be debated by all E.U. member nations' culture ministers.[61]

Late in 1995, E.U. culture ministers agreed to leave unchanged the "where practicable" clause and most everything else. The status quo prevailed. Early in 1996, the European Parliament voted 292 to 195 (25 abstentions) that the 50 percent rule should be enforced by "legally effective means." It also wished to extend the television rules to any and all new media that arrived in the future, such as video on demand. The European Parliament had the powers to decide jointly with the national governments on changes to the TWF directive. Hollywood, of course, lobbied furiously against restrictions. However, it was not then law. The E.U.'s executive body, the European Commission, had to decide whether or not to take on any of the Parliament's proposals. If those commissioners did, it put more pressure on individual cultural ministers. On June 11, 1996, the E.U. cultural chiefs voted not to tighten existing quotas. Those culture ministers also threw out a European Parliament amendment that would have excluded program genres such as game shows and talk shows from the directive's scope. It set the culture ministers on a collision course with the Parliament as the issue bounced back and forth and continues to do so.[62]

When researcher William Ware did a metanalysis of available literature dealing with the effects of U.S. television entertainment programming on foreign audiences, he found mixed results in terms of U.S. programming's either turning people more favorably to U.S. culture or more unfavorably to their own. Ware concluded, "It appears, though, that one of the largest effects of U.S. program exposure is an 'advertising' effect for U.S. or Western products which would then support the consumerism aspect of the media imperialism thesis."[63]

The much-touted "free flow of information" and the "audience making the decision" theory has little evidence to back it up. Testimony before a U.S. Senate subcommittee in 1971 by the Writers Guild of America indicated otherwise. In their statement the writers — who at the time wrote all the network television drama, comedy and variety shows produced in America — declared, "It is our contention that the networks have deliberately and almost totally shut off the flow of ideas, have censored and continue to censor the writers who work for them." The guild's account contained numerous examples of scripts altered by higher echelons. It also contained a finding from a poll of its members that 86 percent of them suffered censorship of their work. The United Nations Educational, Scientific and Cultural Organization (UNESCO) in the 1960s, at the urging of the U.S., endorsed a principle that supported and ennobled the expansion of the U.S. cultural industries — the doctrine of the "free flow of information." Ironically, the U.S. withdrew from UNESCO in 1984 at least in part because of an American belief, as former U.S. UNESCO employee Colleen Roach put it, that UNESCO had a "supposed intent of promoting government-controlled media." None of that fit in with the American drive to deregulation and privatization of the media and other sectors around the world. That corporate deregulatory ethos sought to promote and protect the general commercial information activities of the transnational corporate system; to satisfy the specific marketing needs of those corporations, especially those in the consumer goods and services production and whose sales required having a continued access to national media systems; to protect the interest of large transnational media firms to operate globally without restrictions. National ownership of television systems was considered a roadblock to such goals that had to be eliminated or greatly reduced.[64]

Media critic George Gerbner remarked, "When communication is turned into a business, whatever is said has to be said profitably." Commenting on the American dominance of the world's cinemas and television screens, he said, "Free trade is not a solution to the problem; it is the cause."[65]

Back in 1973, Finnish president Urho Kekkonen said about the free flow of information, "Could it be that the prophets who preach unhindered communication are not concerned with equality between nations, but are on the side of the stronger and wealthier?... More and more it can be seen that a mere liberalistic freedom of communication is not in everyday reality a neutral idea, but a way in which an enterprise with many resources at its disposal has greater opportunities than weaker brethren to make its own hegemony accepted."[66]

Appendix:
U.S. Television Sales
Offshore

(in millions of dollars)

1957	$14	1967	$78	1978	$284
1958	$15	1968	$80	1979	$350
1959	$25	1970	$97	1980	$365
1960	$30	1971	$85	1984	$500
1961	$44	1972	$94	1987	$1,300
1962	$55	1973	$136	1989	$1,700
1963	$66	1974	$124	1994	$2,250
1964	$70	1975	$160	1995	$3,000
1965	$76	1976	$190		
1966	$70	1977	$240		

Sources: Chapter 1, notes 110–112
Chapter 3, notes 101–102
Chapter 5, notes 55, 59
Chapter 7, notes 96, 104
Chapter 9, notes 34, 78, 80

Notes

Chapter 1

1. "Bob Hope envisions global TV networks as aid to understanding." *Variety* 196 (December 1, 1954):2.
2. "Possibilities of transoceanic TV to be explored by 9-man group." *Variety* 195 (July 28, 1954):1, 119.
3. A. E. Hotchner. "Global TV is on the way." *Reader's Digest* 66 (May 1955):61–63.
4. Ibid., pp. 63–65.
5. "Transatlantic TV via micro relay." *Variety* 187 (June 18, 1952):1, 61.
6. Erik Barnouw. *Tube of Plenty*. New York: Oxford, 1975, p. 232.
7. "International television may foster world peace." *Science News Letter* 62 (September 27, 1952):200.
8. Franklin Dunham. "International television." *School Life* 39 (October 1956):2.
9. "World-wide TV: a dynamic fact." *Sponsor* 15 (June 19, 1961):41, 54.
10. Norman Katz. "Those foreign pastures grow greener and greener." *Variety* 215 (July 8, 1959):38.
11. "Possibilities of transoceanic TV to be explored by 9-man group." *Variety* 195 (July 28, 1954): 1, 119; George Wallach. "TV's 'Global Challenge.'" *Variety* 209 (January 22, 1958):30, 55.
12. "Weaver's global TV formula to give the lie to Commies." *Variety* 200 (November 23, 1955):26, 41.
13. Jean Tweed. "American 'dumped' films can kill Canadian television industry." *Saturday Night* 64 (May 17, 1949):6.
14. "Brazilian TV gets a JWT hotfoot." *Variety* 186 (April 16, 1952):29–30.
15. "Aussie market's vidpix potential even tops Britain." *Variety* 196 (October 20, 1954):35.
16. "Australia's TV tastes similar to U.S." *Variety* 209 (February 5, 1958):26.
17. George Rosen. "Japanese TV: the Ginza beat." *Variety* 220 (October 19, 1960):21; "U.S. tempo strong in Nigerian TV where Brod Crawford's a nat'l hero." *Variety* 221 (February 15, 1961):27, 48.
18. "Poland TV's heavy U.S. accent." *Variety* 225 (February 21, 1962):23, 40.
19. "Merle Jones bullish on Japan TV potential on vidpix import." *Variety* 221 (November 30, 1960):26, 49; "Ralph Baruch on TV image abroad." *Variety* 226 (April 18, 1962):26.
20. Hans Hoehn. "West German TV in major strides." *Variety* 211 (June 5, 1958):46.
21. "Transatlantic TV via micro relay." *Variety* 187 (June 18, 1952):61.
22. "Ad men's global TV primer." *Variety* 196 (November 24, 1954):25.

23. "$230,000,000 in o'seas billings for five agencies during '57." *Variety* 210 (March 19, 1958):26.

24. "TV: the international picture." *Broadcasting* 53 (November 18, 1957):118.

25. George Rosen. "Japanese TV: the Ginza beat." *Variety* 220 (October 19, 1960):40.

26. "Yank clients take lead." *Variety* 225 (February 14, 1962):27.

27. "U.S.-style TV looks good to Canadian execs, study shows." *Advertising Age* 30 (December 21, 1959):86.

28. Donald Coyle. "ABC Int'l plays role in Central American culture." *Variety* 217 (February 24, 1960):32; "World-wide TV: a dynamic fact." *Sponsor* 15 (June 19, 1961):53–54.

29. Herm Schoenfeld. "Don Coyle envisions int'l TV as giant ad medium." *Variety* 224 (September 13, 1961):35, 50.

30. "Possibilities of transoceanic TV to be explored by 9-man group." *Variety* 195 (July 28, 1954):1, 119; "SG's $9,000,000 vidpix budget." *Variety* 196 (November 17, 1954):49, 52.

31. Murray Horowitz. "SG's $8,000,000 o'seas biz." *Variety* 223 (August 9, 1961):23.

32. "Cuba, Mexico into NBC-TV affiliate family via kines." *Variety* 186 (April 23, 1952):21; "NBC's Wales, Cuba, Spain, Jamaica aspirations in global video setup." *Variety* 204 (October 3, 1956):1, 78.

33. "Central America TV network." *Variety* 217 (December 9, 1959):29; Donald Coyle. "ABC Int'l plays role in Central American culture." *Variety* 217 (February 24, 1960):32.

34. Murray Horowitz. "CBS is less concerned about percent in o'seas television than in U.S. product sale." *Variety* 217 (December 9, 1959):29, 40; "NBC's 'Have money, will help' in bid for stake in Mex TV." *Variety* 223 (May 31, 1961):1.

35. "Seoul goes ga-ga over teevee." *Variety* 203 (June 20, 1956):21, 28.

36. "CBS & Spain TV in telefilm pact." *Variety* 208 (September 18, 1957):23, 38.

37. "Irish TV operational pattern eyed by other govt. systems in Europe." *Variety* 226 (March 28, 1962):20, 36.

38. "Latin American stake." *Variety* 225 (December 20, 1961):23, 36.

39. "UA finalizes ZIV buyout." *Variety* 218 (March 9, 1960):37; "WB, Col, Metro, 20th in command." *Variety* 222 (April 12, 1961):23, 35.

40. Richard Bunce. *Television in the Corporate Interest.* New York: Praeger, 1976, pp. 76, 79.

41. "Block-booking evidence heard in distribs trial." *Variety* 218 (March 9, 1960):37, 58.

42. "Get on vidpix and see the world." *Variety* 225 (January 31, 1962):31; "NBC resolves residual fee on foreign repeats." *Variety* 213 (October 8, 1958):23, 38.

43. Art Woodstone. "Foreign markets intriguing." *Variety* 200 (October 26, 1955):31, 34.

44. "TV films' MPAA counterpart." *Variety* 206 (March 13, 1957):25.

45. Murray Horowitz. "Vidpix export assn.—when?" *Variety* 210 (April 30, 1958):47.

46. "Vidpixers will try again to get rolling on export assn." *Variety* 214 (April 8, 1959):30.

47. "For U.S. TV, a Commodore Perry?" *Broadcasting* 57 (September 21, 1959):33–34.

48. "TV film exporters set organization." *Advertising Age* 30 (December 21, 1959):83; "TV film exporters organize." *Broadcasting* 57 (December 7, 1959):86.

49. "McCarthy heads TPEA as MPAA inks Fineshriber." *Variety* 218 (May 11, 1960):23; "McCarthy's Latino tour." *Variety* 223 (June 14, 1961):36; "McCarthy in beef to British over protective quota stance on telepix." *Variety* 225 (November 29, 1961):35.

50. "TV in 23 foreign countries." *Variety* 191 (August 12, 1953):27, 34; "The world and TV." *Newsweek* 47 (January 23, 1956):92–93.

51. "Screen Gems' $3,000,000 foreign billings: exposure in 21 countries." *Variety* 205 (February 20, 1957):29; "Screen Gems' Latin American push." *Variety* 206 (April 3, 1957):34.

52. "Telefilms' $6,000,000 o'seas." *Variety* 206 (May 8, 1957):21.

53. Ralph M. Cohn. "Next stop on the global vidpix circuit—the Moon." *Variety* 209 (January 8, 1958):99, 106.

54. "50-country telefilm horizon to open up in '58, sez Fineshriber." *Variety* 209 (January 1, 1958):22.

55. "Zivideo in 9 tongues." *Variety* 215 (June 17, 1959):27.

56. "100 U.S. TV shows circle globe." *Variety* 213 (November 26, 1958):29.

57. "U.S. TV taps worldwide market." *Business Week*, September 27, 1958, pp. 158–160, 162, 164.

58. "World laps up U.S. TV fare." *Business Week*, April 23, 1960, pp. 129, 131.

59. "Building TV chains to span continents." *Printer's Ink* 270 (March 11, 1960): 80–81.

60. "TV abroad thrives on U.S. ways." *Business Week*, September 3, 1960, pp. 105–106.

61. "Potential of foreign revenue spurs distribs to 'global look' operations." *Variety* 196 (December 1, 1954):48.

62. "Latin America's big $$ potential for U.S. telefilms cited by Manson." *Variety* 206 (May 1, 1957):28, 50.

63. "Robt. Sarnoff bullish on Europe TV prospects." *Variety* 207 (July 10, 1957):29.

64. "The foreign market for TV films." *Broadcasting Telecasting* 52 (May 6, 1957):27.

65. "W Germany seen as lucrative area for vidfilm sales." *Variety* 222 (April 5, 1961):31.

66. "Europe's trend to com'l TV." *Variety* 225 (December 27, 1961):23, 32.

67. "Yank telepix distribs reaping lotsa moola in Canadian market." *Variety* 195 (September 1, 1954):52; "New $6,000,000 TV replay system gives Canada more Yank shows." *Variety* 190 (May 20, 1953):31.

68. "½-hour Canadian TV show costs $5,000 in contrast to 35G in U.S." *Variety* 198 (March 30, 1955):35.

69. Art Woodstone. "Inter-American b'casters carry on fight against the 'Little tyrants.'" *Variety* 202 (May 16, 1956):24, 38.

70. "Mestre's Latino dubbing & distrib." *Variety* 198 (July 20, 1955):29.

71. "Argentine TV upsurge forcing govt. hand in return to private ownership." *Variety* 213 (December 3, 1958):55.

72. "Comm'l British TV would spark global vidpix market, sez Towers." *Variety* 192 (September 30, 1953):26.

73. "Curb on U.S. TV asked by British stage folk." *New York Times*, March 23, 1954, p. 34.

74. Bob Chandler. "O'seas sales now key factor." *Variety* 200 (September 14, 1955):35, 44.

75. "N.Y.-to-London TV traffic." *Variety* 200 (September 14, 1955):47; "Vidpix bundles from Britain." *Variety* 210 (December 14, 1955):39, 48.

76. "Telefilms' $6,000,000 o'seas." *Variety* 206 (May 8, 1957):21.

77. "Com'l Swiss TV still 10 yrs. off." *Variety* 209 (January 8, 1958):104.

78. "French TV rules out com'l setup when 2d channel bows." *Variety* 215 (June 24, 1959):83.

79. Hank Werba. "Spanish TV entertains a whole nation on annual budget of 400G." *Variety* 223 (August 2, 1961):25.

80. Hazel Guild. "W. Germans dote on com'l tv." *Variety* 221 (February 22, 1961):43, 46.

81. "TV overseas market limited." *Broadcasting* 58 (February 1, 1960):89.

82. "50-country telefilm horizon to open up in '58, sez Fineshriber." *Variety* 209 (January 1, 1958):34.

83. "NBC's Stern talks co-production with Japan, vidpix payment rules." *Variety* 213 (February 18, 1959):36.

84. "Global glint in Screen Gems' orbit." *Variety* 223 (August 30, 1961):26.

85. "Aussies miffed at U.S. brushoff on tv coproduction." *Variety* 223 (August 16, 1961):30.

86. "NBC's formula for tv program exchange with foreign countries." *Variety* 210 (March 26, 1958):35.

87. "Russo–U.S. exchange — zero." *Variety* 215 (August 19, 1959):27, 42.

88. "H'Wood telepix as no. 1 villain." *Variety* 217 (February 3, 1960):52; "TV overseas market limited." *Broadcasting* 58 (February 1, 1960):89.

89. Murray Horowitz. "Two-way TV: U.S. and o'seas." *Variety* 225 (December 6, 1961):1, 42.

90. Murray Horowitz. "Big 'E' in TV's Common Market." *Variety* 227 (June 6, 1962):23, 40.

91. "The plot to 'overthrow' Latin America." *Variety* 213 (December 10, 1958):22.

92. "Acad told foreign producers of TV shows gunning for U.S. market." *Variety* 221 (February 1, 1961):34.

93. "Foreign vidpix distribs out of 'millionaire's spectrum.'" *Variety* 225 (January 31, 1962):31, 45.

94. "Features invade foreign TV." *Variety* 207 (June 12, 1957):33.

95. Murray Horowitz. "Global cinematic TV market." *Variety* 214 (April 15, 1959):113, 128.

96. "43% of stations devote 10–20 hours weekly to feature pix." *Variety* 215 (July 8, 1959):29.

97. "Snail's pace for U.S. features on o'seas channels." *Variety* 218 (July 6, 1960: 31; "12,209 features into TV." *Variety* 222 (April 26, 1961):185; Murray Horowitz. "NBC-CBS news pubaffairs shows in global TV orbit." *Variety* 224 (October 25, 1961):31, 44.

98. "Adviser to go to Germany." *New York Times*, September 5, 1953, p. 4.

99. "Ziv hosting o'seas TV execs in Cincy." *Variety* 200 (November 9, 1955):31.

100. Eric Gorrick. "Yank TV looks up down under as Aussie buyers comb U.S. for shows." *Variety* 203 (July 11, 1956):25, 39.

101. "U.S. tempo strong in Nigerian TV where Brod Crawford's a nat'l hero." *Variety* 221 (February 15, 1961):27, 48.

102. Giraud Chester. *Television and Radio*. 4th ed. New York: Appleton–Century–Crofts, 1971, pp. 214–215.

103. "50,000,000 TV sets abroad by 1962." *Variety* 213 (December 3, 1958):1.

104. "Global count: 70,000,000 TV sets." *Variety* 213 (February 25, 1959):25.

105. Werner Wiskari. "Iceland's isolation nearly ended as foreign influences increase." *New York Times*, April 1, 1962, p. 20.

106. Giraud Chester. *Television and Radio.* 4th ed. New York: Appleton–Century–Crofts, 1971, p.v; "3 out of every 4 U.S. households have TV." *Variety* 203 (August 1, 1956):23.

107. "European TV 'still in infancy.'" *Variety* 198 (March 23, 1955):20, 38.

108. "European tv in one fell swoop." *Variety* 202 (May 2, 1956):26, 46.

109. "O'seas TV set count: 38,650,000." *Variety* 221 (November 30, 1960):46; $50,000,000 TV sets outside U.S." *Variety* 224 (August 30, 1961):26.

110. Murray Horowitz. "TV's a wide, wide world for U.S. telepix." *Variety* 207 (July 31, 1957):35; "$20,000,000 foreign take." *Variety* 217 (December 23, 1959):26.

111. "Foreign vidpix gross seen topping $30,000,000 mark in '61." *Variety* 221 (February 1, 1961):34; "U.S. telefilms o'seas gross could hit $50,000,000 in '62." *Variety* 223 (July 19, 1961):25; Murray Horowitz. "Foreign sales $43,500,000." *Variety* 225 (November 29, 1961):35.

112. "TV's $50,000,000 o'seas gross." *Variety* 226 (May 2, 1962):143.

Chapter 2

1. "U.S. vidpix eyeing Argentine market." *Variety* 200 (October 12, 1955):2, 27; "Caputo sez Lastinos 'hostile' toward U.S. telefilm imports." *Variety* 203 (July 4, 1956):34.

2. "Cagan raps TPEA, sez more stations key to expansion of Latin market." *Variety* 220 (October 26, 1960):26.

3. "Foreign vidpix gross seen topping $30,000,000 mark in '61." *Variety* 221 (February 1, 1961):34.

4. "Brazilian TV's slapdown on U.S. product in restrictions on film use." *Variety* 222 (April 26, 1961):185; "U.S. vidfilmers expect lifting of Brazil decree." *Variety* 225 (November 29, 1961):35; "Brazilian telepix restrictions eased." *Variety* 226 (March 7, 1962):38.

5. "Mex's snowballing campaign to curb invasions of U.S. telepix." *Variety* 217 (February 10, 1960):30, 50; "Vidpix distribs feel depressed Latino prices." *Variety* 218 (April 13, 1960):29.

6. "Mex union asks ban on TV shows dubbed elsewhere." *Variety* 220 (November 23, 1960):26.

7. "Minow sparks echo in Mexico; stations warned." *Variety* 223 (June 14, 1961):29, 36.

8. "Nigerian urges better U.S. films." *Broadcasting* 61 (August 14, 1961):83.

9. T. J. Allard. *Straight Up: Private Broadcasting in Canada: 1918–1958.* Ottawa: Canadian Communications Foundation, 1979, pp. 204–209.

10. Peter Morris. "Electronic free trade." *Cinema Canada* no. 136:6–10, December 1986.

11. T. J. Allard. *Straight Up: Private Broadcasting in Canada: 1918–1958.* Ottawa: Canadian Communications Foundation, 1979, pp. 210, 214, 223, 225.

12. Ibid., pp. 230–235, 252.

13. Erik Barnouw. *Tube of Plenty.* New York: Oxford, 1975, pp. 235–236; Harry Rasky. "Canada's most successful export: TV talent." *Saturday Night* 74 (June 6, 1959): 14–15.

14. "Imported programs limited." *Broadcasting* 57 (November 23, 1959):110; Tania Long. "Homemade TV pushed." *New York Times,* December 27, 1959, sec. 2, p. 13.

15. Dean Walker. "Canada's TV dilemma: The American influence." *Saturday Night* 75 (July 23, 1950):15–17.

16. "Canada's April 1 edict 45% program content must be homegrown." *Variety* 221 (February 22, 1961):27; "Canadian content rule is now cued to prime time." *Variety* 226 (March 14, 1962):30.

17. George Rosen. "Japanese TV; the Ginza beat." *Variety* 220 (October 19, 1960):21.

18. "MCA rep sour on Japanese market." *Variety* 210 (April 30, 1958):26.

19. "NBC's Stern talks co-production with Japan, vidpix payment rules." *Variety* 213 (February 18, 1959):21.

20. "New Japan ceiling no cause for glee say U.S. vidpixers." *Variety* 218 (May 11, 1960):22, 38.

21. "Warren Lewis in Japan TV dickers." *Variety* 219 (August 3, 1960):44.

22. "Japan provisions governing vidpix get clarification." *Variety* 222 (April 26, 1961):184; "Japan's 100G for 54 Untouchables." *Variety* 223 (June 7, 1961):35.

23. "Screen Gems mulls TV production in Japan." *Variety* 224 (October 25, 1961):30.

24. "Dennis go home!" *Newsweek* 59 (March 19, 1962):82.

25. "Aussie budget for U.S. telepix runs out as TPA sells four more series." *Variety* 202 (May 23, 1956):57, 60.

26. "Australia's TV tastes similar to U.S." *Variety* 209 (February 5, 1958):26.

27. "Aussie election a break for U.S. vidpix producers." *Variety* 213 (December 10, 1958):22; "U.S. telefilmeries can't keep up with Aussie demand for product." *Variety* 216 (October 14, 1959):25, 40.

28. Erik Barnouw. *Tube of Plenty.* New York: Oxford, 1975, p. 234.

29. "Aussie TV edict: 40% home fare." *Variety* 218 (March 30, 1960):51.

30. Eric Gorrick. "Rap made-in-Australia TV fare as too costly vs. imported 'best.'" *Variety* 218 (April 13, 1960):36, 42.

31. "Perils of the quota." *Variety* 225 (December 6, 1961):33.

32. "Paisano Hopalong." *Newsweek* 41 (March 30, 1953):66.

33. "France's TV poser." *Variety* 221 (February 22, 1961):43.

34. Gene Moskowitz. "France eyeing 1960 for bigtime emergence of TV." *Variety* 209 (January 8, 1958):104, 106.

35. "West Germany key to continental Europe's potential for U.S. vidpix." *Variety* 213 (December 10, 1958):50.

36. Murray Horowitz. "TV throughout Europe screening U.S. entries for violence." *Variety* 223 (June 14, 1961):25, 42.

37. "Claim U.S. 'dumping' of TV films ruining Europe markets for others." *Variety* 227 (June 20, 1962):30.

38. Erik Barnouw. *Tube of Plenty.* New York: Oxford, 1975, pp. 229–231.

39. "Fear British telepix quota." *Variety* 197 (March 2, 1955):31.

40. "Brit skirmish on U.S. telepix import." *Variety* 201 (February 8, 1956):31; "TV imports cost Britain $3,750,000." *Variety* 201 (February 29, 1956):30.

41. "ITA may cut time for U.S. TV films." *Broadcasting* 50 (February 20, 1956):104.

42. "British TV goes U.S." *U.S. News & World Report* 41 (July 20, 1956):110–111.

43. "Invasion by film." *Time* 69 (May 6, 1957):53–54.

44. "Film violence on television." *Times* (London), March 10, 1958, p. 7.

45. Harold Myers. "U.S. TV influence irks Brit." *Variety* 211 (July 30, 1958): 27, 98.

46. "Too much Yank accent on Brit. TV: Beaverbrook." *Variety* 217 (December 30, 1959):24.

47. "Easing of Brit. on U.S. TV shows may get State Dept. assist." *Variety* 219

(August 10, 1960):27; "Sir Robert Fraser holds no truck with film quotas for British TV." *Variety* 220 (November 23, 1960):26, 47.

48. "BBC and British com'l TV told to stop 'Americanization' medium" *Variety* 221 (February 22, 1961):43; "Call to reduce U.S. influence on TV programmes." *Times* (London), March 31, 1961, p. 4.

49. "Commercial TV isn't cricket for Britons." *Business Week*, July 7, 1962, p. 38.

50. "H'Wood telepix as No. 1 villain." *Variety* 217 (February 3, 1960):1, 52.

51. "Susskind carries his 'TV smells' campaign to Canadian audience." *Variety* 221 (February 22, 1961):43.

52. George Rosen. "Buy Minow & save the world." *Variety* 222 (May 17, 1961): 23, 56.

53. Murray Horowitz. "TV shows tarnishing U.S. image abroad?" *Variety* 223 (May 31, 1961):23, 44.

54. "Ralph Baruch on TV image abroad." *Variety* 226 (April 18, 1962):26.

55. "Murrow's TV image torch." *Variety* 226 (April 4, 1962):27, 52.

56. Murray Horowitz. "More and more restrictions face U.S. telepix distribs in peddling their programs." *Variety* 220 (September 7, 1960):27, 34.

57. "Middle East yens U.S. TV product but blocked currency major snag." *Variety* 225 (February 14, 1962):27, 38.

58. "Global TV via satellite just a matter of weeks." *Variety* 226 (April 4, 1962):27.

59. "MGM-TV's Spires is dubious about bonanza potential of int'l market." *Variety* 227 (July 4, 1962):68.

Chapter 3

1. "World TV: a click premiere." *Variety* 227 (July 18, 1962):27.

2. Harland Manchester. "Here comes world-wide television!" *Reader's Digest* 81 (July, 1962):77–80.

3. "Telstar—for all the world to see." *Newsweek* 60 (July 23, 1962):13–14.

4. "UNESCO paints a rosy picture of global TV via satellite." *Variety* 232 (November 13, 1963):27.

5. Murray Horowitz. "Paul Levitan envisions satellite era of instant television." *Variety* 236 (September 30, 1964):1, 48.

6. "Don Coyle: 'Think global.'" *Variety* 237 (December 2, 1964):31.

7. Donald Coyle. "TV's global future awaits those who take the opportunity today." *Variety* 245 (January 4, 1967):93.

8. "Gen Sarnoff warns of danger in future satellite b'cast era." *Variety* 240 (September 22, 1965):30; Dave Jampel; "CBS's Kany, in Asia, sees English becoming int'l language via TV." *Variety* 241 (December 15, 1965):52.

9. "General Sarnoff puts 'English' on talk in Australia." *Variety* 249 (January 31, 1967):52.

10. "USIA's bid for global info grid." *Variety* 250 (February 28, 1968):28.

11. Les Brown. "TV webs spurn Bundy's bird." *Variety* 244 (August 24, 1966): 33, 46.

12. "Don't be ashamed of o'seas image sez Ralph Baruch." *Variety* 227 (August 22, 1962):26.

13. "Limitation of free market for U.S. TV shows o'seas assailed." *Variety* 233 (February 12, 1964):42.

14. "McCarthy's aim: a free world open market in program field." *Variety* 228 (November 7, 1962):24.

15. Albert R. Kroeger. "International television." *Television Magazine* 20 (July 1963):78.

16. Erik Barnouw. *Tube of Plenty.* New York: Oxford, 1975, p. 408.

17. "Busy, dizzy o'seas market." *Variety* 228 (September 5, 1962):23; "H'Wood $200,000,000 TV ride." *Variety* 231 (July 31, 1963):27.

18. Barry R. Litman. "The economics of the television market for theatrical movies." *Journal of Communication* 29 (Autumn 1979):23.

19. Ibid., pp. 24–25.

20. Wilson P. Dizard. *Television: A World View.* Syracuse: Syracuse University Press, 1966, pp. 156–158.

21. Ibid., pp. 168, 171.

22. "Distribution rights vital." *Broadcasting* 63 (October 15, 1962):82.

23. Sanford Markey. "Thai TV: Weapon for West vs. Communism." *Variety* 231 (July 21, 1963):32.

24. "NBC Int'l officially hands over Nigerian TV service after 5 years." *Variety* 246 (April 19, 1967):77, 85; Joseph Lapid. "TV no. 1 in Israeli show biz after only 18 months." *Variety* 258 (January 7, 1970):74.

25. "ABC Int'l in $3,600,000 'feed' to foreign affiliates in past year." *Variety* 232 (November 13, 1963):31.

26. "ABC shows off its overseas TV lineup." *Broadcasting* 63 (November 5, 1962): 72–73.

27. "Boom for foreign television." *Broadcasting* 63 (October 15, 1962):75–78.

28. "Global TV network is target of symposium." *Broadcasting* 68 (March 29, 1965):102–103.

29. "U.S. media aid New Zealand on radio–TV bill." *Advertising Age* 39 (April 8, 1968):26.

30. "Television is the message down in Rio." *Business Week*, June 17, 1967, pp. 87–88.

31. Ibid.

32. Domingo di Nubila. "Focus on Time-Life Rio TV stake as Arg. meet eyes foreign influences." *Variety* 247 (June 14, 1967):45.

33. Albert R. Kroeger. "International television." *Television Magazine* 20 (July 1963): pp. 82–83; Ralph Tyler. "Television around the world." *Television Magazine* 23 (October 1966):61.

34. Ralph Tyler. "Television around the world." *Television Magazine* 23 (October 1966):33, 61.

35. Maximo Humbert. "ABC-TV has just bought Latin America." *Atlas* 19 (January 1970):37–39.

36. "Ban sales pitches at 4-day Oct meet of Europe–U.S. b'casters." *Variety* 227 (June 27, 1962):35.

37. Art Woodstone. "ABC's 'commercial' a sour note at EBU's staid opening session." *Variety* 228 (October 24, 1962):30, 54.

38. "ABC Int'l has own 'global meet' & it's strictly hardsell." *Variety* 228 (October 31, 1962):29.

39. "NBC Int'l cuffos pubaffairs o'seas to TV novitiates." *Variety* 227 (July 4, 1962):69.

40. "London jammed with Yank reps pitching product." *Variety* 233 (January 22, 1964):42; "Japanese market for foreign TVers on upswing as domestic costs soar." *Variety* 242 (February 23, 1966):49; "O'seas: old series never die." *Variety* 242 (May 11, 1966):39.

41. "UA-TV first to notch 100 mark offshore." *Variety* 243 (July 20, 1966):35.

42. "It's 'U.S. or Bust' for Britain's tint productions as nut goes up 20%." *Variety* 242 (April 27, 1966):31; "Color TV issue stirs controversy in Italy; slow progress is seen." *Variety* 243 (July 6, 1966):31.

43. "Screen Gems; Canadian caper to plug 'good neighbor star flights' 4 ways." *Variety* 247 (May 24, 1967):39.

44. Albert R. Kroeger. "International television." *Television Magazine* 20 (July 1963):80.

45. Herbert I. Schiller. "The U.S. hard sell." *The Nation* 203 (December 5, 1966):609.

46. Ibid., pp. 610–611.

47. "Worldvision symposium speakers optimistic on overcoming ad obstacles of world TV." *Advertising Age* 37 (November 21, 1966):38.

48. Neil P. Hurley. "Tele-culture and the third world." *Commonweal* 88 (April 19, 1968):131–132.

49. "One spot commercial may someday cover the globe." *Broadcasting* 71 (December 19, 1966):23.

50. "Residual talent fees don't apply to overseas' sales." *Broadcasting* 63 (October 15, 1962):80.

51. Albert R. Kroeger. "International television." *Television Magazine* 20 (July 1963):49.

52. "TV scripters now cut in on foreign take." *Variety* 231 (July 17, 1963): 49, 56; Dave Kaufman. "New SAG pact gives actors % of o'seas take." *Variety* 235 (July 15, 1964):26.

53. "As BBC goes (on U.S. buys) so goes European television webs." *Variety* 231 (August 7, 1963):47.

54. Lloyd Garrison. "Nigeria doing home-grown television shows." *New York Times*, September 8, 1963, sec. 2, p. 15.

55. "Better prices for U.S. programs campaign." *Broadcasting* 64 (March 25, 1963):28.

56. Albert R. Kroeger. "International television." *Television Magazine* 20 (July 1963):78; Murray Horowitz. "Two faces east and west." *Variety* 230 (May 8, 1963): 187, 190.

57. Albert R. Kroeger. "International television." *Television Magazine* 20 (July 1963):77–78.

58. Murray Horowitz, "Two faces east and west." *Variety* 230 (May 8, 1963):187.

59. Murray Horowitz. "Who speaks for America?" *Variety* 233 (November 27, 1963):31.

60. Murray Horowitz. "Valenti eager to keep TV healthy as integral part of picture biz." *Variety* 244 (November 9, 1966):1, 65; "Valenti & Nizer o'seas TV pitch." *Variety* 244 (October 5, 1966):27.

61. "80,000,000 o'seas TV sets." *Variety* 235 (June 17, 1964):31; Eric Barnouw. *Tube of Plenty.* New York: Oxford, 1975, p. 407.

62. Dave Kaufman. "Adams: Don't get too over-zealous on foreign sales." *Variety* 230 (March 13, 1963):33, 50.

63. Albert R. Kroeger, "International television." *Television Magazine* 20 (July 1963):48.

64. "MCA-TV finds Europe situations not what it's cracked up to be." *Variety* 233 (February 19, 1964):31.

65. Abel Green. "Foreign mkt. leveling off?" *Variety* 242 (April 13, 1966):39, 49.

66. Dave Kaufman. "Syndies garner global gold." *Variety* 246 (April 12, 1967): 39, 47.

67. Dave Jampel. "Silverbach eyes 20th–TV coprod. o'seas; sees changing global mkt." *Variety* 249 (December 27, 1967):28, 31.

68. "Swiss TV turns to commercials." *New York Times*, February 2, 1965, p. 67.

69. "Dutch issue: commercial TV." *Variety* 238 (March 17, 1965):51.

70. Hazel Guild. "Station debts may cue hiked fees for German sets." *Variety* 244 (September 7, 1966):36.

71. Hazel Guild. "Private com'l TV in Germany's Saar up for grabs." *Variety* 251 (July 24, 1968):39.

72. Fradley Garner. "Scandinavian TV's foreign accent." *Variety* 249 (January 24, 1967):46.

73. "FC&B's foreign legion views European TV." *Broadcasting* 70 (June 6, 1966): 82–83.

74. "BBC states its case against the acceptance of video commercials." *Variety* 242 (July 13, 1966):33.

75. Jack Hellman. "L.A.'s features-to-tv stockpile." *Variety* 235 (July 29, 1964):37.

76. "Hour reruns vs. features." *Variety* 230 (February 27, 1963):24.

77. Murray Horowitz. "TV's $52-mil insurance." *Variety* 244 (August 31, 1966): 1, 62.

78. "O'seas dilemma on pre–'48s." *Variety* 227 (July 11, 1962):43.

79. "O'seas pix-to-tv expansion." *Variety* 230 (February 27, 1963):25, 40; "O'seas marts shun U.S. pix." *Variety* 235 (June 24, 1964):29; "Features abroad play minor role." *Variety* 230 (March 13, 1963):33.

80. "French TV goal: Fewer U.S. pix." *Variety* 236 (September 30, 1964):32, 46.

81. "Pic prices round TV globe." *Variety* 242 (February 23, 1966):39.

82. "CBS Films' global breakthrough in sale on news-cultural shows." *Variety* 233 (November 27, 1963):31.

83. Jack Pitman. "U.S. sports girdling globe." *Variety* 248 (October 11, 1967):69.

84. "Foreign syndie biz: 50% mark." *Variety* 228 (November 21, 1962):23, 30.

85. Albert R. Kroeger. "International television." *Television Magazine* 20 (July 1963):81.

86. "SG's Burns mulls potentials of Japanese shows for world market." *Variety* 230 (March 20, 1963):35; Dave Jampel. "Silverbach eyes 20th–TV coprod. o'seas; sees changing global mkt." *Variety* 249 (December 27, 1967):28, 31.

87. "Brit vidpix no threat in U.S.: Dann." *Variety* 250 (April 3, 1968):42.

88. Brian Mulligan. "U.K.-U.S. romance." *Variety* 253 (January 8, 1969):87.

89. "USIA eases 'image' barrier in export of TV shows to Iron Curtain nations." *Variety* 228 (October 17, 1962):25.

90. "For a wasteland, U.S. gets big play from TV dignitaries abroad." *Variety* 228 (September 5, 1962):37; "Overseas visitors 'oversee' U.S. television." *Sponsor* 18 (December 7, 1964):40–41.

91. Giraud Chester. *Television and Radio.* 4th ed. New York: Appleton–Century–Crofts, 1971, p. 215.

92. Connie Soloyanis. "Prep for TV bow in Saudi Arabia." *Variety* 237 (January 6, 1965):87, 112.

93. Hazel Guild. "Yank Army TV so hot in Iceland it's forcing govt. to bow own operation." *Variety* 240 (September 15, 1965):42.

94. "GI network bans 'Combat'; Germans may be watching." *Variety* 255 (August 6, 1969):1, 53.

95. Sanford Markey. "TV comes to Vietnam." *Variety* 242 (March 16, 1966): 32, 44.

96. "Turkey TV trot dates March for debut in Ankara." *Variety* 248 (October 4, 1967):30.

97. "Take retired TV execs to o'seas consultant jobs." *Variety* 248 (October 4, 1967):35.

98. "TV's $311,600,000 profits in '62." *Variety* 232 (September 25, 1963):39; Bill Greely. "3-webs' O&O's earn $135,000,000." *Variety* 256 (October 22, 1969):43, 53.

99. Erik Barnouw. *Tube of Plenty.* New York: Oxford, 1975, p. 407.

100. Albert R. Kroeger. "International television." *Television* Magazine 20 (July 1963):44; "Overseas program sales hit $52 million." *Broadcasting* 63 (October 15, 1962): 78–80.

101. "Overseas market: $73,500,000." *Variety* 237 (February 3, 1965):35; "See $74,500,000 offshore mkt. for all U.S. video fare." *Variety* 242 (February 23, 1966):46; "U.S. programs hot items overseas." *Broadcasting* 73 (December 18, 1967):28.

102. "The global market: tough nut." *Television Magazine* 23 (August 1966):68; "World market for U.S. TV up 6%." *Broadcasting* 70 (May 16, 1966):28; George Friedman. "Eye $80-mil offshore gross." *Variety* 249 (January 10, 1968):35.

Chapter 4

1. "Brazil: tough nut to crack." *Variety* 232 (October 16, 1963):26.

2. "Arg house passes bill imposing local dubbing on foreign telepix." *Variety* 241 (November 24, 1965):35.

3. Roger Bower. "Nigeria TV gets H'Wood hoopla on official bow." *Variety* 230 (March 13, 1963):44.

4. Sanford Markey. "Taiwan TV, on 27 months, now into profit era." *Variety* 237 (January 13, 1965):43, 56.

5. Jay Walz. "Cairo TV invaded by cowboys, and the children just love it." *New York Times*, November 25, 1962, p. 8.

6. Sanford Markey. "Korean television relies on its U.S. telefilms." *Variety* 239 (June 2, 1965):39, 49.

7. Joseph Lapid. "Israel's TV pact—winnowing out plus those winning ways of CBS." *Variety* 244 (September 21, 1966):44.

8. Jack Agnew. "Israel TV, born of six-day war, careful about its U.S.-U.K. imports." *Variety* 254 (February 26, 1969):57; "TV export assn. sights $88,000,000 in U.S. overseas sales this year." *Variety* 250 (April 3, 1968):39.

9. Albert R. Kroeger. "International television." *Television Magazine* 20 (July 1963):78; Dave Kaufman. "Adams: Don't get too over-zealous on foreign sales." *Variety* 230 (March 13, 1963):33, 50.

10. Dave Jampel. "McCarthy deplores failure to get fair price shake in Japan." *Variety* 230 (February 27, 1963):24, 44.

11. "Japan lifts $3,300,000 ceiling on imports of U.S.-made telefilms." *Variety* 230 (April 3, 1963):28.

12. "SG's Burns mulls potentials of Japanese shows for world market." *Variety* 230 (March 20, 1963):35.

13. Albert R. Kroeger. "International television." *Television Magazine* 20 (July 1963):48.

14. "Japanese TV now on level with U.S. TV, sez Tokyo's Imamichi." *Variety* 230 (March 20, 1963):26.

15. Dave Jampel. "Decline of U.S. vidpix product on Japanese TV." *Variety* 236 (August 26, 1964):26, 40.

16. "U.S. TV sales in Japan reverse slide." *Variety* 238 (March 10, 1965):53; "If not web-sold in U.S., 'Dead' for tightened-up Japan." *Variety* 246 (March 22, 1967):41, 54.

17. Charles Lazarus. "U.S. TV heft squeezes CBC." *Variety* 238 (March 31, 1965):39.

18. "CBC, financially healthy, yearns to ditch some U.S. 'escapist' fare." *Variety* 239 (July 14, 1965):31, 34.

19. Albert R. Kroeger. "International television." *Television Magazine* 20 (July 1963):48.

20. "The global market: tough nut." *Television Magazine* 23 (August, 1966):90, 92, 102.

21. Charles Lazarus. "Can. TV hot seat cools off." *Variety* 242 (March 30, 1966):45, 64.

22. "Both TV webs in Canada warned by State Secretary to 'shape up.'" *Variety* 246 (February 22, 1967):49.

23. "Foreign control of CATV cut sharply in Canada." *Variety* 252 (October 2, 1968):38.

24. Paul Gardner. "CATV feeds from U.S. would wreck Canadian b'casting." *Variety* 257 (December 10, 1969):40, 54.

25. "Canadian cabler, others hit ukase vs. micro from distant U.S. cities." *Variety* 257 (December 17, 1969):38.

26. "TVer in N'west U.S. border burg milks auds and ads from Canada." *Variety* 257 (December 24, 1969):33; "Canadian cabler, others hit ukase vs. micro from distant U.S. cities." *Variety* 257 (December 17, 1969):38.

27. George Malko. "Australian TV: the wasteland down under." *Saturday Review* 45 (August 11, 1962):42–43.

28. Wilson P. Dizard. *Television: A World View.* Syracuse: Syracuse University Press, 1976, p. 162; "Aussie TV's big politico squeeze on U.S. imports." *Variety* 230 (March 13, 1963):44.

29. Murray Horowitz. "Aussie mart breaking open." *Variety* 231 (July 10, 1963): 35, 48.

30. "TV's expanding world mart." *Variety* 232 (October 16, 1963):27; Albert R. Kroeger. "International television." *Television Magazine* 20 (July 1963):80–81.

31. "Australian TV using fewer U.S. shows." *Variety* 236 (October 28, 1964):30.

32. Eric Gorrick. "Australia resists high prices on U.S. product; Brit shows are up." *Variety* 242 (April 30, 1966):39.

33. "The global market: tough nut." *Television Magazine* 23 (August, 1966):102.

34. "Aussies 'boycotting' U.S. product; possible peace with Nov. Nielsens." *Variety* 243 (August 17, 1966):27, 38.

35. "Yank-Aussie cold war." *Variety* 243 (August 17, 1966):27.

36. "See Aussie Labor Party asking curb on TV dollars for imports." *Variety* 244 (September 21, 1966):51.

37. "Australia edicts 50% local TV to break American stranglehold." *Variety* 244 (September 28, 1966):28.

38. Eric Gorrick. "Aussie television rounds out 12 years; U.S. shows back in favor." *Variety* 247 (July 26, 1967):58.

39. "Aussie TV bought 75% of imported shows from America last year." *Variety* 256 (October 15, 1969):47.

40. "Aussie court upholds appeal ending pact on pool buy of U.S. television product." *Variety* 256 (October 22, 1969):46; "Court kibosh on 4-web consortium in Aussie spurs U.S., U.K. TV thrust." *Variety* 256 (November 5, 1969):42.

41. Hazel Guild. "West German television—one gripe after another." *Variety* 231 (July 31, 1963):33, 90; "Americanization of German television." *Variety* 230 (April 10, 1963):44.

42. "Disenchantment with French TV." *Variety* 253 (December 4, 1968):46.

43. "Yank exec sees no upswing in view on Italo TV's U.S. product drought." *Variety* 250 (April 17, 1968):32.

44. "Scandinavia co-buys Jerry Lewis." *Variety* 254 (April 23, 1969):56.

45. Sigurd Lindal. "Wasteland in Iceland." *Atlas* 11 (April 1966):241–242.

46. "Pilkington report under attack for skirting issue on foreign imports." *Variety* 227 (July 25, 1962):53.

47. Giraud Chester. *Television and Radio.* 4th ed. New York: Appleton–Century–Crofts, 1971, p. 190; "BBC-TV services notice on distribs: We'll be using fewer U.S. shows." *Variety* 228 (November 21, 1962):22.

48. "British TV's scramble for top 20 entries invites top prices for U.S. shows." *Variety* 232 (September 25, 1963):29.

49. "Britain's 14% quota on outside TV product blasted by McCarthy." *Variety* 231 (October 9, 1963):27; "British TV expressed concern over McCarthy's quota pressures." *Variety* 233 (November 27, 1963):31.

50. Roger Watkins. "Fading role of telefilms in British TV market." *Variety* 233 (January 25, 1964):34, 48.

51. Harold Myers. "British TV floodgate open." *Variety* 236 (October 7, 1964): 29; U.S. film exporters ask State Dept. to try again on Brit. TV quota." *Variety* 240 (November 10, 1965):38.

52. "CBS Films won't cutrate programs in tough U.K. market, says Baruch." *Variety* 243 (June 1, 1966):41.

53. "Brit majors paying new top for U.S. series; Batman broke the ice." *Variety* 243 (June 15, 1966):37; "Aussies 'boycotting' U.S. product; possible peace with Nov. Nielsens." *Variety* 243 (August 17, 1966):38.

54. "U.S. hopes up on U.K. quota." *Variety* 246 (April 19, 1967):75, 86.

55. Roger Watkins. "Yanks gain points but lose game as British stand fast on TV quota." *Variety* 247 (May 31, 1967):32; "U.S. hopes up on U.K. quota." *Variety* 246 (April 19, 1967).

56. "U.S. still stuck with 14% quota on British TV." *Variety* 247 (May 24, 1967):31.

57. Albert R. Kroeger. "International television." *Television Magazine* 20 (July 1963):74.

58. "McCarthy charges D.C. attacks on U.S. TV damaging 'image' abroad." *Variety* 229 (February 6, 1963):34, 48.

59. Brian Mulligan. "Fred Friendly's warning in Britain." *Variety* 248 (October 25, 1967):24, 40.

60. "The global market: tough nut." *Television Magazine* 23 (August 1966):90.

61. "U.S. product responsible for violence on Canada's airwaves says CBC Prexy." *Variety* 254 (March 19, 1969):35.

Chapter 5

1. William Boulton. "Broad horizon for global CATV; most countries already pay fees." *Variety* 258 (April 8, 1970):54, 96.

2. Larry Michie. "Ameribird may soar in 1973." *Variety* 267 (June 21, 1972): 31, 50.

3. Philip J. Klass. "U.S. reviews satellite telecast policy." *Aviation Week & Space Technology* 108 (January 23, 1978):66.

4. Hedrick Smith. "Soviet asks U.N. to bar intrusion by satellite TV." *New York Times*, August 11, 1972, p. 1.

5. Philip J. Klass. "U.S. reviews satellite telecast policy." *Aviation Week & Space Technology* 108 (January 23, 1978):66–67; William H. Read. "Multinational media." *Foreign Policy* no. 18 (Spring 1975):157–158.

6. "New race for space." *Forbes* 118 (September 1, 1976):28.

7. Whitney Williams. "Brazil & probably Chile to receive Oscarcast in live ABC-TV beaming." *Variety* 258 (March 25, 1970):41.

8. "A buyer's market; ORTF limits series to 13 episodes." *Variety* 258 (April 8, 1970):88.

9. "TV biz tops $1-bil in earnings." *Variety* 288 (August 31, 1977):43, 56.

10. Dave Kaufman. "H'wood majors (35 hours) vs. 'minors' (8)." *Variety* 262 (March 31, 1971):38.

11. Barry R. Litman. "The economics of the television market for theatrical movies." *Journal of Communication* 29, no. 4 (Autumn 1979):27–28.

12. "Cox cable gets wired in Denmark." *Variety* 276 (October 2, 1974):46; Harold Myers. "Europe 'examining' cable TV." *Variety* 266 (March 15, 1972):39, 52.

13. "NBCI filling up o'seas stocking." *Variety* 265 (December 15, 1971):40; "Worldvision off & running, nears $10,000,000 mark in syndie sales." *Variety* 271 (May 16, 1973):96.

14. "Mixed view of American TV in France." *Variety* 266 (April 12, 1972):80.

15. Dave Kaufman. "How goes U.S. TV o'seas?" *Variety* 280 (August 13, 1975):34.

16. Jack Pitman. "U.S. series licensing for Britain rising to average 10G per hour." *Variety* 282 (April 21, 1976):39, 66.

17. "Program costs per Bob Howard." *Variety* 287 (May 18, 1977):1.

18. John J. O'Connor. "Will they buy it in Brazil." *New York Times*, March 12, 1972, sec. 2, p. 17.

19. "Aussie TV TEN nixes 'package' deals from U.S." *Variety* 261 (November 25, 1970):34.

20. "Unions demand foreign resid coin; webs claim telecasts were pirated." *Variety* 270 (February 14, 1973):64.

21. "World TV set census 251-mil; U.S. has 30%" *Variety* 266 (April 12, 1972):1; Dave Kaufman. "U.S. world vidpix mkt. down." *Variety* 266 (March 15, 1972):37, 54; "Global color TV at 100-mil mark." *Variety* 281 (January 7, 1976):104, 109.

22. "Fresh grumblings by U.S. majors on 'depressed' prices for pix, programs." *Variety* 270 (April 18, 1973):45, 54.

23. "Kojak: The all–American image?" *Senior Scholastic* 110 (September 8, 1977):15.

24. Joyce Nelson. "One way street." *Cinema Canada* no. 54 (April 1979):11.

25. Hank Werba. "Politics buffeting RAI-TV." *Variety* 258 (April 8, 1970):57, 72.

26. Gene Moskowitz. "Profile of Finnish TV." *Variety* 259 (July 8, 1970):49.

27. "Life without tyranny of ratings common in television — outside U.S." *Variety* 258 (April 8, 1970):76.

28. "Subtle minds of the East find U.S. television commercials too sly for their taste." *Variety* 259 (May 6, 1970):84.

29. Joan Dupont. "Life in a country without overnights." *Variety* 294 (March 28, 1979):51, 76.

30. Hazel Guild. "Made-in America movies as the best and cheapest for German video." *Variety* 258 (April 6, 1970):83; "$50-mil foreign films in 8 years on German video." *Variety* 262 (April 14, 1971):55, 60.

31. Hazel Guild. "German TV's $5-mil splurge on pix ires freelance craftsmen, cinemas." *Variety* 269 (January 17, 1973):52.

32. Jack Pitman. "Update on TV movies in Europe." *Variety* 269 (February 7, 1973):60.

33. "French dig U.S. features, $6,000 per pic average, used 370 in 1970." *Variety* 262 (April 14, 1971):62.

34. "U.S. distribs crack freeze on film prices by Europe TV." *Variety* 273 (December 26, 1973):1, 40.

35. Larry Michie. "Movie prices on TV go up the tube." *Variety* 287 (July 20, 1977):1, 102; "Japanese TV cuts back features as oil crisis reduces airtime." *Variety* 277 (February 5, 1975):62; "France's new rules for pix-to-video." *Variety* 292 (October 25, 1978):50.

36. "U.S. tops list of suppliers of feature pix to German TV." *Variety* 296 (October 10, 1979):43.

37. "U.S. films 'not available' to TV in Israel — not at $800 per pic." *Variety* 294 (February 28, 1979):49, 90.

38. "U.S. majors end pix boycott vs. Swedish TV." *Variety* 294 (April 18, 1979):59.

39. Jack Pitman. "Canada's new quotas, U.S. cutback in primetime brighten Brit. o'seas sell." *Variety* 259 (July 29, 1970):35; "Yankee dollar inspires U.S.-angled productions by British television outfits." *Variety* 260 (October 28, 1970):49.

40. Les Brown. "New selling opening in U.S. for selling overseas TV productions." *Variety* 262 (april 14, 1971):40.

41. Andrew Bailey. "Sitcoms from Yankeeland are alive and doing well in crossover to U.K." *Variety* 258 (April 8, 1970):75, 100.

42. "Yorkin & Lear plot Yank version of 'Steptoe' as followup to bigot." *Variety* 262 (March 3, 1971):32.

43. "French TV longs for U.S. mart; a problem is lingo." *Variety* 266 (April 12, 1972):77.

44. "Dominance of foreign programs on public TV rapped by CIO-AFL council." *Variety* 270 (March 7, 1973):38, 52.

45. Joyce Nelson. "One way street." *Cinema Canada* no. 54 (April, 1979):11.

46. Les Brown. "Cracking the U.S. TV market." *Variety* 270 (April 4, 1973):1, 66, 78.

47. Philippe Baraduc. "New direction for television, with quality as common denominator." *Variety* 270 (April 4, 1973):97.

48. Bob Knight. "Scorecard on U.S. TV imports: It helps if show's in English." *Variety* 270 (April 4, 1973):66.

49. Larry Michie. "International TV's 1-way traffic." *Variety* 274 (April 17, 1974): 1, 86.

50. Larry Michie. "British brigade aims for sales." *Variety* 290 (March 1, 1978): 113, 118.

51. "35 TV execs of Japan visit U.S., told of hurdles on show swap." *Variety* 290 (February 15, 1978):41, 62.

52. "Duo's how-to on selling of TV pix o'seas." *Variety* 296 (September 5, 1979): 68, 80.

53. Les Brown. "BBC comedy series' odd format rejected by U.S. commercial TV." *New York Times*, March 3, 1977, p. 67.

54. "TV sales & profits hit new peaks." *Variety* 258 (April 22, 1970):33.

55. "U.S. TV exports in 1970 hit 20% of gross sales." *Variety* 262 (April 28, 1971):1, 70.

56. Tapio Varis. "Global traffic in television." *Journal of Communication* 24 (1) (Winter 1974):102–107.
57. William H. Read. "Multinational media." *Foreign Policy* no. 18 (Spring, 1975):157–167.
58. "American TV abroad." *New York Times*, January 18, 1981, sec. 3, p. 18; "The U.S. as TV programmer to the world." *Broadcasting* 92 (April 18, 1977):48–50, 52.
59. Jack Valenti. "Valenti values film–TV coin in o'seas mart." *Variety* 289 (January 4, 1978):1, 64.
60. Joyce Nelson. "One way street." *Cinema Canada* no. 54 (April 1979):13–14.

Chapter 6

1. Malcolm W. Browne. "Latin nationalists annoyed by Yankees on TV." *New York Times*, March 5, 1971, p. 4.
2. Dave Kaufman. "U.S. declines in Latino TV markets; Mexican-made soapers cleaning up." *Variety* 268 (August 16, 1972):36, 44.
3. Domingo di Nubila. "Argentina TV pampering locals with 80% home-grown product." *Variety* 263 (May 5, 1971):49–50.
4. H. J. Maidenberg. "Peruvians decree state control for all TV and radio stations." *New York Times*, November 11, 1971, p. 11; H. J. Maidenberg. "Why Peru seized TV." *New York Times*, November 14, 1971, sec. 3, p. 11.
5. "Kojack: the all–American image?" *Senior Scholastic* 110 (September 8, 1977):15.
6. Hans Ehrmann. "Chile trims state TV subsidies." *Variety* 279 (July 9, 1975): 47, 59; Hans Ehrmann. "After 16 years, Chile struggling to get out of the basement." *Variety* 290 (March 22, 1978):82.
7. Ira Lee. "Brazil govt. mulls going 70% native." *Variety* 287 (June 1, 1977):43; Ira Lee. "Brazil's Globo TV cuts back on imports to meet govt. quotas." *Variety* 288 (August 10, 1977):42, 50.
8. Edgar Koh. "TV in a developing nation: Singapore's U.K.-U.S." *Variety* 279 (July 9, 1975):58.
9. "Turkish TV: still striving for larger role at age 11." *Variety* 296 (October 10, 1979):100, 107.
10. Jack Pitman. "Deadbeat Nigeria worries syndicators." *Variety* 295 (July 18, 1979):31, 36.
11. Ernest Weatherall. "Indian TV & 'cultural imperialism.'" *Variety* 292 (October 11, 1978):147.
12. Harold Myers. "U.S. movies, but not series, are big on Japanese TV." *Variety* 294 (April 18, 1979):109.
13. "Canada may ease microwaving from States via selectivity." *Variety* 257 (January 21, 1970):49.
14. Charles Lazarus. "Canada tightens TV vs. U.S." *Variety* 258 (February 18, 1970):37, 56.
15. Paul Gardner. "Prexy of Canadian b'casters assn. worried about exports from U.S." *Variety* 258 (April 15, 1970):56.
16. Herschel Hardin. *Closed Circuits: The Sellout of Canadian Television.* Vancouver: Douglas & McIntyre, 1985, pp. 18–19.
17. "CBC topper wonders about budget in facing sked of fewer U.S. skeins." *Variety* 258 (April 22, 1970):37.

18. "Prez of Canada's indie TV web warns of big loss via curb on U.S. shows." *Variety* 258 (April 22, 1970):37.

19. Paul Gardner. "Issue of Canadian program content gets a going-over in Parliament." *Variety* 259 (May 27, 1970):43.

20. Paul Gardner. "Not trying to build 'electronic wall' around Canada, says CRTC's Juneau." *Variety* 259 (June 3, 1970):29, 43; "Canada may up U.S. content." *Variety* 263 (May 12, 1971):211.

21. Herschel Hardin. *Closed Circuits: The Sellout of Canadian Television.* Vancouver: Douglas & McIntyre, 1985, pp. 30-31.

22. "Ban U.S.-fed ads on Can. CATV." *Variety* 263 (July 28, 1971):28.

23. "U.S. TV influence too much in life of Canadians: poll." *Variety* 279 (June 18, 1975):48.

24. Paul Gardner. "Rule 'Yankee dollar' out of Canadian air." *Variety* 277 (January 29, 1975):42.

25. Paul Gardner. "Boyle-ing point in Canadian television." *Variety* 285 (November 24, 1976):62, 75.

26. Paul Harris. "U.S.–Canada's heated TV-film flap." *Variety* 284 (August 18, 1976):1, 68.

27. Paul Gardner. "Boyle-ing point in Canadian television." *Variety* 285 (November 24, 1976):75; Paul Harris. "U.S.–Canada's heated TV-film flap." *Variety* 284 (August 18, 1976):68.

28. Paul Gardner. "U.S. police shows a must in Canada." *Variety* 281 (November 19, 1975):39, 50.

29. Paul Gardner. "Hit U.S.'s dominant TV role in Canada." *Variety* 281 (November 26, 1975):35, 42.

30. Sid Adilman. "CBC's plan for fewer foreign shows." *Variety* 287 (June 22, 1977):75, 86.

31. "The border war." *Macleans* 89 (October 18, 1976):17; "A confrontation with Canada over TV ads." *Business Week*, November 6, 1978, pp. 142, 147.

32. "Limit U.S. channels for Canada cablers." *Variety* 291 (August 2, 1978):45; T. J. Allard. *Straight Up: Private Broadcasting in Canada: 1918–1958.* Ottawa: Canadian Communications Foundation, 1979, p. 272.

33. "Ontario govt. panel hits American TV, pix violence." *Variety* 287 (June 22, 1977):75, 86.

34. Earl Green. "Camu quits as CRTC boss; can't cope with flood of U.S. shows into Canada." *Variety* 296 (September 19, 1979):36.

35. Joyce Nelson. "One way street." *Cinema Canada* no. 54 (April 1979):11–13.

36. "Rise in Aussie-made content figures to add $1-mil to TV stations' nut." *Variety* 261 (December 9, 1970):41, 44; Eric Gorrick. "G.M. of Aussie com'l TV body warns control board of risks in quotas." *Variety* 263 (June 2, 1971):38; "Screen Gems producing TV series down under for Australian mkt." *Variety* 263 (June 9, 1971):30.

37. "Aussie official cautions TVers on foreign buys." *Variety* 270 (March 14, 1973):50–51.

38. "Aussie stations nix Board's bid on o'seas buying." *Variety* 272 (October 24, 1973):46; "Aussie cabinet nixes plan for govt. pool on TV program buys." *Variety* 273 (January 2, 1974):30.

39. "Australian TV goes to point system meant to hypo native production." *Variety* 271 (July 11, 1973):46.

40. Miles F. E. Wright. "Aussie b'casting control board beset by obstacles in trying to upgrade shows." *Variety* 282 (May 5, 1976):80.

41. Raymond Stanley. "Aussie TV imports status quo at 73% from U.S., 24%

from Brit." *Variety* 276 (October 16, 1974):56; Raymond Stanley. "Aussie's stead U.S.-U.K. buys." *Variety* 280 (October 29, 1975):52; Raymond Stanley. "Aussie air control board issues annual TV report; U.S. buys up." *Variety* 284 (October 20, 1976):170.

42. "See Aussie TV critical unless imports curbed." *Variety* 283 (June 16, 1976): 35, 50; "Aussie TV webs put accent on home prod, cut imported shows." *Variety* 282 (May 5, 1976):90.

43. Frank Beerman. "U.S.-based reps assess market for Australian television product here." *Variety* 288 (September 21, 1977):30; Elizabeth Riddell. "Aussie TV imports put at 18% of U.S. foreign TV sales." *Variety* 288 (September 21, 1977):30, 58.

44. "Aussie TVers spending more for local prod." *Variety* 295 (June 27, 1979):48.

45. Mike Nicolaidi. "New Zealand's 2-channel setup under fire." *Variety* 296 (October 3, 1979):57, 61.

46. Billy Kocian. "German TV in deep financial trouble." *Variety* 280 (August 20, 1975):45, 55.

47. "First German net lowers the boom on U.S. TV violence." *Variety* 291 (July 26, 1978):50, 57.

48. Margo Hammond. "Greek TV is at turning point." *Variety* 296 (October 10, 1979):82.

49. "Syndicate of directors claims French TV losing 'service' image." *Variety* 279 (May 14, 1975):133, 146.

50. Ted Clark. "French TV in uptrend for U.S. shows." *Variety* 280 (October 1, 1975):85, 102.

51. Ted Clark. "Creativity crisis in French TV." *Variety* 283 (June 16, 1976):34, 48.

52. Ted Clark. "French TV has a lot of Gaul: Program quotas are imposed." *Variety* 283 (July 28, 1976):39, 48.

53. "Toward reform of French TV." *Variety* 286 (April 20, 1977):60.

54. Hank Werba. "Italy as worst market for U.S. show exports." *Variety* 262 (April 14, 1971):41, 47.

55. "Private TV burgeoning in Italy but still unready." *Variety* 286 (April 20, 1977):48; "Private TV-radio in Italy." *Variety* 291 (April 25, 1978):142.

56. "Publishers now dominate Italian comm'l TV." *Variety* 298 (April 16, 1980): 96, 106.

57. Jack Pitman. "U.S. TV series fail to make dent on Brit viewers." *Variety* 262 (January 13, 1971):41, 54.

58. Jack Pitman. "British com'l TV making time." *Variety* 265 (January 26, 1972):1, 62.

59. "U.S. TV's sour U.K. future?" *Variety* 266 (April 26, 1972):33; "Scrapping of 'outer quota' by Brit's indie TV authority a blow to U.S." *Variety* 267 (July 26, 1972):42.

60. "Foreign TV quotas remain as is in U.K. as other lands tighten up." *Variety* 270 (April 4, 1973):78; Jeremy Isaacs. "This earth this realm this England." *Variety* 281 (January 7, 1976):105, 126.

61. Dave Kaufman. "CPT execs see world peak for U.S. TV & theatre pix." *Variety* 284 (October 20, 1976):171, 178.

62. Jack Pitman. "Brit ITV cuts foreign quota to 12%." *Variety* 289 (November 16, 1977):59, 68.

63. Jack Pitman. "U.K.'s second thoughts on o'seas quota." *Variety* 291 (July 12, 1978):43; "Yank shows in sharp decline on British television screens." *Variety* 297 (January 9, 1980):169, 178.

64. "Cable entering satellite & Superstation era." *Variety* 289 (November 16, 1977):58, 72; "Superstation breakthrough." *Broadcasting* 95 (October 30, 1978):25–26.

65. Paul Harris. "TV-to-cable via satellite blasted hard by MPAA." *Variety* 288 (August 31, 1977):45.

Chapter 7

1. John Eger. "TV program producers in need of global outlook." *Advertising Age* 56 (September 9, 1985):26.
2. James H. Rosenfield. "The age of abundance for television worldwide." *Vital Speeches of the Day* 52 (January 15, 1986):211–212.
3. John M. Eger. "Global television: an executive overview." *Columbia Journal of World Business* 22 (Fall 1987):5–7.
4. Ibid., pp. 7–10.
5. "Turner vows worldwide CNN as cable's coming tops Edinburgh agenda." *Variety* 308 (September 8, 1982):96, 101.
6. Tom Girard. "CNN set to bow in Japan; Turner is eyeing global setup." *Variety* 314 (March 7, 1984):376, 392.
7. Bill Grantham. "Turner takes on Europe." *Variety* 320 (September 4, 1985): 46, 65.
8. "Turner claims advances made in markets CNN to Europe." *Variety* 324 (September 24, 1986):43, 46.
9. Bill Grantham. "CNN finally leaps Euro TV barrier; signs four deals." *Variety* 323 (April 30, 1986):131.
10. "How cable–TV success hinges on satellites." *Business Week*, September 14, 1981, pp. 89–90.
11. Roger Watkins. "European TV: It's a whole new ballgame." *Variety* 313 (January 25, 1984):41, 80.
12. Bill Grantham. "Sky Channel's hefty schedule of U.S. programs play better in North than Southern Europe." *Variety* 322 (March 12, 1986):51.
13. Richard Collins. "Wall-to-wall 'Dallas'? The U.S.-U.K. trade in television." *Screen* (U.K.) 27 (no. 3/4, 1986):67.
14. "Panel knocks Euro television prospects." *Variety* 330 (February 10, 1988):92.
15. John Lippman. "Murdoch: Pay-movie channel's profitability answered mid-'89." *Variety* 332 (November 9, 1988):48.
16. Elizabeth Guider. "Sky has limits, media analysts believe, with dishes selling at 3,000 per week." *Variety* 335 (May 10, 1989):83.
17. "MTV Europe now up and running." *Variety* 328 (August 5, 1987):2, 84.
18. Steve Knoll. "Int'l homevid builds." *Variety* 304 (October 7, 1981):167.
19. "Spain flashes its checkbook, but majors not ready to deal." *Variety* 304 (October 21, 1981):58, 82; Hank Werba. "Films Yank fare on Italian TV biggest roadblock to homevideo." *Variety* 303 (May 13, 1981):353.
20. "Homevid fees in some o'seas areas exceed TV rights." *Variety* 304 (October 21, 1981):58, 82.
21. "Valenti sees homevideo woes as an international horror story." *Variety* 302 (March 25, 1981):124, 144.
22. Michael Silverman. "Negative reaction from U.S. distribs to Europe decision." *Variety* 319 (July 17, 1985):43.
23. Tom Bierbaum. "U.S. TV programs get set to invade Scandi HV scene." *Variety* 328 (August 5, 1987):1, 84.
24. Tom Bierbaum. "Yank vidcassetter industry weights impact of European gang of 12." *Variety* 333 (January 11, 1989):91.

25. James Melanson. "U.S. majors now ready to face Latin America." *Variety* 316 (October 3, 1984):1, 101.

26. "Despite Latino HV's undertow, CBS/Fox will wade in further." *Variety* 330 (March 23, 1988):91.

27. "TV Asahi, one of the big four, boasts several links with U.S." *Variety* 319 (May 29, 1985):108; Jack Loftus. "Viacom a partner in Japan cable." *Variety* 312 (August 17, 1983):52, 67.

28. "Program suppliers face snares in cabled Holland." *Variety* 320 (October 2, 1985):114.

29. "U.S. Cashing in on U.K. feevee, as MGM/UA, Par and U venture leads to second partnership." *Variety* 311 (July 13, 1983):51.

30. Roger Watkins. "Show biz in int'l power play." *Variety* 313 (November 9, 1983):1, 68.

31. "CBS nixes foreign venture." *Variety* 313 (December 14, 1983):60.

32. Roger Watkins. "Big Yank guns aiming at tiny paycable market in the U.K." *Variety* 314 (March 21, 1984):116, 122; Tom Girard. "Pay-TV rivals turn chummy for U.K. deal." *Variety* 314 (March 21, 1984):116, 123.

33. "North American investors revive cable biz." *Variety* 338 (January 24, 1990):95, 108.

34. "Not-so-innocents abroad: U.S. webs in Italy." *Variety* 314 (April 18, 1984): 113, 136; Hank Werba. "Yank in Italy to consult on television strategies." *Variety* 311 (July 13, 1983):43, 70.

35. "Not-so-innocents abroad: U.S. webs in Italy." *Variety* 314 (April 18, 1984): 113, 136.

36. "Basketball started it all for CBS Intl." *Variety* 331 (April 27, 1988):84.

37. Elizabeth Guider. "NBC creates European division for program sales, coprods." *Variety* 335 (May 31, 1989):58.

38. Larry Michie. "Shut out of U.S. pay TV, Hollywood takes Europe for piece of the action." *Variety* 317 (January 9, 1985):77.

39. "Economy attitudes vary widely among major U.S. TV suppliers." *Variety* 310 (March 30, 1983):63, 92.

40. Syd Silverman. "Entertainment in the satellite era." *Variety* 312 (October 26, 1983):13, 99.

41. Jack Loftus. "U.S. distributors bit MIP's cable apple." *Variety* 315 (May 2, 1984):129, 149.

42. "CBS signs TV link with China for programs, blurbs, coprods." *Variety* 311 (June 1, 1983):29, 52.

43. "Global TV: Wave of the future or an industry pipe dream?" *Advertising Age* 55 (December 3, 1984):48.

44. "Prime time in Peking." *New Yorker* 61 (April 1, 1985):30–31; "CBS sends 30 telepics to China; part of unique barter package." *Variety* 321 (Dec. 11, 1985):45, 146.

45. James H. Rosenfield. "The age of abundance for television worldwide." *Vital Speeches of the Day* 52 (January 15, 1986):212.

46. Philip S. Gutis. "China gets a 30-second message." *New York Times*, January 12, 1986, sec. 3, p. 11.

47. Charles Kipps. "In flat fee markets, b'casters lean to old world pitch: barter." *Variety* 324 (October 15, 1986):47, 100.

48. Edward Gargan. "Donald Duck learns Chinese." *New York Times*, October 24, 1986, p. D1.

49. "Par, MCA license 100 drama hours to China TV web." *Variety* 326 (February 11, 1987):54, 68.

50. Ted Clark. "Foreign broadcasters dicker over ancillary licensing of TV program characters." *Variety* 327 (May 13, 1987):94.

51. "Foreign markets fill gaps for U.S. showbiz merchandisers." *Variety* 327 (June 10, 1987):4, 21.

52. John Dempsey. "Overseas coin more essential in greenlighting Yank syndie." *Variety* 332 (October 12, 1988):3, 178.

53. Henry Giniger. "J. R. Ewing and Captain Furillo in Paris." *New York Times*, November 21, 1987, p. 27.

54. Alfred J. Jaffe. "CBS Worldwide Enterprises aiming to supply programming for advertisers around the globe." *Television/Radio Age* 32 (October 15, 1984):54–55.

55. Roger Watkins. "Euro hassle on broadcast ads." *Variety* 319 (July 3, 1985): 1, 61.

56. "World TV market." *Broadcasting* 111 (August 18, 1986):65.

57. Earl Jones. "Coming: Global growth in television advertising." *Broadcasting* 113 (October 12, 1987):28.

58. "'Volume sales' moves goods in small mkts." *Variety* 303 (May 6, 1981):1, 54.

59. Jack Loftus. "Minis lure MIP to U.S." *Variety* 314 (April 18, 1984):47.

60. Jack Loftus. "U.S. distributors bit MIP's cable apples." *Variety* 315 (May 2, 1984):149; Morrie Gelman. "Syndies eye o'seas sales boom." *Variety* 330 (February 17, 1988):47, 164.

61. Bruce Alderman. "Europe's cross-border program war." *Variety* 330 (February 17, 1988):47, 164.

62. Janet Stilson. "U.S. distribs point to Europe as the fastest growing market." *Variety* 324 (October 15, 1986):48.

63. Hank Werba. "Popularity of U.S. series stalks the halls of Euro-Teleconfronto." *Variety* 311 (June 8, 1983):38.

64. Morrie Gelman. "TV indies see o'seas sales boom." *Variety* 328 (October 14, 1987):3, 144.

65. "European appetite for U.S. programming grows." *Broadcasting* 113 (October 12, 1987):66, 68.

66. Richard W. Stevenson. "TV boom in Europe is aiding Hollywood." *New York Times*, December 28, 1987, pp. D1, D3.

67. Jack Kindred. "As Germans scrap for TV fare, they find films in short supply." *Variety* 328 (October 14, 1987):49, 136.

68. Merv Adelson. "Global markets looming as bigger slice of TV pic." *Variety* 329 (January 20, 1988):186.

69. Laurence Michie. "Europe is Klondike for TV gold rush." *Variety* 329 (January 20, 1988):175, 191.

70. John Dempsey. "H'wood says go!" *Variety* 331 (June 15, 1988):1, 33.

71. Roger Watkins. "Commercial TV sweeping Europe." *Variety* 298 (April 16, 1980):1, 60.

72. "Satellites, homevideo hovering over Scandinavia; commercials, pay–TV seen viable solutions." *Variety* 308 (October 13, 1982):143, 146.

73. Paul Hepher. "Sartori's outlook gloomy as U.S. dominates world-wide TV." *Cinema Canada* no. 79 (November, 1981):17.

74. Jack Loftus. "Yanks are comin', TV drums drumming." *Variety* 322 (February 5, 1986):114.

75. Steven S. Wildman. "The privatization of European television." *Columbia Journal of World Business* 22 (Fall 1987):72–76.

76. Willem Hoos. "Commercial TV in Holland grim prospect as partial study reveals domestic's favored, costs high." *Variety* 329 (October 28, 1987):52.

77. "U.S.-style TV turns on Europe." *Broadcasting* 115 (April 13, 1987):96–98.

78. John Marcom Jr. "Le Defi Disney." *Forbes* 143 (February 20, 1989):39–40.

79. "Video bidders sending film prices sky-hi." *Variety* 314 (March 7, 1984): 338, 372.

80. "Italian govt. crimps pic imports; RAI-1 taking it on the chin." *Variety* 314 (April 18, 1984):47, 64.

81. Jane Galbraith. "Chinese hills will be alive with the first sound of Fox U.S. pics." *Variety* 327 (July 8, 1987):57, 95; "Syndicator movie TV has plans for ESPN and deals with China." *Variety* 328 (September 23, 1987):96.

82. Elizabeth Guider. "Brit ITV in multimillion-$ deal for 20th Century pic package." *Variety* 335 (May 10, 1989):83.

83. Jack Loftus. "CBS eyes Global network stance." *Variety* 309 (November 24, 1982):1, 99.

84. Edmond M. Rosenthal. "U.S. TV news deals now proliferating around the world." *Television/Radio Age* 34 (April 13, 1987):35–37.

85. John Lippman. "Italian web buys 'NBC Nightly News'; first complete sale." *Variety* 333 (November 2, 1988):52, 68.

86. James Forkan. "Selling U.S. news and sports abroad." *Television/Radio Age* 37 (October 30, 1989):38–39.

87. Syd Silverman. "Entertainment in the satellite era." *Variety* 312 (October 26, 1983):99.

88. Roger Watkins. "Euros angling to crack U.S. TV market." *Variety* 313 (November 2, 1983):45, 58.

89. "Foreign distribs get U.S. advice." *Variety* 326 (January 28, 1987):39.

90. "German TV networks discover it's hard to sell to U.S. market." *Variety* 318 (February 13, 1985):81.

91. John Dempsey. "Odds against foreign fare in U.S." *Variety* 331 (April 27, 1988):123.

92. Roger Watkins. "Mainstream U.S. syndication still a major goal for foreign producers." *Variety* 334 (February 1, 1989):50, 76.

93. "Gershman foresees U.S.-Euro crisis if Yanks reject European shows." *Variety* 334 (February 15, 1989):5.

94. Richard A. Melcher. "How do you say 'Thirtysomething' in Flemish?" *Business Week*, May 8, 1989, pp. 55, 58.

95. Elizabeth Guider. "European TV must gain 'power of size' to match U.S., sez Booz-Allen report." *Variety* 336 (August 30, 1989):79.

96. "Towards freer trade in services: audiovisuals." *OECD Observer*, July, 1986, pp. 23–25.

97. Sig Paul. "Europe opens its pocketbook to U.S. program suppliers." *Television/Radio Age* 36 (October 17, 1988):8.

98. "Grosses, licenses, budget breakdowns." *Variety* 333 (November 9, 1988):32.

99. Tapio Varis. *International Flow of Television Programs*. Paris: UNESCO, 1985, pp. 15–23.

100. Ibid., pp. 13, 25–27.

101. Ibid., pp. 29–33, 44.

102. Ibid., pp. 53–54.

103. Colin Hoskins. "Reasons for the US dominance of the international trade in television programmes." *Media, Culture and Society* 10 (1988):509.

104. Peter Larsen, ed. *Import/Export: International Flow of Television Fiction*. Paris: UNESCO, 1990, pp. 9, 43–44.

Chapter 8

1. Maria C. Wert. "Global television flow to Latin American countries." *Journalism Quarterly* 65 (Spring, 1988):182–185.

2. Livia Antola. "Television flows in Latin America." *Communication Research* 11 (no. 2, April, 1984):184–198.

3. Ibid., pp. 199–201.

4. Noreene Janus. "Transnational advertising: the Latin American case." in George Gerbner, ed. *World Communications: A Handbook.* New York: Longman, 1984, pp. 137–140.

5. Ibid., pp. 141–142.

6. Shirley Christian. "South Americans use U.S. TV programming." *New York Times*, March 27, 1989, p. C15.

7. "Egypt's TV steady client of U.S. fare." *Variety* 307 (May 12, 1982):396; "Arab TV: a pain in arrears." *Variety* 306 (April 21, 1982):147.

8. "'Dallas' bombs on Japan TV despite heavy dose of promos." *Variety* 306 (April 21, 1982):149, 151; "U.S. TV shows flop in Japan." *Variety* 319 (May 29, 1985):108.

9. Blake Murdoch. "U.S. product going soft in Far East and Asia." *Variety* 320 (August 7, 1985):46.

10. "Aussies yawn at U.S. TV series, yet accept 14% price increase." *Variety* 317 (December 19, 1984):41, 66.

11. "Kiwi TV to up pay for U.S. programs." *Variety* 323 (April 30, 1986):125–126; "New Kiwi web to use mostly Yank programs." *Variety* 331 (July 20, 1988):1.

12. "Sky's the limit for U.S. shows on Canada's private TV stations." *Variety* 299 (May 7, 1980):582.

13. Patricia Green. "Canadian TV hearings focus on content—keeping U.S. out." *Variety* 305 (December 16, 1981):38.

14. Patricia Green. "Canada may open the door to American superstations via cable as hedge against DBS." *Variety* 308 (September 15, 1982):60.

15. Sid Adilman. "Crying Yankee TV go home, CBC producers and directors proposed an all–Canadian sked." *Variety* 310 (February 23, 1983):56.

16. Douglas Martin. "Canadian broadcasters win awards but not big audiences." *New York Times*, May 15, 1983, sec. 4, p. 8.

17. "Winners & losers in Canadian TV's kulchur sweepstakes." *Cinema Canada* no. 102 (December 1983):5.

18. Joyce Nelson. "Very distant signals: Canadian content minimalism." *Cinema Canada* no. 117 (April 1985):25.

19. "Cablers asking for increased Yank imports." *Variety* 318 (April 17, 1986): 86.

20. Joyce Nelson. "U.S. TV dumping." *Cinema Canada* no. 132 (July/August, 1986):32.

21. Brian D. Johnson. "TV boils over." *Macleans* 99 (September 22, 1986):38–40.

22. Al Johnson. "Fifty-fifty TV." *Policy Options Politiques* 9, no. 3 (April 1988): 20–21.

23. "Yank showbiz grasp on Canada." *Variety* 333 (November 23, 1988):36.

24. Rick Salutin. "Free trade and television: A cautionary tale." *Thismagazine* 22, no. 3 (June/July 1988):33–37.

25. "'Horrors' of U.S. TV a big draw for Dutch aud." *Variety* 299 (May 14, 1980):1, 134.

26. Willem Hoos. "Dutch bemoan Yank TV glut that'll worsen with new media." *Variety* 307 (June 9, 1982):44.

27. "American programming dominates among Spanish TV foreign fare." *Variety*

326 (April 15, 1987):97, 136; "Turkish TV programmers move away from their reliance on U.S. shows." *Variety* 326 (February 25, 1987):355.

28. "U.S. series are losing German viewers—no cops, less segs." *Variety* 302 (February 11, 1981):79, 82; "German TV cuts will spawn more offshore purchases." *Variety* 307 (July 7, 1982):32; Hazel Guild. "German web favors U.S. prods; in house ventures too expensive." *Variety* 317 (December 5, 1984):70.

29. Jack Kindred. "German private-net television is here to stay, and U.S. programmers love it." *Variety* 334 (April 19, 1989):100.

30. Ted Clark. "Blast film companies, limit TV quota." *Variety* 304 (September 23, 1981):1, 34.

31. Will Tusher. "French television moratorium on imports may have little immediate effect on U.S. fare." *Variety* 304 (September 23, 1981):47.

32. Jack Monet. "French cable limits imports via 30% quota." *Variety* 315 (May 2, 1984):1, 175; Jack Monet. "France to lift imports quotas to help cable." *Variety* 318 (January 30, 1985):51, 68.

33. Richard Bernstein. "Plan for private French TV stirs wide criticism." *New York Times*, August 14, 1985, p. C18.

34. Carlo Sartori. "TV around the world." *World Press Review* 33 (December 1986):27–30.

35. "French net TF-1 eager to buy till its production machine rolls." *Variety* 330 (February 3, 1988):46.

36. Bruce Alderman. "French TF-1 cancels overnight fare; U.S. programs are affected." *Variety* 334 (February 8, 1989):138.

37. Bruce Alderman. "French program quotas spell trouble for U.S. distribs." *Variety* 334 (April 5, 1989):43, 45.

38. Jack Pitman. "Brits up foreign quotas." *Variety* 312 (August 24, 1983):44.

39. Jack Pitman. "British clamor for tight quota on cable fare." *Variety* 312 (August 31, 1983):89, 96; Bert Baker. "U.K. directors, producers lobby against 'No quota' bill for cable." *Variety* 313 (December 21, 1983):44.

40. Bert Baker. "British audiences are watching 30 hours of peaktime U.S. TV." *Variety* 316 (October 17, 1984):92; Richard Collins. "Wall-to-wall 'Dallas'? The U.S.-U.K. trade in television." *Screen* (U.K.) 27, no. 3/4 (1986):69.

41. Elizabeth Guider. "British gov't's white paper set; broadcast deregulations at last." *Variety* 332 (November 9, 1988):32, 48.

42. "Brits now buy foreign shows faster as competition for hot shows grows." *Variety* 334 (April 19, 1989):65.

43. "Majors more wary of selling product to Italian privates." *Variety* 298 (April 16, 1980):105–106.

44. "Italo competish aids MPEA bid to up TV rates." *Variety* 298 (April 16, 1980):105–106.

45. "Vintage U.S. series add depth to REA programming bench." *Variety* 300 (October 8, 1980):75, 92; "U.S. distribs benefit Italo private TV." *Variety* 301 (November 12, 1980):52, 64; Hank Werba. "Italo TV: U.S. prod. export to tube heavy." *Variety* 305 (February 4, 1981):95, 122.

46. "Commercial TV competition with RAI is boosting Yank majors' price for Italo buy." *Variety* 304 (October 14, 1981):271, 298.

47. Hank Werba. "MPEA, RAI reach agreement on new TV & film price scale." *Variety* 307 (July 7, 1982):32; "Backlash to Yank product and pricing boosts Italo prod'n." *Variety* 308 (October 6, 1982):63.

48. Ibid. "Will U.S. product control Italian commercial TV?" *Variety* 310 (April 20, 1983):107, 122, 124.

49. "Program pricing stabilizes in Italy after MPEA pact." *Variety* 314 (April 18, 1984):113, 136; "Italy's foreign program tab put at $150-mil; 80% from U.S." *Variety* 314 (April 18, 1984):115.

50. Hank Werba. "Italo TV ends its Yank program spree." *Variety* 324 (October 15, 1986):125, 146.

51. Hank Werba. "American suppliers are on easy street as Italians scramble to lock product." *Variety* 330 (February 3, 1988):45, 104.

52. Richard Collins. "Wall-to-wall 'Dallas'? The U.S.-U.K. trade in television." *Screen* (U.K.) 27 (no. 3/4, 1986):67.

53. Jack Kindred. "German private-net TV is here to stay, and U.S. programmers love it." *Variety* 334 (April 19, 1989):100.

54. Bruce Alderman. "U.K.'s Maxwell sez quotas due on European TV networks." *Variety* 331 (May 4, 1988):3, 546.

55. Bruce Alderman. "Europe cries whoa!" *Variety* 331 (June 15, 1988):1, 33.

56. Richard Evans. "EEC television moves threaten new channels." *Times* (London), August 23, 1988, p. 1.

57. "Common Market ministers reach compromise on TV quotas, ad breaks." *Variety* 334 (March 15, 1989):7.

58. Bruce Alderman. "France's Lang sez quotas for television not protective, but competitive." *Variety* 335 (May 3, 1989):1–2.

59. Bruce Alderman. "European pic powers pushing to lift TV quotas past 50%." *Variety* 335 (May 31, 1989):58; Bruce Alderman. "Euro Commission is fighting against 'obligatory and enforceable' program quotas." *Variety* 335 (May 31, 1989):58; Fred Hift. "European television quotas: angry Yanks and a community divided." *Variety* 335 (May 24, 1989):1, 4; Lenny Borger. "EC quotas show down in surprise move; deal with Yanks could be reason." *Variety* 335 (June 21, 1989):1, 8.

60. Clyde H. Farnsworth. "U.S. fights Europe TV-show quota." *New York Times*, June 9, 1989, pp. D1–D2.

61. Steven Greenhouse. "The television Europeans love, and love to hate: *New York Times*, August 13, 1989, sec. 4, p. 24.

62. Bruce Alderman. "Valenti, Carla Hills talk Euro quotas with Lang; no breakthrough near." *Variety* 336 (September 13, 1989):5.

63. Bruce Alderman. "E.C. quota vote Oct. 3; Yank fallout minimal." *Variety* 336 (September 27, 1989):4.

64. "E.C. adopts quota directive to take effect in 18 mos." *Variety* 336 (October 4, 1989):1–2.

65. "Aggressive U.S. stance on quotas may have hurt more than helped." *Variety* 336 (October 4, 1989):2.

66. "It's a knockout." *Times* (London), October 4, 1989, p. 19.

67. Steven Greenhouse. "Europe reaches TV compromise." *New York Times*, October 4, 1989, p. D20; "Rationing 'Dallas' in Europe." *New York Times*, October 24, 1989, p. A26.

68. Morrie Gelman. "Warner's Solomon hammers away at Lang over European quotas." *Variety* 337 (October 18, 1989):72; Daniel Pedersen. "A 'grenade' aimed at Hollywood." *Newsweek* 114 (October 16, 1989):58.

69. John Marcom, Jr. "Empty threat?" *Forbes* 144 (November 13, 1989):43.

70. Bruce Alderman. "France's Lang laments his solitary role as hardline advocate of Euro culture." *Variety* 337 (December 6, 1989):130.

Chapter 9

1. "Television." Special survey, *The Economist* 330 (February 12, 1994):T4, T11–T12.
2. Carl Bernstein. "The leisure empire." *Time* 136 (December 24, 1990):56–58.
3. Ithiel de Sola Pool. "Direct broadcast satellites and cultural identity." *Society* 12 (September 1975):55.
4. David Webster. "Direct broadcast satellites: proximity, sovereignty and national identity." *Foreign Affairs* 62 (Summer 1984):1169–1174.
5. Richard Evans. "New satellite channels in danger of purveying American views." *Times* (London), February 2, 1990, p. 3.
6. Steve Clarke. "Sat booms in Britain as pay–TV provider." *Variety* 349 (December 7, 1992):56.
7. Don Groves. "New programmers vie for a piece of the sky." *Variety* 349 (December 7, 1992):55, 60.
8. Richard Bruner. "HBO extends reach." *Advertising Age* 62 (November 25, 1991):28.
9. Don Groves. "Pay TV biz paying off." *Variety* 352 (October 18, 1993):46.
10. Ibid., pp. 46–47.
11. Melinda Wittsock. "North Americans wise up to £10bn potential of U.K. cable." *Times* (London), May 21, 1990, p. 26.
12. Adam Dawtrey. "Cablers test waters in U.K." *Variety* 351 (July 19, 1993): 33–34, 78.
13. John Dempsey. "Cablers eye global pie." *Variety* 353 (December 6, 1993):17, 41.
14. Richard L. Hudson. "Common market." *Wall Street Journal*, March 26, 1993, p. R15.
15. "Economic upswing brightens the market prospect." *Variety* 356 (October 3, 1994):1, M5–M6; Elizabeth Guider. "U.S. merger mania with global impact." *Variety* (October 2, 1995):M4; Adam Dawtrey. "U.S. mergers make Euros rethink links." *Variety* 360 (September 4, 1995):86.
16. John Horn. "Sharing the high cost of making a profit in films." *Vancouver Sun*, April 19, 1996, p. C1.
17. "Yank tubers plotting to step up Euro ties." *Variety* 338 (February 7, 1990): 104, 136; Chris Fuller. "At crossroads, conglom redefines goals, thrust." *Variety* 356 (October 24, 1994):57, 58.
18. Elizabeth Guider. "Execs say: When in Europe, you better watch out." *Variety* 339 (April 18, 1990):S1, S102.
19. Rebecca Lieb. "CNN spreads news in Germany with N-TV." *Variety* 349 (December 21, 1992):31.
20. Mark Robichaux. "Cable-ready." *Wall Street Journal*, March 26, 1993, pp. R14–R15.
21. Elizabeth Jensen. "Networks move to add stakes in foreign TV." *Wall Street Journal*, November 17, 1993, p. B12; Joe Mandese. "NBC peacock wings around globe." *Advertising Age* 64 (October 11, 1993):4.
22. Lynn Elder. "U.S. TV networks expand interests overseas." *Marketing* 28 (November 7, 1994):7.
23. Adam Dawtrey. "U.S. eyes digital toehold." *Variety* (April 29, 1996):35, 41.
24. "Warner Bros. to launch promo campaign to boost shows sagging Euro ratings." *Variety* 338 (February 7, 1990):96.
25. "Yanks starting to export marketing support." *Variety* 344 (October 7, 1991):M4, M88.

26. Faye Brookman. "U.S. gameshows fit foreign slots." *Variety* 339 (April 18, 1990):S8, S98.

27. Adam Dawtrey. "Rivals see red over free TV." *Variety* 346 (February 10, 1992):1, 100.

28. Blake Murdoch. "Oz webs want out of output deals with U.S." *Variety* 349 (January 25, 1992):55–56.

29. Marlene Edmunds. "Belgium needs plenty of product." *Variety* 358 (April 3, 1995):A20; Elizabeth Guider. "TW extends int'l TV arm." *Variety* 360 (October 9, 1995):35–36.

30. Erik Kirschbaum. "Key players pick up the pace in German market." *Variety*, April 15–21, 1996, p. M8.

31. Lorraine Johnson. "Television's future has a foreign accent." *American Demographics* 17 (May 1995):14–16.

32. Randall Rothenberg. "Is Europe a common TV market?" *New York Times*, June 11, 1990, p. D11.

33. Elizabeth Guider. "Yank distribs read signs of growth abroad." *Variety* 346 (February 3, 1992):39, 54.

34. Elizabeth Guider. "U.S. TV exports to rise, study says." *Variety* 342 (February 4, 1991):70.

35. Terry Ilott. "Yanks still fill Europe's bill." *Variety* 349 (December 7, 1992): 1, 90.

36. Peter Besas. "Yanks seek TV El Dorado." *Variety* 350 (March 29, 1993):74, 80.

37. Elizabeth Guider. "U.S. TV distribs explore new outlets, alliances." *Variety* 350 (April 12, 1993):48–49.

38. Marlene Edmunds. "New channels create Dutch product chase." *Variety* 358 (April 3, 1995):A16; Peter Besas. "Forget the rest, Spaniards want those TV rights." *Variety* 342 (February 25, 1991):A26; Peter Besas. "No TV bidding war in Portugal." *Variety* 346 (February 17, 1992):51.

39. Meredith Amdur. "Cable industry wants world on a wire." *Broadcasting & Cable* 124 (January 24, 1994):116.

40. John Marcom, Jr. "Mickey Mouse to the rescue." *Forbes* 146 (November 12, 1990):41.

41. Adam Dawtrey. "Rubles for Rather in TV deal." *Variety* 346 (February 17, 1992):1, 92.

42. J. Max Robins. "West to test Czech web." *Variety* 353 (December 6, 1993): 1, 42.

43. Laurence H. Gross. "German TV's appetite runs to U.S. pics." *Variety* 346 (February 24, 1992):108, 234; "Fewer slots for U.S. pix on Italo television." *Variety* 344 (September 2, 1991):35, 38.

44. Jonathan Karp. "Who needs news?" *Far Eastern Economic Review* 157 (March 24, 1994):58.

45. James McBride. "World games: growing U.S. export market." *Variety* 346 (February 3, 1992):60.

46. David J. Stern. "The whole world wants American sports." *Fortune* 121 (March 26, 1990):128, 132; John Dempsey. "Globetrotting part of NBA game plan." *Variety* 360 (October 9, 1995):35–36.

47. "ESPN: We're happy we were here first." *Variety* 342 (March 25, 1991):62; "Noted." *Wall Street Journal*, October 17, 1995, p. B10.

48. Brian Lowry. "Euro TV buyers looking to turn the tables." *Variety* 355 (June 6, 1994):27.

49. Anne Swardson. "Alliance focuses more attention due south." *Vancouver Sun*, April 26, 1996, p. C8.

50. Adam Dawtrey. "U.S. mergers make Euros rethink links." *Variety* 360 (September 4, 1995):86.

51. Bill Carter. "MTV's international beat brings a sound of dollars." *New York Times*, May 7, 1990, p. D8.

52. "How MTV plays around the world." *New York Times*, July 7, 1991, sec. 2, p. 22.

53. Jeremy Coopman. "MTV has Europe's ear." *Variety* 344 (August 26, 1991):5, 103.

54. "Rock around the world." *Newsweek* 125 (April 24, 1995):65.

55. Mark Landler. "Media." *New York Times*, March 25, 1996, p. D7; "MTV makes global feeds regional." *Variety* 362 (March 25–31, 1996):24.

56. Elizabeth Guider. "CNN packs global wallop." *Variety* 339 (April 18, 1990): 50, 60.

57. Paul Lenti, "Turner takes Latin twist." *Variety* 342 (March 25, 1991):62.

58. "Europe plan by Turner." *Wall Street Journal*, March 9, 1993, p. D18.

59. Adam Dawtrey. "Turner in overdrive for satellite launch." *Variety* 352 (September 20, 1993):23–24.

60. Alexandra Frean. "Cartoons raise few chuckles in Brussels." *Times* (London), September 16, 1993, p. 3.

61. Michael Williams. "French gov't resists Turner's sat invasion." *Variety* 352 (September 20, 1993):24; Michael Williams. "France braces for a new invasion." *Variety* 352 (October 11, 1993):M4.

62. Andy Stern. "Pinheiro still waves flag at Turner charge into Europe." *Variety* 355 (May 2, 1994):44.

63. Meredith Amdur. "The boundless Ted Turner: road to globalization." *Broadcasting & Cable* 124 (April 11, 1994):34–35.

64. Bianca Ford and James Ford. *Television and Sponsorship*. Oxford: Focal, 1993, pp. 94–97.

65. Todd Gitlin. "World leaders: Mickey, et al." *New York Times*, May 3, 1992, pp. B1, B30.

66. Mark Shapiro. "Lust-greed-sex-power. Translatable anywhere." *New York Times*, June 2, 1991, sec. 2, pp. B29, B32.

67. Stephan Buck. "Golden girls, or fool's gold?" *Times* (London), August 28, 1991, p. 27.

68. "Best of a bad job." *Times* (London), August 28, 1991, p. 15.

69. Ken Auletta. "TV's new gold rush." *New Yorker* 69 (December 13, 1993): 82–88.

70. Rich Brown. "NBC cable dons seven-league boots." *Broadcasting & Cable* 124 (October 10, 1994):90.

71. Richard W. Stevenson. "Lights! Camera! Europe!" *New York Times*, February 6, 1994, sec. 3, pp. 6.

72. Jonathan Karp. "Ready for prime time." *Far Eastern Economic Review* 158 (January 26, 1995):56.

73. Lawrie Mifflin. "Can the Flintstones fly in Fiji?" *New York Times*, November 27, 1995, pp. D1, D4.

74. Don Groves. "MPEA prez Karlin slams French, Spanish trade restrictions." *Variety* 339 (June 20, 1990):10.

75. Ibid.; Michael Vatikiotis. "U.S. threat to pull the plug." *Far Eastern Economic Review* 154 (October 24, 1991):64.

76. Elizabeth Guider. "Execs say: When in Europe, you better watch out." *Variety* 339 (April 18, 1990):S76; Elizabeth Guider. "U.S. TV exports to rise, study says." *Variety* 342 (February 4, 1991):70; "$5 bil intl. TV market predicted for 1995." *Variety* 342 (February 8, 1991):43.

77. Elizabeth Guider. "MIP hip to nets' new game." *Variety* 343 (April 22, 1991):1, 75; Hy Hollinger. "Indies offshore television sales booming as theatrical film biz fizzles." *Variety* 333 (December 7, 1988):1, 36.

78. Elizabeth Guider. "U.S. sellers see green as 'A' product pulls top coin." *Variety*, October 2, 1995, p. M3.

79. Don Groves. "Global vidiots' delight." *Variety* 358 (April 15, 1996):1, 43.

80. Elizabeth Guider. "How'd nets $2 bil from o'seas TV." *Variety* 358 (April 15, 1996):45, 52.

Chapter 10

1. Peter Besas. "Satellite shakeup rocks Latin TV biz." *Variety* 342 (March 25, 1991):59, 80; "Sorting out numbers and prices on cable." *Variety* 346 (March 23, 1992):92.

2. Meredith Amdur. "Cable networks head south." *Broadcasting & Cable* 124 (January 24, 1994):118, 120.

3. Andrew Paxman. "Accent on originality means Latin success." *Variety* 358 (April 24, 1995):27, 30; Andrew Paxman. "Investment grade." *Variety* 358 (March 27, 1995):70.

4. Andrew Paxman. "HBO Ole's Pagani pioneers Latin America cable." *Variety* 357 (January 30, 1995):70.

5. Mark Landler. "Murdoch and 3 others set Latin satellite–TV effort." *New York Times*, November 21, 1995, p. D6; Andrew Paxman. "Region does the dishes." *Variety* 362 (March 25–31, 1996):37, 62.

6. Peter Warg. "Oatar bars dishes, mandates state cable." *Variety* 351 (June 21, 1993):39.

7. Gwen Robinson. "Japan cracks sky for Star, Turner." *Variety* 358 (April 24, 1995):20.

8. Mary Lee. "Mega TV deal set to aid Malaysia's English fluency." *Variety*, June 26, 1995, p. 32.

9. Uma da Cunha. "It's the real thing for MTV India." *Variety* 357 (December 12, 1994):51.

10. Jonathan Karp. "Do it our way." *Far Eastern Economic Review* 157 (April 21, 1994):68–70; Fred Hift. "Asian TV survives without U.S. aid." *Variety* 358 (March 6, 1995):62.

11. Larry Leventhal. "U.S. cablers go intl." *Variety* 358 (October 2, 1995):M8, M12.

12. Faith Keenan. "Battle of the titans." *Far Eastern Economic Review*, April 4, 1996, pp. 56–57.

13. Marseli Sumarno. "Indonesia raps foreign TV fare." *Variety* 355 (May 16, 1994):35, 37.

14. Don Groves. "Despite blackout, execs hope to make pay TV pay." *Variety* 359 (June 26, 1995):32.

15. Elizabeth Guider. "Indonesia mines MGM Gold." *Variety* 359 (June 26, 1995):32.

16. Faith Keenan. "Won't you join us?" *Far Eastern Economic Review*, April 4, 1996, p. 57.

17. Jonathan Karp. "Cast of thousands," *Far Eastern Economic Review* 157 (January 27, 1994):46–48, 50.

18. Louis Kraar. "TV is exploding all over Asia." *Fortune* 129 (Jan. 24, 1994): 99–101.

19. Don Groves. "Asian TV sales: still uphill for U.S. firms." *Variety* 354 (February 14, 1994):35, 37.

20. William Cook. "The great Asian TV sweepstakes." *U.S. News & World Report* 116 (March 28, 1994):69, 71.

21. Don Groves. "HBO Asia looks to pact with Col/Tristar and U." *Variety* 356 (September 26, 1994):24.

22. Joseph Man Chan. "National responses and accessibility to Star TV in Asia." *Journal of Communication* 44 (Summer 1994):123, 128.

23. "Aliens invade Asia." *The Economist* 333 (October 8, 1994):33–34.

24. Geraldine Fabrikant. "MTV and PolyGram starting Asian channels." *New York Times*, April 20, 1995, p. D8.

25. Don Groves. "Premier Sports web to launch Jan. 26 Down Under." *Variety* 357 (December 12, 1994):53–54.

26. Tom O'Regan. *Australian Television Culture.* Sydney: Allen & Unwin, 1993, p. 67.

27. Colleen Fuller. "Fade to black: culture under free trade." *Canadian Forum* 70 (August 1991):5–6.

28. Suzan Ayscough. "Class of cultures: Canadians vs. MPAA." *Variety* 344 (August 19, 1991):35, 42.

29. Suzan Ayscough. "Price sends Yank programs across border to Canada." *Variety* 346 (March 23, 1992):53.

30. Diane Brady. "Competing channels." *Macleans* 106 (March 22, 1993): 36–37.

31. Lorne Gunter. "A free market for TV at last." *Alberta Report* 20 (March 22, 1993):20–21.

32. Karen Murray. "Canada to regulate foreign sat shows." *Variety* 351 (June 14, 1993):45, 67; Karen Murray. "Canada, U.S. tussle over DBS." *Variety* 350 (March 15, 1993):51.

33. "U.S. response to recent Canadian trade-related decisions." *U.S. Dept. of State Dispatch* 6 (January 9, 1995):21.

34. Justin Martin. "Truce declared in the Canadian country music war." *Fortune* 132 (August 21, 1995):26.

35. Vic Parsons. "U.S. appeal over film rights seen as attack on Canada's sovereignty." *Vancouver Sun*, February 8, 1996, p. C7.

36. Alex Strachan. "CBC ensures Canadian identity, says Heritage chair." *Vancouver Sun*, January 26, 1996, p. C6.

37. Elizabeth Guider. "Romania's pleas for price break fall largely on deaf ears." *Variety* 339 (May 2, 1990):300, 304.

38. Haluk Sahin. "Global media and cultural identity in Turkey." *Journal of Communication* 43 (Spring 1993):32–37.

39. Michael T. Malloy. "America, go home." *Wall Street Journal*, March 26, 1993, p. R7.

40. Jeremy Coopman. "U.S. may be shut out by new ITV quotas." *Variety* 341 (December 10, 1990):42.

41. Jeremy Coopman. "Status quota on ITV on foreign shows." *Variety* 342 (February 25, 1991):71.

42. "Home is best." *Times* (London), November 1, 1995, p. 23.

43. Paul Harris. "MPAA breaks out GATT-ling guns." *Variety* 349 (November 23, 1992):70.

44. Tom Walker. "Hollywood takes exception to French block on the box." *Times* (London), May 3, 1993, p. 34.

45. Michael Williams. "France adamant on GATT." *Variety* 352 (October 18, 1993):41–42.

46. Michael Williams. "French still gun for GATT exemptions." *Variety* 353 (November 15, 1993):28.

47. Chris Fuller. "Audiovisual gums up GATT talks." *Variety* 353 (December 20, 1993):27–28.

48. Christian Moerk. "Moguls swat GATT-flies." *Variety* 353 (December 20, 1993):1, 62.

49. Don Groves. "Aussies brace for battle with U.S. over TV quotas." *Variety* 353 (December 27, 1993):49.

50. Michael Williams. "GATT spat wake-up on Yank market muscle." *Variety* 353 (December 27, 1993):45.

51. Matthew Fraser. "A question of culture." *Macleans* 106 (December 27, 1993): 50–51.

52. "Valenti stumps against European quotas." *Broadcasting* 119 November 12, 1990):72–73.

53. Jeremy Coopman. "Poor prospects predicted for Yank programs o'seas." *Variety* 342 (April 1, 1991):24.

54. Stuart Miller. "Euro TV boom seems a steady thing." *Variety* 343 (April 15, 1991):M2.

55. Elizabeth Guider. "Tit for tat: U.S. ticked on EC program quotas." *Variety* 343 (May 6, 1991):317, 322.

56. "E.C., French agree on program quotas." *Variety* 344 (August 5, 1991):41.

57. Dennis Wharton. "Valenti rips NAB E.C. quota report." *Variety* 346 (March 16, 1992):32.

58. "Valenti sees 'World War of Trade.'" *Variety* 347 (June 1, 1992):23.

59. Andy Stern. "EC may boost TV quotas." *Variety* 357 (November 21, 1994):33–34.

60. "Frontier vision." *Times* (London), January 11, 1995, p. 19.

61. Andy Stern. "E.U. partners won't back tighter foreign controls." *Variety* 358 (February 20, 1995):173–174; Alan Riding. "New curbs proposed on foreign TV programs in Europe." *New York Times*, March 23, 1995, p. D8.

62. "E.U. votes today on limiting U.S. film imports." *Vancouver Sun*, February 14, 1996, p. C4; "E.U. votes to limit foreign films on TV." *Vancouver Sun*, February 15, 1996, p. C2; Brian Coleman. "E.U. proposes curbs on TV from the U.S." *Wall Street Journal*, February 16, 1996, p. B3A (East ed); Andy Stern. "2 years on, E.U. maintains status quotas." *Variety* 359 (June 17, 1996):30.

63. William Ware. "Effects of U.S. television programs on foreign audiences: a meta-analysis." *Journalism Quarterly* 71 (Winter 1994):955.

64. Herbert I. Schiller. *Culture Inc.* New York: Oxford, 1989, pp. 8, 115, 118.

65. George Gerbner. "International circulation of U.S. theatrical films and television programming." in George Gerbner ed. *World Communication: A Handbook*. New York: Longman, 1984, pp. 154, 161.

66. William Preston Jr. *Hope & Folly: The United States and UNESCO, 1945– 1985.* Minneapolis: University of Minnesota Press, 1989, p. 293.

Bibliography

"ABC Int'l has own 'global meet' and it's truly hardsell." *Variety* 228 (October 31, 1962):29.

"ABC Int'l in $3,600,000 'feed' to foreign affiliates in past year." *Variety* 232 (November 13, 1963):31.

"ABC shows off its overseas TV lineup." *Broadcasting* 63 (November 5, 1962):72–73.

"Acad told foreign producers of TV shows gunning for U.S. market." *Variety* 221 (February 1, 1961):34.

"Ad men's global TV primer." *Variety* 196 (November 24, 1954):25.

Adelson, Merv. "Global markets looming as bigger slice of TV pic." *Variety* 329 (January 20, 1988):186.

Adilman, Sid. "CBC's plan for fewer foreign shows." *Variety* 287 (June 22, 1977): 75, 86.

_____. "Crying Yankee TV go home, CBC producers and directors propose an all–Canadian sked." *Variety* 310 (February 23, 1983):56.

"Adviser to go to Germany." *New York Times*, September 5, 1953, p. 4.

"Africa TV yields to life & death imminent issues." *Variety* 228 (September 5, 1962):23.

"Aggressive U.S. stance on quotas may have hurt more than helped." *Variety* 336 (October 4, 1989):2.

Agnew, Jack. "Israel TV, born of six-day war, careful about its U.S.–U.K. imports." *Variety* 254 (February 26, 1969):57.

Alderman, Bruce. "E.C. quota vote Oct. 3; Yank fallout minimal." *Variety* 336 (September 27, 1989):4.

_____. "Euro Commission is fighting against 'obligatory and enforceable' program quotas." *Variety* 335 (May 31, 1989):58.

_____. "Europe cries whoa!" *Variety* 331 (June 15, 1988):1, 33.

_____. "European pic powers pushing to lift television quotas past 50%." *Variety* 335 (May 31, 1989):58.

_____. "Europe's cross-border program war." *Variety* 330 (February 17, 1988):47, 164.

_____. "France's Lang laments his solitary role as hardline advocate of Euro culture." *Variety* 337 (December 6, 1989):130.

_____. "France's Lang sez quotas for television not protective, but competitive." *Variety* 335 (May 3, 1989):1–2.

_____. "French program quotas spell trouble for U.S. distribs." *Variety* 334 (April 5, 1989):43, 45.

_____. "French TF-1 cancels overnight fare; U.S. programs are affected." *Variety* 334 (February 8, 1989):138.

_____. "Valenti, Carla Hills talk Euro quotas with Lang; no break through near." *Variety* 336 (September 13, 1989):5.

"Aliens invade Asia." *The Economist* 333 (October 8, 1994):33–34.

Allard, T. J. *Straight Up: Private Broadcasting in Canada: 1918–1958.* Ottawa: Canadian Communications Foundation, 1979.

Amdur, Meredith. "The boundless Ted Turner: road to globalization." *Broadcasting & Cable* 124 (April 11, 1994):34–36.

_____. "Cable industry wants world on a wire." *Broadcasting & Cable* 124 (January 24, 1994):114, 116, 118.

_____. "Cable networks head south." *Broadcasting & Cable* 124 (January 24, 1994): 118, 120.

"American programming dominates among Spanish TV foreign fare." *Variety* 326 (April 15, 1987):97, 136.

"American TV abroad." *New York Times*, January 18, 1981, sec. 3, p. 18.

"Americanization of German television." *Variety* 230 (April 10, 1963):44.

Antola, Livia. "Television flows in Latin America." *Communication Research* no. 2: 183–202.

"Arab TV: a pain in arrears." *Variety* 306 (April 21, 1982):147.

"Arg house passes bill imposing local dubbing on foreign telepix." *Variety* 241 (November 24, 1965):35.

"Argentine TV upsurge forcing govt. hand in return to private ownership." *Variety* 213 (December 3, 1958):55.

"As BBC goes (on U.S. buys) so goes European TV webs." *Variety* 231 (August 7, 1963):47.

Auletta, Ken. "TV's new gold rush." *New Yorker* 69 (December 13, 1993):81–88.

"Aussie budget for U.S. telepix runs out as TPA sells four more series." *Variety* 202 (May 23, 1956):57, 60.

"Aussie cabinet nixes plan for govt. pool on TV program buys." *Variety* 273 (January 2, 1974):30.

"Aussie court upholds appeal ending pact on pool buy of U.S. TV product." *Variety* 256 (October 22, 1969):46.

"Aussie election a break for U.S. vidpix producers." *Variety* 213 (December 10, 1958):22.

"Aussie market's vidpix potential even tops Britain." *Variety* 196 (October 20, 1954): 35, 38.

"Aussie official cautions TVers on foreign buys." *Variety* 270 (March 14, 1973):50–51.

"Aussie stations nix Board's bid on o'seas buying." *Variety* 272 (October 24, 1973):46.

"Aussie TV bought 75% of imported shows from America last year." *Variety* 256 (October 15, 1969):47.

"Aussie TV edict: 40% home fare." *Variety* 218 (March 30, 1960):51.

"Aussie TV TEN nixes 'package' deals from U.S." *Variety* 261 (November 25, 1970):34.

"Aussie TV webs put accent on home prod, cut imported shows." *Variety* 282 (May 5, 1976):90.

"Aussie TVers spending more for local prod." *Variety* 295 (June 27, 1979):48.

"Aussie TV's big politico squeeze on U.S. imports." *Variety* 230 (March 13, 1963):44.

"Aussies 'boycotting' U.S. product; possible peace with Nov. Nielsens." *Variety* 243 (August 17, 1966):27, 38.

"Aussies miffed at U.S. brushoff on TV coproduction." *Variety* 223 (August 16, 1961):30.

"Aussies yawn at U.S. television series, yet accept 14% price increase." *Variety* 317 (December 19, 1984):41, 66.

"Australia edicts 50% local TV to break American stranglehold." *Variety* 244 (September 28, 1966):28.

"Australian TV goes to point system meant to hypo native production." *Variety* 271 (July 11, 1973):46.

"Australian TV using fewer U.S. shows." *Variety* 236 (October 28, 1964):30.

"Australia's TV tastes similar to U.S." *Variety* 209 (February 5, 1958):26.

Ayscough, Suzan. "Clash of cultures: Canadian vs. MPAA." *Variety* 344 (August 19, 1991):35, 42.

_____. "Price sends Yank programs across border to Canada." *Variety* 346 (March 23, 1992):53, 66.

"Backlash to Yank product and pricing boosts Italo prod'n." *Variety* 308 (October 6, 1982):63.

Bailey, Andrew. "Sitcoms from Yankeeland are alive and doing well in crossover to U.K." *Variety* 258 (April 8, 1970):75, 100.

Baker, Bert. "British audiences are watching 30 hours of peaktime U.S. TV." *Variety* 316 (October 17, 1984):92.

_____. "U.K. directors, producers lobby against 'no quota' bill for cable." *Variety* 313 (December 21, 1983):44.

"Ban sales pitches at 4-day Oct. meet of Europe–U.S. b'casters." *Variety* 227 (June 27, 1962):35.

"Ban U.S.-fed ads on Can. CATV." *Variety* 263 (July 28, 1971):28.

Baraduc, Philippe. "New direction for television, with quality as common denominator." *Variety* 270 (April 4, 1973):97.

Barnouw, Erik. *Tube of Plenty.* New York: Oxford, 1975.

"BBC and British com'l TV told to stop 'Americanizing' medium." *Variety* 221 (February 22, 1961):43.

"BBC states its case against the acceptance of video commercials." *Variety* 242 (July 13, 1966):33.

"BBC-TV serves notice on distribs: We'll be using fewer U.S. shows." *Variety* 228 (November 21, 1962):22.

Beerman, Frank. "U.S.-based reps assess market for Australian TV product here." *Variety* 288 (September 21, 1977):30.

Bernstein, Carl. "The leisure empire." *Time* 136 (December 24, 1990):56–59.

Bernstein, Jack. "$230,000,000 in o'seas billings for five agencies during '57." *Variety* 210 (March 19, 1958):26.

Bernstein, Richard. "Plan for private French TV stirs wide criticism." *New York Times*, August 14, 1985, p. C18.

Besas, Peter. "Forget the rest, Spaniards want those TV rights." *Variety* 342 (February 25, 1991):A26.

_____. "No TV bidding war in Portugal." *Variety* 346 (February 17, 1992):51.

_____. "Satellite shakeup rocks Latin TV biz." *Variety* 342 (March 25, 1991):59, 80.

_____. "Yanks seek TV El Dorado." *Variety* 350 (March 29, 1993):47, 74, 80.

"Best of a bad job." *Times* (London), August 28, 1991, p. 15.

"Better prices for U.S. programs campaign." *Broadcasting* 64 (March 25, 1963):28.

Bierbaum, Tom. "Yank vidcassette industry weighs impact of European gang of 12." *Variety* 333 (January 11, 1989):91.

"Block-booking evidence heard in distribs trial." *Variety* 218 (March 9, 1960):37, 58.

"Bob Hope envisions global TV networks as aid to understanding." *Variety* 196 (December 1, 1954):2.

"Boom for foreign television." *Broadcasting* 63 (October 15, 1962):75–78.

Borger, Lenny. "E.C. quotas show down in surprise move; deal with Yanks could be reason." *Variety* 335 (June 21, 1989):1, 8.

"Both TV webs in Canada warned by State Secretary to 'shape up.'" *Variety* 246 (February 22, 1967):49.

Boulton, William. "Broad horizon for global CATV; most countries already pay fees." *Variety* 258 (April 8, 1970):54, 96.

Bower, Roger. "Nigeria TV gets H'wood hoopla on official bow." *Variety* 230 (March 13, 1963):44, 52.

Brady, Diane. "Competing channels." *Macleans* 106 (March 22, 1993):36–37.

"Brazil: tough nut to crack." *Variety* 232 (October 16, 1963):26.

"Brazilian telepix restrictions eased." *Variety* 226 (March 7, 1962):38.

"Brazilian TV gets a JWT hotfoot." *Variety* 186 (April 16, 1952):29–30.

"Brazilian TV's slapdown on U.S. product in restrictions on film use." *Variety* 222 (April 26, 1961):185.

"Brit majors paying new top for U.S. series; Batman broke the ice." *Variety* 243 (June 15, 1966):37.

"Brit skirmish on U.S. telepix import." *Variety* 201 (February 8, 1956):31.

"Brit vidpix no threat in U.S.: Dann." *Variety* 250 (April 3, 1968): 42.

"Britain's 14% quota on outside TV product blasted by McCarthy." *Variety* 231 (October 9, 1963):27.

"British TV expresses concern over McCarthy's quota pressures." *Variety* 233 (November 27, 1963):31.

"British TV goes U.S." *U.S. News & World Report* 41 (July 20, 1956):110–111.

"British TV's scramble for top 20 entries invites top prices for U.S. shows." *Variety* 232 (September 25, 1963):29.

"Brits now buy foreign shows faster as competition for hot shows grows." *Variety* 334 (April 19, 1989):65.

Brookman, Faye. "U.S. gameshows fit foreign slots." *Variety* 339 (April 18, 1990):S8, S98.

Brown, Les. "BBC comedy series' odd format rejected by U.S. commercial TV." *New York Times*, March 3, 1977, p. 67.

_____. "Cracking the U.S. TV market." *Variety* 270 (April 4, 1973):66, 78.

_____. "New selling opening in U.S. for selling overseas TV productions." *Variety* 262 (April 14, 1971):40.

_____. "TV webs spurn Bundy's Bird." *Variety* 244 (August 24, 1966):33, 46.

Brown, Rich. "NBC cable dons seven-league boots." *Broadcasting & Cable* 124 (October 10, 1994):90.

Browne, Malcolm W. "Latin nationalists annoyed by Yankees on TV." *New York Times*, March 5, 1971, p. 4.

Bruner, Richard. "HBO extends reach." *Advertising Age* 62 (November 25, 1991):28.

Buck, Stephan. "Golden girls, or fool's gold?" *Times* (London), August 28, 1991, p. 27.

"Building TV chains to span continents." *Printer's Ink* 270 (March 11, 1960):80–81.

Bunce, Richard. *Television in the Corporate Interest.* New York: Praeger, 1976.

"Busy, dizzy o'seas market." *Variety* 228 (September 5, 1962):23.

"A buyer's market; ORTF limits series to 13 episodes; features go for $2–$10,000 for one screening." *Variety* 258 (April 8, 1970):88.

"Cable entering satellite & superstation era." *Variety* 289 (November 16, 1977):58, 72.

"Cablers asking for increased Yank imports." *Variety* 318 (April 17, 1986):86.

"Cagan raps TPEA, sez more stations key to expansion of Latin market." *Variety* 220 (October 5, 1960):26.

"Call to reduce U.S. influence on TV programmes." *Times* (London), March 31, 1961, p. 4.

"Canada may ease microwaving from States via selectivity." *Variety* 257 (January 21, 1970):49.

"Canada may up U.S. content." *Variety* 263 (May 12, 1971):211.

"Canada's April 1 edict: 45 % program content must be home-grown." *Variety* 221 (February 22, 1961):27.

"Canadian cabler, others hit ukase vs. micro from distant U.S. cities." *Variety* 257 (December 17, 1969):38.

"Canadian content rule is now cued to prime time." *Variety* 226 (March 14, 1962):30.

"Canadian satellite bid for TV space slots shot down by FCC." *Vancouver Sun*, October 30, 1996, p. D5.

"Caputo sez Latins 'hostile' toward U.S. telefilm imports." *Variety* 203 (July 4, 1956):34.

Carter, Bill. "MTV's international beat brings a sound of dollars." *New York Times*, May 7, 1990, p. D8.

"CBC, financially healthy, yearns to ditch some U.S. 'escapist' fare." *Variety* 239 (July 14, 1965):31, 34.

"CBC topper wonders about budget in facing sked of fewer U.S. skeins." *Variety* 258 (April 22, 1970):37.

"CBS & Spain TV in telefilm pact." *Variety* 208 (September 18, 1957):23, 38.

"CBS Films' global breakthrough in sale on news-cultural shows." *Variety* 233 (November 27, 1963):31.

"CBS Films won't cutrate programs in tough U.K. market; says Baruch." *Variety* 243 (June 1, 1966):41.

"CBS nixes foreign venture." *Variety* 313 (December 14, 1983):60.

"CBS sends 30 telepics to China; part of unique barter package." *Variety* 321 (December 11, 1985):45, 146.

"CBS signs TV link with China for programs, blurbs, coprods." *Variety* 311 (June 1, 1983):29, 52.

"Central America TV network." *Variety* 217 (December 9, 1959):29.

Chan, Joseph Man. "National responses and accessibility to Star TV in Asia." *Journal of Communication* 44 (Summer 1994):112–131.

Chandler, Bob. "O'seas sales now key factor." *Variety* 200 (September 14, 1955):35, 44.

_____. "Telepix distribs eye o'seas." *Variety* 193 (February 10, 1954):27, 42.

Chester, Giraud. *Television and Radio*. 4th ed. New York: Appleton–Century–Crofts, 1971.

Christian, Shirley. "South Americans use U.S. TV programming." *New York Times*, March 27, 1989, p. C15.

"Claim U.S. 'dumping' of TV films ruining Europe markets for others," *Variety* 227 (June 20, 1962):30.

Clark, Ted. "Blast film companies, limit TV quota." *Variety* 304 (September 23, 1981): 1, 34.

_____. "Creativity crisis in French TV." *Variety* 283 (June 16, 1976):34, 48.

_____. "French TV has a lot of Gaul: Program quotas are imposed." *Variety* 283 (July 28, 1976):39, 48.

_____. "French TV in uptrend for U.S. shows." *Variety* 280 (October 1, 1976):85, 102.

Clarke, Steve. "Sat booms in Britain as pay–TV provider." *Variety* 349 (December 7, 1992):56.

Cohn, Ralph M. "Next step on the global vidpix circuit — the Moon." *Variety* 209 (January 8, 1958):99, 106.

Coleman, Brian. "E.U. proposes curbs on TV from the U.S." *Wall Street Journal*, February 16, 1996, p. B3A.

Collins, Richard. "Wall-to-wall 'Dallas'? The U.S.–U.K. trade in television." *Screen* (U.K.) 27 (no. 3/4, 1986):66–77.

"Color TV issue stirs controversy in Italy; slow progress is seen." *Variety* 243 (July 6, 1966):31.

"Com'l British TV would spark global vidpix market, sez Towers." *Variety* 192 (September 30, 1953):26, 44.

"Com'l Swiss TV still 10 yrs. off." *Variety* 209 (January 8, 1958):104.

"Commercial TV competition with RAI is boosting Yank majors' price for Italo buy." *Variety* 304 (October 14, 1981):271, 298.

"Commercial TV isn't cricket for Britons." *Business Week*, July 7, 1962, p. 38.

"Common Market ministers reach compromise on television quotas, ad breaks." *Variety* 334 (March 15, 1989):7.

"A confrontation with Canada over TV ads." *Business Week*, November 6, 1978, pp. 142, 147.

Cook, William. "The great Asian TV sweepstakes." *U.S. News & World Report* 116 (March 28, 1994):68–69, 71.

Coopman, Jeremy. "MTV has Europe's ear." *Variety* 344 (August 26, 1991):5, 103.

_____. "Poor prospects predicted for Yank programs o'seas." *Variety* 342 (April 1, 1991):24.

_____. "Status quota on ITV on foreign shows." *Variety* 342 (February 25, 1991):71.

_____. "U.S. may be shut out by new ITV quotas." *Variety* 341 (December 10, 1990):42.

"Court kibosh on 4-web consortium in Aussie spurs U.S., U.K. TV thrust." *Variety* 256 (November 5, 1969):42.

"Cox cable gets wired in Denmark." *Variety* 276 (October 2, 1974):46.

Coyle, Donald. "ABC Int'l plays role in Central American culture." *Variety* 217 (February 24, 1960):32.

_____. "TV's global future awaits those who take the opportunity today." *Variety* 245 (January 4, 1967):93.

"Cuba, Mexico into NBC-TV affiliate family via kines." *Variety* 186 (April 23, 1952):21.

"Curb on U.S. TV asked by British stage folk." *New York Times*, March 23, 1954, p. 34.

da Cunha, Uma. "It's the real thing for MTV India." *Variety* 357 (December 12, 1994): 51.

"'Dallas' bombs on Japan TV despite heavy dose of promos." *Variety* 306 (April 21, 1982):149, 151.

Dawtrey, Adam. "Cablers test waters in U.K." *Variety* 351 (July 19, 1993):33–34, 78.

_____. "Rivals see red over free TV." *Variety* 346 (February 10, 1992):1, 100.

_____. "Rubles for Rather in TV deal." *Variety* 346 (February 17, 1992):1, 92.

_____. "U.S. mergers make Euros rethink links." *Variety* 360 (September 4, 1995):86.

Dawtrey, Michael. "Turner in overdrive for satellite launch." *Variety* 352 (September 20, 1993):23–24.

Dempsey, John. "Cablers eye global pie." *Variety* 353 (December 6, 1993):17, 41.

_____. "Globetrotting part of NBA game plan." *Variety* 360 (October 9, 1995):35–36.

_____. "H'wood says go!" *Variety* 331 (June 15, 1988):1, 33.

_____. "Odds against foreign fare in U.S." *Variety* 331 (April 27, 1988):123.

_____. "Overseas coin more essential in greenlighting Yank syndie." *Variety* 332 (October 12, 1988):3, 178.

"Dennis go home!" *Newsweek* 59 (March 19, 1962):82.

de Sola Pool, Ithiel. "Direct broadcast satellites and cultural identity." *Society* 12 (September, 1975):47–56.

"Despite Latino HV's undertow, CBS/Fox will wade in further." *Variety* 330 (March 23, 1988):91.

di Nubila, Domingo. "Argentine TV pampering locals with 80% home-grown product." *Variety* 263 (May 5, 1971):49–50.

_____. "Focus on Time–Life Rio TV stake as Arg. meet eyes foreign influences." *Variety* 247 (June 14, 1967):45.

"Disenchantment with French TV." *Variety* 253 (December 4, 1968):46.

"Distribution rights vital." *Broadcasting* 63 (October 15, 1962):82.

Dizard, Wilson P. *Television: A World View.* Syracuse: Syracuse University Press, 1966.
"Dominance of foreign programs on public TV rapped by CIO-AFL council." *Variety* 270 (March 7, 1973):38, 52.
"Don Coyle: 'Think global.'" *Variety* 237 (December 2, 1964):31.
"Don't be ashamed of o'seas image sez Ralph Baruch." *Variety* 227 (August 22, 1962):26.
Dunham, Franklin. "International television." *School Life* 39 (October, 1956):2.
"Duo's how-to on selling of TV pix o'seas." *Variety* 296 (September 5, 1979):68, 80.
Dupont, Joan. "Life in a country without overnights." *Variety* 294 (March 28, 1979): 51, 76.
"Dutch issue: commercial TV." *Variety* 238 (March 17, 1965):51.
"Easing of Brit. on U.S. TV shows may get State Dept. assist." *Variety* 219 (August 10, 1960):27.
"E.C. adopts quota directive to take effect in 18 mos." *Variety* 336 (October 4, 1989).
"E.C., French agree on program quotas." *Variety* 344 (August 5, 1991):41.
"Economic upswing brightens the market prospect." *Variety* 356 (October 3, 1994):1, M5–M6.
"Economy attitudes vary widely among major U.S. TV suppliers." *Variety* 310 (March 30, 1983):63, 92.
Edmunds, Marlene. "Belgium needs plenty of product." *Variety* 358 (April 3, 1995):A20.
_____. "New channels create Dutch product chase." *Variety* 358 (April 3, 1995):A16.
Eger, John M. "Global television: an executive overview." *Columbia Journal of World Business* 22 (Fall 1987):5–10.
_____. "TV program producers in need of global outlook." *Advertising Age* 56 (September 9, 1985):26.
"Egypt's TV steady client of U.S. fare." *Variety* 307 (May 12, 1982):396.
Ehrmann, Hans. "After 16 years, Chile struggling to get out of the TV basement." *Variety* 290 (March 22, 1978):82.
_____. "Chile trims state TV subsidies." *Variety* 279 (July 9, 1975):47, 59.
"80,000,000 o'seas TV sets." *Variety* 235 (June 17, 1964):31.
Elber, Lynn. "U.S. TV networks expand interests overseas." *Marketing* 28 (November 7, 1994):7.
"ESPN: We're happy we were here first." *Variety* 343 (March 25, 1991):62.
"E.U. votes to limit foreign films on TV." *Vancouver Sun*, February 15, 1996, p. C2.
"E.U. votes today on limiting U.S. film imports." *Vancouver Sun*, February 14, 1996, p. C4.
"Europe plan by Turner." *Wall Street Journal*, March 9, 1993, p. D18.
"European appetite for U.S. programming grows." *Broadcasting* 113 (October 12, 1987): 66, 68.
"European TV in one fell swoop." *Variety* 202 (May 2, 1956):26, 46.
"European TV 'still in infancy.'" *Variety* 198 (March 23, 1955):20, 38.
"Europe's trend to com'l TV." *Variety* 225 (December 27, 1961):23, 32.
Eutis, Philip S. "China gets a 30-second message." *New York Times*, January 12, 1986, sec. 3, p. 11.
Evans, Richard. "EEC television moves threaten new channels." *Times* (London), August 23, 1988, p. 1.
_____. "New satellite channels in danger of purveying American views." *Times* (London), February 2, 1990, p. 3.
Fabrikant, Geraldine. "MTV and PolyGram starting Asian channels." *New York Times*, April 20, 1995, p. D8.
Farnsworth, Clyde H. "U.S. fights Europe TV-show quota." *New York Times*, June 9, 1989, pp. D1–D2.

"FC&B's foreign legion views European TV." *Broadcasting* 70 (June 6, 1966):82–83.
"Fear British telepix quota." *Variety* 197 (March 2, 1955):31, 46.
"Features abroad play minor role." *Variety* 230 (March 13, 1963):33.
"Features invade foreign TV." *Variety* 207 (June 12, 1957):33.
"Fewer slots for U.S. pix on Italo TV." *Variety* 344 (September 2, 1991):35, 38.
"50-country telefilm horizon to open up in '58 sez Fineshriber." *Variety* 209 (January 1, 1958):22, 34.
"$50-mil foreign films in 8 years on German video." *Variety* 262 (April 14, 1971):55, 60.
"50,000,000 TV sets abroad by 1962." *Variety* 213 (December 3, 1958):1.
"50,000,000 TV sets outside U.S." *Variety* 224 (August 30, 1961):26.
"Film violence on television." *Times* (London), March 10, 1958, p. 7.
"First German net lowers the boom on U.S. TV violence." *Variety* 291 (July 26, 1978): 50, 57.
"$5 bil intl. television market predicted for 1995." *Variety* 342 (February 8, 1991):43.
"For a wasteland, U.S. gets big play from TV dignitaries abroad." *Variety* 228 (September 5, 1962):67.
"For U.S. TV, a Commodore Perry?" *Broadcasting* 57 (September 21, 1959):33–34.
Ford, Bianca and James Ford. *Television and Sponsorship*. Oxford: Focal, 1993.
"Foreign control of CATV cut sharply in Canada." *Variety* 252 (October 2, 1968):38.
"Foreign distribs get U.S. advice." *Variety* 326 (January 28, 1987):39.
"The foreign market for TV films." *Broadcasting & Telecasting* 52 (May 6, 1957):27–30.
"Foreign markets fill gaps for U.S. showbiz merchandisers." *Variety* 327 (June 10, 1987):4, 21.
"Foreign syndie biz: 50% mark." *Variety* 228 (November 21, 1962):23, 30.
"Foreign TV quotas remain as is in U.K. as other lands tighten up." *Variety* 270 (April 4, 1973):78.
"Foreign vidpix distribs out of millionairess spectrum." *Variety* 225 (January 31, 1962):31, 45.
"Foreign vidpix gross seen topping $30,000,000 mark in '61." *Variety* 221 (February 1, 1961):34.
Forkan, James. "Selling U.S. news and sports abroad." *Television/Radio Age* 37 (October 30, 1989):38–39.
"43% of stations devote 10–20 hours weekly to feature pix." *Variety* 215 (July 8, 1959):29.
"France's new rules for pix-to-video." *Variety* 292 (October 25, 1978):50.
"France's TV poser." *Variety* 221 (February 22, 1961):43.
Fraser, Matthew. "Question of culture." *Macleans* 106 (December 27, 1993):50–51.
Frean, Alexandra. "Cartoons raise few chuckles in Brussels." *Times* (London), September 16, 1993, p. 3.
"French dig U.S. features, $6,000 per pic average, used 370 in 1970." *Variety* 262 (April 14, 1971):62.
"French net TF-1 eager to buy till its production machine rolls." *Variety* 330 (February 3, 1988):46.
"French TV goal: fewer U.S. pix." *Variety* 236 (September 30, 1964):32, 46.
"French TV longs for U.S. mark; a problem is lingo." *Variety* 266 (April 12, 1972):76.
"French TV rules out com'l setup when 2d channel bows." *Variety* 215 (June 24, 1959):83.
"Fresh grumblings by U.S. majors on 'depressed' prices for pix, programs." *Variety* 270 (April 18, 1973):45, 54.
Friedman, George. "Eye $80-mil offshore gross." *Variety* 249 (January 10, 1968):35.
"Frontier vision." *Times* (London), January 11, 1995, p. 19.

Fuller, Chris. "At crossroads, conglom redefines goals, thrust." *Variety* 356 (October 24, 1994):51, 58.

_____. "Audiovisual gums up GATT talks." *Variety* 353 (December 20, 1993):27–28.

Fuller, Colleen. "Fade to black: culture under free trade." *Canadian Forum* 70 (August, 1991):5–10.

Galbraith, Jane. "Chinese hills will be alive with the first sound of Fox U.S. pics." *Variety* 327 (July 8, 1987):57, 95.

Gardner, Paul. "Boyle-ing point in Canadian television." *Variety* 285 (November 24, 1976):62, 75.

_____. "CATV feeds from U.S. would wreck Canadian b'casting." *Variety* 257 (December 10, 1969):40, 54.

_____. "Hit U.S.'s dominant TV role in Canada." *Variety* 281 (November 26, 1975): 35, 42.

_____. "Issue of Canadian program content gets a going-over in Parliament." *Variety* 257 (January 24, 1970):22.

_____. "Not trying to build 'electronic wall' around Canada, says CRTC's Juneau." *Variety* 259 (June 3, 1970):29, 43.

_____. "Prexy of Canadian b'casters assn. worried about exports from U.S." *Variety* 258 (April 15, 1970):56.

_____. "Rule 'Yankee dollar' out of Canadian air." *Variety* 277 (January 29, 1975):42.

_____. "U.S. police shows a must in Canada." *Variety* 281 (November 19, 1975):39, 50.

Gargan, Edward A. "Donald Duck learns Chinese." *New York Times*, October 24, 1986, pp. D1, D24.

Garner, Fradley. "Scandinavian TV's foreign accent." *Variety* 249 (January 24, 1967):46.

Garrison, Lloyd. "Nigeria doing home-grown television shows." *New York Times*, September 8, 1963, sec. 2, p. 15.

Gelman, Morrie. "Syndies eye o'seas sales boom." *Variety* 326 (February 18, 1987):1, 130.

_____. "TV indies see o'seas sales boom." *Variety* 328 (October 14, 1987):3, 144.

_____. "Warners' Solomon hammers away at Lang over European quotas." *Variety* 337 (October 18, 1989):72.

"Gen Sarnoff warns of danger in future satellite b'cast era." *Variety* 240 (September 22, 1965):30.

"General Sarnoff put 'English' on talk in Australia." *Variety* 249 (January 31, 1967):52.

Gerbner, George, ed. *World Communication: A Handbook.* New York: Longman, 1984.

"German TV cuts will spawn more offshore purchases." *Variety* 307 (July 7, 1982):32.

"German TV networks discover it's hard to sell to U.S. market." *Variety* 318 (February 13, 1985):81.

"Gershman foresees U.S.–Euro crisis if Yanks reject European shows." *Variety* 334 (February 15, 1989):5.

"Get our vidpix and see the world." *Variety* 225 (January 31, 1962):31.

"GI network bans 'Combat': Germans may be watching." *Variety* 255 (August 6, 1969):1, 53.

Giniger, Henry. "J. R. Ewing and Captain Furillo in Paris." *New York Times*, November 21, 1987, p. 27.

Girard, Tom. "CNN set to bow in Japan; Turner is eyeing global setup." *Variety* 314 (March 7, 1984):376, 392.

_____. "Pay-TV rivals turn chummy for U.K. deal." *Variety* 314 (March 21, 1984):116, 123.

Gitlin, Todd. "World leaders: Mickey, et al." *New York Times*, May 3, 1992, pp. B1, B30.

"Global color TV at 100-mil mark." *Variety* 281 (January 7, 1979):104, 109.

"Global count: 70,000,000 TV sets." *Variety* 213 (February 25, 1959):25.

"Global glint in Screen Gems' orbit." *Variety* 223 (August 30, 1961):26.

"The global market: tough nut." *Television Magazine* 23 (August, 1966): 68–70+.

"Global TV network is target of symposium." *Broadcasting* 68 (March 29, 1955):102–103.

"Global TV via satellite just matter of weeks." *Variety* 226 (April 4, 1962):27.

"Global TV: Wave of the future or an industry pipe dream?" *Advertising Age* 55 (December 3, 1984):48–49, 58.

Gorrick, Eric. "Aussie television rounds out 12 years; U.S. shows back in favor." *Variety* 247 (July 26, 1967):58.

_____. "Aussie TV booming, see color in 1970." *Variety* 243 (July 27, 1966):40.

_____. "Australia resists high prices on U.S. product; Brit shows are up." *Variety* 242 (April 20, 1966):39.

_____. "G.M. of Aussie com'l TV body warns control board of risks in quotas." *Variety* 263 (June 2, 1971):38.

_____. "Rap made-in-Australia TV fare as too costly vs. imported 'best.'" *Variety* 218 (April 13, 1960):36, 42.

_____. "Yank TV looks up down under as Aussie buyers comb U.S. for shows." *Variety* 203 (July 11, 1956):25, 39.

Grantham, Bill. "CNN finally leaps Euro TV barrier; signs four deals." *Variety* 323 (April 30, 1986):131.

_____. "The global pillage." *New Statesman & Society* 1 (August 26, 1988):14–15.

_____. "Sky channel's hefty schedule of U.S. programs play better in North than Southern Europe." *Variety* 322 (March 12, 1986):51.

_____. "Turner takes on Europe." *Variety* 320 (September 4, 1985):46, 65.

Greely, Bill. "3-webs' O&O's earn $135,000,000." *Variety* 256 (October 22, 1969):43, 53.

Green, Abel. "Foreign mkt. leveling off?" *Variety* 242 (April 13, 1966):39, 49.

Green, Earl. "Camu quits as CRTC boss; can't cope with flood of U.S. shows into Canada." *Variety* 296 (September 19, 1979):36.

Green, Patricia. "Canada may open the door to American superstations via cable as hedge against DBS." *Variety* 308 (September 15, 1982):60.

_____. "Canadian TV hearings focus on content — keeping U.S. out." *Variety* 305 (December 16, 1981):38.

Greenhouse, Steven. "Europe reaches TV compromise." *New York Times*, October 4, 1989, pp. A1, D20.

_____. "The television Europeans love, and love to hate." *New York Times*, August 13, 1989, sec. 4, p. 24.

Gross, Laurence H. "German TV's appetite runs to U.S. pics." *Variety* 346 (February 24, 1992):108, 234.

"Grosses, licenses, budget breakdowns." *Variety* 333 (November 9, 1988):32.

Groves, Don. "Asian TV sales; still uphill for U.S. firms." *Variety* 354 (February 14, 1994):35, 37.

_____. "Aussies brace for battle with U.S. over TV quotas." *Variety* 353 (December 27, 1993):49.

_____. "Despite blackout, execs hope to make pay TV pay." *Variety* 359 (June 26, 1995):32.

_____. "Global vidiots' delight." *Variety* 358 (April 15, 1996):1, 43.

_____. "HBO Asia looks to part with Col/Tristar and U." *Variety* 356 (September 26, 1994):24.

_____. "MPEA prez Karlin slams French, Spanish trade restrictions." *Variety* 339 (June 20, 1990):10.

_____. "New programmers vie for a piece of the sky." *Variety* 349 (December 7, 1992):55, 60.

_____. "Pay TV biz paying off." *Variety* 352 (October 18, 1993):46–47.

_____. "Premier Sports web to launch Jan. 26 Down Under." *Variety* 357 (December 12, 1995):53–54.

Guider, Elizabeth. "Brit ITV in multimillion-$ deal for 20th Century pic package." *Variety* 335 (May 10, 1989):83.

_____. "British gov't's white paper set; broadcast deregulations at last." *Variety* 332 (November 9, 1988):32, 48.

_____. "CNN packs global wallop." *Variety* 339 (April 18, 1990):50, 60.

_____. "European TV must gain 'power of size' to match U.S., sez Booz–Allen report." *Variety* 336 (August 30, 1989):79.

_____. "Execs say: when in Europe, you better watch out." *Variety* 339 (April 18, 1990):S1, S76, S102.

_____. "Indonesia mines MGM Gold." *Variety*, June 26, 1995, p. 32.

_____. "MIP hip to nets' new game." *Variety* 343 (April 22, 1991):1, 75.

_____. "NBC creates European division for program sales, coprods." *Variety* 335 (May 31, 1989):58.

_____. "Romania's pleas for price break fall largely on deaf ears." *Variety* 339 (May 2, 1990):300, 304.

_____. "Sky has limits, media analysts believe, with dishes selling at 3,000 per week." *Variety* 335 (May 10, 1989):83.

_____. "Tit for tat: U.S. ticked on E.C. program quotas." *Variety* 343 (May 6, 1991): 317, 322.

_____. "TW extends int'l TV arms." *Variety* 360 (October 9, 1995):36–36.

_____. "U.S. merger mania with global impact." *Variety* 360 (October 2, 1995):M4.

_____. "U.S. sellers see green as 'A' product pulls top coin." *Variety* 360 (October 2, 1995):M3–M4.

_____. "U.S. TV distribs explore new outlets, alliances." *Variety* 350 (April 12, 1993): 48–49.

_____. "U.S. TV exports to rise, study says." *Variety* 342 (February 4, 1991):70.

_____. "Yank distribs read signs of growth abroad." *Variety* 346 (February 3, 1992): 39, 54.

Guild, Hazel. "German TV's $5-mil splurge on pix ires freelance craftsmen, cinemas." *Variety* 269 (January 17, 1973):52.

_____. "German web favors U.S. prods; in-house ventures too expensive." *Variety* 317 (December 5, 1984):70.

_____. "Made-in America movies as the best and cheapest bet for German video." *Variety* 258 (April 8, 1970):83.

_____. "Private com'l TV in Germany's Saar up for grabs." *Variety* 251 (July 24, 1968):39.

_____. "Station debts may cue hiked fees for German sets; France ups 'em." *Variety* 244 (September 7, 1966):36.

_____. "W. Germans dote on com'l TV." *Variety* 221 (February 22, 1961):43, 46.

_____. "West German television — one gripe after another." *Variety* 231 (July 31, 1963): 33, 90.

_____. "Yank Army TV so hot in Iceland it's forcing govt. to bow down operation." *Variety* 240 (September 15, 1965):42.

Gunter, Lorne. "A free market for TV at last." *Alberta Report* 20 (March 22, 1993): 20–23.

"½-hour Canadian TV show costs $5,000 in contrast to 35G in U.S." *Variety* 198 (March 30, 1955):35.

Hammond, Margo. "Greek TV is at turning point." *Variety* 296 (October 10, 1979):82.

Hardin, Herschel. *Closed Circuits: The Sellout of Canadian Television.* Vancouver: Douglas & McIntyre, 1985.

Harris, Paul. "MPAA breaks out GATT-ling guns." *Variety* 349 (November 23, 1992):70.

_____. "TV-to-cable via satellite blasted hard by MPAA." *Variety* 288 (August 31, 1977):45.

_____. "U.S.–Canada's heated TV-film flap." *Variety* 284 (August 18, 1976):1, 68.

Hellman, Jack. "L.A.'s features-to-tv stockpile." *Variety* 235 (July 29, 1964):37.

Hepner, Paul. "Sartori's outlook gloomy as U.S. dominates worldwide TV." *Cinema Canada* no. 79 (November, 1981):17.

Hift, Fred. "Asian TV survives without U.S. Aird." *Variety* 358 (March 6, 1995):62.

_____. "European television quotas: angry Yanks and a community divided." *Variety* 335 (May 24, 1989):1, 4.

Hoehn, Hans. "West German TV in major strides." *Variety* 211 (June 5, 1958):46.

Hollinger, Hy. "Indies offshore TV sales booming as theatrical film biz fizzles." *Variety* 333 (December 7, 1988):1, 36.

"Home is best." *Times* (London), November 1, 1995, p. 23.

"Homevid fees in some o'seas areas exceed TV right." *Variety* 304 (October 21, 1981):58, 82.

Hoos, Willem. "Commercial TV in Holland grim prospect as partial study reveals domestic's favored, costs high." *Variety* 329 (October 28, 1987):52.

_____. "Dutch bemoan Yank TV glut that'll worsen with new media." *Variety* 307 (June 9, 1982):44.

Horn, John. "Sharing the high cost of making a profit in films." *Vancouver Sun*, April 19, 1996, p. C1.

Horowitz, Murray. "Aussie mart breaking open." *Variety* 231 (July 10, 1963):35, 48.

_____. "Big 'E' in TV's common market." *Variety* 227 (June 6, 1962):23, 40.

_____. "CBS is less concerned about % in o'seas TV than in U.S. product sale." *Variety* 217 (December 9, 1959):29, 40.

_____. "Foreign sales $43,500,000." *Variety* 225 (November 29, 1961):35.

_____. "Global cinematic TV market." *Variety* 214 (April 15, 1959):113, 128.

_____. "More and more restrictions face U.S. telepix distribs in peddling their programs." *Variety* 220 (September 7, 1960):27, 34.

_____. "NBC–CBS news pubaffairs shows in global TV orbit." *Variety* 224 (October 25, 1961):31, 44.

_____. "Paul Levitan envisions satellite era of instant TV." *Variety* 236 (September 30, 1964):1, 48.

_____. "SG's $8,000,000 o'seas biz." *Variety* 223 (August 9, 1961):23.

_____. "TV shows tarnishing U.S. image abroad?" *Variety* 223 (May 31, 1966):23, 44.

_____. "TV throughout Europe screening U.S. entries for violence." *Variety* 223 (June 14, 1961):25, 42.

_____. "TV's a wide, wide world for U.S. telepix." *Variety* 207 (July 31, 1957):35.

_____. "TV's $52-mil pix insurance." *Variety* 244 (August 31, 1966):1, 62.

_____. "Two faces east and west." *Variety* 230 (May 8, 1963):187, 190

_____. "Two-way TV: U.S. and o'seas." *Variety* 225 (December 6, 1961):1, 42.

_____. "Valenti eager to keep TV healthy as integral part of picture biz." *Variety* 244 (November 9, 1966):1, 66.

_____. "Vidpix export assn.—when?" *Variety* 210 (April 30, 1958):47.

_____. "WB, Col, Metro, 20th in command." *Variety* 222 (April 12, 1961):23, 35.

_____. "Who speaks for America?" *Variety* 233 (November 27, 1963):31, 40.

"'Horrors' of U.S. TV a big draw for Dutch aud." *Variety* 299 (May 14, 1980):1, 134.

Hoskins, Colin. "Reason for the US dominance of the international trade in television programmes." *Media, Culture and Society* 10 (1988):499–515.

Hotchner, A. E. "Global TV is on the way." *Reader's Digest* 66 (May 1955):61–65.

"Hour reruns vs. features." *Variety* 230 (February 27, 1963):24.

"How cable–TV success hinges on satellites." *Business Week*, September 14, 1981, pp. 89–90.

"How MTV plays around the world." *New York Times*, July 7, 1991, sec. 2, p. 22.

Hudson, Richard L. "Common market." *Wall Street Journal*, March 26, 1993, p. R15.

Humbert, Maximo. "ABC-TV has just bought Latin America." *Atlas* 19 (January 1970):37–39.

Hurley, Neil P. "Tele-culture and the third world." *Commonwealth* 88 (April 19, 1968): 131–133.

"H'wood telepix as no. 1 villain." *Variety* 217 (February 3, 1960):1, 52.

"H'wood $200,000,000 TV ride." *Variety* 213 (July 31, 1963):27.

"If not web-sold in U.S. 'dead' for tightened-up Japan." *Variety* 246 (March 22, 1967): 41, 54.

Ilott, Terry. "Yanks still fill Europe's bill." *Variety* 349 (December 7, 1992):1, 90.

"Imported programs limited." *Broadcasting* 57 (November 23, 1959):110.

"International television may foster world peace." *Science News Letter* 62 (September 27, 1952):200.

"Invasion by film." *Time* 69 (May 6, 1957):53–54.

"Irish TV operational pattern eyed by other govt. systems in Europe." *Variety* 226 (March 28, 1962):20, 36.

Isaacs, Jeremy. "This earth this realm this England." *Variety* 281 (January 7, 1976):105, 126.

"ITA may cut time for U.S. TV films." *Broadcasting* 50 (February 20, 1956):104.

"Italian govt. crimps pic imports; RAI-1 taking it on the chin." *Variety* 314 (April 18, 1984):47, 64.

"Italo competish aids MPEA bid to up TV rates." *Variety* 298 (April 16, 1980):105–106.

"Italy's foreign program tab put at $150-mil; 80% from U.S." *Variety* 314 (April 18, 1984):115.

"It's 'U.S. or bust' for Britain's tint productions as nut goes up 20%." *Variety* 242 (April 37, 1966):31.

Jaffe, Alfred J. "CBS worldwide enterprises aiming to supply programming for advertisers around the globe." *Television/Radio Age* 32 (October 15, 1984):54–55+.

Jampel, Dave. "CBS's Kany, in Asia, sees English becoming int'l language via TV." *Variety* 241 (December 15, 1965):52.

_____. "Decline of U.S. vidpix product on Japanese TV." *Variety* 236 (August 26, 1964):26, 40.

_____. "McCarthy deplores failure to get fair price shake in Japan." *Variety* 230 (February 27, 1963):24, 44.

_____. "Silverbach eyes 20th–TV coprod. o'seas; sees changing global mkt." *Variety* 249 (December 27, 1967):28, 31.

"Japan lifts $3,300,000 ceiling on imports of U.S.-made telefilms." *Variety* 230 (April 3, 1963):28.

"Japan provisions governing vidpix get clarification." *Variety* 222 (April 26, 1961):184.

"Japanese market for foreign TVers on upswing as domestic costs soar." *Variety* 242 (February 23, 1966):49.

"Japanese TV cuts back features as oil crisis reduces airtime." *Variety* 277 (February 5, 1975):62.

"Japanese TV now on level with U.S. TV, sez Tokyo's Imamichi." *Variety* 234 (May 20, 1964):26.

"Japan's 100G for 54 Untouchables." *Variety* 223 (June 7, 1961):35.

Jensen, Elizabeth. "Networks move to add stakes in foreign TV." *Wall Street Journal,* November 17, 1993, p. B12.

Johnson, Al. "Fifty-fifty TV." *Policy Options Politiques* 9 no. 3 (April 1988):18–22.

Johnson, Brian D. "TV boils over." *Macleans* 99 (September 22, 1986):38–40.

Johnson, Lorraine. "Television's future has a foreign accent." *American Demographics* 17 (May 1995):14–16.

Jones, Earl. "Coming: global growth in television advertising." *Broadcasting* 113 (October 12, 1987):28.

Karp, Jonathan. "Cast of thousands." *Far Eastern Economic Review* 157 (January 27, 1994):46–48, 50.

_____. "Do it our way." *Far Eastern Economic Review* 157 (April 21, 1994):68–70.

_____. "Ready for prime time." *Far Eastern Economic Review* 158 (January 26, 1995):56.

_____. "Who needs news?" *Far Eastern Economic Review* 157 (March 24, 1994):58.

Katz, Norman. "Those foreign pastures grow greener & greener." *Variety* 215 (July 8, 1959):38.

Kaufman, Dave. "Adams: don't get too over-zealous on foreign sales." *Variety* 230 (March 13, 1963):33, 50.

_____. "CPT execs see world peak for U.S. TV & theatre pix." *Variety* 284 (October 20, 1976):171, 178.

_____. "How goes U.S. TV o'seas?" *Variety* 280 (August 13, 1975):34.

_____. "H'wood majors (35 hours) vs. 'minors' (8)." *Variety* 262 (March 31, 1971):38.

_____. "New SAG pact gives actors % of o'seas take." *Variety* 235 (July 15, 1964):26, 34.

_____. "Syndies garner global gold." *Variety* 246 (April 12, 1967):39, 47.

_____. "U.S. declines in Latino TV markets; Mexican-made soapers cleaning up." *Variety* 268 (August 16, 1972):36, 44.

_____. "U.S. world vidpix mkt. down." *Variety* 266 (March 15, 1972):37, 54.

Keenan, Faith. "Battle of the titans." *Far Eastern Economic Review,* April 4, 1996, pp. 56–57.

_____. "Won't you join us." *Far Eastern Economic Review,* April 4, 1996, p. 57.

Kindred, Jack. "As Germans scrap for TV fare, they find films in short supply." *Variety* 328 (October 14, 1987):49, 136.

_____. "German private-net TV is here to stay, and U.S. programmers love it." *Variety* 334 (April 19, 1989):100.

Kipps, Charles. "In flat fee markets, b'casters lean to old world pitch; barter." *Variety* 324 (October 15, 1986):47, 100.

Kirschbaum, Erik. "Key players pick up the pace in German market." *Variety* 358 (April 15, 1996):M8.

"Kiwi TV to up pay for U.S. programs." *Variety* 323 (April 30, 1986):125–126.

Klass, Philip J. "U.S. reviews satellite telecast policy." *Aviation Week & Space Technology* 108 (January 23, 1978):66–67.

Knight, Bob. "Scorecard on U.S. TV imports: it helps if show's in English." *Variety* 270 (April 4, 1973):66.

Knoll, Steve. "Int'l homevid builds." *Variety* 304 (October 7, 1981):167, 186.

Kocian, Billy. "German TV in deep financial trouble." *Variety* 280 (August 20, 1975):45, 55.

Koh, Edgar. "TV in a developing nation: Singapore's U.K.–U.S. yen." *Variety* 279 (July 9, 1975):58.

"Kojak: the all–American image?" *Senior Scholastic* 110 (September 8, 1977):14–15, 24.

Kraar, Louis. "TV is exploding all over Asia." *Fortune* 129 (January 24, 1994):98–101.

Kroeger, Albert R. "International television." *Television Magazine* 20 (July 1963): 43–49+.

Landler, Mark. "Media." *New York Times*, March 25, 1966, p. D7.

_____. "Murdoch and 3 others set Latin satellite–TV effort." *New York Times*, November 21, 1995, p. D6.

Lapid, Joseph. "Israel's TV pact — winnowing out plus those winning ways of CBS." *Variety* 244 (September 21, 1966):44.

_____. "TV no. 1 in Israeli show biz after only 18 months." *Variety* 258 (January 7, 1970):74.

Larsen, Peter, ed. *Import/Export: International Flow of Television Fiction*. Paris: UNESCO, 1990.

"Latin American stake." *Variety* 225 (December 20, 1961):23, 36.

"Latin America's big $$ potential for U.S. telefilms cited by Manson." *Variety* 206 (May 1, 1957):28, 50.

Lazarus, Charles. "Can. TV hot seat cools off." *Variety* 242 (March 30, 1966):45, 64.

_____. "Canada tightens TV vs. U.S." *Variety* 258 (February 18, 1970):37, 56.

_____. "U.S. TV heft squeezes CBC." *Variety* 238 (March 31, 1965):39, 46.

Lee, Ira. "Brazil govt. mulls going 70% native." *Variety* 287 (June 1, 1977):43.

_____. "Brazil's Globo TV cuts back on imports to meet govt. quotas." *Variety* 288 (August 10, 1977):42, 50.

Lee, Mary. "Mega TV deal set to aid Malaysia's English fluency." *Variety* 359 (June 26, 1995):32.

Lenti, Paul. "Turner takes Latin twist." *Variety* 342 (March 25, 1991):62.

Leventhal, Larry. "U.S. cablers go intl." *Variety* 360 (October 2, 1995):M8, M12.

Lieb, Rebecca. "CNN spreads news in Germany with N-TV." *Variety* 349 (December 21, 1992):31.

"Life without tyranny of ratings common in television — outside U.S." *Variety* 258 (April 8, 1970):76.

"Limit U.S. channels for Canada cablers." *Variety* 291 (August 2, 1978):45.

"Limitation on free market for U.S. TV show o'seas assailed." *Variety* 233 (February 12, 1964):42.

Lindal, Sigurd. "Wasteland in Iceland." *Atlas* 11 (April 1966):241–242.

Lippman, John. "Murdoch: pay-movie channel's profitability answered mid-'89." *Variety* 332 (November 9, 1988):48.

_____. "Italian web buys 'NBC Nightly News'; first complete sale." *Variety* 333 (November 2, 1988):52, 68.

Litman, Barry R. "The economies of the television market for theatrical movies." *Journal of Communication* 29 (no. 4 Autumn 1979):20–33.

Loftus, Jack. "CBS eyes global networks stance." *Variety* 309 (November 24, 1982):1, 99.

_____. "Minis lure MIP to U.S." *Variety* 314 (April 18, 1984):47, 187.

_____. "U.S. distributors bit MIP's cable apple." *Variety* 315 (May 2, 1984):129, 149.

_____. "Viacom a partner in Japan cable." *Variety* 312 (August 17, 1983):52, 67.

_____. "Yanks are coming, TV drums drumming." *Variety* 322 (February 5, 1986):49, 114.

"London jammed with Yank reps pitching product." *Variety* 233 (January 22, 1964):42.

Long, Tania. "Homemade TV pushed." *New York Times*, December 27, 1959, sec. 2, p. 13.

Lowry, Brian. "Euro TV buyers looking to turn the tables." *Variety* 355 (June 6, 1994):27.

Maidenberg, H. J. "Peruvians decree state control for all TV and radio stations." *New York Times*, November 11, 1971, p. 11.

"Majors more wary of selling product to Italian privates." *Variety* 298 (April 16, 1980):105–106.

Malko, George. "Australian TV: the wasteland down under." *Saturday Review* 45 (August 11, 1962):42–43.

Malloy, Michael T. "America, go home." *Wall Street Journal*, March 26, 1993, p. R7.

Manchester, Harland. "Here comes worldwide television!" *Reader's Digest* 81 (July, 1962):77–80.

Mandese, Joe. "NBC peacock wings around globe." *Advertising Age* 64 (October 11, 1993):4.

Marcom, John Jr. "Empty threat?" *Forbes* 144 (November 13, 1989):43.

_____. "Le defi Disney." *Forbes* 143 (February 20, 1989):39–40.

_____. "Mickey Mouse to the rescue." *Forbes* 146 (November 12, 1990):41–42.

Markey, Sanford. "Korean television relies on its U.S. telefilms." *Variety* 239 (June 2, 1965):39, 49.

_____. "Taiwan TV, on 27 months, now into profit era." *Variety* 237 (January 13, 1965):43, 56.

_____. "Thai TV: weapon for West vs. Communism." *Variety* 231 (July 21, 1963):32.

_____. "TV comes to Vietnam: GIs' sets bought in PX worth 5 times more in Saigon." *Variety* 242 (March 16, 1966):32, 44.

Martin, Douglas. "Canadian broadcasters win awards but not big audiences." *New York Times*, May 15, 1983, sec. 4, p. 8.

Martin, Justin. "Truce declared in the Canadian country music war." *Fortune* 132 (August 21, 1995):26.

"MCA rep sour on Japanese market." *Variety* 210 (April 30, 1958):26.

"MCA-TV finds Europe situation not what it's cracked up to be." *Variety* 233 (February 19, 1964):31, 46.

McBride, James. "World games: growing U.S. export market." *Variety* 346 (February 3, 1992):60.

"McCarthy charges D.C. attacks on U.S. TV damaging 'image' abroad." *Variety* 229 (February 6, 1963):34, 48.

"McCarthy heads TPEA as MPAA inks Fineshriber." *Variety* 218 (May 11, 1960):23.

"McCarthy in beef to British over protective quota stance on telepix." *Variety* 225 (November 29, 1961):35.

"McCarthy's aim: a free world open market in program field." *Variety* 228 (November 7, 1962):24.

"McCarthy's Latino tour." *Variety* 223 (June 14, 1961):36.

Melanson, James. "U.S. majors new ready to face Latin America." *Variety* 316 (October 3, 1984):1, 101.

Melcher, Richard A. "How do you say 'Thirtysomething' in Flemish?" *Business Week*, May 8, 1989, pp. 55, 58.

"Merle Jones bullish on Japan TV potential on vidpix import." *Variety* 221 (November 30, 1960):26, 49.

"Mestre's Latino dubbing & distrib." *Variety* 198 (July 20, 1955):29.

"Mex union asks ban on TV shows dubbed elsewhere." *Variety* 220 (November 23, 1960):26.

"Mex's snowballing campaign to curb invasion of U.S. telepix." *Variety* 217 (February 10, 1960):30, 50.

"MGM-TV's Spires is dubious about bonanza potential of int'l market." *Variety* 227 (July 4, 1962):68.

Michie, Larry. "Ameribird may soar in 1973." *Variety* 267 (June 21, 1972):31, 50.
_____. "British brigade aims for sales." *Variety* 290 (March 1, 1978):113, 118.
_____. "International TV's 1-way traffic." *Variety* 274 (April 17, 1974):1, 86.
_____. "Movie prices on TV go up the tube." *Variety* 287 (July 20, 1977):1, 102.
_____. "Shut out of U.S. pay–TV, Hollywood takes Europe for piece of the action." *Variety* 317 (January 9, 1985):77.
Michie, Laurence. "Europe is Klondike for TV gold rush." *Variety* 329 (January 20, 1988):175, 191.
"Middle East yens U.S. TV product but blocked currency major snag." *Variety* 225 (February 14, 1962):27, 38.
Mifflin, Lawrie. "Can the Flintstones fly in Fiji?" *New York Times*, November 27, 1995, pp. D1, D4.
Miller, Stuart. "Euro TV boom seems a steady thing." *Variety* 343 (April 15, 1991):M2.
"Minow sparks echo in Mexico; stations warned." *Variety* 223 (June 14, 1961):29, 36.
"Mixed view on American TV in France." *Variety* 266 (April 12, 1972):80.
Moerk, Christian. "Moguls swat GATT-flies." *Variety* 353 (December 20, 1993):1, 62.
Monet, Jack. "France to lift import quotas to help cable." *Variety* 318 (January 30, 1985):51, 68.
_____. "French cable limits imports via 30% quota." *Variety* 315 (May 2, 1984):1, 175.
Morris, Peter. "Electronic free trade." *Cinema Canada* no. 136 (December 1986):6–10.
Moskowitz, Gene. "France eyeing 1960 for bigtime emergence of TV." *Variety* 209 (January 8, 1958):104, 106.
_____. "Profile of Finnish TV." *Variety* 259 (July 8, 1970):49.
"MTV Europe now up and running." *Variety* 328 (August 5, 1987):2, 84.
"MTV makes global feeds regional." *Variety* 362 (March 25–31, 1996):24.
Mulligan, Brian. "Fred Friendly's warning in Britain." *Variety* 248 (October 25, 1967): 24, 40.
_____. "U.K.–U.S. romance." *Variety* 253 (January 8, 1969):87.
Murdoch, Blake. "Oz webs want out of output deals with U.S." *Variety* 349 (January 25, 1993):55–56.
_____. "U.S. product going soft in Far East and Asia." *Variety* 320 (August 7, 1985):46.
Murray, Karen. "Canada to regulate foreign sat shows." *Variety* 351 (June 14, 1993): 45, 67.
_____. "Canada, U.S. tussle over DBS." *Variety* 350 (March 15, 1993):51.
"Murrow's TV image torch." *Variety* 226 (April 4, 1962):27, 52.
Myers, Harold. "British TV floodgate open." *Variety* 236 (October 7, 1964):29.
_____. "Europe 'examining' cable television." *Variety* 266 (March 15, 1972):39, 52.
_____. "U.S. movies, but not series, are big on Japanese TV." *Variety* 294 (April 18, 1979):109.
_____. "U.S. TV influence irks Brit." *Variety* 211 (July 30, 1958):27, 98.
"NBC Int'l cuffos pubaffairs o'seas to TV novitiates." *Variety* 227 (July 4, 1962):69.
"NBC Int'l officially hands over Nigerian TV service after 5 years." *Variety* 246 (April 19, 1967):77, 85.
"NBCI filling up o'seas stocking." *Variety* 265 (December 15, 1971):40.
"NBC's formula for TV program exchange with foreign countries." *Variety* 210 (March 26, 1958):35.
"NBC's 'have money, will help' in bid for stake in Mex TV." *Variety* 223 (May 31, 1961):1.
"NBC's Stern talks co-production with Japan, vidpix payment rules." *Variety* 213 (February 18, 1959):21, 36.
"NBC's Wales, Cuba, Spain, Jamaica aspirations in global video setup." *Variety* 204 (October 3, 1956):1, 78.

"NBC-TV resolves residual fee on foreign repeats." *Variety* 212 (October 8, 1958):23, 38.

Nelson, Joyce. "One way street." *Cinema Canada* no. 54 (April 1979):10–16.

_____. "U.S. TV dumping." *Cinema Canada* no. 132 (July/August 1986):32.

_____. "Very distant signals: Canadian content minimalism." *Cinema Canada* no. 117 (April 1985):25.

"New Japan ceiling no cause for glee say U.S. vidpixers." *Variety* 218 (May 11, 1960): 22, 38.

"New Kiwi web to use mostly Yank programs." *Variety* 331 (July 20, 1988):1.

"New race for space." *Forbes* 118 (September 1, 1976):28, 31.

"New $6,000,000 TV relay system gives Canada more Yank shows." *Variety* 190 (May 20, 1953):31.

"Nicaragua gov't takes over stations." *Variety* 297 (November 28, 1979):38, 54.

Nicolaidi, Mike. "New Zealand's 2-channel setup under fire." *Variety* 296 (October 3, 1979):57, 61.

"Nigeria urges better U.S. films." *Broadcasting* 61 (August 14, 1961):83.

"North American investors revive cable biz." *Variety* 338 (January 24, 1990):95, 108.

"Not-so-innocents abroad: U.S. webs in Italy." *Variety* 314 (April 18, 1984):113, 136.

"Noted." *Wall Street Journal*, October 17, 1995, p. B10.

"N.Y.-to-London TV traffic." *Variety* 200 (September 14, 1955):47.

O'Connor, John J. "Will they buy it in Brazil?" *New York Times*, March 12, 1972, sec. 2, p. 17.

"100 U.S. TV shows circle globe." *Variety* 213 (November 26, 1958):29.

"One spot commercial may someday cover the globe." *Broadcasting* 71 (December 19, 1966):23.

"Ontario govt. panel hits American television, pix violence." *Variety* 287 (June 22, 1977):75, 86.

O'Regan, Tom. *Australian Television Culture.* Sydney: Allen & Unwin, 1993.

"O'seas dilemma on pre–'48s." *Variety* 227 (July 11, 1962):43.

"O'seas marts shun U.S. pix." *Variety* 235 (June 24, 1964):29.

"O'seas: old series never die." *Variety* 242 (May 11, 1966):39.

"O'seas pix-to-TV expansion." *Variety* 230 (February 27, 1963):25, 40.

"O'seas TV set count: 38,600,000." *Variety* 221 (November 30, 1960):46.

"Overseas market: $73,500,00." *Variety* 237 (February 3, 1965):35.

"Overseas program sales hit $52 million." *Broadcasting* 63 (October 15, 1962):78–82.

"Overseas visitors 'oversee' U.S. television." *Sponsor* 18 (December 7, 1964):40–41.

"Paisano Hopalong." *Newsweek* 41 (March 30, 1953):66–67.

"Par, MCA license 100 drama hours to China TV web." *Variety* 326 (February 11, 1987):54, 68.

Parsons, Vic. "U.S. appeal over film rights seen as attack on Canada's sovereignty." *Vancouver Sun*, February 8, 1996, p. C6.

Paul, Sig. "Europe opens its pocketbook to U.S. program suppliers." *Television/Radio Age* 36 (October 17, 1988):8.

_____. "It's a knockout." *Times* (London), October 4, 1989, p. 19.

Paxman, Andrew. "Accent on originality means Latin success." *Variety* 357 (January 30, 1995):42–43.

_____. "HBO Olé's Pagani pioneers Latin America cable." *Variety* 357 (January 30, 1995):42–43.

_____. "Investment grade." *Variety* 358 (March 27, 1995):70.

_____. "Region does the dishes." *Variety* 362 (March 25–31, 1996):37, 62.

Pedersen, Daniel. "A 'grenade' aimed at Hollywood." *Newsweek* 114 (October 16, 1989):58.

"Perils of the quota." *Variety* 225 (December 6, 1961):33.

"Pic prices round TV globe." *Variety* 242 (February 23, 1966):39, 46.

"Pilkington report under attack for skirting issue on foreign imports." *Variety* 227 (July 25, 1962):53.

Pitman, Jack. "Brit ITV cuts foreign quota to 12%." *Variety* 289 (November 16, 1977):59, 68.

_____. "British clamor for tight quota on cable fare." *Variety* 312 (August 31, 1983): 89, 96.

_____. "British com'l TV making time." *Variety* 265 (January 26, 1972):1, 62.

_____. "Brits up foreign quotas." *Variety* 312 (August 24, 1983):44.

_____. "Canada's new quotas, U.S. cutback in primetime brighten Brit o'seas sell." *Variety* 259 (July 29, 1970):35.

_____. "Deadbeat Nigeria worries syndicators." *Variety* 295 (July 18, 1979):31, 36.

_____. "U.K.'s second thoughts on o'seas quota." *Variety* 291 (July 12, 1978):43.

_____. "Update on TV movies in Europe." *Variety* 269 (February 7, 1973):60.

_____. "U.S. series licensing for Britain rising to average 10G an hour." *Variety* 282 (April 21, 1976):39, 66.

_____. "U.S. sports girdling globe." *Variety* 248 (October 11, 1967):69, 88.

_____. "U.S. TV series fail to make dent on Brit viewers." *Variety* 262 (January 13, 1971):41, 54.

"The plot to 'overthrow' Latin America." *Variety* 213 (December 10, 1958):22.

"Poland TV's heavy U.S. accent." *Variety* 225 (February 21, 1962):23, 40.

"Possibilities of transoceanic TV to be explored by 9-man group." *Variety* 195 (July 28, 1954):1, 119.

"Potential of foreign revenue spurs distribs to 'global look' operations." *Variety* 196 (December 1, 1954):48.

Preston, William Jr. *Hope & Folly: The United States and UNESCO, 1945–1985.* Minneapolis: University of Minnesota Press, 1989.

"Prez of Canada's indie TV web warns of big loss via curb on U.S. shows." *Variety* 258 (April 22, 1970):37.

"Prime time in Peking." *New Yorker* 61 (April 1, 1985):30–31.

"Private TV burgeoning in Italy but still unsteady." *Variety* 286 (April 20, 1977):48.

"Private TV-radio in Italy." *Variety* 291 (April 25, 1978):142.

"Program costs per Bob Howard." *Variety* 287 (May 18, 1977):1.

"Program pricing stabilizes in Italy after MPERA pact." *Variety* 314 (April 18, 1984): 113, 136.

"Program suppliers face snares in cabled Holland." *Variety* 320 (October 2, 1985):114.

"Programmers down under get ground under from two sides." *Variety* 254 (March 26, 1969):62.

"Publishers now dominate Italian comm'l television." *Variety* 298 (April 16, 1980): 96, 106.

"Ralph Baruch on TV image abroad." *Variety* 226 (April 18, 1962):26.

Rasky, Harry. "Canada's most successful export: TV talent." *Saturday Night* 74 (June 6, 1959):14–15.

"Rationing 'Dallas' in Europe." *New York Times*, October 24, 1989, p. A26.

Read, William H. "Multinational media." *Foreign Policy* no. 18 (Spring 1975):155–167.

"Residual talent fees don't apply to overseas' sales." *Broadcasting* 63 (October 15, 1962):80.

Riddell, Elizabeth. "Aussie TV imports put at 18% of U.S. foreign TV sales." *Variety* 288 (September 21, 1977):30, 58.

Riding, Alan. "New curbs proposed on foreign TV programs in Europe." *New York Times*, March 23, 1995, p. D8.

"Rise in Aussie-made content figured to add $1-mil to TV stations' nut." *Variety* 261 (December 9, 1970):41, 44.

Robichaux, Mark. "Cable-ready." *Wall Street Journal*, March 26, 1993, pp. R14–R15.

Robins, J. Max. "West to test Czech web." *Variety* 353 (December 6, 1993):1, 42.

Robinson, Gwen. "Japan cracks sky for Star, Turner." *Variety*, April 24, 1995, 20.

"Robt. Sarnoff bullish on Europe TV prospects." *Variety* 207 (July 10, 1957):29, 104.

"Rock around the world." *Newsweek* 125 (April 24, 1995):65.

Rosen, George. "Buy Minow & save the world." *Variety* 222 (May 17, 1961):23, 56.

_____. "Japanese TV: the Ginza beat." *Variety* 220 (October 19, 1960):21, 40.

Rosenfield, James H. "The age of abundance for television worldwide." *Vita Speeches of the Day* 52 (January 15, 1986):210–213.

Rosenthal, Edmond M. "U.S. television news deals now proliferating around the world." *Television/Radio Age* 34 (April 13, 1987):35–37, 67.

Rothenberg, Randall. "Is Europe a common TV market?" *New York Times*, June 11, 1990, p. D11.

"Russo–U.S. exchange — zero." *Variety* 215 (August 19, 1959):27, 42.

Sahin, Haluk. "Global media and cultural identity in Turkey." *Journal of Communication* 43 (Spring 1993):31–41.

Salutin, Rick. "Free trade and television: a cautionary tale." *ThisMagazine* 22, no. 3 (June/July, 1988):33–37.

Sartori, Carlo. "TV around the world." *World Press Review* 33 (December 1986):27–30.

"Satellites, homevideo hovering over Scandinavia; commercials, pay–TV seen viable solutions." *Variety* 308 (October 13, 1982):143, 146.

"Scandinavia co-buys Jerry Lewis." *Variety* 254 (April 23, 1969):56.

Schapiro, Mark. "Lust-greed-sex-power. Translatable anywhere." *New York Times*, June 2, 1991, sec. 2, pp. B29, B32.

Schiller, Herbert I. *Culture, Inc.* New York: Oxford, 1989.

_____. "The U.S. hard sell." *The Nation* 203 (December 5, 1966):609–612.

Schoenfeld, Herm. "Don Coyle envisions int'l as giant ad medium." *Variety* 224 (September 13, 1961):35, 50.

"Scrapping of 'outer quota' by Brit's indie TV authority a blow to U.S." *Variety* 267 (July 26, 1972):42.

"Screen Gems' Canadian caper to plug 'good neighbor star flights' 4 ways." *Variety* 247 (May 24, 1967):39.

"Screen Gems Latin American push." *Variety* 206 (April 3, 1957):34.

"Screen Gems mulls TV production in Japan." *Variety* 224 (October 25, 1961):30.

"Screen Gems' producing TV series down under for Australian mkt." *Variety* 263 (June 9, 1971):30.

"Screen Gems' $3,000,000 foreign billings: exposure in 21 countries." *Variety* 205 (February 20, 1957):29.

"See Aussie Labor Party asking curb on TV dollars for imports." *Variety* 244 (September 21, 1966):51.

"See Aussie TV critical unless imports curbed." *Variety* 283 (June 16, 1976):35, 50.

"See $74,500,000 offshore mkt. for all U.S. video fare." *Variety* 242 (February 23, 1966):46.

"Seoul goes ga-ga over teevee." *Variety* 203 (June 20, 1956):21, 28.

"SG's Bruns mulls potentials of Japanese shows for world market." *Variety* 230 (March 20, 1963):35, 58.

"SG's $9,000,000 vidpix budget." *Variety* 196 (November 17, 1954):49, 52.

Silverman, Michael. "Negative reaction from U.S. distribs to Europe decision." *Variety* 319 (July 17, 1985):43.

Silverman, Syd. "Entertainment in the satellite era." *Variety* 312 (October 26, 1983): 13, 99.

"Sir Robert Fraser holds no truck with film quotas for British TV." *Variety* 220 (November 23, 1960):26, 47.

"Sky's the limit for U.S. shows on Canada's private TV stations." *Variety* 299 (May 7, 1980):582.

Smith, Hedrick. "Soviet asks U.N. to bar intrusion by satellite TV." *New York Times*, August 11, 1972, pp. 1, 4.

"Snail's pace for U.S. features on o'seas channels." *Variety* 218 (July 6, 1960):31.

Soloyanis, Connie. "Prep for TV bow in Saudi Arabia." *Variety* 237 (January 6, 1965): 87, 112.

"Sorting out numbers and prices on cable." *Variety* 346 (March 23, 1992):92.

"Spain flashes its checkbook, but majors not ready to deal." *Variety* 304 (October 21, 1981):58, 82.

Stanley, Raymond. "Aussie air control board issues annual TV report; U.S. buys up." *Variety* 284 (October 20, 1976):170, 180.

_____. "Aussie TV imports status quo at 73% from U.S., 24% from Brit." *Variety* 276 (October 16, 1974):56.

_____. "Aussie's stead U.S.–U.K. buys." *Variety* 280 (October 29, 1975):52.

Stern, Andy. "E.C. may boost TV quotas." *Variety* 357 (November 21, 1994):33–34.

_____. "E.U. partners won't back tighter foreign controls." *Variety* 358 (February 20, 1995):173–174.

_____. "Pinheiro still waves quota flag at Turner charge into Europe." *Variety* 355 (May 2, 1994):44.

Stern, David J. "The whole world wants American sports." *Fortune* 121 (March 26, 1990):128, 132.

Stevenson, Richard W. "Lights! Camera! Europe!" *New York Times*, February 6, 1994, sec. 3, pp. 1, 6.

_____. "TV boom in Europe is aiding Hollywood." *New York Times*, December 28, 1987, pp. D1, D3.

Stilson, Janet. "U.S. distribs point to Europe as the fastest growing market." *Variety* 324 (October 15, 1986):48.

Strachan, Alex. "CBC ensures Canadian identity, says Heritage Canada." *Vancouver Sun*, January 26, 1996, p. C6.

"Subtle minds of the East find U.S. TV commercials too sly for their taste." *Variety* 259 (May 6, 1970):84.

Sumarno, Marselli. "Indonesia raps foreign TV fare." *Variety* 355 (May 16, 1994):35, 37.

"Superstation breakthrough." *Broadcasting* 95 (October 30, 1978):25–26.

"Susskind carries his 'TV smells' campaign to Canadian audience." *Variety* 221 (February 22, 1961):43.

Swardson, Anne. "Alliance focuses more attention due south." *Vancouver Sun*, April 26, 1996, p. C8.

"Swiss TV turns to commercials." *New York Times*, February 2, 1965, p. 7.

"Syndicate of directors claims French TV losing 'service' image." *Variety* 279 (May 14, 1975):133, 146.

"Take retired television execs to o'seas consultant jobs." *Variety* 248 (October 4, 1967):35.

"Telefilms' $6,000,000 o'seas." *Variety* 206 (May 8, 1957):21, 38.

"Television." Sp. summary *The Economist* 330 (February 12, 1994):T2+.

"Television is the message down in Rio." *Business Week*, June 17, 1967, pp. 86–88.

"Telstar — for all the world to see." *Newsweek* 60 (July 23, 1962):13–14.

"35 TV execs of Japan visit U.S., told of hurdles on show swap." *Variety* 290 (February 15, 1978):41, 62.

"3 out of every 4 U.S. households have TV." *Variety* 203 (August 1, 1956):23.

"Too much Yank accent on Brit. TV: Beaverbrook." *Variety* 217 (December 30, 1959):24.

"Toward reform of French TV" *Variety* 286 (April 20, 1977):60.

"Towards freer trade in services: audiovisuals." *OECD Observer*, July 1986, pp. 23–26.

"Transatlantic TV via micro relay." *Variety* 187 (June 18, 1952):1, 61.

"Turkey TV trot dates March for debut in Ankara." *Variety* 248 (October 4, 1967):30.

"Turkish TV: still striving for larger role at age 11." *Variety* 296 (October 10, 1979):100, 107.

"Turkish TV programmers move away from their reliance on U.S. shows." *Variety* 326 (February 25, 1987):355.

"Turner claims advances made in marketing CNN to Europe." *Variety* 324 (September 24, 1986):43, 46.

"Turner vows worldwide CNN as cable's coming tops Edinburgh agenda." *Variety* 308 (September 8, 1982):96, 101.

Tusher, Will. "French television moratorium on imports may have little immediate effect on U.S. fare." *Variety* 304 (September 23, 1981):47.

"TV abroad thrives on U.S. ways." *Business Week*, September 3, 1960, pp. 105–107.

"TV Asahi, one of the big four, boasts several links with U.S." *Variety* 319 (May 29, 1985):108.

"TV biz tops $1-bil in earnings." *Variety* 288 (August 31, 1977):43, 56.

"The TV border war." *Macleans* 89 (October 18, 1976):17.

"TV export assn. sights $88,000,000 in U.S. overseas sales this year." *Variety* 250 (April 3, 1968):39.

"TV film exporters organize." *Broadcasting* 57 (December 7, 1959):86.

"TV film exporters set organization." *Advertising Age* 30 (December 21, 1959):83.

"TV films' MPAA counterpart." *Variety* 206 (March 13, 1957):25.

"TV imports cost Britain $3,750,000." *Variety* 201 (February 29, 1956):30.

"TV in 23 foreign countries." *Variety* 191 (August 12, 1953):27, 34.

"TV overseas market limited." *Broadcasting* 58 (February 1, 1960):89–90.

"TV sales & profits hit new peaks." *Variety* 258 (April 22, 1970):33.

"TV scripters now cut in on foreign take." *Variety* 231 (July 17, 1963):49, 56.

"TV: the international picture." *Broadcasting* 53 (November 18, 1957):118.

"TVer in N'west U.S. border burg milks auds and ads from Canada." *Variety* 257 (December 24, 1969):33.

"TV's expanding world mart." *Variety* 232 (October 16, 1963):27.

"TV's $50,000,000 o'seas gross." *Variety* 226 (May 2, 1962):143.

"TV's $311,600,000 profits in '62." *Variety* 232 (September 25, 1963):29.

Tweed, Jean. "American 'dumped' films can kill Canadian television industry." *Saturday Night* 64 (May 17, 1949):6–7.

"12,209 features into TV." *Variety* 222 (April 26, 1961):185.

"$20,000,000 foreign 'take.'" *Variety* 217 (December 23, 1959):26.

Tyler, Ralph. "Television around the world." *Television Magazine* 23 (October, 1966): 32–35+.

"UA finalizes ZIV buyout." *Variety* 218 (March 9, 1960):37.

"UA-TV first to notch 100 mark offshore." *Variety* 243 (July 20, 1966):35.

"UNESCO paints a rosy picture of global TV via satellites." *Variety* 232 (November 27, 1963):27.

"Unions demand foreign resid coin; webs claim telecasts were pirated." *Variety* 270 (February 14, 1973):64.

"The U.S. as TV programmer to the world." *Broadcasting* 92 (April 18, 1977):48–50+.
"U.S. cashing in on U.K. feevee, as MGM/UA, Par and U venture leads to second partnership." *Variety* 311 (July 31, 1983):51.
"U.S. decision on Telesat raises Manley's dander." *Vancouver Sun*, October 31, 1996, p. D6.
"U.S. distribs benefit Italo private TV." *Variety* 301 (November 12, 1980):52, 64.
"U.S. distribs crack freeze on film prices by Europe TV." *Variety* 273 (December 26, 1973):1, 40.
"U.S. film exporters ask State Dept. to try again on Brit. TV quota." *Variety* 240 (November 10, 1965):38.
"U.S. films 'not available' to TV in Israeli; not at $800 per pic." *Variety* 294 (February 28, 1979):49, 90.
"U.S. hopes up on U.K. quota." *Variety* 246 (April 19, 1967):75, 86.
"U.S. majors end pix boycott vs. Swedish TV." *Variety* 294 (April 18, 1979):59.
"U.S. media aid New Zealand on radio–TV bill." *Advertising Age* 39 (April 8, 1968):26.
"U.S. product responsible for violence on Canada's airwaves says CBC prexy." *Variety* 254 (March 19, 1969):35.
"U.S. programs hot items overseas." *Broadcasting* 73 (December 18, 1967):27–30.
"U.S. response to recent Canadian trade-related decisions." *U.S. Dept. of State Dispatch* 6 (January 9, 1995):21.
"U.S. series are losing German viewers — no cops, less segs." *Variety* 302 (February 11, 1981):79, 82.
"U.S. still stuck with 14% quota on British TV." *Variety* 247 (May 24, 1967):31.
"U.S.-style TV looks good to Canadian execs, study shows." *Advertising Age* 30 (December 21, 1959):86.
"U.S.-style TV turns on Europe." *Broadcasting* 115 (April 13, 1987):96–98.
"U.S. telefilmers can't keep up with Aussie demand for product." *Variety* 216 (October 14, 1959):25, 40.
"U.S. telefilms o'seas gross could hit $50,000,000 in '62." *Variety* 223 (July 19, 1961):25.
"U.S. tempo strong in Nigerian TV where Brod Crawford's a nat'l hero." *Variety* 221 (February 15, 1961):27, 48.
"U.S. tops list of suppliers of feature pix to German TV." *Variety* 296 (October 10, 1979):43.
"U.S. TV exports in 1970 hit 20% of gross sales." *Variety* 262 (April 28, 1971):1, 70.
"U.S. TV influence too much in life of Canadians: poll." *Variety* 279 (June 18, 1975):48.
"U.S. TV sales in Japan reverse slide." *Variety* 238 (March 10, 1965):53.
"U.S. TV shows flop in Japan." *Variety* 319 (May 29, 1985):108.
"U.S. TV taps worldwide market." *Business Week*, September 27, 1958, pp. 158–160, 162, 164.
"U.S. TV's sour U.K. future?" *Variety* 266 (April 26, 1972):33.
"U.S. vidfilmers expect lifting of Brazil decree." *Variety* 225 (November 29, 1961):35.
"U.S. vidpix eyeing Argentine market." *Variety* 200 (October 12, 1955):2, 27.
"USIA eases 'image' barrier in export of TV shows to Iron Curtain nations." *Variety* 228 (October 17, 1962):25, 37.
"USIA's bid for global info grid." *Variety* 250 (February 28, 1968):28.
Valenti, Jack. "Valenti values film–TV coin in Oseas mart." *Variety* 289 (January 4, 1978):1, 64.
"Valenti & Nizer o'seas TV pitch." *Variety* 244 (October 5, 1966):27.
"Valenti sees homevideo woes as an international horror story." *Variety* 302 (March 25, 1981):124, 144.
"Valenti sees 'World War of Trade.'" *Variety* 347 (June 1, 1992):23.

"Valenti stumps against European quotas." *Broadcasting* 119 (November 12, 1990): 72–73.

Varis, Tapio. "Global traffic in television." *Journal of Communication* 24 (1) (Winter 1974):102–109.

_____. *International Flow of Television Programs.* Paris: UNESCO, 1985.

Vatikiotis, Michael. "U.S. threat to pull the plug." *Far Eastern Economic Review* 154 (October 24, 1991):64.

"Video bidders sending film prices sky-hi." *Variety* 314 (March 7, 1984):338, 372.

"Vidpix bundles from Britain." *Variety* 201 (December 14, 1955):39, 48.

"Vidpix distribs feel depressed Latino prices." *Variety* 218 (April 13, 1960):29.

"Vidpixers will try again to get rolling on export assn." *Variety* 214 (April 8, 1959):30.

"Vintage U.S. series add depth to REA programming bench." *Variety* 300 (October 8, 1980):75, 92.

"'Volume sales' moves goods in small mkts." *Variety* 303 (May 6, 1981):1, 54.

"W. Germany seen as lucrative area for vidfilm sales." *Variety* 222 (April 5, 1961):31.

Walker, Dean. "Canada's TV dilemma: the American influence." *Saturday Night* 75 (July 23, 1960):15–17.

Walker, Tom. "Hollywood takes exception to French block on the box." *Times* (London), May 3, 1993, p. 34.

Wallach, George. "TV's 'global challenge.'" *Variety* 209 (January 22, 1958):30, 55.

Walz, Jay. "Cairo TV invaded by cowboys, and the children just love it." *New York Times,* November 25, 1962, p. 8.

Ware, William. "Effects of U.S. television programs on foreign audiences: a meta-analysis." *Journalism Quarterly* 71 (Winter 1994):947–949.

Warg, Peter. "Qatar bars dishes, mandates state cable." *Variety* 351 (June 21, 1993):39.

"Warner Bros. to launch promo campaign to boost shows' falling Euro ratings." *Variety* 338 (February 7, 1990):96.

"Warren Lewis in Japan TV dickers." *Variety* 219 (August 3, 1960):44.

Watkins, Roger. "Big Yank guns aiming at tiny paycable market in the U.K." *Variety* 314 (March 21, 1984):116, 122.

_____. Commercial TV sweeping Europe." *Variety* 298 (April 16, 1980):1, 60.

_____. "Euro hassles on broadcast ads." *Variety* 319 (July 3, 1985):1, 61.

_____. "European TV: It's a whole new ballgame." *Variety* 313 (January 25, 1984):41, 80.

_____. "Euros angling to crack U.S. TV market." *Variety* 313 (November 2, 1983):45, 58.

_____. "Fading role of telefilms in British TV market." *Variety* 33 (January 29, 1964): 34, 48.

_____. "Mainstream U.S. syndication still a major goal for foreign producers." *Variety* 334 (February 1, 1989):50, 76.

_____. "Show biz in int'l TV power play." *Variety* 313 (November 9, 1983):1, 68.

_____. "Yanks gain points but lose game as British stand fast on TV quota." *Variety* 247 (May 31, 1967):32.

Weatherall, Ernest. "Indian TV & 'cultural imperialism.'" *Variety* 292 (October 11, 1978):147.

"Weaver's global TV formula to give the lie to Commies." *Variety* 200 (November 23, 1955):26, 41.

Webster, David. "Direct broadcast satellites: proximity, sovereignty and national identity." *Foreign Affairs* 62 (Summer 1984):1161–1174.

Werba, Hank. "American suppliers are on easy street as Italians scramble to lock product." *Variety* 330 (February 3, 1988):45, 104.

_____. "Films, Yank fare on Italian biggest roadblock to homevideo." *Variety* 303 (May 13, 1981):353.

_____. "Italo TV ends its Yank program spree." *Variety* 324 (October 15, 1986):125, 146.

_____. "Italo TV: U.S. prod. export to tube heavy." *Variety* 305 (February 4, 1981): 95, 122.

_____. "Italy as worst market for U.S. show exports." *Variety* 262 (April 14, 1971):41, 47.

_____. "MPEA, RAI reach agreement on new TV & film price scale." *Variety* 307 (July 7, 1982):32.

_____. "Politics buffeting RAI-TV." *Variety* 258 (April 8, 1970):57, 72.

_____. "Popularity of U.S. series stalks the halls at Euro–Teleconfronto." *Variety* 311 (June 8, 1983):38.

_____. "Spanish TV entertains a whole nation – on annual budget of 400G." *Variety* 223 (August 2, 1961):45.

_____. "Will U.S. product control Italian commercial TV?" *Variety* 310 (April 20, 1983):122, 124.

_____. "Yank in Italy to consult on TV strategies." *Variety* 311 (July 13, 1983):43, 70.

Wert, Maria C. "Global television flow to Latin American countries." *Journalism Quarterly* 65 (Spring 1988):182–185.

"West Germany key to continental Europe's potential for U.S. vidpix." *Variety* 213 (December 10, 1958):50.

Wharton, Dennis. "Valenti rips NAB E.C.-quota report." *Variety* 346 (March 16, 1992):32.

Wildman, Steven S. "The privatization of European television." *Columbia Journal of World Business* 22 (Fall 1987):71–76.

Williams, Michael. "France adamant on GATT." *Variety* 352 (October 18, 1993):41–42.

_____. "France braces for a new invasion." *Variety* 352 (October 11, 1993):M4.

_____. "French gov't resists Turner's sat invasion." *Variety* 352 (September 20, 1993):24.

_____. "French still gun for GATT." *Variety* 353 (November 15, 1993):28.

_____. "GATT spat wake-up on Yank market muscle." *Variety* 353 (December 27, 1993):45, 49.

Williams, Whitney. "Brazil & probably Chile to receive Oscarcast in live ABC-TV beaming." *Variety* 258 (March 25, 1970):41.

"Winners & losers in Canadian television's kulchur sweepstakes." *Cinema Canada* no. 102 (December 1983):5.

Wiskari, Werner. "Iceland's isolation nearly ended as foreign influences increase." *New York Times*, April 1, 1960, p. 20.

Wittsock, Melinda. "North Americans wise up to £10bn potential of U.K. cable." *Times* (London), May 21, 1990, p. 26.

Woodstock, Art. "ABC's 'commercial' a sour note at EBU's staid opening session." *Variety* 228 (October 24, 1962):30, 54.

Woodstone, Art. "Foreign markets intriguing." *Variety* 200 (October 26, 1955):31, 34.

_____. "Inter-American b'casters carry on fight against the 'little tyrants.'" *Variety* 202 (May 16, 1956):24, 38.

"The world and TV." *Newsweek* 47 (January 23, 1956):92–93.

"World laps up U.S. TV fare." *Business Week*, April 23, 1960, pp. 129, 131.

"World market for U.S. television up 6%." *Broadcasting* 70 (May 16, 1966):27–29.

"World TV: a click premiere." *Variety* 227 (July 18, 1962):27, 38.

"World TV market." *Broadcasting* 111 (August 18, 1986):65–66.

"World TV set census 251-mil; U.S. has 30%." *Variety* 266 (April 12, 1972):1, 102.

"Worldvision off & running, nears $10,000,000 mark in syndie sales." *Variety* 271 (May 16, 1973):96.

"Worldvision symposium speakers optimistic on overcoming ad obstacles of world TV." *Advertising Age* 37 (November 21, 1966):38.

"Worldwide TV: a dynamic fact." *Sponsor* 15 (June 19, 1961):40–41+.

Wright, Miles F. E. "Aussie b'casting control board beset by obstacles in trying to upgrade shows." *Variety* 282 (May 5, 1976):80.

"Yank–Aussie cold war." *Variety* 243 (August 17, 1966):27.

"Yank clients take lead." *Variety* 225 (February 14, 1962):27.

"Yank exec sees no upswing in view on Italo TV's U.S. product drought." *Variety* 296 (December 14, 1979):22.

"Yank showbiz grasp on Canada." *Variety* 333 (November 23, 1988):36.

"Yank shows in sharp decline on British television screens." *Variety* 297 (January 9, 1980):169, 178.

"Yank telepix distribs reaping lotsa moola in Canadian market." *Variety* 195 (September 1, 1954):52.

"Yank tubers plotting to step up Euro ties." *Variety* 338 (February 7, 1990):104, 136.

"Yankee dollar inspires U.S.-angled production by British TV outfits." *Variety* 260 (October 28, 1970):49.

"Yanks starting to export marketing support." *Variety* 344 (October 7, 1991):M4, M88.

"Yorkin & Lear plot Yank version of 'Steptoe' as followup to bigot." *Variety* 262 (March 3, 1971):32.

"Ziv hosting o'seas TV execs in Cincy." *Variety* 200 (November 9, 1955):31.

"Zivideo in 9 tongues." *Variety* 215 (June 17, 1959):27.

Index